Imperial Affects

War Culture

Edited by Daniel Leonard Bernardi

Books in this new series address the myriad ways in which warfare informs diverse cultural practices, as well as the way cultural practices—from cinema to social media—inform the practice of warfare. They illuminate the insights and limitations of critical theories that describe, explain, and politicize the phenomena of war culture. Traversing both national and intellectual borders, authors from a wide range of fields and disciplines collectively examine the articulation of war, its everyday practices, and its impact on individuals and societies throughout modern history.

Imperial Affects

SENSATIONAL MELODRAMA
AND THE ATTRACTIONS
OF AMERICAN CINEMA

Jonna Eagle

RUTGERS UNIVERSITY PRESS

New Brunswick, Camden, and Newark, New Jersey, and London

Library of Congress Cataloging-in-Publication Data
Names: Eagle, Jonna, 1968- author.
Title: Imperial affects : sensational melodrama and the attractions of American cinema /
Jonna Eagle.
Description: New Brunswick : Rutgers University Press, [2017] | Series: War culture |
Includes bibliographical references and index.
Identifiers: LCCN 2016043417| ISBN 9780813583037 (hardback) | ISBN 9780813583020 (pbk.)
| ISBN 9780813583044 (e-book (epub))
Subjects: LCSH: Action and adventure films—United States—History and criticism. |
Western films—United States—History and criticism. | National characteristics, American,
in motion pictures. | Melodrama in motion pictures. | Violence in motion pictures. |
Imperialism in motion pictures. | BISAC: PERFORMING ARTS / Film & Video / History &
Criticism. | HISTORY / United States / 20th Century.
Classification: LCC PN1995.9.A3 E24 2017 | DDC 791.43/6582—dc23
LC record available at https://lccn.loc.gov/2016043417

A British Cataloging-in-Publication record for this book is available from the
British Library.

∞ The paper used in this publication meets the requirements of the
American National Standard for Information Sciences—Permanence of
Paper for Printed Library Materials, ANSI Z39.48–1992.

www.rutgersuniversitypress.org

Manufactured in the United States of America

For Will, who always encourages me in what is best;
and for Kaia and Theo, the two best things I know.

CONTENTS

Imperial Affects

Introduction

Making Sense

The Moral and Affective
Appeals of Melodrama

[I]f war is to be opposed, we have to understand how
popular assent to war is cultivated and maintained, in
other words, how war waging acts upon the senses so
that war is thought to be an inevitability, something
good, or even a source of moral satisfaction.

—**Judith Butler**, *Frames of War*

On September 11 of each year, Americans observe the officially designated
occasion of Patriot Day. Not to be confused with Patriot's Day, which marks
the Battle of Lexington and Concord and the "shot heard 'round the world,"
Patriot Day was proclaimed by President George W. Bush, in accordance
with a joint congressional resolution, as an opportunity to "remember and
honor those who perished in the terrorist attacks of September 11, 2001."
In his presidential proclamation of September 4, 2002, marking the first
observance of Patriot Day, Bush noted that "we will not forget the events
of that terrible morning" and will "always remember our collective obligation to ensure that justice is done." "Inspired by the heroic sacrifices of our
firefighters, rescue and law enforcement personnel, military service members, and other citizens," he continued, "our Nation found unity, focus,
and strength. We found healing in the national outpouring of compassion
for those lost. . . . From the tragedy of September 11th emerged a stronger

Nation, renewed by a spirit of national pride and a true love of country." In September 2003, marking the day's second observance, Bush proclaimed that in the events and aftermath of the September 11 attacks "we saw the greatness of America in the bravery of victims," and promised that we in America "will continue to bring our enemies to justice or bring justice to them."[1]

That the individual tragedies and images of an assaulted national body to which 9/11 gave rise are here so intimately associated with the obligations and acts of the patriot deserves our further consideration. For, as the occasion of Patriot Day underscores, very often in American culture a feeling of national identity and belonging has derived from a sense of injury, vulnerability, and loss. The nation is unified, in Bush's statement, through the shared experience of suffering and compassion, and national identity is consolidated through the position of the victim and with what Bush designates as the greatness adhering to that position. The insistence upon remembrance and the oft-repeated refrain that "we will not forget" resonate with past appeals—the injunctions to "Remember the Alamo," "Remember the *Maine*," and "Remember Pearl Harbor." In such contexts, to "not forget" is to strike a defiant pose, as the commemorative gesture is inextricable from the promise and the threat of violence. A commitment to violence emerges here as a form of remembrance, manifesting in Bush's proclamation as our "collective obligation to ensure that justice is done." The representation of the assaulted national body thus serves to animate an identification with nationalist violence and its agents. To take pleasure or satisfaction in the representation of such violence becomes the act of a patriot, a particularly zealous and embodied form of commemoration.

As exemplified by Bush's Patriot Day proclamations, political rhetoric after 9/11 turned swiftly and insistently to the spectacle of injury and suffering, both as the foundation of national innocence and goodness and as an irrefutable argument for violence as a righteous and necessary rejoinder to such suffering. Sympathy and aggression operate as twinned affects here: the identification with suffering serves simultaneously as an alignment with and implicit endorsement of state-sponsored violence.[2] The efficacy of this rhetoric after 9/11 was striking; it seemed to resonate broadly and in immediate and instinctual ways, seemed able to focus and consolidate national affect and to organize an orientation toward a future violence cast as both virtuous and inevitable. How to account for this efficacy? What was called forth by this rhetoric, and what did it call upon? What structures of feeling were conditioned and mobilized here? What affective potentials were actualized (and what others were closed down)?

The degree to which the melodramatic conventions framing political discourse after 9/11 felt both natural and right, and the degree to which they primed an expectation of violence as both exciting and virtuous, are questions *Imperial Affects* seeks to address. To do so, we must look to the American cinema, which has functioned as a privileged site for the melodramatic merger of morality and feeling. We must consider, for instance, the spectacular violence and pathetic suffering of a figure like Rambo, who first emerged in 1982 and returned more sensationally in 1985, as a meaningful precursor to the visual and affective logics that structure the televisual discourse of war—briefly during the Persian Gulf War in 1991 and more persistently during the twenty-first-century wars in Afghanistan and Iraq. The success of action blockbusters generally across the 1980s and 1990s, both in theaters and in the burgeoning home video market, speaks to affective postures made both pleasurable and habitual, focused around the intertwined fantasies of embodied vulnerability and technologically enhanced omnipotence. These positions do not emerge fully formed at the century's end but derive from a long history of cinematic melodrama in which action and violence onscreen are constituted as the locus of both visceral thrills and moral goodness and in which identification with the victimized serves as the foundation for righteous violence.

The scenarios of victimization, virtue, and violence mobilized to frame and allegorize the events of September 11 and the subsequent war on terror thus speak to the ongoing work of sensational melodrama in American politics and culture, and in the American cinema in particular. Tracing a genealogy of melodramatic action from the military actualities of the Spanish-American and Philippine-American Wars to the emergence and evolution of the Western and into the late-century action cinema, here I examine how the appeals of omnipotence and vulnerability intertwine in this tradition, analyzing how the cinema works to position its viewers as subjects within specific ideological and affective constellations. Considering the production of what I term imperialist affect, I interrogate the processes by which cinematic action has been constituted as something that *feels* good—both pleasurable and right, thrilling and virtuous.

In arguing for the particular role of cinema in the constitution of a national subject as imperialist subject, I am emphasizing not simply that, through popular film, audiences have been invited to identify with the overlapping positions of agency and vulnerability, but rather that, through cinema itself, the position of the victim-hero has been consolidated as a defining feature of American national identity. As outlined in Benedict Anderson's seminal account of print capitalism and the rise of nationalism, the experience of national belonging is a mediated one, relying on the constitution of imagined communities across dispersed geographical spaces and through a sense of simultaneous time.[3] Through identification with mediated forms of communication and the sense of shared time they construct, disparate populations may come to locate their own experience within an abstract community of others with whom they lack any direct contact. As Lauren Berlant has stated in another context, media are "in the business of making nationality and making it personal to citizens," negotiating and circulating the terms of national identity.[4] Berlant highlights both the role of media in constituting the imagined community of the nation and the way this imagination is incorporated at the level of individual as well as collective bodies. The national feeling constructed through mass-mediated forms is at once public and intimate, social and bodily in nature, as Berlant and others have underscored.

In tracing this genealogy of cinematic action, I add to a growing body of scholarship on melodrama as a dominant mode of popular and political discourse in the United States.[5] Melodrama, as Linda Williams has argued, is protean by nature, as slippery as it is ubiquitous, and the spilling of increasing amounts of ink on the topic has done little to fix its parameters.[6] It has been associated with the constitution of moral discourse in the context of a post-sacred universe; with the rise of industrial modernity and the heightened modes of sensory address with which it is associated; with the negotiation of gendered identity under patriarchy and racialized identity under white supremacy; and with cultural forms including but not limited to the novel, theater, film, and television.

As Williams has emphasized, melodrama pivots around identification with the position of the victim. Suffering functions in this context as the primary signifier of inner goodness; to suffer, and to do so publicly, provides a mark of virtue.[7] As Williams and Ben Singer have both detailed, this identification with suffering, victimization, and abuse alternates, in melodrama, with another set of appeals oriented around sensational action and violence. While there has been some debate about the precise relationship between these poles of pathos and action, the oscillation itself has structured melodrama since the early nineteenth century, in the "movement between absorptive, introverted moments of sympathetic identification and highly spectacular, extroverted scenes of shocking violence."[8]

Within film studies in particular, however, the study of melodrama was for a time focused almost exclusively on its more pathetic forms and cycles, including the women's weepies of the 1930s and 1940s and the domestic or family melodramas of the 1950s and early 1960s.[9] In this context, melodrama was understood to signal a primary emphasis on heightened emotionality, domestic relations and environments, and female protagonists and audiences. In these discussions, melodrama was contrasted quite explicitly to realist representational modes. The association of melodrama with emotionality and the feminine has been a key aspect of its cultural denigration as a non-normative site of excess. Questions of masculine identity, when they were raised, continued the association of melodrama with domestic scenes and relations, assessing the pressures of normative heterosexual identity on the male subject and focusing on issues of father-son relationships in particular.

Starting in the 1990s, however, understandings of melodrama and its role in mainstream American cinema began to move away from an emphasis on pathos, domesticity, and the feminine and toward a greater emphasis on action and sensation. As Linda Williams has suggested, within this expanded view, melodrama is best understood not as a specific genre or cycle but as the dominant mode organizing American cinema from its emergence, "the foundation of the classical Hollywood movie."[10] Alongside film scholars like Steve Neale, Christine Gledhill, Ben Singer, and Tom Gunning, Williams has highlighted action and sensation as central components of melodrama, locating the significance of the form precisely in the vacillation between pathetic and action-based modes of address.[11] As I discuss below, this pivot within film studies is echoed in scholarship on melodrama more broadly, which has shifted toward an emphasis on action as well as pathos, sensation as well as morality, as constituting melodrama's core.

Suggested alongside this shift are a change in the gendered emphasis of melodrama studies and a concomitant move away from an understanding of melodrama and realism as oppositional terms. Steve Neale's research into the American film trade press, for instance, importantly highlights how, in the context of classical Hollywood cinema, a "meller" was the designation given to signal a film's emphasis on thrilling action. Neale cites a 1925 review that asserts, "[M]elodrama, on the screen, is identified almost entirely with fast physical action: cowboys or sheiks or cavalrymen riding madly across the country, men hanging by their teeth from the ledges of skyscrapers."[12] (This last image is suggestive of the precarious conceits of the action cinema sixty years later, which I discuss in chapter 4.) Categorizations such as "hard-boiled, action-crammed melodrama," "rough, tough melodrama," or "virile," "vigorous," or "he-man" melodrama were not uncommon in this context. In fact, as Neale insists, up through 1960, "if there is any marking of the nature or appeal of melodrama in gender terms, that nature and that appeal are almost exclusively specified as male."[13] Williams similarly argues that "prolonged climactic action" has always supplied a central feature of film melodrama and that the "virility" of such action should not "fool us into thinking that it is not melodramatic."[14]

Regardless of these critical pivots, the intertwined status of gender, race, and action in American melodrama has not yet been fully explored. "If male-orientated action movies are persistently termed 'melodrama' in the trade, long after the term is more widely disgraced," Christine Gledhill has suggested, "this should alert us to something from the past that is alive in the present and circulating around the masculine."[15] To date, however, these comments have remained more provocative than explicated, as the relationship of melodrama to male-identified genres and modes of address has been acknowledged and asserted more than it has been directly addressed or analyzed.

In *Imperial Affects*, I offer the first sustained account of the relationship of melodrama to male-identified action-based cinema, arguing for the tremendous influence of this tradition on attitudes toward imperialist violence across the twentieth century. The conventions of sensational action have developed only in and through broader social, cultural, and political negotiations around questions of gender, race, and nation; and the significance of rapid motion and violence onscreen—the central features of "thrilling" action in the cinema—can be apprehended only within these terms. Through the genealogy of melodramatic action that I trace, injury and suffering are linked to the mobilization of violent agency, soliciting identification with a national subject who is constituted as at once vulnerable and powerful, victimized and invincible. Nationalist violence is produced as both righteous and retributive, always already defensive in nature; and the spectacular display of such violence, which both relies upon and refutes the premise of violability, is sanctioned as a site of mediated pleasure. Exploring the invitation to identify with positions of both vulnerability and violent agency as they shape imperialist representation— an invitation issued not simply at the level of narrative but also and importantly at the level of form—*Imperial Affects* offers an account of affective structures produced and naturalized across a century of cinema, a legacy powerfully mobilized in support of the project of American Empire at the twenty-first century's turn.

The Felt Good of Melodrama

Peter Brooks's seminal account of the emergence of the melodramatic imagination does crucial work in helping us to identify the specific relationship of melodrama to the constitution of moral feeling, or morality as feeling. Brooks argues that the function of melodrama as it first developed in the late eighteenth and early nineteenth centuries is the production of moral legibility in the face of the diminished authority of both church and crown. In a post-sacred universe, in which traditional guarantors of moral meaning no longer hold sway, a new system for producing and recognizing the signs of good and evil is required.[16]

Brooks explores melodrama's impulse to give expression to what resides beneath or beyond the surface of the world—the intensity of affective experience, for one, but also the idea of a moral truth that animates the social world but cannot be apprehended solely within its terms. Emerging in the theaters of revolutionary France and soon after in England, melodrama can be distinguished from official theatrical forms through its incorporation of nonverbal modes of expression—pantomime, tableau, gesture, and, significantly, music (melos)—to give to moral meaning a fullness of expression not available through spoken language alone. Through the nonverbal signs of music and gesture, melodrama seeks to provide a "language of presence and immediacy,"[17] a plenitude of feeling that corresponds to and replaces, one might argue, the realm of the sacred that has been lost. In the context of melodrama as Brooks discusses it, this fullness of feeling is mobilized in the interests of virtue, producing signs of an underlying moral order that comes to be expressed through and as emotional states, "so that the expression of emotional and moral integers is indistinguishable."[18]

In contrast to Brooks's emphasis on moral legibility, more recent accounts have highlighted the significance, or even the primacy, of sensationalism to melodrama's form and function. Already in the context of its early emergence, an emphasis on sensation may have overshadowed any moral imperative. Rather than a "redemptive social vision," Matthew Buckley asserts that "a primary basis of the genre's appeal and a shaping imperative of its formal development almost from the start . . . [was] its capability to produce affective and emotional sensations of great intensity."[19] Buckley's proposition resonates with the insights of other scholars: Tom Gunning's emphasis on the importance of "non-cognitive affects, thrills, sensations" in late nineteenth-century stage melodrama;[20] Ben Singer's seminal account of the sensationalism of American melodrama on stage and screen in the late nineteenth and early twentieth centuries; and Neale's research on the significance of sensation to melodrama in classical Hollywood cinema.

We might consider that the fullness and plenitude that Brooks attributes to the expression of moral feeling in melodrama depend upon the interlacing of cognitive with other affective appeals. For what is most significant about melodrama—and arguably about its more sensational forms in particular—is its ability to produce the terms of morality precisely at the level of feeling, to articulate morality as and through feeling.[21] It is the merger of morality and sensation that makes melodrama such an efficacious mode of representation—the conjunction of a visceral, affectively rich address with the project of excavating the signifiers of good and evil from amid the modern ruins of sacred and monarchical authority.

Sensational melodrama developed most fully in the context of its migration to the United States, married to an official ideology of democracy and supported by a burgeoning investment in increasingly sophisticated stagecraft. In general, the United States has been understood as particularly fertile ground for the growth of melodrama, which offers propitious materials for the articulation of an emergent national identity. As Daniel C. Gerould has noted, melodrama and the United States emerged from a shared historical moment, both born of the radical political and philosophical reorientations of the eighteenth century. For Gerould, in his focus on the Americanization of what was originally a continental form, this twin birth is highly significant: melodrama's individualistic emphasis on spirited underdogs who prevail over adversity and its explicit address to a mass rather than an elite audience resonate in powerful ways in the nineteenth-century United States. Animated by technologically driven special effects, which Gerould associates with American materialism and entrepreneurial capitalism, "melodrama became a direct expression of American society and national character," one that in turn shaped the imagination of national identity.[22]

In the context of American melodrama, national identity is forged in and through a relationship to violence. As Christine Gledhill has suggested, although performances earlier in the nineteenth century mined European melodramatic traditions to articulate a growing dissonance between city and country, a "truly American melodrama" did not emerge until the 1880s, through Civil War and frontier stories that stage the fantasy of national unity through violence.[23] This theatrical tradition feeds directly into early cinema and the narrative conventions upon which it draws. Tracing the ongoing impact of melodrama on political and popular discourse, Linda Williams takes the argument of melodrama's particular intimacy with American national identity even further, suggesting melodrama's status as "the best example of American culture's (often hypocritical) notion of itself as the locus of innocence and virtue"; she considers melodrama's paradoxical power of identification with victimhood as "one of the great unexamined moral forces of American culture."[24] These are points to which I return in chapter 2.

Even as the mass appeal of melodrama has been associated with the consolidation of American national identity, the form's popular success has been more complex, raising anxieties among social and political elites about the changing nature of the country itself. As Singer's account of sensationalism suggests, the denigration of melodrama as a cultural form in the late nineteenth and early twentieth centuries drew upon suspicions surrounding the status of the mass—mass society and culture and mass spectatorship as a phenomenon of this new social and cultural sphere. Such suspicions engaged centrally with issues of class, ethnicity, and power during a period of intensive immigration to a newly industrialized and urbanized nation.

The ascendance of mass culture and the imagined role and function of the spectator within it were issues to which popular and political discourse frequently returned. Cultural and political sites often merged in these discussions; class-based forms of resistance could be expressed through new activities of leisure and consumption, and the anxieties of social reformers and others in the face of these activities often expressed broader concerns about the status and political organization of the working class. In this context, the urban crowd was figured as "affectively effervescent," as William Mazzarella has suggested, unstable, suggestible, and subject to both violence and manipulation.[25]

The cinema was primary within these debates, as the mimetic power of film was a focus of reformist concern. This influence was theorized by Hugo Munsterberg, in one of the first works of film theory, as a kind of "psychical infection," to which young people, women, and the working class were thought to be particularly susceptible.[26] The effects of film were imagined as explicitly bodily in nature; in addition to imitative behaviors, vulnerable spectators were "inclined to experience touch or temperature or smell or sound impressions from what they see on the screen."[27] Cinema in this context is aligned with a kind of affective intensity that is feared to exceed or undermine a dominant social and political order based on a presumption of rational rather than bodily ways of knowing. The early cinema's emphasis on a direct, visceral mode of address also associates it with the body, as I discuss in chapter 1. In addition to the medium itself, with the advent of the nickelodeon, the very site of exhibition was identified with modes of affective response that reform efforts both inside and outside the nascent film industry sought to discipline.

In this discourse, the dubious status of the mass is articulated through the categories of gender and race: mass response, a mimetic process pathologized through the language of contagion and hysteria, is cast as both feminine and primitive. The image of the mass or crowd governed by a contagious kind of bodily responsiveness stands in implicit opposition to the construction of a national subject, whose well-bounded sovereignty is coded as a feature of both his masculinity and his whiteness. What we see in the association of melodrama with mass culture (and with the notion of a working-class audience in particular) is an alignment of melodrama with bodily modes of engagement and responsiveness understood to exceed socially sanctioned forms and with ways of knowing and being in the world that stand in contrast to the normative construction of the rational, enlightened subject—an association, that is to say, with affect. In Singer's account, for instance, melodrama is signaled by "a kind of sensory excess" or a "mode of visceral excess," which Singer himself designates as "primal."[28] This early association of melodrama with mimetic bodily response persists across the twentieth century, as the ability of genres like melodrama, horror, and pornography to solicit responses that mirror those represented onscreen (tears, screams, sexual arousal) has served as the marker of their low cultural status.[29]

The sensationalism of melodrama is understood to bear an essential relationship to modernity (with this latter term as variously conceived as the former). On the one hand, for instance, Brooks's discussion of plenitude relates to the persistent sense that modernity lacks the means for giving expression to a fullness of feeling, a fullness often associated with the spiritual, the numinous, or the sacred. In this view, which circulates widely in scholarship on the spectacular and sensational aspects of popular attractions from the late nineteenth century forward, modernity is understood to be enervating, sapping the vital energies of its subjects through increasingly standardized and mechanized routines.[30] The sensationalism of modern cultural forms is thus viewed as compensatory, its visceral, often aggressive mode of address working to supply the intensity and immediacy of lived experience from which the modern subject has been alienated. This interpretation relates also to notions of realness and authenticity, which often if paradoxically circulate around such cultural forms, as intense sensory stimulation comes to be associated with ideals of manliness, as I discuss in chapter 1.

In another view, one equally familiar, the sensationalism of melodrama echoes the sensory intensity of modern experience rather than compensates for its lack.[31] Sensationalism is understood both to reproduce and to assuage anxieties occasioned by the sensory stimulations of a newly urbanized world, in which rapid social, cultural, and technological change threatens traditional foundations of knowledge and identity and traditional rhythms of lived experience. As Singer details, both the assaultive qualities of melodrama—which help to manage the condition of modern shock even as they reproduce it—and its emphasis on the underlying if often invisible moral ordering of a chaotic universe provide an ameliorative function. Matthew Buckley associates the predominance of sensation with melodrama's historical development. The genre's sensory intensity, in his view, was conditioned by the traumatized status of its contemporary audience, who, having lived through an epoch of spectacular violence and profound social upheaval, required a heightened, distilled mode of representation to signify this experience.[32]

In relation to the history of imperial affect that I trace, what is significant is the production of the white male hero as the iconic embodiment of a national subject through the mode of sensational melodrama. Rather than representing denigrated forms of affective responsiveness, the thrilling appeals of action and violence in male-identified genres like the Western and the war film are naturalized, circulating as normative signifiers of manly pleasure (a position actively constructed and negotiated in the context of an ascendant consumer culture), and linked to a set of explicitly moral and nationalistic claims. Earlier in the twentieth century, action-based forms still circulated with the taint of lower-class entertainment, associating them with an ethnic or racialized otherness. With the advent of the Western in particular, action-based sensationalism becomes a signifier of the national.

Rather than cause for suspicion or alarm, visceral modes of responsiveness are harnessed toward more hegemonic concerns in this context; the intensity they lend to the representation of good and evil is understood as an indicator of the force of true feeling, with which the Western in its moralizing is associated.[33] Here the collective or even contagious state of affective agitation, which in other contexts may signify as a threat to the dominant social order—marked off as feminized, primitive, or regressive and associated with women, racialized others, and the working class—achieves a normative status. Rather than stigmatized, the intensity of shared feeling is naturalized through an association with dominant ideologies of white and male supremacy and works to animate these very ideologies.

Indeed, as Judith Butler has suggested, popular conceptions of moral feeling seem to take particular pride in the idea of morality as instinctive, as prior to or unsullied by processes of ratiocination, which are believed to undercut the obviousness and inherency of moral sentiment. We imagine morality to be lodged most compellingly at the level of feeling rather than of thought, such that virtue calls forth its own instinctive recognition. To think through or think over a problem posed as moral is thus an enterprise met with suspicion or derision, to the extent that such cognitive processes are understood to pervert a purer, more immediate mode of affective responsiveness. Morality emerges here as something that is felt, or felt first and rationalized after.[34] These thoughts echo those explicated in Lauren Berlant's national sentimentality project, in which she traces the "shift from the notion of a rational critical public to an affective public," whereby feelings become the basis of attachment to or identification with a national public sphere.[35] In tracing this shift, Berlant diagnoses the emergence of a visceral politics, at the core of which is the notion of true feeling—the idea that truth itself is the product of a gut kind of knowing rather than, say, the outcome of rational argument or deliberation.

An appreciation of melodrama in its historical and ongoing function can help us better understand this production of moral feeling and the rise of affect as a mode of public address, that is, the invitation to identify with the nation primarily through and on the level of feeling. In melodrama, as Linda Williams has argued, "a visceral sort of ethics" prevails.[36] Indeed, the visceral politics Berlant discusses cannot be appreciated outside the broader ascendance of what Brooks calls the melodramatic imagination.

The assertion of goodness and rightness in this context resides in modes of responsiveness that are never apart from, although at the same time never fully reducible to, socially encoded categories of emotion. The significance of melodrama, in its drive to produce moral goodness as an unequivocal and broadly accessible sign, rests upon the status of feeling as an indicator of truth. Melodramatic discourse works powerfully to naturalize its ideological workings through this insistence upon feeling, which is understood to exist beyond or beneath the processes of cognition or rational consideration.

Melodrama operates at the hinge of cognition and sensation, aimed at making sense in both senses of that term: it channels sensory responsiveness (one mode of sense making) toward particular patterns of cognitive ordering and recognition (the second mode). Thus the notion of a felt good emerges as central to my investigation here—the idea of morality as something animated through visceral as well as intellectual or emotional satisfactions, something in which sensational and cognitive appeals, never coextensive though never neatly separable, forcefully combine. We might think of sensational melodrama as a kind of ordering device, a mechanism through which sensation is both conditioned and narrativized, animated and framed. Visceral sensation within this context is not experienced separately or apart from this ordering, of course, nor is the moral sense these forms work to construct apprehensible outside of the bodily responses they elicit. Nonetheless, these forms of sense making are conventionally understood to be separate, and the extent to which bodily agitations undergird moral conviction is conventionally denied. To account for the efficacy of melodrama, however, is to grapple with their interweaving.

On the one hand, then, melodrama's association with affect has marked it off as threatening, or as other, to hegemonic structures of power and authority. In its ability to solicit a strong affective response, melodrama has been aligned at various times and in various contexts with the feminine, the immigrant, and the working class, with all of these figures constructed in opposition to a normative conception of rational engagement embodied by the white male subject-citizen. On the other hand, the work of melodrama, and of mediated affect more broadly, has been identified as precisely the glue binding hegemonic conceptions like national identity. Excitability itself, as Joseph Masco has recently argued, "is now the foremost duty of all citizens"; the ability to be coordinated by affect at a mass level functions as "a core aspect of modern life."[37] Thus, what is cast off or denigrated is also essential, as intense embodied modes of responsiveness are normalized within the very workings of power that they are imagined, in other contexts, to destabilize. And sensational melodrama in particular, by binding morality to other modes of visceral response, has been central to this process.

Affective Attunement and the Structuring of Feeling

The concept of affect surfaces here as a critical gateway through which to engage the work of melodrama. The study of affect as it has emerged across the past two decades in humanities and social science scholarship seeks to recognize both emotion and, crucially, what remains beyond and in some sense beneath it: visceral modes of responsiveness that exceed and undergird socially recognized and codified categories of emotion; forces and energies, impacts and intensities; the broadly reaching power "to affect and be affected."[38]

At the same time, while speaking to what is excessive to or other than these socially codified categories, affect is never outside the social but is a force that moves it and moves within it. As Brian Massumi asserts, affect should be understood as always already political in nature, embedded within specific social and historical contexts and structures, even as it cannot be fully reduced to the dominant terms of meaning or feeling codified within these at any given time. Affect is thus at once within and beyond these structures, both what is produced or conditioned through them and what animates, drives, challenges, or reshapes them. As William Mazzarella asserts, "any social project that is not imposed through force alone must be affective in order to be effective." Affect, then, operates not as an alterior or excessive force in relation to the ordering of the social but as its very ground, "a necessary moment of any institutional practice with aspirations to public efficacy."[39]

As scholars including Massumi and Berlant have emphasized, however, affect is an amorphous thing, and the subject's affecting encounter with the world does not produce any inevitable reactions. There is a lack of fixity in this encounter; indeed, this instability has made affect rich terrain for the exploration of alternative ways of knowing and being in the world, a site of potentiality that moves against hegemonic assumptions of what is possible. In addition, while my own focus is on the work of melodrama in animating a pleasurable identification with ideologies of American imperialism and the fantasies of agency and vulnerability that undergird it, melodrama does not work in one inexorable direction but opens out onto a range of affective responses and identifications. As a cultural mode, it has been mobilized in the interests of nationalist power as well as in the interests of disenfranchised populations in their struggle to access freedoms and rights historically denied them. Harriet Beecher Stowe's *Uncle Tom's Cabin* is among the most frequently cited examples, and the mobilizing of melodramatic conventions has continued as a central rhetorical, visual, and political strategy of civil rights movements across the twentieth century.[40]

On neither the individual nor the collective level are the affective impacts of cultural works singular or predetermined, although the cultural and political work of affect must nonetheless be reckoned with. In this respect, Massumi has spoken usefully of differential attunement, a concept that addresses the power of media to position us affectively and the lack of fixity that attends this process.[41] In the context of any one instance or encounter, the immediacy of any one event, the media may attune bodies in a particular way but may do so differently, in accordance with the habits and tendencies that organize one individual relative to another.[42] As Massumi highlights, bodily impact is here essential: "Our bodies and our lives are almost a kind of resonating chamber for media-borne perturbations that strike us and run through us." We are collectively "braced" into this experience "in a very direct, bodily way" and prior to any process of rationalization, "at a level where direct bodily reactions and our ability to think are so directly bound up with each other that they can't be separated out yet from each other." Hence, an event attunes us in both collective and individual ways, "snapping us to attention together, and correlating our diversity," even as "we each are taken into the event from a different angle, and move out of it following our own singular trajectories."[43]

In general, Massumi's approach to affect is alive to the processual, the indeterminate, and the potential and to what may be foreclosed in the assumption of any event's unfolding along specific trajectories, whose endpoints are predetermined by dominant modes and structures of signification. His work underscores the pull of affect theory toward an imagination of alterity, of ways of being, feeling, and knowing that exist outside the foreclosures of hegemonic signifying systems. Yet, as Massumi also suggests, there is still a need to theorize the force of collective attunement itself, to account for the ability of particular affective logics to shape or frame the social encounter of subjects with their worlds. As Butler asserts, "affect is, from the start, communicated from elsewhere. It disposes us to perceive the world in a certain way, to let certain dimensions of the world in and to resist others."[44] Crucial questions thus arise: To what are collective or individual bodies being attuned in any given instance? And how might we begin to map the forces and patterns that drive these processes, which dispose us through these processes, at the level of both emotional and political, individual and collective response?

This notion of affect as a force that moves and shapes feeling in meaningfully collective ways has been crucial to the emergence of affect studies, in which the project of public feelings has emerged as central.[45] Raymond Williams's concept of a structure of feeling has served as a provocative challenge here, an invitation to theorize culture as the interactive sum of its parts, not limited to fixed aesthetic forms and functions but open to the interaction of these within the immediate and always unfolding present of social relations, understood as actively lived and experienced rather than ossified in some perpetual pastness. Such social processes, he observes, "exert palpable pressures and set effective limits on experience and on action." Like the concept of affect that emerges under its influence, the notion of structures of feeling breaks down familiar dichotomies between the personal and the social, experience and belief, thought and feeling, asserting "not feeling against thought, but thought as felt, and feeling as thought." Williams points to the status of these structures as related, though in no way reducible, to ideology, ordered by specific internal patterns and relations, while nonetheless encompassing "elements of social and material . . . experience which may lie beyond, or be uncovered or imperfectly covered by, the elsewhere recognizable systematic elements."[46]

Artistic and literary conventions are understood by Williams as specifically social formations, articulating broader "structures of feeling which as living processes are much more widely experienced."[47] Judith Butler makes a resonant point in a discussion of interpretation, noting how "interpretation takes place by virtue of the structuring constraints of genre and form on the communicability of affect."[48] In both cases, a focus on cultural practice as expressing the structuring work of affect moves somewhat against the sense of affective open-endedness that Massumi tends to emphasize. And indeed, by outlining a specific genealogy of melodramatic action, it is such structuring constraints that I seek to trace, to account for the force of generic convention in shaping an affective field to which we are and have been collectively attuned.

The analysis of a cultural text's dominant mode of address or the dominant logic structuring its discourse does not exhaust the possibilities of its uses or deny the extent to which social subjects may react in ways other than those conditioned by the text or discourse. In the face of calls to nationalist violence, for instance, some may—and many do—refuse the terms through which identification is offered, may ignore the invitation to pleasure and react instead with horror or disgust, may rebel against the dominant mode of address or resist its structuring logic, may even turn this logic against itself to open up the possibility of critique. But these structures and these logics nonetheless do their work, channeling and organizing affect in particular ways, working to constitute the broad terms of normalcy or legitimacy. The efficacy of the invitations they offer may be measured by their ubiquity, by the ease with which their logics take effect in the social and political sphere, and by the force of common sense they construct. This efficacy derives from the combination of the affective with the symbolic, the combination of "intensity as well as qualification"—the force of affect as well as its shaping.[49]

Visceral Politics

The scholarly turn to affect has been understood to map a shift in the social and political organization of public life in the United States, to chart the ascendance of affect itself as a means by which subjects—and national subjects in particular—are constituted and addressed. The rise of affect as a means of national address relates to the historical emergence of melodrama and cannot be understood outside of the ascendance of mass media across the nineteenth and twentieth centuries. Berlant traces the emergence of visceral politics to the 1830s, when feeling rather than rationality comes to be constituted as the basis for inclusion into the categories of both the human and the citizen; but it is in the context of the twentieth century that this kind of address comes fully to dominate mainstream political discourse. By the early twenty-first century, as Berlant suggests, the media's emphasis on liveness and on a variety of "you are here" conventions works to intensify a specific repertoire of emotional responsiveness as the basis for national identity and belonging.

I will return to a consideration of these conventions in the Epilogue. For now, it is important to note how they participate in the scene of visceral politics that Berlant discusses. The mediated solicitation to feel in response to an event deemed always already significant in nature—the present stuff of future history—constructs a privatized scene of emotional responsiveness as the basis for identification with a national public. Through the "mass-mediated scene of visceral engagement," the spectator is solicited to experience an emotional impact constituted through its representation as both shared and natural; and the projected collectivity of this impact, intensified through the mediated constructions of simultaneity and liveness, becomes the basis for political subjectivity in this context.[50]

Berlant speaks to the power of the media—in the example above, specifically television—in encouraging a citizenry to tune in together, noting how "the airwaves are saturated with incitements to keep citizens linked to each other" through identification with onscreen representations "composed of . . . the public's own, simultaneous, spontaneous, identical, and fully fleshed-out sensations in response to events deemed clearly worthy of noticing in a particular way."[51] Like Benedict Anderson, Berlant emphasizes the mediated experience of simultaneity in constituting national identity, alongside the function of collective attunement, the incitement to tune in together and "in a particular way." The context of Berlant's discussion, as it happens, is a reference to melodramatic address, which she links also to the early mode of the cinematic attraction, with which my own account begins. The representation of "scenes of intense emotion" serves as a "lubricant" for the experience of belonging, according to Berlant, and the sense of immediacy that the attraction works to produce is important to this process. Even Hugo Munsterberg in 1916, while anxious over the state of suggestibility the cinema was imagined to condition, identified the hegemonic possibilities of the young medium's "incomparable power for the remolding and upbuilding of the national soul."[52]

More specifically, in thinking of the work of melodrama, we might turn to Judith Butler's discussion of framing, in which she emphasizes the crucial role of the media in shaping the collective terms of mourning and violence. As Butler argues, the mediated act of framing constitutes the recognizability of different forms of injury and suffering, channeling the affective intensities of mourning into the retributive energies of nationalist violence. The move from mourning a loss to promising its violent retribution—the move, precisely, of sensational melodrama—forecloses upon other affective and political possibilities of an identification with suffering, as Butler has suggested. Membership in the larger public comes to be founded upon such mass-mediated responses, which themselves work to link feeling—and, as Berlant has argued, most significantly the feeling of pain or suffering—to both moral and political worth. The political implications of such a solicitation are vast, as morality and politics both are understood to derive primarily from the privatized experience of an emotional identification with pain and suffering, the capacity for which has been promoted from the nineteenth century forward as the basis of humanness itself. To question the workings of feeling in this context is to denigrate the very essence of what it is to be human.

In addition to Berlant's account of national sentimentality, other key junctures have been marked in the study of affect and its political function. The Cold War has been emphasized as a key period, as in Joseph Masco's analysis of the advent of national security affect and Elisabeth Anker's discussion of melodramatic political discourse. The period designated as late capitalism or post-Fordism has also been identified, often dated from the economic crises of the early 1970s and marked by the decline of the welfare state, the turbulence of global capital, and labor insecurity. Finally, the era deemed post-9/11 has been a focus of affect studies, marked by national reaction to the attacks on the Pentagon and World Trade Center, the intensification of the national security state, and the ascendance of the political logic of preemption and the ongoing war on terror.[53]

More broadly, Massumi has mapped a shift in the workings of power from disciplinary forms focused on the normalization of subjects and behaviors to affective forms focused on the modulation of feelings. He understands this change in relation to different modes of capitalist power and reads evidence of it in the political climate after 9/11, during which "an American president can deploy troops overseas because it makes a population feel good about their country or feel secure, not because the leader is able to present well-honed arguments that convince the population that it is a justified use of force."[54] Yet, even while Massumi locates visceral politics in a post-9/11 landscape, the significance of affect as a mode of national address structuring the collective identification of what feels good, as well as just, stretches back much further.

Imperial Affects

As feeling comes to constitute the primary means through which national subjects are hailed as such, affect becomes a crucial terrain upon which to interrogate the workings of imperialism. How is a national public attuned to the project of imperialism? How does this project come to feel both good and right, thrilling and rejuvenating? How are innocence and virtue constituted within the imperialist imagination through and in relation to the sensational appeals of action and violence? As the media function as primary mechanisms for these processes of attunement, mediated representations of nationalist violence are a central archive in addressing these questions; and melodrama, as the dominant mode organizing the affective address of American public culture across genres and media, is a key analytic framework. For the cinema in particular, melodrama has provided both a lineage—a set of formal conventions and narrative structures that shape its articulation—and a highly flexible form, able to adapt to a variety of political projects. Within this protean form and across diverse historical periods, however, certain patterns persist.

The relationship between imperialism and melodrama reaches back toward the genre's origins, as evidenced in its quick pivot from a "primarily didactic genre of social restoration to a militant, primarily sensationalist genre of imperial power."[55] Sensational melodrama in particular, with its explicit investment in a visceral, agitating mode of address, has been central in the constitution of imperialist affect across the American twentieth century. As in the early context Buckley discusses, the form has relied upon the vacillation between masochistic and sadistic modes of identification—between the appeals of suffering and vulnerability, agency and violence—although the precise patterns and rhythms governing this relationship, as well as the social contexts through which it circulates and the tensions it expresses and negotiates, have varied.

In the analysis of cinematic invitations to a pleasurable identification with nationalist violence across the twentieth century, the gendering of particular representational conventions emerges as one important theme. In American cinema and cinema studies scholarship alike, aggressive onscreen action has been cast as a signifier of the masculine, a construction that has escaped critical scrutiny with surprising regularity. In *Imperial Affects*, I take sources of cinematic satisfaction often regarded as too obvious to require careful analysis—the pleasure of cavalry charging across the screen, for instance, or an action hero exploding in a frenzy of retributive violence—and attempt to understand how a sense of rightness or inevitability accrues to particular scenarios of action and violence through the reiterative conventions of melodrama. In linking the work of melodrama to imperialism in particular, I seek to understand the way ideologies of white, male, and American supremacy—constituent interlocking features of imperialist discourse in the United States—have been animated by the appeals of both virtue and excitement (with this latter term understood in a broadly affective sense). While male-oriented genres have often been cordoned off from discussions of melodrama through an emphasis on their realism, I interrogate how the sensationalism of these forms takes shape through a discourse of the authentic and the real, tethered to ideas of bodily responsiveness that are themselves both racialized and gendered.

One question that resonates across the book is that of the attraction: the direct, kinesthetic, often aggressive mode of address that has been argued to define the early cinema in particular (and whose reascendance marks the late-century action cinema as well). As I argue, it is the persistence of the attraction within classical as well as post-classical Hollywood cinema that has designated male-identified forms as thrilling, a classification that gestures toward their imagined impact on the body. This question of the body both draws upon and deviates from earlier approaches to the study of spectatorship, raising issues that remained bracketed in feminist discussions of the male gaze, for instance, by considering embodied experience as central to the gendering of particular modes of cinematic representation and address. Like these earlier accounts, however, the present project is not an ethnographic study of audience reaction or an exploration of the myriad ways specifically situated subjects or communities may take up or resist the invitations held out to them by the dominant culture. Instead, it is a reckoning with the shape and force of these invitations themselves, an examination of what has constituted their particular promise of pleasure and what factors—cinematic as well as social—have shaped the satisfactions they offer.

Within the American cinema, a discourse of realness and authenticity works to naturalize the merger of visceral with moral appeals, as I discuss across the first two chapters. Chapter 1 explores the relationship between cinema and imperialism in the crucial early period of their convergence, considering not simply how representations of imperialist pursuits were constituted as appealing spectacles, but also how cinema spectatorship itself was shaped through and within a discourse of imperialism. Focused on representations of the Spanish-American War in newspapers, illustrated weeklies, paintings, and photographs, as well as early moving pictures, the chapter centers on the discourse of the strenuous life as it shaped emergent forms of cinematic representation and address. Rather than naturalize the conjunction of cinematic action with masculine modes of entertainment, the chapter traces the ascendance of a culture of strenuous spectacle, through which a particular repertoire of mass-mediated display came to signify the values of the authentic, the manly, and the American.

Central here is my concept of strenuous spectatorship: a gendered mode of mediated engagement combining voyeuristic distance with an embodied sense of vulnerability, in line with the strenuous life's celebration of intense embodied sensation as balm to the enervations of modern life. Looking to the figures of the war correspondent and the thrill-seeking soldier, alongside the charge films and battle reenactments of the early cinema, the chapter analyzes how such representations function to transform the very act of observation into a specifically manly activity. Situating the attractions of the early cinema within this broader discourse allows for new insights into the gendering of cinematic action, as contemporary fears of white masculine enervation are paradoxically addressed through the visceral appeals of the cinema, helping to negotiate the place of the nascent institution in the social landscape of the twentieth century.

Building on these arguments, chapter 2 analyzes the merger of the thrilling direct address of early cinema with the increasingly moral solicitations of narrative film form in the emergent genre of the Western. Focusing specifically on the status of the Western as melodrama, I examine the sensational appeals of both action and pathos as they structure western representation, from pre-cinematic forms like western action painting and the Wild West show, to the emergence and evolution of the film Western as the most successful of Hollywood genres. Through the melodramatic alignment of visceral thrills with moral authority, the Western produces a powerful felt good in the image of nationalist expansion, which is constituted as both virtuous and thrilling in nature.

In analyzing the felt good of motion and violence in the Western, I emphasize the continuity between expansionist ideologies of the nineteenth century and imperialist aims of the twentieth, understanding these as a shared project of nationalist and white supremacist violence. The conventions inaugurated by the early imperialist actualities are central to the generic pleasures of the Western, which grow out of and extend both an identification with the white masculine hero as the morally endowed agent of expansion and the alignment of this identification with the visceral thrills of an aggressive cinematic address. The chapter interrogates the ideological work performed by the conventional alignment of the Western with the values of the authentic and the real, through which the genre and its hero appear as spontaneous products of American history and cinema alike. Focusing on the genealogy of the charge in particular, I elucidate the cultural and affective force of identification with the Western hero, illuminating how the white supremacist foundations of the genre are both encoded and disavowed through the sensational appeals of motion, from silent Plains War Westerns to the B Westerns of the 1930s and early 1940s.

While the first two chapters analyze the cinematic merger of visceral with moral thrills, chapters 3 and 4 focus on the rise of pathos in action-oriented genres across the second half of the twentieth century, questioning the new affective attachments these forms engender. In chapter 3, I investigate how a focus on the hero's suffering intensifies in the Cold War Westerns of the 1950s and early 1960s, as the white supremacist discourse upon which the genre is founded comes under increased pressure from social and political movements of the postwar period, including the rise of the civil rights movement and the global export of both American films and ideologies of democracy. Breaking with the cinematic lineage of the charge, the affective address of the Western shifts from the visceral and moral appeals of motion toward a pathetic identification with the Western hero as victim. While guilt and shame enter the genre's affective register in a new way in this period, as unapologetic celebrations of white supremacy become more difficult to sustain, a new kind of moral authority accrues to the hero, derived from the formal and thematic emphasis on his suffering. This emphasis maintains this figure as the affective center of the genre, even as the conventions of action that had once assured his moral stature render him increasingly suspect.

Drawing upon Linda Williams's discussion of racial melodrama, the chapter emphasizes the function of racialized victimization in the "pro-Indian" Westerns of the 1950s in particular, in which the Western hero moves from an increasingly intimate alignment with the figure of the Indian as a victim of white racist violence to a complex appropriation of that position. In the hero's suffering and instability, the genre finds an affective solution for the contemporary critique of traditional forms of white masculine authority, inviting a renewed attachment to the image of such authority through gestures of its repudiation. Providing a powerful model for the action hero to come, the Cold War Western hero is produced as the locus of both power and anguish, paradoxically shored up through the image of his breakdown.

The pathetic figure of the Cold War Western hero serves as an important precedent for action films of the 1980s and 1990s, which mobilize the technological apparatus of the cinema to wed spectacular displays of destructive violence to increasingly elaborate scenarios of victimization and abuse.

Chapter 4 considers the status of imperialist subjectivity in this context, both in relation to the action cinema's invitation to identify with techno-logically enhanced powers of mastery and self-extension and in relation to the hero's precarious positioning as it is constructed in physical as well as social and institutional terms. The invitation to identify with both agency and vulnerability structures late-century action at the level of form as well as narrative, returning us to the doubled appeal of both omnipotence and embodied vulnerability that has marked the mediated production of impe-rialist subjectivity across the twentieth century.

In examining the relationship of victimization, virtue, and violence in the late-century action cinema, I consider both the efficacy and the increasing queasiness surrounding their conventional alignment. The chapter opens with a discussion of the *Rambo* films, in which the melodra-matic articulation of action reaches its zenith, and traces this articulation across the canonical *Lethal Weapon* and *Die Hard* franchises and into the purportedly critical works of *Falling Down* and *Unforgiven*. Even as *Rambo* reworks the cultural imaginary of Vietnam through the melodramatic conjunction of thrills with moral innocence, the film suggests the sadistic energies that imperialist affect both invokes and disavows. These impulses rise more explicitly to the surface in late-century action cinema, in which the technological attractions of onscreen violence often escape their melo-dramatic framing, suggesting how these appeals both animate and exceed officially sanctioned modes of aggression. Committed to the dialectical production of both innocence and pleasure, late-century action cinema introduces new notes of ambiguity and ambivalence into the affective reg-ister of sensational melodrama, manifesting in the unstable claims of moral authority on the spectacular appeals of screen violence. Nonetheless, melo-dramatic structures continue to shape cinematic action, as challenges to the conventional conjunction of virtue and violence ultimately seek reso-lution through pleasurable and pathetic identification with the plight of white male victim-heroes.

The felt good of melodrama is borne out of a complicated confluence of factors—morally endowed frameworks of story and character along-side viscerally intense modes of spectatorial address—that involve socially sanctioned states of aggression, gratification, sympathy, and desire along-side less organized forms of affective arousal. It is the work of melodrama to elicit these diverse affects and to integrate and arrange them within broader ideological frames, making particular kinds of sense out of the fields of sensation it invokes. Though the claims of moral authority on the spectacular appeals of screen violence become more unstable by the twentieth century's close, popular and political responses to the attacks of

9/11 suggest the enduring role of melodrama in the production of imperialist affect at the dawn of a new century.

The Epilogue returns to the questions of realness and mediated experience that thread through the previous chapters, evaluating the legacy of sensational melodrama in the appeals of screen-based violence in the early twenty-first century. The genealogy of cinematic action that I trace across the book provides a crucial foundation for understanding the attractions of imperialist violence in the wake of 9/11, as the melodramatic constellation of victimization, virtue, and violence provides a ready and compelling frame for both the 9/11 attacks and the ensuing war on terror. As at the turn of the twentieth century, a discourse of the real continues to frame both the cultural imagination of combat and the appeals of virtual violence. In closing, I consider the affective, ideological, and political functions of realness in this context and its specific relationship to the contemporary military-entertainment complex, in which the screen-based experience of war plays an increasingly prominent and lethal role in the project of U.S. imperialism.

1

A Rough Ride

Cinema, War, and the Strenuous Life

In the early moving picture *Roosevelt's Rough Riders* (AMB 1898), a mounted cavalry unit charges toward the camera, Theodore Roosevelt at the fore (fig. 1). As the riders advance, they loom larger in the frame, bearing down upon the spectator with speed and force, much like the oncoming locomotive in the Lumière brothers' famous *Arrival of a Train at La Ciotat* (1895) three years earlier. The picture is one of many military actualities produced around the Spanish-American and Philippine-American Wars, documentary-style and reenacted films that attest to the centrality of imperialist spectacle to the American film industry in its earliest years. The aggressive mode of address typifies the era's charge films and battle reenactments, in which action and violence are oriented directly out toward the spectator, inviting a visceral response to the novel attractions of motion onscreen. Here, imperialism itself takes a new and appealing form, as the sensational address of the early cinema is harnessed to an ideology of national expansion embodied in the image of the charge. Shot in 1898 at the training ground in Tampa, Florida, before the troops departed for Cuba, the film both anticipates and compensates for Roosevelt's mythic "charge" up San Juan Hill, providing a thrilling image of the Rough Riders in motion that—due to fighting conditions and the technological limitations of early film—the war in Cuba would not itself provide.[1]

A second image, not a film but a journalist's account, offers another take on war and cinema on the eve of the twentieth century. As described by Richard Harding Davis, novelist and fellow war correspondent Stephen Crane stands atop a Cuban hillside, hands stuffed into his raincoat pockets,

Fig. 1. The Rough Riders stage a charge, Roosevelt at the fore. *Roosevelt's Rough Riders* (AMB 1898).

pipe dangling from his lips, coolly surveying the Battle of San Juan. Bullets fly about him, but he does not once duck his head. He appears instead to be absorbed in the scene before him, peering over the crest of the hill "as unconcerned as though he were gazing at a cinematograph." Though Crane's colleagues urge him to take cover, he ignores them until Davis accuses him of "trying to impress us with his courage," at which point Crane finally drops to his knees.[2] This image of Crane circulated in the contemporary press alongside other accounts of the bravery and derring-do of the war correspondents, who offered a powerful point of entry into the fantasy of wartime experience, functioning as both surrogate spectators and heroic would-be soldiers for the audience back home.

Both these images, in different and sometimes surprising ways, speak to the relationship of early American cinema to the contemporary notion of the strenuous life and the imperialist ideology at its core. As articulated in the late nineteenth and early twentieth centuries, the strenuous life represented a host of aspirations and anxieties, driven by the imagination of an American national identity constituted through racialized properties of manliness and against the perceived effeminizing effects of an indus-trialized, commercial culture. A commitment to the strenuous life was advocated as necessary to the health of both individual Anglo-American men and the nation itself, as the former were understood to embody and ensure the latter.

In this chapter, I trace the discourse of the strenuous life as it emerges in the context of an ascendant mass-mediated culture, attending to how these forces shape and inform one another. As suggested by my opening images, I focus on representations of the Spanish-American War in particular and their implications for understanding the nascent technology of the cinema. Ultimately at issue is the emergence of particular modes of cinematic representation and address in which ideologies of imperialism and the thrill-seeking impulses of an ascendant consumer culture combine. Constructing this alignment, the earliest war films encouraged a set of viscerally and ideologically satisfying responses, producing a kind of felt good in the image of imperialist action.

The relevance of the strenuous life to these opening images concerns interrelated issues of representation and spectatorship—what is being imaged and the way this image addresses its imagined audience. On the level of representation, the moving picture of Roosevelt's charge participates in what I term the culture of strenuous spectacle, that is, the widespread performance of a muscular and vigorous Anglo-American masculinity, circulated as evidence of the national strength and imperialist destiny of the United States at the turn of the twentieth century. Physically active male bodies were highlighted in live athletic events and exhibitions, in the military parades, drills, and battle reenactments that crowded the era's fairs and expositions, and, most importantly, through the circulation of these images in the burgeoning mass media of print and film. This circulation pivoted on the conflation of particular male bodies with the body of the nation, naturalizing specific modes of masculine performance and instantiating an ideology of the strenuous as central to an ascendant national mass culture.

The cinema worked to legitimize itself through the image of an active Anglo-American masculinity, just as the strenuous life came into focus through the thrilling and novel appeals of moving pictures. Even before the advent of the cinema, there was a notion that physically active male bodies in athletic and military contexts would offer particularly suitable subject matter for the nascent technology.[3] Indeed, moving forward from the early days of Edison's peep-hole kinetoscope, a range of strenuous pursuits—boxing, wrestling, bodybuilding, gymnastics, football, and war itself—supplied a persistent and ubiquitous theme. And the actualities of the Spanish-American War would provide a crucial boost to the film industry at a key moment in its development, offering powerful early testament to the ability of the medium to solicit an intense affective response on the part of its audience.[4]

At the same time, however, as Davis's accusation of posturing suggests, the performance of masculine strength and courage in an increasingly image-driven world conditioned its own risks and anxieties. Ideas about manliness teetered in a fragile balance with the feminizing implications of conspicuous display. Producing deviant as well as normative modes of masculine spectacle thus becomes one important project of the mass-mediated discourse of war, as African American, Cuban, Filipino, and Spanish men are all offered up as feminized objects of the gaze, working to secure the normative status of Anglo-American masculine spectacle in contrast.

In addition, the aggressive address of *Roosevelt's Rough Riders* suggests another crucial aspect of the cinema's participation in the cultural fantasy of the strenuous life: the mediated production of war as a thrilling and highly consumable experience, one paradoxically aligned with the "authentic" embodied appeals of risk and danger. Like other charge films of its day, noted in the popular and trade press for their thrillingly direct address, the film places the spectator in a position of vulnerability while at the same time inviting identification with the moving image of American imperialist agency.[5] It is this paradoxical appeal of vulnerability and omnipotence to which the second image also refers; Crane's imagined position as a cinema spectator is constituted through a voyeuristic vantage point on the action alongside an embodied vulnerability to assault.

In their doubled roles as both vigorous participants in and privileged observers of war, correspondents like Crane embodied an imagination of spectatorship as both thrilling and manly—a model of what I have deemed strenuous spectatorship, which the charge films and battle reenactments also work to construct. In the discussion to follow, I consider these issues of spectacle, spectatorship, and the strenuous life across a range of sites, including newspapers, paintings, memoirs, and a novel, as well as early moving pictures. At the heart of this investigation is the Spanish-American War correspondent as he suggests the emergent outlines of another figure, one who would gain even greater cultural prominence across the twentieth century: the cinema spectator.

Theodore Roosevelt and the Discourse of the Strenuous Life

Before I move to the Spanish-American War and the images and texts that circulate around it, it is necessary to sketch out something of the cultural fantasy of the strenuous life, which provides the foundation for this chapter's exploration of the relationship between cinema and imperialism in this crucial period of their convergence. At the simplest level of its meaning, the term "strenuous" signifies energetic exertion, with connotations that are strongly gendered, suggesting a muscular straining that, if not explicitly somatic, is at least imagined in relation to an idea of physical effort. Arguably, too, the idea of the strenuous carries an insinuation of positive gain, a whiff of the worthiness of the ultimate goal driving this vigorous effort.

These connotations of both virility and merit derive in important ways from Theodore Roosevelt's tremendously influential articulation of the strenuous life in his many writings and speeches. Most famously, in his 1899 address "The Strenuous Life," Roosevelt introduces an injunction to imperialist action in Hawaiʻi, Puerto Rico, Cuba, and the Philippines through an emphasis on individual men's commitment to vigorous effort and striving and their concomitant eschewal of the seductions of leisure, enjoyment, and "ignoble ease." Linking the fate of the nation to the vigor of its Anglo-American male citizens, he enjoins his listeners to fealty to the virtues of toil, suffering, and risk, casting these as manful pursuits measured against the enfeeblements of base commercialism and pleasure seeking. At the same time, he extols "the mighty lift that thrills 'stern men with empires in their brains,'" conjoining the discourse of commercialized pleasure with the project of empire.[6]

The annexation and occupation of "the great, fair tropic islands" and the broader military investments these commitments entail emerge in Roosevelt's account as consonant with the gendered virtues of action above and against the feminization of both leisure and peace. The failure of individual men to commit to the doctrine of strenuous living directly implicates the health and strength of the nation; muscular, active Anglo-American men will ensure a muscular, active foreign policy, committed to extending the rights and influence of the nation beyond its continental borders while preserving the dominance of Anglo-American men within them. To shirk these responsibilities is to endanger the future of race and nation alike, in Roosevelt's view; the "native" white race will decline in the face of falling birth rates and rising immigration, and aggression from abroad will overwhelm a weakened nation of gender deviants.[7]

Roosevelt's advocacy of the strenuous life as both an individual and a national imperative speaks to widespread anxieties over the changing structural and sensory organization of everyday life at the end of the nineteenth and beginning of the twentieth centuries. The ongoing industrialization, urbanization, and increased corporatization of the United States were rapidly reorganizing the economic and social foundations of the country, and the impact of these changes on ideologies of Anglo-American masculinity was profound.[8] Ever a tenuous proposition, the nineteenth-century ideology of manly self-making became increasingly difficult to sustain as capitalism developed away from a producer-based and toward a consumer-based economy. Alongside the dramatic uncertainties of the market, middle-class men's labor was now entrenched within larger bureaucratic structures offering limited opportunities for individual initiative and advancement. That this labor was often sedentary in nature raised additional concerns about the physical health and vigor of middle-class men.

Meanwhile, the fantasy of separate spheres, which had shored up the Victorian construction of manhood, continued to crumble in the face of women's increasingly visible and vocal participation in the public sphere. While middle-class women participated heavily in Progressive reform movements, extending while challenging assumptions about their proper place and function in the home, working-class and immigrant women circulated prominently in the public sphere as laborers and activists. The growth of consumer society also encouraged the increased activities of women as consumers of essential goods and services as well as new forms of entertainment and leisure (including, of course, moving pictures).[9] At the same time, the influx of immigrants from Southern and Eastern Europe changed the ethnic composition of the fast-growing cities, challenging dominant conceptions of the United States as an Anglo-centric nation; and fears of a Yellow Peril were mobilized to police the boundaries of both nation and neighborhood against the racialized specter of the Chinese immigrant.[10] Energized by industrial growth, the labor unrest of the previous three decades continued, as working-class men and women protested against corporate capitalism's worst abuses, stoking middle-class fears of violent class revolt.

The crowded cities in particular, with their new modes of transit and communication, regimented forms of industrialized labor, and visually explosive landscapes, constituted a profound challenge to traditional modes of temporal, corporeal, and social experience. In a much-explored thesis, modernity itself was understood as constituted through the affective experience of shock or trauma—sudden, disruptive, and often violent encounters that typified the texture and rhythm of urban life in the late nineteenth and early twentieth centuries.[11] The era's burgeoning entertainment industry has been broadly read as reproducing the violent and disruptive experiences of modernity while containing and controlling them, habituating the modern subject to a new relationship to time and space while managing, at least to some extent, the anxieties occasioned by technological, economic, and social change. Like the Coney Island roller coaster for which its attractions are named, the early cinema participated in this process, redeploying sensory assault as a thrilling and consumable experience.[12]

The accelerated pace and heightened sensory stimulations of daily life were felt to imperil the physical and mental health of middle-class men especially. They gave rise to an epidemic of nervous disorders attributed to the cumulative pressures and pace of modern life (a diagnosis offered to many prominent intellectual, political, and cultural figures, Roosevelt among them). The prescriptions for such nervous ailments worked to reinscribe the gendered and racialized differences modern life was imagined to erode; thus, while neurasthenic middle-class white women were recommended an infantilizing regime of bed rest and cessation of all mental labors, middle-class men were directed toward active physical pursuits through which they might be revitalized.[13]

The widespread diagnosis of neurasthenia highlights the uneasy relationship between notions of progress and decline as they structure ideas of Anglo-American masculinity in this period. Nineteenth-century conceptions of middle-class manhood had emphasized the regulation of male bodily economy, imagined as a closed system of limited vital resources whose careful management would ensure both physical health and financial success in a competitive marketplace oriented around the production of goods and the accumulation of capital. Thrift and restraint were valued highly, and self-control emerged as a key signifier of middle-class masculine identity; to expend fruitlessly was deemed both wasteful and unmanly.[14] In the context of an ascendant consumer society, however, the virtues of such self-regulation were less clear. Although middle-class masculinity was still identified with ideals of self-control, concerns emerged as well over excessive productivity, overexertion, and overwork—conditions of an overregulated masculine subject.

Closely aligned with these concerns was the fear of "overcivilization," the anxiety that, by regulating their more "primitive" appetites in the interests of a commercial marketplace, middle-class Anglo-American men (and by extension, the American nation itself) had become less manly. Although the growth of the marketplace was promoted as a testament to the industry and vigor of these same men, commercial society was castigated for undermining the traditional foundations of masculine identity, as in Roosevelt's outcry against the "timidity" and "flaccidity" of commercial interests. The fear of overcivilization expressed a central paradox: even as civilized virtues were represented as the substance of white racial and American national superiority—and the ideological basis for imperialist intervention into geographical spaces and communities deemed unfit for self-governance— these virtues were associated with the values of the feminine. The purportedly civilized nature of Anglo-American men thus signified at once their racial superiority and the vulnerability of that superiority to decay; manliness was understood as a precondition to national progress but was threatened with destruction by that very progress.[15]

The strenuous life emerges within this context. It is presented in political, popular, and medical discourse as a solution to the epidemic of neurasthenia and the general threat of overcivilization. In place of civility and self-restraint, strenuous living was imagined to tap into essential masculine appetites and manly passions repressed by the market and by feminine forces of temperance and reform. A wide range of physical pursuits—including hunting, ranching, fishing, camping, wrestling, boxing, bodybuilding, and football—were promoted to reinvigorate a generation of would-be pussyfoots and mollycoddles. The experience of combat was heralded as a prime opportunity for revitalization through strenuous experience, reconnecting men with an aggressive physicality and homosociality imagined as the legacy of an Anglo-Saxon warrior past. Related to this legacy was the equivalency constructed between western continental conquest and conquest abroad.[16] Whether cowboy or cavalryman, the figure of the white man on horseback was cast as the descendant of the Anglo-Saxon knight, in whose blood ran an inborn impulse toward expansion, the racial imprint of Manifest Destiny.[17]

As Amy Kaplan has observed, it was "the discovery of 'the primitive' as a regenerative force" that underwrote the seemingly diffuse impulses of the strenuous life, from the emphasis on outdoor activity, to the special status of the frontier, to the new craze for spectator sports.[18] In pursuing this life, middle-class men were imagined to ward off the threat of masculine softness, rejecting the sybaritic pleasures and bureaucratic pressures of modern commerce through an embrace of the more primitive virtues of physically demanding, or even punishing, experience. Thus, even as they were encouraged to subdue "savage" and "barbaric" populations both at home and abroad—the multi-ethnic domestic working class, as well as non-Anglo and non-Christian populations overseas—Anglo-American men were encouraged to foster a relationship with the imagined primitive within, the controlled cultivation of which would redress the threat of individual, racial, and national degeneration.

Yet, while the strenuous life was posited in rhetorical opposition to the developments of modern commercial society, it was deeply embedded in ascendant modes of commercialized recreation and consumption and served in many ways as an accommodation to the very modernizing impulses it decried.[19] Though staged against the pressures and seductions of modern life, for instance, the strenuous life was inseparable from its circulation as mass-mediated spectacle.[20] The explosion of visual media in the 1890s revolves significantly around a culture of strenuous spectacle: newspapers, mass-circulation magazines, and early moving pictures centered on images of active and muscular masculinity; and photojournalism emerged and quickly established its prominence through the largely interchangeable representation of sports and war.[21] Articulated against an encroaching consumerism associated in a variety of ways with the feminine, the strenuous life was constituted through a particular repertoire of images of masculine mobility, strength, and agility, which would come to signify the authentic manly substance of both individual men and the nation itself.

Historical actors moved fluidly among diverse registers of strenuous performance in this context, as in the famous example of Buffalo Bill Cody, who shuttled between frontier violence and its spectacular Wild West reenactment. These movements were promoted as an intensification of the realism of cultural attractions, underscoring the imbrication of the authentic with the theatrical. In the case of Roosevelt's First Volunteer Cavalry—composed of eastern blueblood athletes and roughhewn western cowboys, some courtesy of the Wild West show—the credentials of the Wild West cowboys (the original "Rough Riders of the World") brought a degree of manly authenticity to the unit's cultural standing. Such fluidity emphasized that war and its performance were understood as coextensive, located not on disparate or even parallel planes of experience but constituting between them a single plane of strenuous endeavor.

Thus, while authenticity was associated with substance and materiality—"the real thing," in the parlance of the day—a theatrical register of display became the dominant mode of its construction. Roosevelt himself provides perhaps the single best example of this impulse, as the most conspicuous proponent of the strenuous life, for whom technologies of representation were an integral aspect of its construction. His personal transformations—from asthmatic youth to collegiate athlete, for instance, and from dandified eastern dude to frontier rancher—served as a prominent argument for the virtues of strenuous living, even as his near-obsessive documentation of these pursuits registered the centrality of an ascendant mass cultural gaze to the constitution of the strenuous life.[22]

In the context of a war orchestrated to a significant extent as a mass entertainment spectacle, Roosevelt and his First Volunteer Cavalry emerged as ready-made poster boys for the strenuous life. Offered as a testament to the substance of American masculinity in the face of its perceived crisis, the unit achieved a celebrity that highlights war itself as contiguous with other forms of contemporary spectator-driven entertainments.[23] In one account given by Albert Smith, the Vitagraph film company's co-founder and cameraman, Roosevelt halted in the midst of his charge up San Juan Hill to "strike a pose" for the moving picture camera. Though the account is spurious, it is significant as a testament to the way mass-mediated spectacle was imagined not apart from but deeply interwoven with even the most deadly serious of strenuous pursuits.[24] And while there is no photographic record of the charge, there are—not incidentally—many pictures of men "striking tough poses for the camera."[25]

Roosevelt's promiscuous relationship to the media became the stuff of both legend and satire, highlighting an instability at the core of the culture of strenuous spectacle. Hostage within this culture is the insurgent sense of gender as a constellation of surface acts, a set of ritualized and costumed displays in which difference and identity are continually reinscribed, a reiterative structure in which failure and inadequacy emerge as constitutive possibilities. This sense is conditioned by the development of new technologies of representation and their increasing integration into everyday existence, as well as by the erosion of the myth of economic self-making, in the face of which the ideology of normative masculinity begins to shift to the register of cultural representation.

The more anxious implications of this process are often highlighted in contemporary comic representations. Some herald Roosevelt's strenuous commitments by representing his aggression, strength, and mobility in contrast to a feminized or infantilized corporate body; others underscore the more unstable aspects of these commitments through images of hysteria (Roosevelt as a grinning madman adorned with an excess of phallic weaponry) or infantile theatrics (Roosevelt as a small boy in knickers, mounted atop a hobby horse rather than a strapping stallion). That one popular series represents the petulant young Teddy in blackface further underscores the instability of his strenuous performances and suggests the function of racialized bodies in marking off the borders of normative masculine display. These images lampoon the very premise of strenuous spectacle, classifying Roosevelt's theatrics in direct opposition to the normative category of manliness that the strenuous life worked to construct (fig. 2).

Though historical accounts of the strenuous life most often emphasize its commitment to physicality, muscularity, and hardness as manly balm to the enervating impact of modern life, understandings of strenuous experience also revolved in important ways around ideas of physical vulnerability, receptivity, and openness. As expressed in Roosevelt's emphasis on "strife and . . . hard and dangerous endeavor," the strenuous life encompassed ideas of suffering as well as triumph. Exposure to bodily risk emerged in this context as a keystone of individual and national regeneration—a crucial aspect of the strenuous life that aligns it with the sensationalist discourse of the thrill in ways that will prove central to my argument. While the simultaneous emphasis on hardness and openness, strength and vulnerability, might appear contradictory, when encountered in an appropriately strenuous context (a battle, say, as opposed to an industrial accident), overwhelming sensation was understood to harbor revitalizing potential. In contrast to the feminizing impulses of civilization—the seductions of affluence and ease, as well as the restrictions and routinizations of industrialization—the immediacy of intense embodied sensation was conceptualized as a more primitive, more real, and hence more manly mode of experience.

Fig. 2. Roosevelt's courtship of the gaze, both racialized and infantilized. Frederick Opper, *New York Journal*, March 2, 1901. Courtesy of the Library of Congress.

Thus, the overcivilized man might be reinvigorated if, instead of simply hardening himself, he remained open and receptive to overwhelming bodily sensations. War, with its imminent dangers and physical deprivations, was cast as the most opportune environment for manly reinvigoration through strenuous experience, as well as—and inseparable from this—the most prominent stage for mass-mediated strenuous display. And so we return to the thrilling image of Roosevelt charging toward us and to Crane on the hilltop, immersed in the spectacle of battle below.

Strenuous Spectacle in the Theater of War

In the theater of the Spanish-American War, the relationship of strenuous spectacle to ideas about the nature and substance of American men was negotiated against a field fraught with the lethal implications of seeing and being seen. "The history of battle," Paul Virilio has famously argued, "is primarily the history of radically changing fields of perception," a fact made particularly explicit in the context of this conflict, in which emergent technologies governed changing modes of visuality.[26] Guerilla tactics, more accurate long-range rifles, and smokeless powder obscured the location of Spanish adversaries, while an American observation balloon baldly announced troop movements and the smoking guns of the U.S. volunteers gave "the regimental line away to the enemy as plainly as an illuminated sign."[27] Like the American soldiers who "cursed and raved because they could see nothing to shoot at," reporters, illustrators, and photographers—dispatched in unprecedented numbers to cover the conflict—decried the lack of scenes corresponding to a traditional imagination of war. Without vast, amassed armies moving to confront each other across clearly marked plains of battle beneath clouds of billowing smoke, the view of war lacked, according to photojournalist J. C. Hemment, "the same romantic spectacle that one is accustomed to seek and find in past war pictures."[28]

Hemment and his peers expressed disappointment over the limitations of photographic technology in this changing landscape of war; in particular, the new moving picture camera proved too cumbersome to shoot footage of the fighting. Already associated with the culture of strenuous spectacle through his innovative "instantaneous" work in sports photography, Hemment yearned for the capacity to capture the speed and motion of war. He fantasized, "if a shutter can be made fast enough to take the bullets as they whiz through the air, then war scenes may again become very vivid, picturesque, and romantic. . . . This is, of course, but a dream . . . but we know there must be something that will give that vividness and reality which the absence of smoke now deprives."[29] In another passage, Hemment remarks on the Spanish Mauser bullets as they sliced through the air overhead. Their incessant whine was a regular source of terror among the troops, but "I could not prevent my head turning upward when they hissed by, and I could not restrain the idea from arising in me that I ought to photograph them as they flew."[30]

In his persistent impulse to photograph the bullets—to render the image of war through an affecting reference to the force of its violence—Hemment gives expression to the contemporary collapse of realism and sensationalism, founded in the presumption that the "vividness and reality" of war are best represented through an intensely visceral mode of mediated address.

In this, he identifies the central impulse animating the early charge films and battle reenactments and anticipates conventions that would persist across twentieth- and into twenty-first-century screen cultures. In contrast to these fantasies of speed and motion, however, which governed contemporary written as well as illustrated accounts, actual photographs of the war represent more static and mundane scenes. Rather than the explosive energy of the bullets, we witness fields of action too distant to discern, the gradual, gathering movements of large groups of men, and tableaus of the aftermath of battles or the periods of waiting that precede them.

Thus it is against the much-maligned backdrop of "nothing to see" that the spectacle of strenuous action comes into focus, compensating for the failures of modern technologies of both photography and war to fulfill the ideological requirements of imperialism, with its emphasis on the inexorable force—the violence and motion—of American expansion. Contemporary written and visual representations of the war emphasize the heightened visibility and definitive movements of figures like Roosevelt, transposing the "suicidal conspicuousness" of the mismanaged ground campaign into a register of Anglo-American heroics.[31] The fantasy of motion organizing these images represented and confirmed the war as a site of white masculine reinvigoration and the inevitability of national expansion both embodied and ensured by this reinvigoration.

An innate and enduring compulsion toward motion was attributed to both the masculine and the national body, a compulsion that was imagined to find its natural expression in the Manifest Destiny of imperial warfare.[32] This emphasis on motion makes itself felt most acutely in the battle reenactments and charge films, which represent the war as a viscerally thrilling spectacle in a way live footage could not. Images of the mythic charge up San Juan Hill—anticipated by *Roosevelt's Rough Riders* and reproduced widely in newspapers, illustrated weeklies, and paintings—highlight the figure of Roosevelt as the focal point of action, as in the Frederic Remington portrait commissioned by Roosevelt himself, which features the colonel on horseback, saber drawn, leading the way. In the most hyperbolic of these images, Roosevelt's mount bursts forward from amid a visual field overflowing with energy and motion, the cavalry exploding into action behind him (though in truth cavalry units had been dismounted at the outset of the campaign) (fig. 3).

Other accounts extend the theme of heightened visibility as a signifier of manliness, celebrating the bravery of soldiers and officers willing to expose themselves under fire. In a description of the Santiago campaign, for instance, correspondent Edward Marshall notes proudly that "neither Colonel Wood nor any other officer that I saw made any effort to hide from the Spaniards." Instead, Wood "wandered slowly about on horseback

Fig. 3. The popular imagination of the Rough Riders' charge emphasized energy, force, and motion, in contrast to the scramble described by correspondents on the scene. W. G. Read, "Teddy's Rough Riders." Exact date unknown. Courtesy of the Library of Congress.

among his men with the bullets continuously shrieking their devilish song in his ears, and playing their infernal tattoo on the ground near him. . . . It was wonderful."[33] This recasting of suicidal conspicuousness as heroic spectacle became a convention of the correspondents' reports, suggesting how, in a conflict noted for the lethal invisibility of its adversaries, "the promise of being seen" may serve a compensatory function, helping to allay insecurities occasioned by the "confusion and the fear of not seeing."[34]

Many of the images of the Battle of San Juan Hill draw their inspiration from correspondent Richard Harding Davis's much-cited account, in which Roosevelt "was without doubt the most conspicuous figure in the charge . . . mounted high on horseback, and charging the rifle-pits at a gallop and quite alone, [he] made you feel that you would like to cheer."[35] Davis casts the appeal of the charge through an alignment of war with spectator sports, emphasizing a common reaction to the thrilling image of motion around which this conjunction pivots. Yet, even as he highlights the theatrical register of the charge, in which Roosevelt's blue polka-dot handkerchief "float[s] out straight behind his head like a guidon," Davis makes a point to stress the soldiers' strenuous efforts, the scrappy substance of their unlikely yet intractable progress up the hill.[36] While "in the picture papers the men are running up hill swiftly and gallantly, in regular formation, rank after rank, with flags flying . . . their bayonets fixed, in long, brilliant lines, an invincible, overpowering weight of numbers," Davis emphasizes that what was in fact impressive about the advance was that the men were so few:

> They had no glittering bayonets, they were not massed in regular array. There were a few men in advance, bunched together, and creeping up a steep, sunny hill, the tops of which roared and flashed with flame. The men held their guns pressed across their breasts and stepped heavily as they climbed. Behind these first few, spreading out like a fan, were single lines of men, slipping and scrambling in the smooth grass, moving forward with difficulty, as though they were wading waist high through water, moving slowly, carefully, with strenuous effort. It was much more wonderful than any swinging charge could have been. . . . It was inevitable as the rising tide. When it had reached the halfway point, and we saw they would succeed, the sight gave us such a thrill as can never stir us again. It was a miracle of self-sacrifice, a triumph of bull-dog courage, which one watched breathless with wonder.[37]

In his emphasis on "bull-dog courage" and self-sacrifice, Davis locates the charge within Roosevelt's own lexicon of manly effort and war. At the same time, and not incidentally, he infuses the thrill of ultimate victory with a pathetic appeal. At first the charge appears not heroic but "merely terribly pathetic. The pity of it . . . was what held you." Emphasizing the men's underdog advance and the spectator's thrill as pathos shades inexorably to triumph, Davis sounds the affective registers of melodrama, a mode of representation central to the theatrical figuring of heroic action, as I shall discuss.

Davis's refutation of the more patently spectacular image of the charge—brilliant, orderly, invincible—and his insistence instead on the straining, scrambling effort it entailed speak to broader tensions attending the culture of strenuous spectacle. Constituting the normativity of mass-mediated display as a signifier of masculine substance required the regular production of deviant modes of spectacle in contrast, to distinguish strenuous heroics from (in Crane's words) the "gallantry of Reginald Marmaduke Maurice Montmorenci Sturtevant" (a stand-in for the blueblood Rough Riders, who, like Roosevelt, were both celebrated and lampooned for their theatrics). Thus the figures of the dandy and the minstrel haunt accounts of the war, marking off the margins of strenuous spectacle even as they threaten to destabilize its premise.

The Spanish were frequently conjured to help secure the distinction between effete theatrics and more authentic expressions of masculine strength and courage. Paradoxically, in light of their lethal invisibility, they were reported to stage military spectacles "worthy of an opera bouffe," their conspicuous visibility signifying not heroics but vain posturing. Crane, for instance, described one Spanish officer who was "wont to promenade during lulls and negligently gossip" through the Battle of San Juan. Decked out in a "summer-resort straw hat," the officer "did a deal of sauntering in the coolest manner possible, walking out in the clear sunshine and gazing in our direction. He seemed to be carrying a cane."[38] Unlike similar accounts of American officers, whose "coolness" under fire was constituted as an affirmation of their valor (or of correspondents like Crane himself, whose similar conspicuousness was tempered only by the charge of vain posturing), heightened visibility here signals the masculine and military inadequacy of the Spanish officer; with his hat and cane, his sauntering and gossip, he is cast in the feminized role of the dandy. This construction was in keeping with the broader discourse of civilization, in which the Spanish Empire served as a cautionary tale, an effete example of a degenerated Old World power in an inexorable state of decline.[39]

Other racialized figures appear at the margins of contemporary accounts focused on the vigorous movements of Anglo-American soldiers. In catalog copy for the 1898 Edison actuality *Tenth U.S. Infantry, Second Battalion, Leaving Cars*, for instance, we witness again the eagerness to distinguish between the strenuous spectacle of the soldiers and the dandification of other modes of display. The picture, which features troops moving slowly across the frame, is advertised as "full of vigorous life." The Edison catalog announces the soldiers' arrival through an insistence on the indices of rugged experience: "Hurrah-here they come! Hot, dusty, grim and determined! Real soldiers, every inch of them! No gold lace and chalk belts and shoulder straps, but fully equipped in full marching order: blankets, guns, knapsacks and canteens." Downplaying more ornamental accoutrements of battle in favor of the strenuous accessories of the camping trip or hunting expedition, the copy also emphasizes the figure of a "comical looking 'nigger dude' with a sun-umbrella," who "strolls languidly in the foreground." In the film itself this figure flits briefly across a visual field dominated by the bodies of the disembarking soldiers. In the catalog copy, his presence is constructed as an anti-strenuous mode of display through the intertwining of racialized and sexualized tropes. Like the promenading Spanish officer in his summer-resort hat, the "nigger dude" with his sun-umbrella is made to embody a feminizing solicitation of the gaze, confirming the instability of strenuous spectacle while his otherness works to deflect it.[40]

To invite the gaze with too eager an appetite was to play the part of the dandy or the dude; but to refuse it completely was to intimate cowardice. Thus, while the conspicuous visibility of the Spanish signaled their feminized status, they were likewise impugned as cowards for sniping at

American soldiers from the dense, concealing vegetation. The charge of cowardice attending these guerilla tactics was racialized in its association with the Cuban pickets, whose invisibility was naturalized through a discourse of the primitive. In this discourse, men who "so closely resemble the bark of a royal palm or stump of an old dead tree in color" merged seamlessly into the landscape of which they were perceived to be an intimate part.[41]

In their primitive state, the Cubans were represented as inadequately manly and therefore unfit for self-governance, just as the Spanish, in their degeneracy, were unfit to rule over them. The strenuous spectacle of American soldiers, in contrast, served as confirmation of their manly and moral fitness to rule. Within this paradigm, the refusal to make oneself visible could constitute the failure of Anglo-American masculinity, as in a morality tale offered by Roosevelt himself. As the colonel charges past on horseback during the Battle of San Juan, he cajoles a soldier lying prone behind a bush to rise: "Are you afraid to stand up while I am on horseback?" At just this moment a bullet "aimed at the colonel . . . by some freak of ballistics missed him completely," slicing instead through the body of the prone man "lengthwise from head to foot." Thus the coward gets his due, as manliness—constituted here through codes of heightened visibility—provides providentially for its own protection.[42]

These negotiations around the condition of visibility and its implications emerge in the context of a newly intensified mass cultural gaze that shapes the landscape and experience of war. In addition to the emergence of photojournalism, the appearance of the new moving picture camera, and the unprecedented presence of newspapermen on the field of battle, over three-quarters of U.S. soldiers reportedly brought the popular Kodak "pocket cameras" with them to Cuba. The "massification of the gaze" through technologies like the portable camera helped to produce "unprecedented anxieties about the condition of being visible," as Bill Brown has suggested, and these anxieties registered in the instabilities of strenuous spectacle itself.[43] In the context of the new conditions of visibility, the implications of action or inaction are imagined through the structural dynamics of the gaze, highlighting the central function of spectatorship to their constitution.[44]

The significance of the gaze as a constitutive if unstable force is compellingly suggested by the internal predicaments of Henry Fleming, protagonist of *The Red Badge of Courage*, Crane's seminal novel of wartime experience. Though offered as an account of the Civil War, the novel resolutely locates its imagination of the conflict within the cultural and political contexts of the 1890s. As Amy Kaplan and Bill Brown have argued, the novel explores the manifestly theatrical experience of combat and the mechanisms of spectatorship through which it is constituted. According to Kaplan, "Crane transforms the representation of war . . . into an exotic spectacle that must be viewed by a spectator and conveyed to an audience." The novel not only renders sensory experience in photographic terms, Brown maintains, but also "materializes the psyche and the very process of mentation as a spectatorial apparatus."[45]

Manhood—or its denial—emerges in this context not in the medium of conflict but, in Kaplan's words, "in the medium of spectacle, from the relationship to a spectator," a dynamic that highlights manhood itself as an inherently unstable proposition.[46] The novel emphasizes what Crane would later refer to as the "absolute longing for the spectator" experienced by soldiers in battle, a longing fraught with anxiety and dread. For Henry is a protagonist agonizingly aware of his own status as spectacle, a status conferred through his identification with a mass cultural gaze before which he constantly performs (a propensity resonant with Roosevelt's own strenuous commitments).[47] This gaze is projected out across the novel's mise-en-scène, residing in a landscape imbued with eyes that watch and judge Henry and in an audience of comrades and corpses vested with the power to confer his manhood or deny it.

Identified as he is with this gaze, Henry, too, stands "as if apart from himself," "to look . . . in spectator fashion" at his own actions, and finds "considerable joy [and occasional distress] in musing upon his performances." Although Henry's "compulsion to picture" is gently mocked throughout the novel, he is described, even in his most decisive gestures, as "deeply absorbed as a spectator."[48] Like Roosevelt's, Henry's heroic gestures are defined by their conspicuous visibility, as when he races forward at the vanguard of a desperate charge, taking up the fallen color bearer's flag. Yet, rather than purifying him of the "compulsion to picture"—a compulsion represented as both constitutive and compensatory—this defining action secures his relationship to a manliness understood as and through its status as spectacle.

As Kaplan suggests in her reading of *The Red Badge of Courage*, the fantasy of heroic action and the strenuous discourse that underwrites it mediate the more mechanistic image of battle that Crane likewise insists upon. In the latter view, the individual soldier operates as a cog in the greater industrial and bureaucratic machine of war. While Henry may be "unaware of the machinery of orders," they nonetheless dictate his movements, a tension Crane highlights in his vacillation between mechanistic metaphors—the battle as "an immense and terrible machine" whose "grim processes" fascinate Henry, who "must go close and see it produce corpses"—and the chivalric discourse of the strenuous life in its emphasis on romantic images of martial heroics.

This tension surfaces three years later in the context of the Spanish-American War, where the compensatory function of strenuous spectacle manifests in relation to the "spectacle of efficiently massed efforts" onboard the modern battleships, themselves definitive in the American victories in Cuba and the Philippines.[49] Like the bureaucratic structures against which the strenuous life rebelled, the image of naval organization stressed the incorporation of the individual into larger bodies of effort. In contrast to the notorious confusion of the land campaign and the much-maligned mismanagement of the ground troops, the force and efficiency of the naval organization were widely celebrated. As David Axeen has argued, for Secretary of War Elihu Root and his allies, the "symbolic heroes of the war were the modern battleships and the professional principles of organization embodied in their crews and machinery."[50] The metaphors that defined these principles located the individual soldier or sailor as the necessary outcome of a mechanized process of production. Government policy was transformed "as by electrical converters," according to Root in a 1899 speech, into the strategy and tactics of the field "and into the action of the man behind the gun," who is "fed, clothed, transported and armed, equipped and housed" as "part of a great machine we call military organization."[51]

Retooled as the passive material over which the military machine works, the individual soldier is deprived of the vigorous energy and initiative celebrated in the image of Roosevelt's charge. Even in the firing of his gun, the soldier merely attests to the success of a mechanized process of conversion, whereby energy is transformed and transferred from government policy into military action. Photographs and illustrations of the "efficiently massed efforts" aboard the battleships confirmed this sense, offering images of coordinated action that signify the industry and enterprise of American men as a collective rather than an individual force. Even while the war was staged as a "warrior critique of business civilization," images of the navy suggest a heroic type at one with modern bureaucratic structures.[52] At the same time, sailors toiling away in the blasting heat of the engine room could not be easily absorbed into the chivalric image of martial heroism extolled by the strenuous life. Thus the celebration of naval force helped to condition the nostalgic spectacle of individual heroic action embodied in the charge, as a testament to the endurance of manly virtues in the face of modernizing technologies of work and war.

Strenuous Spectatorship and the Early Cinema of Assaults

According to Amy Kaplan, Henry Fleming's initial flight from battle in *The Red Badge of Courage* is motivated in part by a desire "to trade the role of actor for spectator, to gain both a sense of control and a vicarious thrill from observing the battle at a safe enough distance not to be crushed by it."[53] The sense of control that Kaplan suggests Henry is seeking provides useful insight into the function of spectatorship throughout the novel, as it works to contain the disordering sensations of battle with which Crane is also emphatically concerned. For *The Red Badge of Courage* articulates the experience of war through two primary tropes: war as sensory dislocation and war as spectacle, with the latter functioning as a framework to contain and organize the former. As Alan Trachtenberg describes, Henry's predicament across the novel is "to connect his body's [often overwhelmingly confusing] experience with the dreams of martial glory with which he sped to battle."[54] While the novel underscores the discrepancy between Henry's fantasies of martial glory and both the mundaneness and the brutal immediacy of war, the function of these fantasies is nonetheless suggestive. For Henry himself, once his exploits are constituted in the register of strenuous spectacle, "It was pleasure to watch these things."

When Henry eventually returns to the intensity and immediacy of the fighting, however, his renewed participation represents not a rejection of the spectator position but a more complete collapse of the boundary between observation and experience; even in the heat of battle, he continues to look as a spectator upon his own actions. In this doubling of the roles of spectator and actor, Henry resembles the figure of Crane himself, observing the Battle of San Juan as if "gazing at a cinematograph" while bullets whiz about his head. In the image of Crane on the hilltop, offered by Davis as a paean to the war correspondents' courageous feats, the sense of removal implied by Crane's position as cinema spectator is contrasted to the sense of his embodied vulnerability. Like Henry, Crane inhabits simultaneously the poles of distance and danger, voyeurism and vulnerability, as they structure the modern experience of war. His position is defined both by his absorption in the scene before him and by the degree to which this state harbors the possibility of violent rupture. In Crane's case as in Henry's, the experience of spectatorship itself is located within the terrain of the strenuous life.

In combining a voyeuristic gaze with the fantasy of heroic action, Crane and his fellow war correspondents adumbrate a position that would become central to the apparatus of the cinema and the constitution of the position of the spectator within it. In this, they are key to the construction of what I have termed strenuous spectatorship, suggesting how dominant conceptions of masculinity are being recast in this period through and in relation to the mediated experience of action and violence. Emerging in the late nineteenth century at the intersection of cinema and war, the strenuous spectator constructs a gendered mode of engaging with the appeals of an ascendant screen culture.[55] He embodies a set of contradictory appeals, negotiating the passivity and relative immobility of the spectator position by emphasizing risk as inherent to it. Like Crane on the hilltop—at once impervious and vulnerable, removed from the scene of violence in which he is at the same time intimately engaged—the strenuous spectator occupies a privileged vantage point on action alongside a fantasy of assault. Rather than cordoned off from an embodied sense of threat, as some early cinema theorists have argued, here the spectatorial body—and the white male body in particular—is imagined as very much on the line.

This doubled position of vulnerability and voyeurism shapes the charge films and battle reenactments of the Spanish-American and Philippine-American Wars as they circulated within the broader discourse of the strenuous life. In these films, the early cinematic convention of the attraction is rendered in its more assaultive form, incorporating the spectator—in formal and visceral terms—into the terrain of battle. Understanding the significance of strenuous spectatorship to these earliest war films is important to a consideration of the embodied appeals of screen culture across the twentieth century; the mediated fantasy of "being there," which direct, visceral modes of address work to construct, continues to mark screen violence with the assertion of an access to the real. This fantasy of "being there" pivots around the persistence of the attraction within narrative cinematic forms and the steadfast association of direct, aggressive modes of address with masculine-identified proclivities (a point to which I return in my discussion of the Western).

Strenuous spectatorship attests to the centrality of embodiment to the construction of a mode of cinematic engagement that—far from disappearing with the advent of narrative cinema—persists as a marker of male-identified genres and the pleasures they are thought to proffer. To emphasize the significance of embodiment to the construction of a masculinized cinematic address, however, is to deviate from influential discussions of the status of the gendered body in modernity and in the context of early cinema in particular.[56] In these discussions, the white masculine body has been imagined as most vulnerable to, and most threatened by, the physically and psychically jolting experiences of modern assault. As Mary Ann Doane has argued, "what is at stake in the early stages of development of the cinema is very much the body, but it is a body which is preeminently masculine, a body which is threatened and haunted by the specter of flaw or failure and by an anxiety generated by a conception of modernity as an assault on the body and its perceptual powers."[57]

In Doane's account, the cinematic apparatus comes to function as a prosthetic device, albeit imperfect, fashioned to assuage a masculine lack intensified through encounters with a host of modern shocks. Through a "refusal of contingency and embodiment," the white male subject is sheltered from modernity's blows, taking up residence in an increasingly disembodied identification with the apparatus, while the "burdens of contingency" are assigned to feminine and/or racialized bodies onscreen.[58] This argument is echoed in Lauren Rabinovitz's discussion of the early structures of screen exhibitionism and the function of the female body onscreen as it works to activate "a specifically cinematic *male spectator* as an implied aspect of the text" (italics in original).[59] In this account, the more familiar coordinates of Laura Mulvey's voyeuristic male spectator are associated with the emergent institution of the cinema,[60] a line of argument that tends to overlook the simultaneous role of embodiment in the masculinization of the spectator position in this early period.

Early films often thematize this imagination of modernity as an assault on the white male subject. In the trick films and story films of the cinema's first decade, for instance, the white male protagonist is regularly made to bear the brunt of modernity's blows, harassed, beaten, and literally blown apart in a series of assaults that the cinema is seen both to condition and to represent. Bodily peril provides these films with form as well as content, as the conventions of direct address and the appeals of trick photography are used to demonstrate the aggressive force of modern technology upon bodies both onscreen and off.

As Lynn Kirby has suggested, the protagonist's vulnerability in such films is sometimes associated specifically with his position behind the camera, as in the example of *The Photographer's Mishap* (Edison 1901), in which a photographer is run over by an oncoming train whose still image he is trying to capture. In Kirby's view, the film represents an "assault on vision" through the "aggression of the apparatus," confirming the collusion of the cinema in the masculine undoing that is signified by the photographer's subsequent hysteria.[61] Animated by the technological magic of moving pictures, even the most mundane of objects could collude in this kind of assault: deviously liberated from their quotidian functions, beds, chairs, and clothing climb walls and sail about rooms with the steadfast intent of harassing an increasingly hysterical white male protagonist. Like other early trick and story films, these scenarios highlight the complicity of cinema in a new visual, social, and technological regime associated here as elsewhere with the interarticulated threats of the feminine and the modern.

While the tendency of the early cinema to empower as well as to hystericize its male subject has been fruitfully explored by Doane, Rabinovitz, Kirby, and others, both the association of the white male subject with the disembodied gaze of the apparatus and the emphasis on bodily peril as a site of masculine undoing neglect the centrality of embodied experience itself to dominant social constructions of masculinity in this period.

To consider more fully the question of gender and spectatorship within the early cinema, we must first return to ideas about the rejuvenating potential of intense embodied sensation and to the figure of the war correspondent as he straddles the poles of spectatorship and risk. As an author, for instance, Crane made clear his disappointment in Civil War memoirs that failed to tell him much of the subjective experience of war, and he sought in *The Red Badge of Courage* to rectify this absence, focusing on an imaginative account of how war *feels* (inseparable, as it happens, from an account of how war looks—or, more precisely, of how it has been imaged, as Crane drew inspiration from Civil War photographs, among other sources).

Crane was far from alone. The embodied sensations of battle provided a particular focus of the burgeoning military literature of the late nineteenth and early twentieth centuries, in which Civil War veterans and soldiers recently returned from Cuba and the Philippines offered breathless, harrowing accounts of their extreme battle experiences. The imminent dangers and physical deprivations of war were imagined in relation to the fantasy of a more primitive warrior past; in his renunciation of sensual gratification, the resurrected Anglo-Saxon warrior would throw off the yoke of modern softness and ward off the specter of degeneration. But the purifying power of pain was driven by its own kind of sensual fantasy, an imagination of the loss of boundaries and a merging with immediate sensation, in which war was conceived "not so much as being a means of making others suffer as an occasion for giving ourselves up to suffering."[62] Soldiers detailed "how it feels to be under fire," "how it feels to be shot," "the awful sensations of a Naval encounter," and other "realistic" experiences of combat that emphasized the overwhelming physical and sensory impact of war, its powers of dismemberment and obliteration.[63] In these accounts, the ability of war to overwhelm sensory organization was celebrated, as it was the way in which combat "expands and strains the functions of sensation," "lifts [a man] out of himself," and "permeates his receptive facilities" that constituted its regenerative possibilities.[64]

In these representations of combat, we witness again the extent to which the strenuous life was constituted within the terms of an ascendant consumer culture, the agitations of war understood through a logic of consumption, in which thrill circulates as a desirable unit of experience to be quantified and consumed. The experience of being under fire was understood in this context as "the thrill we had come for."[65] This notion of combat as thrilling, echoed compulsively across contemporary accounts of war, complicates an understanding of thrill as that which "promises an excitation of the body without the accompanying threat of breaching its integrity," as here the excitations of consumer culture are aligned with the very real physical risks of battle.[66] The experience of combat was heralded for its potential to open overcivilized men to sensations more authentic, or more primitive, than those available in modern urban life, with the modern serving as a figure of alienation and abstraction, the primitive as a figure of embodiment and immediacy (though there was nothing inherently less immediate about the sensations of urban life, of course). Through the discourse of the thrill, however, the sensations of battle are aligned with those of the theater, the amusement park ride, or even the cinema itself. As in the broader culture of sensationalism, here notions of realness and authenticity are tightly bound to the process of their commodification, the appeal of the real operating not in opposition to but as a central aspect of an ascendant consumer culture.[67]

In his negotiation of pleasure, vulnerability, and aggression, the thrill-seeking soldier suggests the emergent position of the strenuous spectator, teetering on the brink of action and entertainment. He embodies a masculinized accommodation to a consumer culture aligned with the feminine, representing visual and sensory pleasure in and through the fantasy of violence and reading in this fantasy an assurance of the authentic and the manly. We might usefully consider this late-century image as it both extends and works to supplant the nineteenth-century tradition of *flânerie*, in which the urban male subject of a proliferating visual culture—the "perfect spectator" in Baudelaire's famous description—roams the streets of Paris, Brussels, or New York, collecting impressions. The flâneur is said to "idle in the city because, if he keeps himself purely receptive, the city prints each instant a fresh picture in his brain."[68] Like the flâneur, the thrill-seeking soldier is a mobile, touristic subject, open and receptive to sensory impression and positioned in significant ways as a consumer of the novel and the sensational. While in the case of the flâneur it is the visual stimulations of an urban world of commerce that impress themselves upon him, the soldier's receptivity to sensory impression is intended to signify his allegiance to the antimodern cult of authentic experience. The flâneur remains contemplative while the soldier asserts a more aggressive stance, echoing the flâneur's receptivity but refuting any association with the effete tastes of a mobile yet still passive urban subject.

Even more than the thrill-seeking soldier, the war correspondent helps to displace the image of flânerie, transforming the very act of observation into a specifically manly activity. The correspondents played multifaceted roles in the war, positioned as privileged spectators while actively involving themselves in the conflict, undertaking scouting expeditions, accompanying troops to the front, and helping to stage theatrical quasi-military missions in which they also took part (and on which they then reported). Echoing the impulse of Henry Fleming, the correspondents "pictured themselves as actors on a real-life stage; they strutted and posed, championed the downtrodden, and risked their necks as if they were heroes in a melodrama."[69]

Offering regular accounts of their own and their colleagues' heroism under fire, the correspondents worked to produce a model of masculinity in which modern professionalism and strenuous heroics were effectively combined. Contemporary representations of the correspondent as military hero worked to assert an image of strenuous masculinity that the correspondents' own function as agents of a mass cultural gaze helped to destabilize. As Bill Brown has argued, the heroization of the correspondent enacts a transformation that "effectively condenses the whole business of war's modern representation—the bureaucratic newspaper system, the telegraphic, photographic, and cinematic apparatuses—and displaces it onto the individualized American male."[70] Amy Kaplan has argued that the media's focus on the war reporter as hero "turned writing into a strenuous activity and the reporter into a virile figure who rivaled the soldiers."[71] Yet, it is not in his function as a writer but in his function as a spectator that the correspondent is represented as heroic, not writing so much as spectating that constitutes his strenuous credentials.

Contemporary accounts regularly define the role of the correspondent through an emphasis on the preeminence of his vision. Davis celebrates Crane's status as the correspondent best able "to make the public see what he sees," commending his willingness to sit at the feet of a solider under fire, "close enough to watch his lips move."[72] Crane himself described his function as that of "a sort of cheap telescope," an apparatus "whose business it was to transfer . . . visual impressions to other minds."[73] Another account identifies the correspondents' responsibility as "nothing beyond using the wonderful photographic plate of their memory for everything that passes before the lens of their eyes."[74] Although such images ascribe an aspect of passivity or disengagement to the correspondent's function, casting him in the technologized role of apparatus, these same accounts also emphasize the active incorporation of the correspondent into the strenuous field of battle. Davis pays homage to the correspondent "who watches the battle from an elevation in the rear" and thus "can obtain a much better view," for instance, but he also celebrates the one who chooses "to stand on the firing-line in order to see what is going forward close at hand."[75]

As in the case of Crane, it is precisely through the collapse of these positions that the correspondent's function is constructed, the privileged vantage of the voyeur merging with the authenticating credentials of the firing line. Photojournalists like Hemment make this imbrication of vision and violence explicit, as the gestures of the photojournalist and the soldier mirror and confirm one another.[76] Unlike the reporter, who could conceivably fake his dispatches while remaining far from the front, the indexical quality of the photograph served as proof of the photojournalist's bravery in "being there" amid the action.[77] Celebrated for the strenuous virtues understood to be necessary to his service, the photojournalist absorbs the masculine credentials of authenticity associated with photography and combat both, while asserting a manly agent "behind" the mass technologies of representation and war.

Embodying the collapse of action and observation, the war correspondent offers a compelling site of identification for the mass audience back home, mediating concerns over the feminizing implications of spectatorship itself. The contemporary association of mass spectatorship with women and with the feminine more broadly is evident in the gendered construction of the consumer gaze as well as in widely expressed anxieties over the role and influence of women as a cultural audience.[78] Even the popular pocket cameras carried by soldiers to the front were marketed heavily to women, providing them "with 'a look' just as that other craze, the bicycle, provided them with a new degree of mobility."[79]

The uncertain implications of male spectatorship in this context are hinted at in the description of a football crowd offered by Harvard president Charles Eliot in 1894. Eliot decries the football spectator's "disposition to 'hysterical excitement'" as "evidence, not of physical strength and depth of passion, but of feebleness and shallowness," an affective instability and excitability associated at once with the "uproarious mob" and the savage "Indian village."[80] Circulating as a suggestive amalgam of gendered, classed, and racialized deviance, here the mass spectator is clearly marked off from normative ideals of white masculine subjectivity. While the hysterical or savage spectator represents a feminized loss of control, the war correspondent as strenuous spectator works to organize an affective response that, though implicated in the action, at the same time retains a distance from it. The correspondent speaks to what J. A. Hobson in a 1902 treatise on imperialism deemed the "lust of the spectator," a desire, as Kaplan has noted, that "is both gratified and further aroused only in the act of watching, which distances the viewer while tantalizing him with the possibility of action."[81]

It is this tantalizing sense of possibility that the charge films and battle reenactments of the Spanish-American and Philippine-American Wars work to construct, as they locate spectatorship within a thrilling and specifically somatic field of experience. The military actualities were responsible for a dramatic surge in the popularity of moving pictures, whose initial appeal as a technological novelty had begun to wane by the end of 1897. The conflict that was to assist in the regeneration of Anglo-American men thus provided as well for the invigoration of the American film industry, which found in the buildup to war a steady stream of subjects that lent themselves particularly well to the novel attractions of motion onscreen.

With the intensified production of war-related subjects—military drills and parades, U.S. battleships, the routines of camp life, bathtub renditions of famous naval battles, the popular raising of the flag over Morro Castle, as well as the charge films and battle reenactments—moving picture engagements were renewed at vaudeville houses and middle-class establishments like New York's Eden Musee. Storefront theaters, circuses, and traveling picture shows headlined the technological attraction of the cinema projector, newly christened as the "Wargraph" or "Warscope." Cameramen from the production companies of American Mutoscope and Edison (with the substantial aid of the Hearst organization) made their way to Tampa and then on to Cuba to film footage of the conflict. Although the action itself proved elusive and the technology ill-suited for capturing live images of the fighting, military actualities filled program bills across the country (fig. 4).

Associating the film industry with the strenuous spectacle of war granted a new kind of legitimacy to the infant medium. At the same time, the appeal of war itself was significantly constituted through the novel attractions of motion, in which an ideology of imperialist expansion found particularly affecting form. Arranged together in proto-narrative form and combined with stereopticon slides as part of a full-length evening's program, the films played to packed houses and boisterous crowds, who "cheered . . . to the echo as they watched the War-graph throw [pictures of the war in Cuba] upon the giant screen."[82]

To the extent that their direct aggressive mode of address elicits a specifically visceral response, the charge films and battle reenactments in particular provide compelling testament to the appeal to embodiment through which cinema spectatorship takes shape, complicating (as I have suggested) the theoretical tendency to emphasize the institutionalization of a disembodied male gaze. In these films, the body of the spectator is imagined as situated within the contemporary terrain of battle—a terrain that, as Kristin Whissel has deftly argued, emerges only in and through this presence.[83] Returning, then, to the question of masculinity and the early cinema, it is worth considering these earliest war films alongside discussions of the attraction as the mode of address organizing the relationship of the early apparatus to its spectator.

As Tom Gunning has famously argued, in contrast to classical conventions of narrative integration and voyeuristic structures of looking, the early cinema of attractions demonstrates strong sadistic and exhibitionist tendencies as it directly solicits, acknowledges, and plays to the viewer's gaze, seeking to agitate and astonish its audience through a succession of shocking and immediate encounters.[84] The direct address that typifies this cinema often takes the exaggerated form of an assault, in which the speed and force of bodies in motion are oriented toward the camera and,

Fig. 4. The attractions of battle reenactments and other Spanish-American War actualities invigorated the film industry, an early testament to the affective appeal of moving pictures. *Lyman H. Howe's New Marvels in Moving Pictures* (Buffalo, NY: Courier Co., ca. 1898). Courtesy of the Library of Congress.

by extension, the audience. Such films mediate "how it feels" to be on the receiving end of violent technological assault, as in the aptly titled *How It Feels to Be Run Over* (Hepworth 1900), in which a stationary camera films the approach of a horse-drawn carriage and then a motor car down a stretch of dusty road; the former passes without incident, but the second careens directly into the camera/audience. As in *The Photographer's Mishap*, the technological threat represented by modern forms of rapid transit is redoubled through the technological novelty of the cinema.

Indeed, train films have served as the analytic exemplar of both the convention of cinematic assault and the hysterical spectator it is argued to condition. Among the earliest and most cited examples is the Lumière brothers' *Arrival of a Train at La Ciotat* (1895), from whose hulking locomotive the early spectator is said to have cringed and fled in terror. While the significance of this encounter as an origin myth has been widely debated, it is indisputable that the sense of embodied vulnerability conditioned by films like *Arrival* constituted a large part of their appeal. And we should not underestimate the violence underwriting this appeal, as evidenced in Maxim Gorky's contemporary description of the way the train "seems as though it will plunge into the darkness in which you sit, turning you into a ripped sack full of lacerated flesh and splintered bones."[85] Attractions like the popular Hale's Tours of the World, an early train-ride simulator, also attest to the importance of embodiment to the contemporary spectator position, intensifying the somatic appeals of onscreen motion through the introduction of sensory cues like sound and the agitation of the exhibition space, "locat[ing] meaning in the body of the spectator."[86]

While train films have received the lion's share of critical attention, the charge films and battle reenactments of the cinema's first years offer another prominent example of the convention of assault, one that raises important questions as to how we understand the significance of this convention as well as its persistence. Like the train films, the charge films figured their assault upon the audience through the representation of rapid oncoming motion: the pounding rush of a cavalry unit galloping toward the front of the frame. The charge films' representation of forceful forward motion produces in the spectator a pleasurable apprehension of impending collision, as highlighted in catalog copy for the *Charge of Boer Cavalry* (Edison 1900), which approvingly notes how "the audience makes an involuntary effort to move from their seats in order to avoid being trampled under the horses" as the cavalrymen advance, waving their sabers aloft.[87] These films represented a very popular early subject, at least as common as the train films and, according to Charles Musser, equally characteristic of the early cinema's style.[88] Screened alongside *Arrival* at the 1896 New York City debut of the Lumières' cinematographe, for instance, the *Charge of the Seventh French Cuirassiers* was heralded as "one of the most exciting scenes ever displayed"; nothing "more realistic or thrilling" had been seen in town for many a month.[89] The film's popularity inspired many others, *Roosevelt's Rough Riders* among them.

For all their formal similarity, however, the train and the charge films figure cinematic assault in significantly different terms. For if the image of the train rushing headlong toward the audience activates anxieties about modern technological development—representing through its aggressive address both the technology of the train and the cinema's ability to figure it, as Gunning has suggested—what does it mean to figure cinematic assault through the image of a mounted cavalry charge? As with contemporary attractions like the roller coaster, the train and the charge films both invoke and contain a sense of threat, repackaging the shocking and often violent experience of modernity as a commercialized thrill. In contrast to the more unruly attractions of Coney Island, however, the charge films explicitly align this thrill with the nationalist project of war.

Wolfgang Schivelbusch has discussed the history of shock as this term granted a specifically military significance to the more general concept of collision, initially arising to describe "the encounter of an armed force with the enemy in charge" or "the encounter of two mounted warriors . . . charging one another."[90] In this light, charge films may be seen to restore to the notion of modern shock something of its traditional valence, resituating modern technological encounter within the ideological landscape of the strenuous life, with its image of a rejuvenated knightly warrior. Circulating within the culture of strenuous spectacle, charge films mediate the representation of technological modernity itself, embodied here in an image of traditional martial heroics. The notion of modern technology as threat is thus contained, as the thrilling force of cinematic assault is harnessed to a triumphal assertion of white masculine and American national mobility.[91]

In addition to the cavalry charge, the battle reenactments of the Spanish-American and Philippine-American Wars mobilize the convention of assault through the image of the infantry attack—soldiers rushing forward and firing their weapons, "attacking the camera position as if it were a bastion."[92] In the first two shots of U.S. Infantry Supported by Rough Riders at El Caney (Edison 1899), for instance, infantrymen rush down a dusty road, fall to their knees, aim, and fire toward the front of the frame; the film's third and final shot features the charge of a cavalry unit down the same stretch of road. While the action in U.S. Infantry is angled toward the camera at a slight diagonal and places the spectator in roughly the position of the Spanish adversaries, other films deploy the convention of assault to condition identification with the position of the U.S. soldiers under attack. One of the most suggestive of these is Advance of the Kansas Volunteers at Caloocan (Edison 1899), in which Filipino rebels advance in a line directly toward the camera, firing their guns straight out ahead of them. Although the slow, almost tentative nature of their advance undercuts somewhat the status of the Filipinos as a threat (rendering them less than manly, in

Fig. 5. The melodramatic staging of imperialism as inherently defensive, inviting identification with the U.S. soldier as both the victim and the agent of violent action. *Advance of the Kansas Volunteers at Caloocan* (Edison 1899).

keeping with the racialized construction of their dependent status), the convention of firing toward the audience formally casts their approach as a menacing one.

The directness of the Filipinos' fire conditions a visceral sense of assault while intensifying the spectator's identification with the position of the U.S. soldiers under attack; when the soldiers rise up out of the bottom foreground of the frame, emerging as if from the space of the audience itself, their interruption of the rebels' gunfire functions at once as a moment of triumph and of rescue (fig. 5). Contemporary catalog copy highlights these movements as particularly affecting. The film is lauded as "one of the best battle pictures ever made. . . . The first firing is done directly toward the front of the picture, and the advance of the U.S. troops apparently through the screen is very exciting."[93] A similar strategy can be seen at work in *Sham Battle at the Pan-American Exposition* (Edison 1901), in which a live battle reenactment is shot from "behind the lines" of the U.S. infantrymen. The camera's location encourages identification with the defensive position of the soldiers as they retreat under Indian fire; moving backward into the foreground of the frame, the soldiers' increasing scale emphasizes the camera's placement among their ranks, soliciting identification with the aggressive forward motion of their eventual offensive surge. The substitutability of Indians and Filipinos in these films highlights the ideological equivalence through which imperialism is constructed as an extension of continental westward movement, operating as a new frontier within the cultural imagination of nationalist expansion.

Inviting identification with the experience of battle, these films inscribe the position of the strenuous spectator within the nascent institution of the cinema. As Whissel has argued, they locate their audience "on the scene of history," staging the attractions of battle both to mobilize and to manage an encounter with the technological force of modernity.[94] While Whissel focuses on a more generic figuring of the audience, my concept of strenuous spectatorship seeks to understand more precisely the position of this audience within the ideological web of gender, race, and war. In contrast to Whissel's consideration of the battle reenactments as a means both to figure and to contain the technological trauma of war (an argument more in line with the discussions of modern shock outlined above), the notion of strenuous spectatorship suggests how the aggressive and immersive properties of cinematic assault in this context are contained already within a contemporary discourse of the strenuous. In their impulse to represent "how it feels" to be under fire, the charge films and battle reenactments ask to be read alongside other articulations of the strenuous life, in which the opportunity to experience the violent embodied sensations of battle is understood as central to the broader project of both individual masculine and American national invigoration.

In their emphasis on an aggressive visceral mode of address, these films hold forth the possibility that the rejuvenating fantasy of the battlefield might be extended to include the space of the cinema, that spectatorship—like war itself—might harbor possibilities of masculine regeneration and renewal. This sense of possibility is not simply a function of the films' representational content—triumphal images of strenuous heroics—but equally or more so of the mode of address through which onscreen heroics are figured, as the spectatorial body is explicitly invited into a visceral sense of involvement with the scene of battle. Rather than the denial of embodiment suggested by Doane, these films construct and mobilize a viewing position by animating rather than refusing an imagined relationship to the body. In contrast to Kirby's assertion that "the assaulted spectator is the hysterical spectator," the charge films and battle reenactments masculinize the spectator position precisely through their aggressive mode of direct address. The spectatorial position these films construct resembles that of the war correspondent, constituted through the merger of voyeuristic distance with an embodied sense of threat. Rather than an apparatus of masculine undoing, then, the cinema here incorporates the dominant ideological impulses of the strenuous life, soliciting identification with the imperialist project of war and the fantasy of battlefield experience that underwrites it.

A melodramatic structure of feeling often frames the visceral attractions of these films, a framing that will be essential to my discussion across the remaining chapters. It is suggested in compact but compelling terms in *Advance of the Kansas Volunteers*, in which rudimentary structures of identification appeal to and produce a sense of both embodied vulnerability and aggressive agency. The spectator is invited first into a viscerally charged identification with the position of victim (situated as the locus of the rebels' fire) and then aligned with the forward motion of the U.S. soldiers' efficacious advance. By conditioning an embodied sense of threat, which is then redressed through an identification with violent action, the film highlights the underlying role of melodrama in shaping representations of war and violence in American cinema—the way scenarios of victimization function in both formal and narrative terms to situate the appeals of aggressive action, framing this action as defensive in nature.[95] *Advance of the Kansas Volunteers* sounds an additional note of pathos in the felling of the U.S. color bearer halfway through its forty-five-second battle scene. His death— the battle's only visible casualty—serves to accentuate a sense of triumph when the massive flag is then raised and carried forward, waving across the center of the frame as the U.S. soldiers surge ahead (harkening back to Henry Fleming's own heroic action).

Even charge films like *Roosevelt's Rough Riders* circulate within the melodramatic structure of turn-of-the-century imperialist discourse, in which a maidenly Cuba, subject to the rapacious appetites of a decadent and lecherous Spain, awaits the chivalric intervention of the heroic American cavalryman. The contemporary force and legibility of these films drew from and relied upon this context, lending to the thrilling image of the charge the moral valence of rescue.[96] The charge films and battle reenactments also referenced and recast the melodramatic scenarios of assault and rescue made popular by the Wild West show, in which the image of the cavalry's advance had already been constituted as a nationalistic spectacle at once thrilling and righteous, as I discuss in the next chapter.[97]

In activating popular melodramatic scenarios of war, the charge films and battle reenactments align the attractions of the new medium of moving pictures with morally endowed structures of identification and feeling, while imbuing these familiar scenarios with a novel appeal. In doing so, they contain a provocative suggestion of the pull of the attraction toward rather than simply away from narrative and, in the context of the American cinema, toward narrative of a particular sort. The appeal of such scenarios would be intensified through the formal articulation of film melodrama in the years to come, in which the invitation to identify with victimization and vulnerability is interwoven in increasingly complex and involving ways with the thrilling spectacle of retributive violence. If it is true, then, as Kirby has argued, that narrative cinema will emerge in part as an effort to absorb the "hysterical premise" of early cinema, it is important to note the charge films and battle reenactments as an early front in this campaign.[98]

The discourse of the strenuous life staged its fantasies of primitive masculine substance through the register of mass-mediated display. The Spanish-American War in particular marked the integration of strenuous experience with the commercial enticements of the thrilling and the sensational, securing space within an ascendant consumer culture for manly modes of performance and consumption. The war provided a venue at once theatrical and authentic, in which the rejuvenating effects of intense embodied experience merged with the conspicuous spectacle of white masculine heroics, combining the manly appeals of combat with the commercial discourse of the thrill—"the thrill" the soldiers had come for, as well as the "thrilling" spectacle of the soldiers themselves.

The cultural imagination of war became in this period more intimately wed to mass technologies of visual representation, themselves shaped in significant ways by the imperatives of strenuous spectacle. Innovations in photographic techniques and materials emerged through the spectacularization of sports, and photojournalism established its cultural and ideological influence through the strenuous spectacle of war. While still photography provided one "cultural lens" through which strenuous spectacle was produced, the cinema—burgeoning due to the popularity of Spanish-American War films—would supply a powerful new one, in which the visceral and ideological appeals of motion were more fully realized.[99] It was only within the context of the broader culture of strenuous spectacle that the cinematic image of white masculine motion would emerge and come to signify, working to manage even as it invoked the technological anxieties of a new mass medium.

The conventions inaugurated by the charge films and battle reenactments are central to the generic pleasures of the Western in particular, which would grow out of and extend both an identification with the white masculine hero as a morally endowed agent of nationalist expansion and the alignment of this identification with the visceral thrills of an aggressive cinematic address. The rejuvenating space of the West and the movement of the mythic cowboy across it were already cast within the imperialist terms of the strenuous life, as frontier experience was constituted as a primary site of white masculine and American national invigoration. In its spectacle of Anglo-American masculinity in motion, its investment in the regenerative possibilities of the frontier, and its reliance upon scenarios of conquest and violence, the Western provides a powerful means by which the ideological impulses of the strenuous life are carried forward across the twentieth century. Here the images of strenuous masculinity that dominated the actualities of the 1890s and early 1900s are conventionalized within the context of narrative cinema, increasing the moral and affective force of these representations while retaining their value as thrilling spectacle.

The conflation of thrilling action with the values of the national as well as the masculine would become explicit in the first decade of the twentieth century, as arguments for the authentically American virtues of the early Western were launched in explicitly gendered terms, the thrills of action associated with a more muscular, more manly—and hence more American—style of production.[100] The persistence of the attraction in the context of the Western is key to these claims, as a direct address based in action and violence continues to function as the signifier of a specifically gendered appeal. It is through the sensationalism of the Western that strenuous spectatorship—the paradoxical provision of "authentic" embodied experience through the virtuality of the spectator position—becomes conventionalized, the visceral thrills of action instituted as a mark of male-identified genres and the masculinized modes of pleasure and engagement they are imagined to condition.[101] This notion of authenticity returns us to questions of affect and the body, because it is through an association with embodied experience that the mise-en-scène of the Western comes to be classified (like the West itself) as a landscape of the real, a classification closely aligned with the genre's melodramatic impulses.

2

Manifest Destiny in Action

Sensational Melodrama and the
Advent of the Western

In the photograph, the painter stands erect and intent, brush poised before the canvas. He wears a coat and derby hat, a sharp nose and well-groomed mustache visible beneath its brim. He stands on the rooftop of an apartment building, along which a line of chimneys runs into the distance, suggesting the crowded lives below. Beyond the rooftop are the belching smokestacks of a rapidly industrializing city. In front of the painter kneels another man, this one suited up in a cavalry coat and bandana, a gun belt slung low around his waist. The crouching man's six-shooter is drawn and pointed squarely at the painter and his canvas (fig. 6).

The year is 1903, and the man in the hat is Charles Schreyvogel, best known for his action paintings of the U.S. Cavalry, for which he drew inspiration from his avid attendance at Buffalo Bill's Wild West show. In the photograph, Schreyvogel is working in his outdoor "studio" in Hoboken, New Jersey, above the apartment where he lives. The image distills many of the themes of the last chapter: the fast-changing terrain of social and economic life in the late nineteenth and early twentieth centuries; the impact of these changes on gendered and racialized identity; and a set of cultural responses, which emphasized a visceral, often aggressive mode of address—the ascendance of the thrill as a primary unit of cultural consumption.

The menacing pose suggested by Schreyvogel's model appears in *Breaking Through the Line* (1903), a Plains War portrait in which a

Fig. 6. The image of the West is produced as a thrilling site of violent encounter, associated with the rejuvenating potential of immediate embodied experience. Unknown photographer, *Charles Schreyvogel Painting on the Roof of His Apartment Building in Hoboken, New Jersey,* ca. 1903. By permission of the National Cowboy & Western Heritage Museum, Oklahoma City.

cavalry trooper, charging from the center of the frame, leans across his horse's neck to aim his revolver directly out at the viewer (fig. 7). As in most of Schreyvogel's western images, an emphasis on the force of motion gives the painting a distinctly cinematic feel. The aggressive address apprehends the viewer in immediate and visceral terms in much the same way as the charge films and battle reenactments of the last chapter, reaching beyond the frame to invite the viewer into an embodied imagination of the experience of violence.

The aggressive address staged by Schreyvogel and his model and reiterated in the context of the painting references the violent attractions of the early cinema while suggesting their relevance to the cultural imagination of the West in particular. Against the backdrop of an urban industrial East, the West comes into focus around the turn of the twentieth century as a kind of Rooseveltian landscape of the strenuous, in which a self-conscious and highly mediated performance of violence comes paradoxically to signify a claim on the authentic, the American, and the manly—a provenance nowhere more evident or influential than in the genre of the Western. With his gun drawn and aimed out toward the front of the frame, the trooper in *Breaking Through the Line* bears a striking resemblance to the infamous bandit in the emblematic opening/closing shot of Thomas Edison's

Fig. 7. The visceral emphasis on motion and an aggressive direct address constitute the West as attraction through suggestively cinematic conventions, enveloping the viewer in the space of violence. Charles Schreyvogel, *Breaking Through the Line*, 1903. From the collection of Gilcrease Museum, Tulsa, Oklahoma.

The Great Train Robbery, also produced in 1903 and frequently credited as the first Western.[1] While a viewing of the film may have influenced Schreyvogel's composition here, his earlier use of direct address speaks to the broader significance of the attraction within western representation in this period.

In the emerging contours of the Western as a generic form, the tendency to appeal to the spectator in visceral as well as moral terms locates Schreyvogel within the fantasized terrain of the strenuous life, in which exposure to violence held forth the promise of manly reinvigoration in the interests of Anglo-American empire. It is fitting, then, that the image of the cavalryman in Schreyvogel's painting recalls that of the "cowboy president" and Rough Rider Theodore Roosevelt, one of Schreyvogel's many admirers. The resemblance speaks, like Roosevelt himself, to the close ideological and representational kinship between continental expansion and overseas imperialism, as images of military action in Cuba and the Philippines circulated alongside images of violence on the western plains in mutual tribute to the inexorable force of Manifest Destiny. In imperialist discourse of the time, these spaces were constructed as continuous, providing largely interchangeable sites for the reinvigoration of overcivilized Anglo-American men in the interests of American empire.

The construction of this equivalence is key to the genesis of the Western, in which the cavalry charges and battle reenactments of the cinema's first years find a generic home, instituting the appeals of motion that defined the early cinema's imperialist attractions. Onscreen motion in the early military actualities testified to the power of Anglo-American empire, embodied with particular force and ubiquity in the image of the charge. As discussed in the last chapter, the charge was thrilling both because it offered a dynamic representation of imperialist agency with which the spectator was invited to identify and because it addressed this spectator in a particularly direct and aggressive fashion, inviting a visceral as well as ideologically invested response. To trace the image of the charge from the early military actualities into the genre of the Western is to appreciate how deeply the conventions of cinematic action are implicated in the history of imperialism and how a particular mode of address forms a central aspect of their appeal.[2] For their part, the early charge films and battle reenactments also referred back to the popular attractions of the Wild West show, highlighting again the common visual and ideological terms animating images of nationalist violence on the North American continent and abroad.

As the cultural expression of Manifest Destiny, the Western emerges as a generic form only through this emphasis on motion, which has been central both to its identification as a genre and to its ability to "move" audiences in particular directions. Constant, fast-paced motion was key to the extraordinarily popular attractions of Buffalo Bill's Wild West show; and, as in the example of *Breaking Through the Line*, the genre of western action painting inspired by the Wild West show is likewise distinguished by an intensely kinesthetic rendering of physical movement. As in the Spanish-American War representations of the last chapter, the appeals of motion are ideologically particular here, embodying an invitation to pleasurable identification with the projects of imperialism and Manifest Destiny.

Drawing from the Wild West show as well as the charge films and battle reenactments, the Western is distinguished as a genre on the basis of its relationship to physical movement. As early as 1915, Vachel Lindsay attributed a generative power to Western action, exclaiming over "[t]he whirlwind of cowboys and Indians with which the photoplay began" (an origin Lindsay associated, echoing Roosevelt, with the cinema's embrace of the reinvigorating possibilities of "the primitive").[3] Over half a century later, André Bazin famously pondered the Western in similar terms, noting its close identification with "the essence of cinema" and its status as "the only genre whose origins are almost identical with those of the cinema itself."

According to Bazin, "It is easy to say that because the cinema is movement the western is cinema *par excellence*."[4]

What is striking in these and other accounts is the extent to which the appeals of cinematic motion are naturalized, their association with the Western—and with the imagined space of the West more generally—offered up as an obvious and seemingly inevitable conjunction. Indeed, the alliance between the Western and specific kinds of action-based appeals has escaped critical scrutiny to a striking degree; the charge, the chase, and the fight appear instead as the privileged expressions of some irrefutable essence of the West. And although Bazin, in trying to solve the "secret" of the Western's ongoing appeal, ultimately rejected the idea that this appeal is constituted through the emphasis on movement, his rejection is enabled in part by a failure to account for the ideological specificity of the genre's commitments.

What Bazin overlooks is the work of the Western in naturalizing a particular repertoire of white masculine motion as a cinematic and cultural shorthand for thrilling entertainment underwritten by an assertion of moral virtue. His discussion instead confirms the Western in its own ideological aims, legitimating its historical claims and validating the affective force of the image of morality it works to produce. In making this argument, Bazin emphasizes both the epic and the tragic value of the Western while neglecting entirely its melodramatic structures (despite the extent to which his own comments often draw attention to them). However, as I shall argue across this chapter and the next, it is precisely through its status as melodrama that the Western is able to produce and secure the image of action as at once thrilling and moral, an image to which Bazin's own account fully subscribes.

In tracing the Western's naturalization of moral action, two points emerge as key: the persistence and importance of the attraction in the context of Hollywood narrative cinema; and the centrality of melodrama to the emergence and evolution of the genre. Until recently, the dominant scholarly attitude toward both points has been one of neglect. With respect to the former, studies of classical Hollywood cinema have traditionally overlooked the role of the attraction, identifying it primarily as a marker of early cinema and a measure of the distinction of this cinema from later narrative forms predicated upon voyeurism and a prohibition against direct address.[5] Beyond the early period, consideration of the attraction has been largely limited to avant-garde filmmaking and to "presentational" genres such as pornography and the musical, both of which orchestrate their central numbers for the explicit viewing pleasure of their spectators. While singing cowboys and barroom showgirls provide for a similar address in the Western, the role of the attraction is much more extensive than these instances suggest.

The genealogy of the Western reveals the centrality of the attraction to its affective and ideological appeal, highlighting how a direct and often aggressive address has constituted the basis for its identification as a "manly" and essentially American cultural form. As Richard Abel's research into the early Western suggests, the consolidation of the genre by 1910 around action-based thrills—or "snap and go," in the promotional discourse of the day—was identified as key to its distinctly American character; in this context, making "American film for American people" came to mean making Westerns.[6] The status of thrilling action as a signifier of the American is inextricable from the negotiations of gendered, racial, and national identity so neatly distilled in Roosevelt's notion of the strenuous life (discussed at length in the last chapter). To assert American film production as action-based was to assert its alliance with the cultural values of the strenuous—a commitment to masculine muscularity and physicality coupled with an assertion of Anglo-American superiority—in implicit contrast to the decadent, effete form of production with which foreign producers such at Pathé were increasingly associated.[7]

The persistence of the attraction within the Western speaks to its status as sensational melodrama, a cultural form focused on the making of sense in visceral and kinetic as well as moral and cognitive terms. In wedding the attractions of the early cinema to the traditions of theatrical and literary melodrama, the Western contextualizes cinematic action within a particular narrative and moral frame. Drawing upon frontier melodramas and the Wild West show as well as literary precedents like the dime novel, the popular Leatherstocking tales, and earlier captivity narratives, the genre sites thrilling action and violence within scenarios of victimization, the cornerstone of the melodramatic tradition from which it derives.

In this emphasis, the Western echoes contemporary imperialist discourse as well, playing upon the sensationalism of the yellow press, for instance, while amplifying the impact of melodramatic scenarios of victimized virtue and righteous, redemptive violence through the developing language of the cinema. The charge takes on a new kind of appeal in this context, related not only to the technological novelty and imperialist mobility discussed in the last chapter but also to circuits of identification produced through the emerging codes of narrative cinema. The affective experience of onscreen motion is imbued with a more explicit moral dimension, as the visceral impact of the charge is harnessed to more specific invitations to identify with the positions of both victimization and heroic agency.[8]

It is through the melodramatic interweaving of the thrills of action with the structures of pathetic identification that the Western comes to function as such an extraordinarily influential and enduring cultural form; indeed, in the context of twentieth-century American cultural production, the Western provides one of melodrama's most conspicuous and far-reaching incarnations. Despite the melodramatic foundations of the genre, however, and the ongoing significance of melodramatic conventions to its themes and structure—the emphasis on sensational action, Manichaean conceptions of good and evil, and the moral authority of victim-heroes, for instance—the specific relevance of melodrama to the Western has been little explored. Instead, within film studies in particular, melodrama has most often been examined in relation to its more feminized and stylistically "excessive" cycles, including the women's weepies of the 1930s and 1940s and the domestic or family melodramas of the 1950s and early 1960s. In these contexts, it is associated with female or feminized protagonists (as well as audiences), domestic conflicts and environments, and exaggerated forms of emotional display.[9] The Western, in contrast, has been understood as a realist, tragic, or even epic genre—masculinized cultural forms associated with authenticity, fate, or the broad sweep of myth and history (and with high rather than low cultural productions).

The strong tendency to associate the Western with realist masculine as opposed to excessive feminine cultural values has inhibited inquiry into both the melodramatic conventions that structure the genre and the specific nature of its realist claims.[10] Arguments for the Western's close association with the real have taken a variety of forms, including: a heightened interest in details of the mise-en-scène as signifying both the genre's stylistic realism and its historical verisimilitude; the production of star personas that authenticate the image of the Western hero by blurring the distinction between masculine performance onscreen and off; and an insistence on the unimpeachable visual authority of the western landscape as it lends veracity to the figures and action sited within it. In its association with realism, the genre has been aligned with the evolution of cinema itself, which has been understood as a technologically and stylistically inevitable movement away from an early investment in melodrama toward a more realist mode of representation. This disavowal of the Western as melodrama and the attendant emphasis on its realist virtues serve to mystify the process of representation as such. Rather than representing a set of cultural and aesthetic negotiations, the genre and its hero appear as more spontaneous and inevitable products of American history and cinema, embodiments of the ideology of Manifest Destiny and the inexorable force of white masculine motion that animates it.

As research into late nineteenth- and early twentieth-century popular culture attests, however, the appeals of the sensational are inextricable from a discourse of authenticity and the real.[11] This conjunction is nowhere more prominent than in the American cinema, where, as Linda Williams has deftly argued, "supposedly realist cinematic *effects* . . . most often operate in the service of melodramatic *affects*."[12] And although critical discourse has often cordoned off masculine-identified genres from discussions of melodrama on the basis of their realism, designations of "melodramatic realism" and "ultra-realistic melodrama" circulated in the film industry trade press until 1960 at least. References to "virile," "vigorous," and "heman" melodrama are common in this context, highlighting masculine-identified action and violence as a central aspect of melodramatic structure and appeal.[13]

The Western rehearses its preoccupation with the real in concert with the discourses of gender, race, and modernity that defined the strenuous life at the turn of the twentieth century. Like the strenuous spectacles of the last chapter, the Western asserts the "primitive" values of realness in the context of perceived social and economic encroachments on traditional foundations of Anglo-American masculine authority. And like the culture of strenuous spectacle more broadly, it works to mediate ascendant forms of commercialized experience through an insistence on their status as authentic. Analysis of the genre's preoccupation with realness and authenticity thus requires that we apprehend the very notion of the real as a specifically gendered and racialized construction.

The function of the western landscape in relation to these claims is undeniable. The visual rhetoric of the West—arid desert, rocky butte, forested mountain, or open range—comes by the late nineteenth century to signify a masculine-identified space of the real. Location shooting emerges very early as a privileged marker of the film Western's authenticity. Critics have read western landscapes as expressions and extensions of the character of the Western hero himself. Emphasizing the hardness and austerity of each, they have understood this resonance as an element of the genre's realism, although it is equally available for interpretation as the hysterically expressive mise-en-scène of melodrama.[14]

If the Western's association of sensational attractions with realness suggests that "it is the West *itself* that is authentic, versus existentially inauthentic life lived elsewhere," we are still left to reckon with exactly how and why this is the case.[15] For the West as an ideological and geographical space comes into focus in the latter half of the nineteenth century in significant relationship to the question of Anglo-American masculine vitality. In contrast to the rapidly industrializing East—cast as a site of enervation and racial "mongrelization," in which the abstractions of capital and the sedentary taxations of "brain work" pushed toward a cultural logic of disembodiment—the West was offered as a space of materiality, physicality, and bodily renewal. The authenticity of the Western hero is produced through his distance from these commercial contaminations, forcefully represented as both feminizing and racially impure.[16]

Within this ideological constellation, an emphasis on physical sensation provides the basis for casting some experiences as more real than others. Recalling the strenuous discourse of the twentieth century's turn, Jane Tompkins offers a testament to the role of embodied sensation in constituting the "realness" of the Western: "physical sensations are the bedrock of the experience Westerns afford. . . . For Westerns satisfy a hunger to be in touch with something absolutely real." In describing her own experience of the genre, she notes the particular impact of the charge, highlighting the somatic aspects of spectatorship—her own "breathless" response to onscreen action—in language that recalls contemporary catalog descriptions of the early charge films.[17]

In registering the persistence of the attraction within the conventions of the Western, as well as its association with the masculine virtues of realness, Tompkins emphasizes (even if she fails to fully unpack) the importance of feeling and sensation to the cultural and ideological significance of the genre.[18] As her comments suggest, Westerns, like the military actualities of the last chapter, locate the values of the real within the mass-mediated experience of the cinema, helping to institute and conventionalize the position of strenuous spectatorship. Indeed, through their institutionalization in the Western, visceral thrills themselves are established as an enduring mark of male-identified genres.[19]

These issues will be central to this chapter and the next, as I consider the shifting pleasures of the Western as a melodramatic form—the visceral as well as ideological appeals of a genre anchored by an insistence on victimization and suffering and authorized through an association with authenticity and the real. My interest in the Western revolves around questions of feeling as well as understanding: the kinds of reactions—ideological and affective, cognitive and visceral, significant and sensational—that the genre may be argued to condition and the "felt good" it works to institute in both individual and collective terms. This notion of a felt good is both a subjective and a profoundly social concept, as it highlights the implication of affective response in the complex collective fabric of value, worth, and meaning. The felt good of the Western corrals a range of pleasures and anxieties—both those associated with the experience of cinema and those beyond—bringing them into line with socially sanctioned categories of moral identity and worth and with the self-evidence of truths of a particular kind. In her seminal work on melodrama as a dominant mode of American cultural production, Linda Williams has asked how it succeeds in moving people and, most importantly, what it moves them toward.[20]

In interrogating the significance of the Western as a melodramatic form, these are ultimately the questions I seek to engage.

Sensational Melodrama and Western Attractions

The melodramatic origins of the Western derive from popular culture of the late nineteenth century and draw from cultural reservoirs much older and deeper than that. The assault on the settler's cabin, stagecoach, or wagon train, the ambush of the cavalry, the poignant last stand, or the ultimate ride to the rescue—these set pieces emerge across an array of late nineteenth- and early twentieth-century popular entertainments, including dime novels, paintings, frontier melodramas, and, in their most spectacular and influential incarnation, Buffalo Bill's Wild West show. Dime novels and frontier plays featured dashing heroes, odious villains, and captive damsels in distress; plots revolved around mistaken identities, implausible coincidences, and suspense-ridden, death-defying rescues presented in vivid and "lifelike" detail. Years before the emergence of cinema, such entertainments constructed a melodramatic imagination of the American West, emphasizing the plight of innocent victims and the thrill of spectacular, last-minute rescues.

In line with Peter Brooks's account of melodrama, these entertainments revolved around the revelation of moral virtue, producing signs of an underlying moral truth as the animating force of a secular and modernizing world.[21] As David Mayer has explained, in place of an overarching religious authority, melodrama substitutes "a secular explanatory narrative of causality which attributes public disaster and private calamity, peril, or tribulation to the malign operation of evil seeking to overcome goodness."[22] Central to this melodramatic tradition is an emphasis on the individual protagonist as an innocent victim whose virtue is established through the public display of his or her suffering; in melodrama, indeed, victimization functions as the privileged signifier of moral worth, that which makes virtue legible as such. While Brooks locates the emergence of melodrama in revolutionary France, its emphasis on spirited underdogs who prevail over adversity and its democratic mode of address in contrast to early theatrical forms make it uniquely well suited to the cultural and political context of the United States.[23]

But where Brooks focuses on the revelation of a "moral occult" as melodrama's primary function, Tom Gunning has argued for the relative dominance of sensation over the production of moral legibility in stage melodrama by the end of the nineteenth century.[24] As he suggests, the modernization of melodrama in this period may be best understood in relation to an intensified address at the level of the body, as sensational melodrama weds the noncognitive (somatic and affective) thrills of action and violence to cognitive categories of moral worth (good and evil, guilt and innocence, virtue and villainy). Like Ben Singer, whose account of melodrama and modernity informs both Gunning's and my own, Gunning suggests how melodrama worked to represent and to negotiate the "new abrasive" experiences of urban modernity in particular.[25]

This function is most evident in the "sensation scenes" around which late-century stage melodramas pivoted, the large-scale spectacles featuring chaotic action and violence, rendered with an eye toward realistic detail. As Gunning has discussed, these scenes mobilized a "powerful assault on the senses of the audience"; while their spectacular displays could be tethered to the moral expressivity of a performance, their success depended more upon their immediate visceral impact than on their revelation of any underlying moral order.[26] Although Gunning maintains an analytical distance between the terms of sensation and significance, it is difficult to disentangle their functions as discrete modes of response. In a form like the Western, for instance, the power of the genre relates precisely to the intertwining of these appeals: the excitations of action and violence are coded and experienced through categories of moral worth, while categories of moral worth and value derive their force and impact through the affective intensities of their display.

The contemporary insistence on the realism of the sensation scenes—which commonly included natural and technological disasters such as earthquakes, avalanches, volcanoes, fires, explosions, and train and ship wrecks—located their emphasis on the spectacular and sensational within the ongoing quest for ever more lifelike and "authentic" re-creations. The efficacy of such scenes relied on both their perceived level of authentic detail and the sensory intensity of their address, highlighting how verisimilitude was valued primarily as a means of amplifying the thrilling impact of such performances. Contemporary western entertainments were particularly insistent on this alignment of the real with the sensational; they sought to deliver, in the promotional discourse of the day, a "realism that quickens the blood," testifying to the intimate relationship between realism and a visceral, affective response.[27] Like other strenuous spectacles of the day, Westerns offered thrilling representations of action and violence at a time when opportunities for intense embodied experience were feared to be eroding, signifying the cultural status of the West as an imagined site of active physicality and immediacy, made broadly accessible through the commercialized growth of national amusements.

The most lucrative and successful of the western-themed attractions of the late nineteenth and early twentieth centuries—and one of the most influential examples of the interlacing of the categories of the real and the authentic with the theatrical and the sensational—was Buffalo Bill Cody's

Wild West show. Cody's life experiences as a buffalo hunter for the Kansas Pacific Railroad, a Pony Express rider, and an Indian scout for the U.S. Army inspired hundreds of dime novels and a successful stage career, in which Cody appeared in theatrical reenactments of his own mythicized exploits on the western frontier. As in the culture of strenuous spectacle more broadly, Cody's authenticity was produced through these performative contexts, even as a significant aspect of the Wild West's appeal derived from his perceived status as a genuine relic of the recent past.[28] The inclusion of other historical actors—frontier cowboys, Spanish-American War Rough Riders, recently de-territorialized Native Americans, including briefly but notoriously the Lakota chief Tatanka Iyotanka (Sitting Bull)—worked also to assert the show's unique claims upon the real, while heightening the sense of fluidity between the registers of historical and theatrical performance.

That Cody worked persistently to blur any sense of distinction between these two registers—donning his stage costume when employed as a government scout so that he might later promote its historical authenticity, in one well-known example—did not undermine the popular sense of the Wild West's realism, but rather intensified the show's appeal by creating a greater intimacy between historical actors and arena showmen, historical violence and its sensational reenactment. The self-consciousness of Cody's performances (resonant with Roosevelt's less candid but no less persistent displays) underscores the extent to which, by the closing decades of the nineteenth century, the category of authenticity was itself produced through the conventions of sensational melodrama. Western film would follow in this tradition; its narratives would be recognized as authentic on the basis of their resemblance to wild west show conventions, and theatrical experience would align Western stars with the authentic virtues of the West. The onscreen personas of Tom Mix and later B cowboys were validated by their past careers as performers in Wild West shows, and a decade-long career in the Bs provided the foundation for John Wayne's emergence as the paragon of authenticity in later feature Westerns.

The Wild West show drew directly upon Cody's theatrical experience, distilling the sensational conventions of stage melodrama by amplifying the kinesthetic thrills of fast-paced, frenetic action and large-scale violence and wedding these to conventional scenarios of Anglo-American settlers or cavalry under siege. Promotional discourse highlighted the Wild West's visceral impact as an explicit aspect of its appeal. The smells and sounds of gunpowder and horses, the "terrific whoops of the painted warriors," the blur of fantastically colorful costumes—all contributed to a multifaceted assault that "bombilated" Wild West audiences, overwhelming them on a number of sensory fronts.[29] Underscoring the show's diverse stimuli was the melos of melodrama. Buffalo Bill's Cowboy Band accompanied the action-packed spectacles with tunes both martial and sentimental, "control[ing] the multiple energies of each performance" to create a sense of continuity "in a diversified extravaganza that seemed to hover throughout on the precipice of chaos."[30] The melodramatic status of the show's structure and appeal were broadly promoted; advertising campaigns boasted of its "popular, sensational, melodramatic" attractions, and press coverage breathlessly described the "rescue party of dashing, dare-devil cowboys" that arrives "just in the nick of time."[31]

Structuring the Wild West's sensory agitations was a narrative and thematic emphasis on victimization, rescue, and retribution, as in the largely interchangeable scenarios of the "Attack on the Wagon Train," the "Attack on the Settler's Cabin," and the "Attack on the Deadwood Stage." In these and similar centerpiece attractions, the Wild West rehearsed the melodrama of Manifest Destiny, in which frontier satellites of civilized progress and Anglo-American domesticity were imperiled by savage assault. Although the particulars could vary, the general contours remained consistent: the protagonists are viciously attacked by an adversary marked as racially other; though outnumbered by the "marauding" hordes, they fight back valiantly until—just when hope seems finally lost—they are rescued in a spectacular show of action and violence by the advance of white men on horseback.

Imperialist exploits abroad were represented as the natural extension of such western frontier heroics: the "Attack on the Settler's Cabin" gave way in 1899 to the timely spectacle of the "Battle of San Juan Hill" as the show's grand finale (giving new resonance to the linkages between Roosevelt's Rough Riders and the Wild West's original Rough Riders of the World); and the "Attack on the Deadwood Stage" was featured alongside "The Rescue at Pekin" as equivalent representations of innocent whites imperiled. Cowboys and cavalrymen served as interchangeable embodiments of heroic white male action in these contexts, while Spaniards or "Chinamen" played the part of racialized adversaries, standing in place of (and most often performed by) Native Americans.[32] Featuring the imperialist attractions of Roosevelt's Rough Riders in a performance context dedicated to western scenes and iconography, the Wild West show underscores the ideological equivalence between continental and overseas expansion (suggested also in Roosevelt's adoption of the moniker Rough Riders for his cavalry unit).

In general, the Wild West audience was invited to take pleasure in the show's reenactments through the interweaving of pathos with action; an anxious identification with the assaulted protagonists moved the spectator alongside the fast-paced thrills of action and violence. The sensory appeals of the Wild West were thus articulated within (even if not fully contained by) the moralizing project of melodrama, as the thrill of action emerged within these specific narrative and ideological frames. And while the conventional satisfactions of such scenarios included both the anxiety of the attack and the exhilaration of the rescue, a variation on the pattern could work to emphasize the pathetic intensity of the scene. In the popular long-standing attraction of "Custer's Last Fight," for example, a reenactment of the Battle of the Little Big Horn concluded with the arrival of Buffalo Bill upon the scene of massacre, while projected upon a screen behind him appeared the conventional melodramatic lament, "Too late."

Indeed, as Linda Williams has argued, the insistence with which the show staged its narrative of Manifest Destiny through the framing of white settlers and soldiers as innocent victims of Indian attacks underscores the significance of racial melodrama to such attractions: "The white settlers are not just victims in this scenario; they are racially beset victims who acquire moral legitimacy through the public spectacle of their suffering."[33] Such scenarios point to the paradoxical power of identifying with victimhood, which Williams has deemed "one of the great unexamined moral forces of American culture."[34] The positioning of the white protagonists as the victims of a brutal Indian assault would carry over into the narrative and affective structures of the film Western, of course, constituting one of its most ubiquitous attractions. And while the resonance of this scenario of assault, rescue, and retribution extends broadly across American culture and politics, it has nowhere been more conspicuous, or arguably more influential, than in the conventions established in the Wild West reenactments.

The Wild West show was not the first or the only western-themed attraction in this period, but its influence upon the contemporary imagination of the West is impossible to overstate. The emphasis on frenetic motion and sensory excitation, coupled with the melodramatics of Cody's literary and theatrical appearances, worked to produce a particular imagination of the West as a space defined by sensational action and violence. This vision would influence men like Schreyvogel, whose western portraits reproduce the intense visceral address of the Wild West attractions that inspired him.

With its insistent claims to authenticity, the Wild West reenactments provided eastern painters like Schreyvogel and Frederic Remington with both a style and a subject matter. Like the Wild West show, the popular genre of western action painting in the late nineteenth and early twentieth centuries composed an image of the West as a space of narrative drama defined by the melodramatic poles of action and pathos and paired an overarching concern with the values of realism and authenticity with an emphasis on visceral and kinesthetic renderings of motion and violence. Such paintings would help to define the popular imagination of the West to a degree rivaled only by the Wild West show itself, exerting a "controlling influence . . . upon the formation of the idea of 'the West' and subsequently upon the Western as a cinematic genre," and helping to determine, in the years before the cinema's emergence, "what 'the West' could be taken to mean."[35]

The organization of western action painting around moments of intense action and violence contrasts with earlier images of the West, which tend to emphasize tranquil, bucolic scenes of Indians or Anglo-American settlers or the majestic and ethereal wonders of the natural landscape.[36] These earlier representations downplay a sense of speed, motion, and the impact of violence, whereas the sensationalism of turn-of-the-century popular culture offered a new way to imagine the West.[37] Rather than invite a state of ethnographic contemplation or intellectual or spiritual revelation, the aim of later western paintings is to make an immediate visceral impact on their viewers.

Remington was explicit on this point: "I have always wanted to be able to paint running horses so you would *feel* the details and not see them" (my italics).[38] An early example of this impulse can be found in *In a Stampede* (1888)—which illustrated Roosevelt's writings in *Century Magazine* and later his *Ranch Life and the Hunting Trail*—in which a cowboy charges directly toward the front of the frame, the white head of his mount dramatically offset against a dark sea of stampeding cattle. Remington returned to this composition repeatedly throughout his career; in *A Saber Charge* (1895), for example, Native American warriors are trampled under the pounding hooves of a cavalry onslaught. The force and direction of the charge are emphasized by the placement of the lead horse in the center of the frame, its forward-facing head rendered in clean, geometric lines, signaling (as Alex Nemerov has argued in relation to other Remington images) the righteous orderliness of the cavalry's advance.[39] Such paintings provide early examples of the direct aggressive mode of address that would become increasingly common in western painting at the turn of the twentieth century, influencing the emerging medium of moving pictures in *Roosevelt's Rough Riders* and other early charge films.

Aligned with the so-called "school of Remington," Schreyvogel's work is particularly striking for its resonance with, and in some cases anticipation of, early cinematic conventions. Schreyvogel was recognized primarily as a painter of the Indian-fighting U.S. Cavalry, although before ever traveling West (where he, like Roosevelt and so many of his contemporaries, sought refuge from ill health), his knowledge of the Indian Wars was gained through regular attendance and extensive sketching at the Wild West show. The subject matter of Schreyvogel's work was directly informed by the Wild West reenactments, some of which he reproduced in his paintings.

The formal characteristics of his style are oriented around an intensification of the sense of speed and motion: energy is represented through detailed rendering of muscular straining; white bursts of gunfire explode across the canvas; horses charge toward the front of the frame or rear up in the foreground, bursting out of the visual field to address the viewer with a visceral immediacy.[40] Rather than taking in an overview of a battle scene, the viewer is enveloped within the space of action, drawn into—and implicated in—the graphic spectacle of violence.

As noted above, in *Breaking Through the Line* (1903) Schreyvogel brings this aggressively direct mode of address to the image of the cavalry charge, forcefully recalling the charge films of a few years earlier. Here the cavalry stampedes directly toward the viewer, horses' hooves raised in mid-air, clouds of dust shooting up from the arid ground. Heightening the sense of momentum and immediacy, the lead rider (in suggestively Rooseveltian spectacles) leans forward from the center of the frame. His gaze, like the pistol in his outstretched arm, is aimed squarely out at the viewer—a motif Schreyvogel had incorporated in *How Kola!* (1901) and would mobilize again in later paintings such as *Protecting the Emigrants* (1906) and *Pickets* (1907).

Alongside this kind of address, Schreyvogel's work mines the tensions of melodrama, the action frozen in a teetering balance between the poles of "too late" and "in the nick of time." Though such paintings necessarily lack the temporal suspense of the race to the rescue (featured in the Wild West show and intensified through the cinematic convention of cross-cutting), the impulse to visualize western violence as a thrilling melodramatic spectacle nonetheless serves to animate them. In *The Summit Springs Rescue* (1908), for instance, the temporal dimensions of theatrical melodrama are collapsed within the frame, the affective intensity of suspense displaced onto other planes, including the dramatic use of color, the visceral emphasis on motion, and the graphic representation of violence at its moment of greatest impact.[41]

The painting references an actual event via a Wild West reenactment. As in the arena attraction, Buffalo Bill charges into the midst of a frenzied battle scene, his white horse centered in the frame. The panicked eyes of his mount accentuate his own steady calm as he fires a close-range shot at an Indian in the painting's left foreground. In one hand, the Indian grasps the hair of an ashen-faced woman, whose pale skin and closed eyes signify her death ("too late"); crumpled at his feet with face cradled in her hands is another woman, who will be spared a similar fate ("in the nick of time"). In his other hand, the Indian clutches a raised tomahawk above the dead woman's scalp; even as his neck bends back in an agonizing death throw, he is imaged as a threat, highlighting the overlapping of assault and rescue in this context.[42]

Like the Wild West show reenactments they reference, western action paintings are organized around the appeals of pathos as well as action.

In Remington's *Downing the Nigh Leader* (1907), for instance, the pathos of "too late" provides the central visual drama. A present-day description of the painting suggests how the image calls forth an impulse toward melodramatic narrativization: "The Indian has driven his lance into the falling left horse. . . . The other horses will be down in a moment, the stagecoach will crash to a halt, and all will be at the mercy of the attacking Indians. They haven't a chance."[43]

In Remington's famous Last Stand compositions in particular, the appeals of pathos and action combine to significant effect: a small party of cowboys or cavalrymen stands stoically centered in the frame, making a valiant final show of resistance while Indians circle on the distant horizon.[44] Earlier iterations like *Last Lull in the Fight* (1889) and *The Last Stand* (1891) leave their protagonists posed and static, available for our sincere if somewhat distant regard; in later representations, however, like *The Intruders* (1900) and *Caught in a Circle* (1906), Remington moves the beleaguered group into the foreground and animates these figures through their active resistance. The long horizontal barrels of their rifles and bursts of gunfire across the canvas join with the men's rigid erect frames to qualify their status as victims (a status the composition at the same time confers).[45] As I argue at length in the next chapter, the operation of pathos is central to the moral authority of these figures, whose righteousness is signified not just by the rigid lines of the composition—the "tight grid of verticals and horizontals" constructed through their upright bodies and steadily drawn rifles[46]—but also by their status as victims. Their appeal is constituted through their strength and their vulnerability and, most poignantly, through the joining of these two seemingly disparate positions—a central conjunction in the traditions of sensational melodrama that concern me here.

In images like these, western painters like Remington and Schreyvogel paid close attention to the naturalistic rendering of artifacts and accessories, weapons foremost among them. This kind of visual verisimilitude was understood to constitute the basis of a painting's broader claims to legitimacy; the merit of any individual painting could be undermined by the perception of an inauthentic detail—the precise shade of blue of a cavalry officer's trousers, an anachronistic pistol holder, a misshapen stirrup cover, or an oversized saddlebag.[47] As Alex Nemerov has suggested, the obsessive attention to the detailed rendering of such objects suggests their power "to testify to the reality of the historical world of which [they are] a fragment."[48]

Like the Wild West show's promotion of the signs of the real—the very coat Cody wore when he shot Yellow Hand, the very presence of Cody himself—the visually and historically accurate representation of trousers and rifles in western action painting served to authenticate the specific image alongside the scene in which it appeared. This convention would carry over forcefully into the cinema, where the authenticity of props and costumes would be widely celebrated as a sign of the genre's broader realist commitments. The ideological importance of realism becomes clearer in this context: the sensational rendering of the West as a space defined through the appeals of pathos and action is naturalized through this insistence on verisimilitude, as are the gendered and racialized images through which such appeals are constituted.

Western action painting would exert a strong influence on the film Western in other ways, too. Though these works could not reproduce the temporal suspense of theatrical melodrama and lacked the sensory intensity of a Wild West show, their ability to impose particular angles of vision provided a powerful model for emergent point-of-view structures in the cinema. Remington's compositions would be particularly influential, both in moments of direct homage and in the dominant lines of vision organizing cinematic action and violence.[49] For while the sensory pleasures of the Wild West show were intense, they were also disorganized; the action flew by in a blur of color and speed, and the views available to the audience were necessarily multiple and fluid. Consider, in contrast, the precise and particular rendering of the action in Remington's *Opening of the Fight at Wounded Knee* (1891). Unlike Remington's Last Stand compositions, in which subjects are collected in the center of the frame and face forward for the viewer's regard, here a sense of identification is heightened by the placement of the viewer within the space of the action itself. Positioned just behind the line of fire, the sketch constructs the image of the fight by aligning the viewer's sights with those of the soldiers and their rifles, an orientation that would be echoed in numerous later images and would come to dominate Hollywood representations of Indian assault (fig. 8).

In its composition, *Opening of the Fight at Wounded Knee* encourages identification with the soldiers as both the victims and the agents of violence—a melodramatic convention that would become even more emphatic with the emergence of the Western as a film genre. In the sketch, the line of soldiers is broken by a figure falling backward toward the viewer, about to topple onto another who lies dead in the lap of a comrade. That the tumbling body of the soldier, the pale face of his dead comrade, and another crumpled figure just beyond represent the only visible casualties within the frame is important to note in what is, after all, the representation of a massacre of Native American men, women, and children at the hands of a well-armed U.S. force.

This kind of composition becomes particularly prevalent in Remington's work just after Wounded Knee, as Ben Vorpahl argues, suggesting how the impulse to align the viewer's gaze with the soldiers' violence and to cast this violence as essentially defensive in nature intensifies in the face of

Fig. 8. Within the conventions of Western melodrama, even the massacre of Native men, women, and children is represented through the image of U.S. soldiers under attack, their violence coupled with an emphasis on their vulnerability. Frederic Remington, *The Opening of the Fight at Wounded Knee, Harper's Weekly*, January 24, 1891. Courtesy of Yale Collection of Western Americana, Beinecke Rare Book and Manuscript Library.

white culpability and aggression.[50] This point brings us back to the tendency of imperialist melodrama to solicit pathetic identification with its victim-heroes even as they are represented as the agents of aggressive force. The early military actualities produced similar point-of-view structures, as in *Advance of the Kansas Volunteers* (Edison 1899), in which the camera is positioned directly behind the U.S. soldiers as they rise up out of the foreground to advance upon the encroaching Filipino rebels. Here, too, the gunning down of the color guard produces the film's only casualty, mirroring the falling soldier in Remington's rendering of Wounded Knee and adding a note of pathos even to this single-shot film.[51] Such point-of-view structures, which engage the spectator in the image of battle by encouraging identification with white victim-heroes defending themselves against the violence of others defined as more savage—and, importantly, the historical conditions under which these structures emerge—are crucial to consideration of the Western as a film genre.

Ultimately, the resonance between the Wild West show and western action paintings highlights the degree to which a sensational mode of representation came to define images of the West across a range of media by the end of the nineteenth century. It suggests the extent to which the

cultural imagination of the West was brought into focus through the iteration of "thrilling" scenarios of victimization, violence, and heroic action,
constituted through a visceral mode of address. As Nemerov has suggested,
the prevalence of citation in western representation speaks to the ability of
iteration across media to compel conviction in the truth of such scenes.[52]

While live entertainment spectacles and western action paintings participated in wedding the popular imagination of the West to the formal and thematic conventions of sensational melodrama, it was through the emerging
medium of moving pictures that the merger of melodramatic conventions
and western thematic material would be most fully naturalized. Like the Wild
West show, the cinema was able to produce large-scale spectacles that emphasized motion and speed; like western painting, it was able to control the angle
of vision through which such action was organized and perceived. At the
same time, the formal and technological resources of cinema allowed for an
intensification of the melodramatic rhythms that had long underscored western representation, deepening identification both with the position of those
under assault and with the heroic violence that would save them.

The Visceral and Moral Thrills of Western Action

While scholarly accounts of the Western generally open with *The Great
Train Robbery*, the charge films and battle reenactments provide an earlier
precedent in their emphasis on cinematic motion and violence as vehicles
of a specifically nationalist pleasure. The conventions these films inaugurated would come to constitute defining features of the film Western—in
the set pieces of the charge, the chase, and the gunfight, for instance—
soliciting identification with white masculine and American nationalist
action through the visceral and kinesthetic appeals of cinema. With the
industrial move toward narrative integration in the 1910s, the moral authority of these early attractions would be drawn increasingly into the body of
the film itself, dependent less on the extratextual discourse of imperialism
and more on the emergent formal and generic structures of Hollywood.
Nonetheless, the appeals of an aggressive direct address inaugurated by the
imperialist actualities would continue to form a key aspect of the genre,
central to its identification as a form of cinema both thrilling and manly.

The consolidation of western themes and scenarios into a distinct category of film production was a process that drew upon different impulses
of the early cinema, including the culture of strenuous spectacle itself.
Cowboys and Indians, shooting and riding stunts, and views of the western landscape had provided subjects for moving pictures from the first:
in Edison's kinetograph views of Wild West show stars and attractions,
for instance, and in the actualities, comic shorts, and scenic Hale's Tours

films that populated the early years of projection. The first story films, too, often exploited western scenes and scenarios for dramatic content, most famously in *The Great Train Robbery* and other films inspired by its success. These early films evidenced a range of tendencies, from the sensationalist to the ethnographic and touristic.

By 1908, the western picture had emerged as a distinct and extremely popular category of narrative film production, accounting for at least one-fifth of all domestic releases. Around this time, film began to take over as the dominant medium through which popular western images and scenarios were produced, while live spectacles such as the Wild West show fell into a slow decline. The narrative western film evidenced a fair amount of ideological fluidity in its first few years, though association with "Wild West drama" was its dominant and enduring trend.[53] Such "Wild West subjects," according to one reviewer in 1909, provided "the foundation of American moving picture drama," the basis for industrial as well as ideological claims for American exceptionalism.

The prominence of western subjects was conditioned in part by the shift in production from the Northeast and Chicago to the South and, most significantly, the West; though some films simply repositioned familiar scenarios before the scenic backdrop of the western landscape, location shooting in the West was felt to benefit the cowboy and Indian films in particular. The move westward was associated with new kinds of formal and visual conventions; the "wide open spaces" of California and the Rockies inspired greater camera mobility and the use of extreme long shots to capture action across a broadened visual field. The visual assertion of the emptiness of the West had an ideological as well as a formal significance, of course, as shots of vast "empty" spaces participated directly in the discourse of Manifest Destiny and the amnesia of settler colonialism, anticipating subsequent shots in which the open space was filled with the industrious activity of white civilization on the move.[54]

The Western hero began to emerge in this period as a persona defined through his relationship to the "thrilling" representation of Wild West–style action and violence. An example, fittingly enough, is *The Making of Broncho Billy* (1913), an Essanay one-reeler featuring the "first western star," Gilbert "Broncho Billy" Anderson (appearing, in the tradition of Buffalo Bill, as himself). The film is suggestive of how the impulse of the early attraction is woven into the formal language of narrative cinema, as Billy's transformation from harassed eastern dude to formidable western cowboy is effected through a shift in the film's mode of address.

The picture opens on the scene of a milk-drinking Billy taunted by roughneck cowboys before the painted set of a western barroom. A subsequent sequence moves outdoors, where Billy engages in target practice, learning to shoot so that he might face off with the cowboys' ringleader. The shift from painted set to naturalistic location signals the greater value of manly authenticity accruing to Billy in the latter context, as the ensuing action makes clear. Still in his eastern attire, Billy gingerly places a bottle on a tree stump in the background of the frame; walking into the middleground, he turns his back to the camera to shoot toward the bottle (and miss). After a number of failed attempts, the film cuts to the intertitle "Later"; we then return to another shot of Billy at his target practice. Now, the camera has moved in closer on the action, and Billy has donned his western "Broncho Billy" garb. This time, Billy lines up his bottles on a fence at eye level in the foreground. Firing toward the camera at close range, he proceeds to blast each bottle in sequence (fig. 9). The angle on the action grants a new kind of value to the westernized Billy, who displays a prowess reminiscent of the Wild West's shooting stunts. The cowboy hero is thus "made" through his explicit alignment with a direct and visceral mode of address, encouraging a greater investment in the image of the westernized and masculinized Billy at the level of feeling as well as understanding (we understand him to be effectively transformed and experience this transformation as exciting).

At work in this example is the significance of the attraction as an enduring mode of address in the Western, one aligned in particular ways with the

Fig. 9. The cinematic figure of the cowboy hero takes shape through an explicit alignment with the visceral thrills of a direct address. *The Making of Broncho Billy* (Anderson 1913).

values of the masculine. Even in the context of classical Hollywood cinema, the impulse of the attraction would persist, stitched into the generic fabric of the Western in a variety of ways. In one set of conventions, for instance, shots of aggressive action directed toward the camera are nominally motivated through the presence of an onscreen character, whose point of view these shots may be seen to inscribe, thus preserving the impulse of the attraction alongside classical conventions that dictate against unmediated forms of direct address. Examples of this tendency include fight, chase, and stampede sequences, in which direct shots of guns firing, fists flying, or hooves pounding are associated with the position of an imperiled onscreen character, even though the angle and proximity of the camera to its object may align only loosely with this position. These shots function primarily to intensify the visceral and kinesthetic impact of onscreen action, rather than to promote or exploit identification with a given character, as in conventional point-of-view shots.

In addition, the Western's representation of motion routinely incorporates direct address: both stationary and moving-camera shots offer the image of cowboys, cavalrymen, stagecoaches, or covered wagons racing headlong toward the camera, unmediated by the perspective of any onscreen character (echoing the early charge films and western action paintings). While occasionally available for interpretation as subjective point-of-view shots, these images are generally distinct from any specific character-driven motivation. In a variation on this technique, the camera is sometimes positioned in a hole to intensify the sense of force and impact, recording the charging horses or stampeding cattle from below, their hooves pounding down directly on the camera/audience.

In all these examples, the use of direct address is smoothed over by the placement of such shots within longer and more formally intricate sequences, as well as by the weight of generic convention itself, which has rendered them seemingly immune to critical analysis. Importantly though, such shots are not conditioned or necessitated by the vicissitudes of narrative development or character psychology but relate rather to the ongoing significance of the attraction. Incorporated into longer sequences of action and violence, such shots combine with rapid cuts and pulsating soundtracks to constitute the Western's reputation for visceral and kinesthetic pleasures—pleasures that circulate around ideas about embodiment, sensation, and the real.

The affective force of the Western derives from its situating of this kind of viscerally invested address within the moral framework of melodrama. On the one hand, as I have argued, western representation was already aligned with the sensational pleasures of melodrama—its visceral as well as moral satisfactions—years before the advent of cinema. The development of the Western as a moving picture genre, however, also relates to specific industrial pressures, including the need to assert the still relatively young institution of cinema as a site of moral uplift and middle-class respectability. During the period in which the Western was consolidating around the appeal of Wild West–style attractions, the film industry was subject to the mounting concerns of Progressive and other reform-minded critics.[55] In this context, even as the Western was being hailed as "the quintessential 'American subject,'" the association of sensational action with the dime novel tradition and its perceived working-class audience was cause for criticism and concern.

Harnessing the visceral pleasures of western sensationalism to narrative contexts that emphasized the moral authority underlying their appeal was thus an industrial as well as an ideological necessity, and the Plains War focus of Westerns in the early 1910s can be understood as part of this process. Contextualizing the thrills of cinematic action within narratives of masculine and national reinvigoration in the authenticating space of the West, these films escaped some of the charges of sensationalism attending tales of sordid crime in the overcrowded urban centers of the East.[56] Mining established attractions and articulating them within an invigorated moral framework, Westerns addressed the cinema's need to appeal to a mass audience while presenting itself as an institution of middle-class uplift and reform. Action-oriented thrills were made available through identification with official narratives of Manifest Destiny and the plight of white victim-heroes, emphasizing the moral authority underlying their appeal. Framing its attractions in this way helped the cinema to distance its pleasures from the bodily sensationalism of mass attractions like the Coney Island roller coaster, asserting instead the value of the cinema as a moving apparatus of an altogether different kind.

The moral intensification of western attractions in this context also relied on formal and technological developments, as the increasingly sophisticated language of the cinema brought with it new modes of spectatorial engagement and response. Through more fully articulated storylines, a greater individuation of character, and the temporal extension of suspense, Westerns in the 1910s referenced the familiar themes and iconography of the Wild West show while intensifying their affective force. The use of extreme long shots and wide-angle lenses alongside the emerging convention of the close-up, for instance, generated a spectacle at once more sweeping and more intimate than the Wild West show attractions. At the same time, the developing conventions of cross-cutting and parallel action allowed for the temporal extension of melodramatic suspense—the agonizing pull of "too late" drawn into increasingly intricate and prolonged relation to the thrilling possibility of "in the nick of time."

Cross-cutting between shots of large-scale violence and intimate close-ups of individualized protagonists in moments of suffering allowed for new ways of identifying with familiar scenarios of assault and rescue. As Ben Singer has argued, these developing techniques of narrative integration amplify the "stimulating capacity of attractions" by placing them in more direct relationship with emotionally invested scenarios: "A shot of a speeding locomotive may be arousing, but it is all the more so if the locomotive is carrying the protagonist who is racing to stop the villain from putting a ring on the finger of his childhood sweetheart and ruining her life through a mock marriage."[57] Likewise, a shot of a cavalry charge, while circulating already within the melodramatic discourse of imperialism, may be more arousing when cross-cut with a brutal Indian assault upon a wagon train or a raid upon an Anglo homestead—contexts in which the visceral appeal of the attraction is interwoven with the agitations of melodramatic suspense, fueled by the invitation to identify with those in a position of vulnerability.

Establishing the more intimate space of "home" within the expansive space of the western landscape—and articulating the relationship between these two spaces—is one of the most significant projects of the Western in this period. Long shots attested to the cinema's resources of location and scale, but they also recalled live attractions like wild west shows and battle reenactments as viewed from grandstands and hillsides, with the action largely obscured in the distant smoke- and dust-filled chaos. What the cinema could bring to these familiar spectacles was a greater articulation of the relationship between this large-scale action and the domestic space it threatened, conditioning a more intimate identification with the white settlers and cavalrymen under fire and fusing the image of distant violence with a more affecting and immediate assertion of what it imperiled.

Interior shots of wagons, cabins, and stagecoaches, anchored by the image of women and children huddled against the edges of the frame, articulate what is at stake in action-filled long shots, representing a feminine space of innocence founded upon and maintained through an assertion of sexual and racial purity. In an emerging convention, the image of Indian assault is shot from within these domestic spaces, inviting the spectator's explicit identification with the position of the imperiled white protagonists and framing the violence through this invitation in a way the Wild West show never could. That this domestic point of view comes into focus only through an insistence on its status as imperiled is not an insignificant point, highlighting as it does the function of melodrama in constituting the space of innocence upon which its own moral authority at the same time depends.

The Western's alternation between scenes of suffering and scenes of fast-paced action establishes a particular affective rhythm, in which onscreen action is anticipated as the source of both visceral excitement and deliverance from the anxieties of pathetic identification and suspense. The invitation to identify with and take pleasure in this action is increasingly aligned with the moral righteousness it embodies, as the visceral and kinesthetic pleasures of action emerge as the "fruit of moral energy."[58] The conjunction of visceral pleasure and moral righteousness works to authorize, and even to naturalize, the more unruly thrills of cinematic action and violence—the more disorganized, less socialized, or more sadistic pleasures of identification with violent agency—while addressing reformist anxieties about the nature and implications of cinematic spectatorship.

Jane Tompkins has discussed the state of "moral ecstasy" induced by the Western when virtue, "which up till then had shown itself in long-suffering and restraint," transforms into aggression. Though the term does not figure in her discussion, her comments underscore the affective rhythms of melodrama; highlighting the "satisfying sense of release the plot's culmination in violence affords," she notes that "the violence, by the time it arrives, fills a visceral need."[59] As the Western became established as a major category of film production in the first decades of the twentieth century, the white Western hero was produced in increasingly explicit and affecting ways as the locus of this merger of visceral thrills and moral authority. The point is not simply that the Western asserts the moral legitimacy of the hero's action but that morality itself is embodied in this generic context through a specific set of cinematic images focused around the affectively charged motion of the white masculine hero onscreen.[60]

Although this rhythm is crucial to the efficacy and endurance of the genre, the feature Western in its early years—and its Plains War variant in particular—was most invested in affecting images of suffering and loss rather than triumphalist representations of white masculine violence. This emphasis can be found in the many Last Stand films, for instance, which sound the pathetic register of melodrama within narrative contexts that seek to justify and, more importantly, to exonerate a national history of racial genocide. Like the Plains War films more generally, they tend to end on a note of extended pathos, often encapsulated in a static long take at the graveside of the self-sacrificing hero. These final tableaus reproduce the conventions of nineteenth-century theatrical melodrama, in which the recognition of hidden or misunderstood virtue is prolonged "in the frozen tableau whose picture speaks more powerfully than words."[61]

Among the popular Wild West attractions revisited in such films is the story of General George Armstrong Custer, around which a number of productions were either explicitly or more impressionistically based.[62] These include *Custer's Last Fight* (1912), produced by Thomas Ince and directed by Francis Ford, in which the tableaus that constitute the titular battle sequence reference directly the Last Stand images of western action painting (and include as well a shot of Custer taking direct aim at the audience). Mirroring Remington's use of horizontal and vertical lines, the film emphasizes the orderliness and discipline of the imperiled cavalrymen, virtues signified also in the tidy columns of cavalry threading through the mountains in earlier shots, in contrast to the scattered, scrambling motions of the Indians throughout the film. The heavy use of citation deepens the affective resonance of the film while contributing centrally to its credibility; references to iconic images like Remington's and direct borrowings from Buffalo Bill's popular Last Stand reenactment serve paradoxically to mark the authenticity of *Custer's Last Fight*, its intimate association with the real.[63]

But if *Custer's Last Fight* represents its hero as "the archetypal martyr on the altar of manifest destiny," in Roberta Pearson's suggestive phrasing, it is important to ask why the altar of Manifest Destiny requires such a martyr and what the cultural function of this image of sacrifice might be.[64] The answer relates to the melodramatic production of moral legibility and, more generally, to what Linda Williams has referred to as American culture's need to address "the overwhelming moral burden of having been the 'bad guys.'" Though Williams discusses this burden in relation to the Vietnam-themed *Rambo* films of the 1980s (to which I return in chapter 4), the Last Stand films suggest the extent to which this dilemma has long undergirded the traditions of American cinema and the genre of the Western in particular. Melodrama, as Williams argues, provides "the alchemy whereby we turn our deepest sense of guilt into a testament of our virtue." As she suggests, "the perceived excesses of the mode may in fact be a function of a particularly American insistence on innocence and good, as if American national identity required a constant assertion of innocence."[65]

That the hidden or misunderstood virtue in these films is that of the Anglo protagonists—metonymic of the guilt or innocence of the nation— is suggested more explicitly in D. W. Griffith's *The Massacre* (1912), another reworking of the Custer myth produced and released contemporaneously with Ince's film. Griffith's explorations of form are key to the melodramatic articulation of cinematic action, and films like *Fighting Blood* (1911), *The Last Drop of Water* (1911), and *The Battle of Elderbush Gulch* (1913) provide the most significant examples of the intensification of affect in the Western in this period. In *The Massacre*, this process is suggestively complex. The film invites identification with Indian as well as Anglo figures and raises the question of white culpability by shadowing the events at Little Bighorn, however anachronistically, with those at Wounded Knee. The film has been heralded for its moral and semantic fluidity, as the massacre of its title can be read in reference both to the initial "surprise attack on [an] Indian village" by the

U.S. Cavalry and to the subsequent and much more extensive attack by the Indians on a wagon train and the cavalry assigned to protect it.[66]

The initial massacre sequence destabilizes any simple assignment of moral authority to the film's white protagonists, including the heroic figure of the Scout, whose death will provide for the closing note of pathos. This destabilization takes place through the representational conventions noted above, in which the moral status of onscreen violence is constituted in relation to the production of domestic space. In *The Massacre*, the morally suspect nature of the initial cavalry assault is established through medium shots of an Indian family in their teepee just before the massacre begins. The shots rhyme with a previous sequence featuring the film's white heroine and her husband and baby, underscoring the association of the Indian family with the melodramatic value of home as a locus of innocence.

The massacre sequence replays formal conventions familiar from the representation of Indian assaults on the satellites of Anglo domesticity: shots of the approaching cavalry are intercut with interior shots of the teepee's domestic space; and wide, high-angle shots of the attacking cavalry and fleeing Indians are intercut with shots highlighting violence and death on an individualized scale. The sequence concludes with a desolate long take of a lone dog moving amid the carnage, the corpses of the mother and child featured earlier conspicuous in the foreground. The dog, embodying the desolation of this shot, will later return to signal the vengeful presence of the surviving Indian father as he crouches on a hillside, gazing in an extreme long shot at a wagon train below. While the formal highlighting of the wagon train's vulnerability adheres to generic convention, the presence of the dog draws an associative connection between this image of white settlement and the earlier explosion of white violence; the Indian father is legible to us here not simply as a threat but as a figure of righteous retribution, in keeping with the moral authorization of violence that melodrama constructs.

That the racial melodramatics of the Western have long been able to incorporate a condemnation of white violence alongside a celebration of Manifest Destiny is a useful lesson to be learned from the relative complexities of *The Massacre*. Ultimately, though, the project of the film is to assert rather than qualify the morally purified status of the white protagonists as victims. From the beginning, they provide the individual dimension and scale through which spectacles of large-scale action and violence are interpreted and experienced. Even the brief shots of the domestic space of the teepee, positioned to legitimize the image of the Indian family through association with its white counterpart, visually mark the limitations of this comparison by refusing to employ the convention of the close-up. In contrast, close-ups of the white baby recur throughout the film and function to establish and maintain its affective center.

This focus is particularly significant in the attack on the wagon train, which (in comparison with the initial massacre's three minutes of screen time) takes up almost an entire reel of this two-reel film. Here long shots of violence are intercut with close-ups of individualized anguish and suffering, focusing in particular on the imperiled white mother and baby, whose rescue provides the narrative drive of the film's second half (fig. 10). The insistent return to this image as the visual and affective anchor in the melodramatic production of suspense underscores what is at stake: not simply the life of the baby or, metaphorically, the innocence and vulnerability it represents, but the viability of a "civilized" western community (which is to say, its racialized identity). In committing himself to save the mother and her child, the Scout, who has been directly implicated in the earlier attack on the Indian village, is exonerated and, through the sacrifice of his own life, saved from any lingering sense of moral culpability. The Indian mother and child, in contrast, serve as narrative motivation only; their deaths provide an impetus to action, but their lives do not function as a site of particular affective investment or represent any larger moral sacrifice for the greater good.

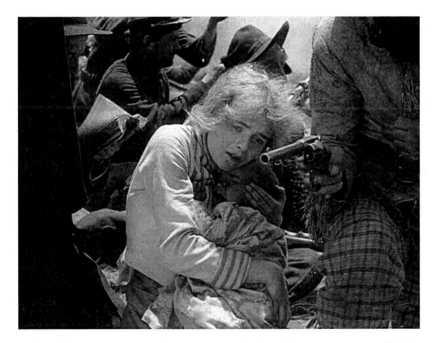

Fig. 10. The image of vulnerable white domesticity under assault anchors the melodramatic spectacle of violence in the early Western. *The Massacre* (Griffith 1912).

The accumulated cultural and affective force of such attack and rescue sequences would inspire Griffith's most famous charge: the notorious ride of the Clansmen in the Civil War epic *The Birth of a Nation* (1915). *Birth* is a foundational text in the history of film melodrama, of course, and its cultural and cinematic significance, both at the time of its release and since, would be hard to overestimate. In this film, the long history of the charge as a thrilling attraction meets up with the developing formal language of film to particularly powerful effect, interweaving the visceral and moral satisfactions of onscreen action in particularly affecting ways.

The efficacy of the film's solicitation to identify with the plight of its protagonists—to cringe at the sight of their suffering, rail at their abuse, and celebrate the thrilling spectacle of their rescue—derives from Griffith's increasingly sophisticated articulation of melodramatic form. As in *The Massacre*, the race-to-the-rescue sequence in *Birth* intercuts between more static images of individualized suffering and anxiety—Elsie Stoneman fending off the leering Silas Lynch, the besieged national "family" of Northerners and Southerners huddled together in the little log cabin, the tableaus of anxious townspeople—and action-filled shots of the Clansmen's ride. The sequence suggests how an identification with the position of those under assault can intensify spectatorial pleasure in the representation of action, as suggested by the visual and visceral satisfactions of the speeding Clansmen as they sweep across the screen, "flushing" blackness as they go.[67] The film makes textually explicit the historical and ideological appeals of white supremacy upon which the image of the charge has been founded and attests to melodrama's power to recast the historical legacy of violence through an insistence on the status of white protagonists as victims. As Linda Williams has argued, the "fundamental impact of *Birth* is as a melodramatic spectacle eliciting an affective response of sympathy" for its racist heroes. Indeed, though the widespread protests that greeted the film's release attest to how these appeals could be adamantly resisted and refused, the overwhelming popularity and success of the film also testify to their efficacy.

The ability of the film to compel a strong affective response relates to the history I have been tracing. Although the film is not a Western, Griffith self-consciously mined the conventions of the genre to produce a text that would resonate powerfully with his audience. In his own account, it was the ubiquity and popularity of "horse opera" sequences in which "the old U.S. Cavalry would gallop to the rescue" that inspired him "to do this ride-to-the-rescue on a grand scale. Instead of saving one poor little Nell of the Plains this would be a ride to save a nation."[68] The familiar conventions through which Griffith shapes this rescue in *Birth* cue the audience to this broader frame of reference, and the subtext of the cavalry charge intensifies identification with the Clansmen's ride as one of national relevance.

The early charge films provide an important precedent, as Amy Kaplan notes: "views of the climactic ride of the Klan echo on a grander scale films made of the Rough Riders on their way to rescue Cuba." Such images, of course, refer back to popular Wild West attractions.[69]

The mining of Western conventions contributed significantly to Griffith's project of nationalizing the image of Confederate suffering, helping to evacuate its regional specificity by associating it iconically (if not narratively) with the space of the West. Thus Griffith recasts the "Attack on the Settler's Cabin" with a band of marauding blacks in the role of Indians, while the "settler" whites—here reconstituted as a union of North and South—maintain their conventional status as innocents under assault.[70] The power of the film to compel conviction does not rest exclusively with the artistic innovations of Griffith the auteur (as many accounts would have it); it also emerges from the ideological and visual history of attack and rescue sequences. If the "whitewashing" of the screen as the Clansmen sweep across it appears as "a natural process of heroic rescue," the force of this naturalization derives from the image of the charge in western entertainments of the late nineteenth and early twentieth centuries and the cinematic development of this image in the decades preceding *Birth*.[71]

As Linda Williams has also argued, the visceral thrills of the final charge sequence are authorized and intensified by the prior identification with protagonist Ben Cameron as the paragon of a once glorious, now downtrodden white Southern manhood. In this respect, *Birth* returns to the theme of white masculine weakness and redemption that animates so many of Griffith's Biograph films, his early Westerns included. The film details Cameron's pathetic plight as, injured in body and spirit, he returns home after the Civil War to a social order in which his traditional claims to authority have been rendered obsolete.[72] In Cameron, the conventional melodramatic identification with victimization is redoubled and—through the explosive action of the charge—ultimately refused.

While even a charge film like *Roosevelt's Rough Riders* may be read at some level as a refutation of white masculine weakness, here the redemptive relevance of onscreen action is made textually explicit and given an individual dimension. Earlier Westerns tended to represent the charge from a distance, emphasizing speed and motion through an aesthetics of scale, the impressive massing of horses and men amid the dramatic western landscape being an early point of pride for western filmmakers. Through the figure of Cameron, Griffith brings to this convention a new kind of affective investment, intensifying both the visceral and the moral appeals of the charge. Though the Clansmen are at times featured as a vast force pouring forth from the deep space of a long shot, the final race-to-the-rescue sequence favors a moving camera that cleaves more closely to

Fig. 11. Through the melodramatics of the charge, the thrills of fast motion animate identification with white supremacist violence. *The Birth of a Nation* (Griffith 1915).

the bodies of the galloping horses and their riders (fig. 11). This technique greatly intensifies the sense of speed and urgency, while the more intimate camera distance locates the action on the same scale as the intercut images of innocents under assault.

The positioning of Cameron at the head of the charge in these shots provides an important link between the assertion of his victimization (and the film's insistent invitation into identification with this state) and the explosion of action onscreen. In making this link thematically as well as visually explicit, the film invites a satisfaction in the image of the charge as both thrilling and redemptive and an identification with Cameron as the agent of this conjunction. As I shall argue below, in the B Westerns of the 1930s and 1940s, the emphasis on thrilling motion would come to constitute the primary content of the genre, beholden to, if increasingly desirous to evacuate, the racist representational history that *The Birth of a Nation* both references and extends.

Moving Men: Heroic Action and the Morality of Motion

The Birth of a Nation speaks powerfully to the coherence of moral authority and visceral thrill in the cinematic image of the charge, as well as to the status of the white masculine hero in motion as the visual signifier of this coherence. The film would influence early stars like William S. Hart, in whose work the Western hero begins to take more specific shape. While Griffith's Westerns (like his Civil War and other films) often focus on issues of masculine transgression and redemption, it is not until Hart that the cowboy hero emerges as an explicit focus of the genre. Continuing in the ideological tradition of Roosevelt and Wister, Hart sought to imbue the rowdy stereotype of the cowboy with a specific moral identity while maintaining his status as a "primitive" antidote to the overcivilized East.

The ideological contradictions of this exercise—in which the racial and moral requirements of "white" masculinity must converge free from the stigma of effeminacy—condition an emphasis on the cowboy hero as a primary site of conflict. Drawing from and extending Broncho Billy Anderson's portrayal of the "good badman," Hart emphasizes white masculinity as both the problem the films set out to solve and the mechanism of their resolution. In films that move away from the Plains War focus of *Custer's Last Stand* and *The Massacre*, the moral and racial legibility of the good badman emerges as the principal site of drama. In this context, Hart serves as the locus of both pathos and action onscreen. As in *The Birth of a Nation*, these registers both authorize and qualify one another: pathetic identification with the hero frames the pleasures of action as morally legitimate, while an insistence on the hero as the agent of such action mediates the feminizing implications that pathetic identification might otherwise entail.

Rather than Wild West–style attack and rescue scenarios, Hart's films revolve around melodramas of identity and disguise, in which the whiteness of the hero may initially dissemble under signs of blackness. The morally divided nature of the hero is often cast in racialized terms; in the guise of the half-breed, the status of the good badman pivots around the issue of divided loyalty, as the films move to establish the hidden identity of whiteness and goodness, which it is their project to construct. The invocation of whiteness as at once a racial and a moral category invariably circulates around a melodramatic moment of revelation, in which Hart's love for a "pure" white woman serves both to catalyze his moral conversion and to assure the audience that such a conversion was inevitable (as the love of the pure white woman establishes the truth of Hart's racial and moral identity as a white man).

Even when the racial identity of the Hart protagonist is not explicitly in question, the rhetorical insistence on whiteness and blackness as moral categories indicates the extent to which a racialized imagination prevails. Hence, in *The Aryan* (1916), Hart will ultimately "run true to the creed of his race," transforming himself from an abductor and wagon train raider—racialized categories of banditry signifying also a sexual threat—to emerge as a guardian and protector of white womanhood.[73] And in *The Toll Gate* (1920), the outlaw Black Deering, whose heart has become "black with the poison of revenge," must work to reestablish his claims to whiteness by transforming himself from a sexual threat to the self-sacrificing savior of the white heroine, "Provin' you can't tell how white a man is by the color of his coat" (as the closing title maintains).

The divided nature of the Hart protagonist conditions a formal shift that establishes the Western hero as the visual center of the genre in new ways. Rather than close-ups of the imperiled heroine, for instance, long takes of Hart's face provide the primary register of pathos and suspense. Issues of masculinity and performance emerge as central in this context; manliness and authenticity (nearly synonymous terms in the Hart Western, as elsewhere) are signified through a rejection of forms of display marked as theatrical.

In *Hell's Hinges* (1916), for instance, the "Weakling" Henley's unfitness for the ministry is visualized in the opening sequence through the inappropriate pleasure he takes in the admiring gaze of an all-female congregation. Cutting from Henley's expressive pronouncements at the pulpit to shots of his rapt, adoring flock, the sequence casts masculine weakness as an issue of vanity: Henley "tak[es] an actor's delight in swaying the audience." The pattern will be repeated when Henley preaches to prostitutes at a saloon out West. In contrast to Henley's broad gesticulations, Hart's Blaze Tracey makes his first appearance on the dusty streets of Hell's Hinges in a display of shooting stunts executed from the back of his horse to the rowdy appreciation of a rough group of western men. Whereas Henley's performances are confined to the interior spaces of the church, drawing room, and saloon, Hart appears within the authenticating mise-en-scène of the western landscape, demonstrating the kinds of Wild West skills that continue to signify the realism of western-themed attractions. The film underscores the different status of these performances through an emphasis on the female gazes they attract: that of the darkly sexual "bad woman" marks out Henley, in contrast to that of the heroine Faith (Henley's sister), whose look at Blaze is first given formal prominence on the heels of his shoot-'em-up stunts.

In keeping with the culture of strenuous spectacle detailed in the last chapter, *Hell's Hinges* associates a certain kind of spectacle with theatricality, falseness, and masculine deviance, while naturalizing the appearance of Hart through a different kind of display, one defined by its violence and a certain restrained repertoire of gesture and expression that signify the virtues of masculine self-control.[74] For the Hart hero emotes not to express himself but in spite of himself, inaugurating a propensity for underplaying that would continue to define the Western hero for decades to come. The minimalism of Hart's expressions paradoxically conditions the camera's closer attention to his face, highlighting his status as an object of the gaze even as the film disavows it. This kind of performance style would emerge as a key signifier of the genre's overall realism: an implicit refutation of its "melodramatic" affect coupled with a persistent disavowal of acting or performance as such.

A concern with the masculine virtues of the real marks Hart's films in other ways as well. The unadorned western town and the violence it engenders are described in *Hell's Hinges* as "The Reality" of the West (in contrast to a shot of Henley's fantasy of the West as an uninhibited space ripe for sexual showboating). Excess in costumes and sets, as well as in performance style, is rejected as a sign of effeminacy and falseness, and certain elements of the mise-en-scène emerge to signify, in contrast, attributes of the masculine and the real. In keeping with the impulses of men like Remington, Hart eschewed the sequined vests and decorated chaps of his contemporary Tom Mix in favor of understated attire selected with an eye toward greater historical fidelity. Sets also were spare and austere, with rickety buildings, dusty main streets, and arid landscapes signifying a rejection of ornamentation and an embrace of the "real"—a virtue, Hart's films suggest, that rightly attends both the space of the West and the process of representing it. The association of an austere mise-en-scène with a male-identified realism would continue across the twentieth century, as when Howard Hawks's *Red River* (1948) is heralded as setting a new standard for western realism—offering a "spectacle . . . as rugged and hard as the men" it represents—while the widescreen, Technicolor compositions of *Shane* (Stevens 1953) are decried as an aestheticizing betrayal of the same.[75]

Although Hart's pathos-infused Westerns are a significant precedent for the postwar features of the next chapter, by the 1920s the dictate of "action for action's sake" would eclipse Hart in favor of former wild west show performers like Mix. In stark contrast to Hart, Mix brought flamboyant showmanship to the genre, evident in his stunt riding as well as in his propensity for sequins and decorative spurs. Rather than a site of pathos, the cowboy hero in the Mix films of the 1910s and 1920s serves as the locus of visual and visceral excitement through fast breakaways, stunts, and extended chase sequences. While the Mix films rely more on stock scenarios of abduction and rescue and less explicitly on issues of racial and moral legibility, "a very white hero" still provides a key part of their conventional formula, highlighting the conjunction of moral goodness, racial identity, and onscreen action.[76]

This action-oriented tradition would inform the B Westerns of the 1930s and 1940s, low-budget assembly-line productions that provided the economic backbone of the industry after the coming of sound temporarily eroded the status of the feature Western.[77] In these Westerns we witness the naturalization of an action-based hero whose moral authority is founded not upon any explicit white supremacist assertion but rather—and perhaps more powerfully—on its prior assumption. Divesting themselves of the explicit racism of Griffith's Clansmen or Hart's anguished paeans to whiteness, the Bs constitute the authority of their hero by wedding him ineluctably to the thrills of fast action and violence onscreen.

In contrast to the Hart films, the goodness and the whiteness of the B hero are taken as the preconditions of his action. If in melodrama the body "speaks" morality, in the context of the B Westerns its diction is unwavering: heroes are white men almost without exception, unmarked by signifiers of non-Anglo ethnic identity. Men marked by foreignness, darkness, or legibly "ethnic" origins are impugned on the basis of their masculine and racial failings. Scott Simmon has discussed the function of John Wayne's body in *The Big Trail* (1930) as representing that film's "deepest, wordless argument for Manifest Destiny."[78] This assertion may be usefully extended to the B Western hero, whose body—defined through its privileged relationship to motion and in explicit contrast to the pantheon of other masculine types in the genre's repertoire—makes implicit arguments about racial identity, moral legitimacy, and the prerogatives of action.

The promise of extended action serves as the genre's defining attraction in this period, and the orchestration of suspense revolves primarily around its anticipation and delay. In this, the melodramatic rhythm of the Bs operates in the more mechanical tradition of the early silent serials and their nineteenth-century theatrical precedents. Films often establish only the most rudimentary context for extended action sequences, and interludes of dialogue serve as minimalist bridges between one sequence and the next. Plots revolve around conventional melodramatic devices of misunderstanding, misrecognition, and disguise and conclude after the orderly reassignment of innocence and guilt through the necessary revelations on the part of misled authorities or love interests. In contrast to its formulaic plot devices, limited production values, disjunctive editing (amplified by the common practice of recycling footage), and relatively wooden scripts and performances, the eruption of motion and violence provides the B Western with its primary source of vitality.[79] It is visceral thrill itself that emerges as the central appeal of the genre in this period, heightened through speed, rapid cuts, an increasing reliance on moving camerawork, and the conventionalization of direct address within charge and chase sequences.

In the context of the Bs, the realist imperative of earlier western entertainments gives way, as low-budget production values and a high degree of incongruity in stories and settings undercut any claims to verisimilitude. Indeed, the B Westerns are largely unconcerned with such issues, notoriously intermixing anachronistic technologies with the exploits of the genre's cowboy heroes. In addition, Mix's emphasis on performance carries over into the Bs, in the explicit example of the singing cowboy, as well as in the ongoing emphasis on stunt riding as a central attraction. Even the western landscape, a traditional authenticating feature, recedes into the distance in many of these films; while a tumbleweed-strewn plain or dusty wagon train may make an occasional appearance, conventional western landscapes and scenarios are not privileged over other settings and plot devices. Instead, action serves as the primary credential of both these films and their stars; it cements the relationship between the formulaic and sometimes farcical storylines of the Bs and the cultural imagination of the West they nonetheless work to fortify.

With their formulaic structures and low production values, the Bs have often seemed unworthy of critical attention, too juvenile and naive, their pleasures too unserious. The films' eschewal of the traditional dictates of realism contributes to this neglect, I would suggest. Their exuberant celebration of onscreen action and more explicit acknowledgment of the showmanship of their heroes highlight their melodramatic status in more obvious ways, stigmatizing the form with the feminizing implications of mass entertainment. But it is precisely the conventionalization of action they effect that makes the Bs important to consider: the seeming innocence (or, alternately, inanity) of the pleasures they proffer helps to mystify the ideological labor they perform in aligning the visceral thrills of onscreen action with an unimpeachable moral authority and embodying this conjunction in the image of the Western hero in motion.

It is in the B Westerns, through constant iteration, that the relationship between righteous action and the cowboy hero is fully naturalized. If in a postwar Western like *Shane* the hero's body can be said to "[arouse] a longing for action," this longing can only be understood in relation to the Bs' conditioning of generic expectation.[80] The eventual sense of breakdown in the relationship between action, moral authority, and the Western hero that dominates critical response to the genre after World War II—the subject of the next chapter—can be apprehended only in relation to this history.

In general, as the representation of action becomes the primary basis for identification with the figure of the hero, the way in which race has functioned to consolidate the moral authority of this figure is elided. The expansionist impulse and racialized scenarios of attack and rescue that historically attended the image of the charge are largely disavowed in the Bs. While epic feature Westerns of the 1920s such as *The Covered Wagon* (Cruze 1923) and *The Iron Horse* (Ford 1924) reference the dictates of Manifest Destiny directly to produce an image of the Western hero as national hero, Indian wars and wagon trains are almost wholly absent from the representational repertoire of the B Western (as are Indians themselves). Rather than rehearsed through the racial melodramatics of the plot, the whiteness and goodness of the hero are secured through the generic weight of thrilling action itself, the serialization of the Bs, and the industrial investment in offscreen star personas who adhere to the mythic moral code of the cowboy (as codified by Gene Autry's Ten Cowboy Commandments).

The Bs' general avoidance of explicitly racialized violence allows them to appear innocent of the legacies upon which the representational conventions of the genre are founded; the charge, chase, and rescue are divested of their white supremacist and imperialist content. Instead, the cowboy hero comes to represent a "classless and uncontroversial image of white supremacy," an image, as Peter Stanfield has argued, that negotiates the controversial associations of Southern culture by recasting them in the space of the West (an impulse at work to some degree in Griffith's *Birth* as well).[81] By deemphasizing the racial conventions of the genre and situating its heroic exploits in temporally indeterminate contexts, the B Western produces a national hero who, though descending from an imagined historical past, is innocent of the legacy of white supremacism this lineage implies. Nonetheless, the identification with the B hero as an embodiment of moral authority, and the constitution of this authority in and through motion and violence, cannot be understood outside of this generic history, which the films work both to affirm and to disavow.

On occasion, the Bs' repudiation of the racist history of the West (and implicitly, the representational history of the Western) is made explicit, though—as with Griffith's *The Massacre*—the limitations of this impulse are worth noting. The Tim McCoy film *End of the Trail* (Lederman 1932), for instance, is unusually insistent in employing its hero as a mouthpiece for Indian grievances and white culpability. ("That's why I'm for the Indian," the McCoy hero asserts, "because in every instance the white man has been to blame.") Foreshadowing later "pro-Indian" Westerns, the film casts the conventional alignment of race and morality as a misreading of the signs of moral legibility (as in the case of the army general who interprets McCoy's status as an "Indian lover" as a sign of his criminality).

The rhetorical insistence on the historical abuse of the Indian forms an interesting and unexpected counterpoint to the film's opening sequence, in which shrieking Indians encircle and massacre first a wagon train and then a unit of outnumbered cavalrymen, recycling the most common scenarios of the silent Western, including the conventional shot of the Indian assault viewed from within the space of a covered wagon. The domesticity of this space is emphasized here through the use of curtains as a framing device, which also draws attention to the attack as a spectacle, underscoring the conventional nature of such images and suggesting a subtle distancing from them. The rehearsal of familiar generic conventions within a film that seeks on some level to repudiate the genre's traditional racist violence has the potential to discredit the conventions themselves. The film moves away from the possibility of critique, however, to find resolution in the reestablishment of a racialized distinction as the basis for the McCoy hero's authority. McCoy ultimately ascends to the post of benevolent Indian agent, evacuating his previous position as a "red brother" to preside "as a father" over a grateful flock of "Indian half-children."[82]

Even while the Bs work to dissociate the thrilling action of the Western from its imperialist, expansionist, and white supremacist content, the representational history of the genre and its defining image of the charge haunt these films on both a narrative and a visual level. One way this haunting surfaces is through a persistent concern with vigilante violence. Indeed, establishing the legitimacy of extralegal violence—the difference between upstanding moral crusaders and outlaw renegades—is an ongoing project of the Bs.[83]

In *Westward Ho* (Bradbury 1935), for instance, John Wayne and his masked vigilante band sing jovially of their "midnight ride of terror" as they comb the darkened streets. Although the film does not evidence any overt discomfort with the representation of the vigilantes, "[t]he dark implications of living by law of their own making isn't so much softened as made more perverse" by the lighthearted tone of the film.[84] The film opens with the desire to "see an Injun," a wish voiced by the Wayne hero's younger brother as the family's wagon train snakes its lonely way across an open expanse of flat, dusty land. While the visuals strongly cue the expectation of an impending Indian assault, the narrative quickly turns toward a concern with "bad men." When it is outlaw whites rather than Indians who descend upon the wagon train, however, the representation of their attack—the abduction of Wayne's brother, massacre of his parents, and burning of their wagons—evokes the conventions of Indian assault that the film both references and disavows. An opening title acknowledges something of the violent history the film's jovial tone belies, dedicating the film "to the Vigilantes . . . builders of the New Empire of the West," a gesture that asserts the plot line of Manifest Destiny that the film otherwise represses.

The concern with vigilante violence produces strong echoes with *The Birth of a Nation*. While *Westward Ho* recalls and represses the conventional Indian assault, for instance, *The Night Riders* (Sherman 1939) produces a striking visual homage to Griffith. In this film (an entry into the Three Mesquiteers series in which Wayne also stars), the heroes organize themselves into a vigilante band to protect a victimized community of farmers and small ranchers and to reclaim the violent masculine prerogatives of what it means to be "an American." Like *The Birth of a Nation*, the film frames its representation of vigilante violence with an explicit assertion of its national significance: the vigilante band is born in response to

Fig. 12. The Bs constitute generic action as the locus of both morality and excitement, mobilizing the appeals of the charge while disavowing their white supremacist lineage. *The Night Riders* (Sherman 1939).

the complaint that "it used to be that being an American *meant* something." The action sequences themselves—composed of moving camera shots of the night riders as they gallop across the country in white hoods and capes—resonate deeply with images of the Klan and with *The Birth of a Nation*'s ultimate ride to the rescue in particular (fig. 12). Such images provide striking testimony to the ongoing influence of Griffith's film and are affectively powerful not despite but as a result of this lineage, I would suggest.[85]

The emphasis on vigilantism draws upon a longstanding inclination to align the Western and its hero against institutionalized forms of authority, an inclination intensified in the Depression-era context of the Bs. In part through the embrace of a contemporary rhetoric of populism, the image of action in this period is distanced from its racist representational past, emphasizing other sources of moral authority for the white Western hero. Hence in the Bs, villains are often bankers or other discredited authority figures, while heroes appear as modern-day Robin Hoods, squarely aligned with the interests of the "common man."[86] Motivations of commercial gain are decried through the figures of the corpulent banker (whose girth signifies his greed) and the dandyish gambler, whose masculine failings are opposed to the virile authenticity and moral authority of the Western hero. The B heroes themselves tend to eschew motives of economic self-interest and devote themselves instead to the service of small-time farmers and ranchers, ordinary folks trying to get by in the face of corporate avarice and ineffectual government protections. The image of the B cowboy as an anti-elite, anti-corporate hero activates the category of class even as the genre's white supremacist underpinnings work to undercut the impetus toward a class-based critique.[87] And while the narrative emphasis on corporate greed and abuse might seem to incline toward capitalist critique, the melodramatic insistence on issues of individual guilt and innocence works in the service of disavowal, representing corruption as a localized rather than a systemic problem.

Asserting the relationship between the visual set pieces of the Western (the chase, the charge, the rescue) and the plight of the struggling common man works to mystify the representational history through which these images have become culturally and morally meaningful. The Bs propose a powerful source of pleasure for their viewers: an identification with the visceral thrills of onscreen action (and with the white Western hero as their agent) that insists upon the status of such action as natural, timeless, and morally unimpeachable. While the Wild West show embraced the discourse of economic expansionism, celebrating the "Anglo-Saxon's commercial necessities" as a further testimony to Manifest Destiny, the B Western disavows its service to the ideologies of expansion and white supremacism upon which its thrilling action has been founded.

The imperialist appeals from which the genre's central images derive are thus rigorously divorced from the materialist aims of expansion itself (evidencing a reluctance to associate heroic white masculinity with commercial motivations that both predates and outlasts the Western's heyday).[88] In 1898, the moving image of Rough Riders charging in the name of American imperialism represented an interwoven appeal to white manhood and American dominion; by the 1930s, the charge has been conventionalized as an embodiment of masculine and moral authority divorced from the history of imperialist and white supremacist violence. Hence the Western binds the energy of the early attraction to the constitution of moral authority and secures the status of the white Western hero as the agent and embodiment of both.[89] The identification invited in this context is not with continental expansionism, overseas imperialism, economic opportunism, or white supremacism, but with the appeals of a populist action hero.

Representing moral agency through the figure of white masculinity is a cultural tradition that neither begins nor ends with the B Western; it is in the Western, however, that the sensational conjunction of thrilling cinematic action with moral and masculine authority finds one of its most efficacious forms. It is this action—and the history of racial violence it encodes—that the genre works to naturalize, conventionalizing its pleasures by codifying them as a mark of American, masculine, and cinematic authenticity. Though the Western grows increasingly uneasy with the inherent instabilities of this alignment, it nonetheless provides the genre with its ideological and visual foundations and conditions generic, cultural, and affective expectations of thrilling righteous action in the Western and beyond.

3

Western Weepies

The Power of Pathos in
the Cold War Western

The conjunction of onscreen action with moral and masculine authority, so endlessly iterated in the B Westerns of the 1930s and early 1940s, begins to fall apart after World War II. Breaking with the cinematic lineage of the charge, the affective address of the genre shifts from the visceral and moral appeals of motion toward a pathetic identification with the Western hero as a man caught within confining circumstances over which he is largely powerless. Extended sequences in which the hero races unfettered across the screen are increasingly rare; instead, feature Westerns after the war come to emphasize the hero's physical and psychological impairment. Indeed, the hero is often without a horse altogether, lacking the thrilling speed and mobility—as well as the moral authority—his status on horseback previously signified.

This new Western hero is frequently injured and often mentally unbalanced, his physical debilities offered as a sign of deeper psychological troubles. Regularly deprived of the authenticating value of landscape shots and the claims to realness these had signified, he is often restricted to the interior spaces of saloons, hotel lobbies, houses, and shops—a mise-en-scène more closely aligned with that of domestic melodrama. In his newly constricted mobility, the hero grows twitchy and restless, uneasy with himself and agitated with others. His face—featured by the 1950s in widescreen, Technicolor close-up—betrays anguish and anxiety. He is as often the pursued as the pursuer, though his primary adversaries have morphed into his

own shadowy doubles and internal demons. He flees his past but is persecuted by it; his journeys lead him back in circles upon himself.[1]

In both thematic and stylistic terms, Westerns of the Cold War era (for
the purposes of this discussion, extending from the late 1940s through the
early 1960s) resonate with other contemporary genres and cycles, including
film noir, the social problem picture, and the domestic or family melodrama.
Each in its own way is oriented around the representation of white masculine instability. Noir stylistics in particular operate as a visual code for white
masculine insecurity and anxiety in this period, and their incorporation into
the Western beginning in the 1940s helps to signal the genre's focus on a
troubled, persecuted, and morally ambiguous protagonist.[2] In addition, contemporary issues and conflicts that provide material for the social problem
pictures of the 1940s—juvenile delinquency, the psychological adjustment of
returning veterans, and, most especially, racism—become central thematic
concerns in the Western by the late 1940s and early 1950s. In the context of
these migrations and generic cross-breedings, the Western takes as its focus
the instability and moral ambiguity of its hero; like the domestic melodrama
to which it is kin, it engages in a critique of traditional modes of white masculine authority while evidencing an anxiety over their absence or decline.

What interests me about this hero and the generic shifts he embodies is the new affective registers they sound and the particular modes of
authorization they represent, as the Western shifts away from the visceral
and moral thrills of action toward pathetic modes of identification and
attachment. In ways that I discuss across this chapter and the next, moral
authority in this context is generated through the status of the hero as the
film's primary victim, one whose victimization often takes on a specifically racialized dimension, derived from the hero's close association with
(and, eventually, his substitution for) the figure of the Indian. Alongside
an emphasis on suffering, shame and guilt emerge as newly central in this
era, working in complex ways both to acknowledge and to alchemize the
genre's racist representational past.

Reestablishing the hero's claim to moral authority through an emphasis on pathos thus becomes the central ideological project of the Western
in this period. The paradigmatic image of the Cold War Western hero—
to whose enduring efficacy political discourse after 9/11 would attest—is
inseparable from the melodramatic function of pathos and the moral
authority that accrues around the spectacle of victimization. In the hero's
suffering and instability, the genre finds an affective solution for the contemporary critique of traditional forms of white masculine authority—a
form of critique that reinvests in the image of the hero through gestures
of his repudiation. Thus the Western hero is paradoxically reinvigorated
through films that emphasize his weakness and vulnerability.[3]

The changing status of action in the Western cannot be understood outside the racialized meanings this action has worked historically to construct. To understand this broad shift, it is necessary to consider the role of pathos in melodrama generally, the specific function of racialized victimization in American cultural discourse, and the significance of political and ideological pressures of the Cold War period. As action once signified the thrilling virtue of imperialist mobility—producing the gendered and racialized identity of the hero through the alignment of this identity with both agency and pleasure—the virtues of this action and the identity it has worked to consolidate become more unstable in the social and political context of the Cold War. Tracing the nature of this instability, and the melodramatic solution the Western provides, is the project of this chapter.

Questioning Authority: Masculinity, Morality, and the Cold War Western

In its gravitation toward images of masculine instability, Hollywood participates in the broader discourse of white masculine crisis. Like the turn of the century, the Cold War period represents a high-water mark in this discourse, a time when dominant conceptions of normative masculinity are challenged by social and economic pressures, and popular and political rhetoric articulates this sense of challenge with a high degree of self-consciousness.[4] In a 1958 essay on "The Crisis of American Masculinity," Arthur Schlesinger Jr. bemoans the degradation of traditional forms of masculine identity and authority, noting a "rising tide of male anxiety" and the increased consciousness "of maleness not as a fact but as a problem"; "something," he maintains, "has gone badly wrong with the American male's conception of himself."[5] Suggestively echoing contemporary film critic Robert Warshow's description of the Western hero as a man whose moral clarity "corresponds to the clarity of his physical image," Schlesinger asserts that "the male role had plainly lost its rugged clarity of outline."[6]

This new fuzziness, according to Schlesinger, is related to the impulses of a mass society toward the conforming and the de-individualized, in stark contrast to ideologies of masculinity rooted in individualism, independence, and self-determination. As noted in the Introduction, the affective orientation of the mass has long raised anxieties, posited in explicit contrast to the self-governing virtues of the white male as a representative national subject. In the contemporary discourse of crisis, the political climate of consensus, the explosive growth of the suburbs, the domestic consumption and conformism these communities housed, and the emergence of the corporate commuter, whose "inner direction" and individuality were sacrificed on the altar of the organization, were all seen as harbingers of the "decline of the American male."[7] As at the turn of the century, the conditions of modern life were seen as anathema to the values of manliness. The "other-directed" man, the organization man, and the man in the gray flannel suit emerged in sociological and cultural texts as embodiments of postwar masculine conformity, representing the eradication of traditional forms of authority and independence. White middle-class men were imagined to be dominated by the women in their lives, domesticated through mass consumption, and enervated by a corporate culture based not on individualist striving and self-determination but on the feminized values of flexibility and teamwork.[8] Schlesinger articulates the opposition in strikingly melodramatic terms, decrying a loss of moral as well as masculine identity in this context. This negative view of group identity would find explicit representation in the Cold War Western's image of the town as mob, an embodiment of unruly affect and moral disorder.

Within this discourse, the very affluence and material abundance to which anticommunist rhetoric turned in its celebration of the free-market economy and the "American way" were articulated as paradoxically corrosive to the virtues upon which ideas of American exceptionalism were founded. Even as the new G.I. Bill underwrote white middle-class masculinity through education and home ownership loans and the construction of the federally funded interstate highway system provided the infrastructure for a postwar suburban boom, cultural commentators voiced concern over the new middle class of white-collar commuters these policies helped to produce. Corporate labor and the suburban prosperity it sponsored—while celebrated as the pinnacle of national and individual achievement—were simultaneously decried as undercutting self-reliance and individualism. A culture that counseled consumption as the key to individual happiness and addressed men as consumers in newly explicit ways continued to wring its hands over the masculine softness affluence was feared to condition.

The war itself helped raise alarm over the softening of American men by investigating their suitability for combat and emphasizing the national implications of their failings, as the bodily vigor of white men continued to serve as a synecdoche for national vitality. The wartime institutionalization of psychiatric screening, designed to forestall a sequel to World War I's shell-shock epidemic, contributed significantly to the cultural authority of Freudian discourse after the war, further destabilizing the image of normative masculine identity.[9] This destabilization fed persistent fears of a subversive potential lurking within the American national (and individual male) body, fears that took shape in the widespread homosexual hysteria of the McCarthy era. The paranoid structure of internal subversion would become central to the Western, as both the hero and the community he is traditionally bound to protect are grievously threatened by weakness and corruption from within—problems that define the genre in this period.

Even as it decried the corrosion of masculine individualism, however, mainstream culture asserted the values of a masculinity rooted in the conventionally feminine virtues of domesticity, cooperation, and togetherness. Men were encouraged to embrace their limited functions within larger bureaucratic structures and to define themselves more centrally in relation to their roles as husbands and fathers (a pressure legible in the Western's new emphasis on the hero's nurturing function). And while the contemporary outcry over lost individualism imbues the Western hero with invigorated appeal, saturating his image with longing and nostalgia, authoritarian masculinity had at the same time been discredited in its association with the moral bankruptcy of the fascist and racist regimes of World War II. Schlesinger suggests this link when he observes (not a little forlornly) that any restoration of "the old masculine supremacy" is both impossible and, ultimately, undesirable, because "[m]asculine supremacy, like white supremacy, was the neurosis of an immature society."[10] Thus the appeals of traditional masculinity are ambivalent at best, producing tensions and contradictions that find powerful expression in the changing melodramatics of the Western.

Although an emphasis on the suffering and anguish of the Western hero is not unprecedented, it comes to dominate generic conventions in new ways after the war. Ever since the newly troubled hero began making his appearance in films such as _Pursued_ (Walsh 1947), _Red River_ (Hawks 1948), _The Gunfighter_ (King 1950), and _High Noon_ (Zinnemann 1952), critics and scholars have noted these generic shifts and often forcefully decried them. A variety of factors have been cited in an attempt to understand this transformation, including the Cold War's general mood of anxiety, discomfort with its conformist pressures, and specific concerns over the fate of masculine individualism. In addition, some critics have argued that the Western as an ideologically conservative genre provided a venue in the age of the Hollywood blacklist for oblique forms of social and political critique (in contrast to the more didactic social problem pictures of the late 1940s, for instance), leading toward themes outside its conventional purview. Meanwhile, the pantheon of aging Western stars raised questions of mortality. And finally, the feature Western's attempt to appeal to a more adult audience, in distinction to the juvenile associations of the Bs, met with the rise of popular Freudianism to condition a greater emphasis on sexuality and character psychology. All of these forces, it has been argued, worked to move the genre away from its traditional emphasis on action.[11]

Closer attention to critical reaction, however, suggests something more and different at stake. Among contemporary accounts, for instance, Robert

Warshow's 1954 "chronicle" of the Westerner is particularly suggestive of
how the shift away from action is understood to implicate the hero's moral
stature specifically. Moral authority, in Warshow's account, derives from
thematic as well as stylistic conventions—from the hero's ability to ride,
shoot straight, and "keep his countenance in the face of death," as well as
from the visual emphasis on "wide expanses of land, the free movement of
men on horses." After the war, according to Warshow, as movement stalls
in the face of new thematic concerns, "[e]ven the horses, no longer . . .
the inspired chargers of knight-errantry, have lost much of the moral significance that once seemed to belong to them in their careering across the
screen."[12] Gesturing toward the genealogy of the charge, Warshow highlights the extent to which moral authority has been constituted through
and in relation to the visceral satisfactions of onscreen motion. The "careering" horses embody this authority not simply because of the moral clarity
of their mission—a sure sense of the value of whom or what they race to
save—but also through the force and speed of their motion, the conventional collapse of visceral with moral appeals.

Precisely this kind of thrilling action changes in the postwar period. It
is not simply that there is less of it—that the genre closes in more tightly
around the figure of the hero as the primary locus of moral conflict,
although this is certainly true—but that its value alters. Rather than an
invitation to unproblematic pleasure, strong action in the postwar Western
becomes an ambivalent signifier, embodying a mode of agency and authority the genre is moved both to celebrate and to critique. The ambivalence
of this relationship to the appeals of fast, aggressive action and violence
comes to shape the genre after the war, conditioning both guilt and longing, shame and the gesture toward redemption.

The ascendance of pathetic identification and the degree to which the
hero's moral and affective claims come to be constituted through it are
Warshow's primary concerns. Although he cites as a virtue the Western
hero's traditional melancholy, he objects to the status of Gary Cooper in
High Noon as a "pathetic rather than a tragic figure" and protests the contemporary "passive" conception of heroism itself, in which "the brave young
men who kill large numbers of our enemies" are neglected in favor of those
"heroic prisoners who endure torture without capitulating." Warshow's
comments register the extent to which representations of violent agency are
coming under critique in this period, operating as an increasingly unstable
and ambiguous signifier, while pathetic modes of identification become
more central. In Warshow's ideal Western "our eyes are not focused on
the sufferings of the defeated but on the deportment of the hero"; in contrast, in the Cold War Western these positions collapse increasingly into
one another. Philip French has identified this transformation in similar

terms, noting the genre's movement from an emphasis on victory toward a preoccupation with losing. In terms of the genre's affective address, however, in losing the Western hero has much to gain, for as Warshow acknowledges, "what we finally respond to is not [the hero's] victory but his defeat."[13] The felt good of the genre shifts in this context, moving away from the visceral appeals of motion and toward the complex pleasures of identification with suffering, failure, and loss.[14]

The Western's new ambivalence toward its hero as an agent of strong action pivots in crucial ways around the issue of race. Warshow's account, though unable to name the racial foundations of its critique, gestures toward the white supremacist lineage of the Western hero in language resonant with Owen Wister's paean to the racial heritage of the Anglo-Saxon cowpuncher half a century earlier.[15] The effort of Warshow's Westerner, as "the last gentleman," to maintain "the purity of his image" is an unquestionably racialized pursuit, as Warshow's rhetoric of purity, honor, and other "knightly" virtues underscores. Among the social, political, and industrial pressures on the genre in this period, however, none is more significant than the challenge to its foundational conjunction of moral authority with white supremacy. While the racism of Henry Fonda's Wyatt Earp in *My Darling Clementine* (Ford 1946) can still be played lightly for laughs, the days of the Western hero as an unrepentant racist are numbered. Racism underwrites Earp's status as a moral agent in cleaning up Tombstone—his repression of racial (and sexual) difference securing the badge of his moral authority—but this violence becomes increasingly problematic in the Western after 1950.[16]

For the Western and its hero, the conjunction of moral authority with the thrills of white supremacist violence is inadequate to the ideological imperatives of the Cold War. The extent to which a racialized purity no longer provides for moral legibility marks one of the most significant changes in the genre, at a time when extratextual pressures on the official avowal of white supremacism transform the conventional alignment of whiteness with morality. The acceleration of the civil rights movement at home and the rhetorical and ideological role of American freedom and equality within Cold War propaganda push against the Western's white supremacist foundations. In the aftermath of a "good war" fought against the forces of fascism and anti-Semitism and in the context of the domestic and international challenges to racism that follow, the hypocrisy of instituted forms of white supremacy becomes increasingly costly to maintain as the public face of American democracy.

At the same time, white racial violence gains a new kind of mediated visibility in this period. With the opening of Emmett Till's casket to the world and the televised attacks on African American schoolchildren in the years after *Brown v. Board of Education*, the hypocrisy of "the American way" as a democratic ideal is subject to greater domestic and international exposure. Widely published incidents of white racial violence in the Jim Crow South and elsewhere provided themes and images for Soviet propaganda campaigns and greatly undermined the moral authority of the United States as a force for democratic change in the world. "Rehabilitating the moral character of American democracy" becomes a dominant ideological project in this context, as Mary Dudziak has asserted. The "telling of a shameful story" emerges as a way of "presenting American history as a story of redemption."[17] Through the witnessing of a shameful past, as Sara Ahmed argues in another context, the nation can reassert the ideals deemed foundational to its identity in the present.[18]

Hollywood cinema, as a major global export and a prime vehicle of nationalist propaganda, responded to these pressures in significant ways, and the Western's turn toward pathos and shame is one articulation of this response. As a genre, the Western is particularly ripe for the kind of redemption story to which Dudziak refers, given the roots of its narrative content in a history of genocide and its formal and industrial genesis in the mediated appeals of imperialism. As Douglas Pye has argued, the "conventions of the Western's generic world became embarrassing" after the war, as an "increased consciousness of what was implied in representations of gender and race made it extraordinarily difficult to use many of the basic character types of the genre in the traditional ways."[19] Under such pressures, the paradigm in which whiteness serves as a signifier of masculine as well as moral integrity begins to shift, explicitly in the so-called pro-Indian cycle of the 1950s, but also more generally, as Warshow's comments suggest.

The ideological casting of white supremacism as anti-American poses a distinct representational challenge, given that whiteness and moral authority have been linked terms since the Western's inception and that the righteousness of the genre's conventional violence has long relied on the positioning of its white protagonists as victims of Indian assault. With a few key exceptions, including D. W. Griffith's Indian pictures for Biograph, early Westerns take shape around a racial paradigm in which "bad" whites can be recognized through their social and sexual alignments with the genre's racialized others. This alignment is produced as the signifier of a moral darkness, with the refusal of such characters to commit to the project of white racial purity signifying a masculine as well as a moral failing.

In the 1950s, however, the genre's racial paradigm undergoes a decisive shift. Articulated through a contemporary rhetoric of tolerance, Westerns in this period value the show of racial sensitivity as a marker of moral integrity and cast overtly racist acts and exclamations as indicators of ignorance, mental instability, or moral laxity. In contrast to conventional Indian assault scenarios, white racism itself is represented as a primary threat to the white community, and cowboy culture is increasingly pathologized as violent and intolerant, the menacing refuge of sadistic and maladjusted men.[20] Even when represented on the rampage, Indians are given a back-story of abuse at the hands of dishonorable whites or the U.S. Cavalry to contextualize and to some extent justify their onscreen violence.

In the pro-Indian cycle in particular, the hero's adversaries are defined on the basis of their racial intolerance. Previously identified through association with racialized otherness, bad whites are now constituted through their racist outbursts and penchant for racially motivated violence. And the hero—once defined by his commitment to racial purity as synonymous with moral "whiteness"—is established through his increasingly intimate alignment with the figure of the Indian. The presence of an Indian wife or lover operates in this context as a signifier of the hero's moral integrity. Although Production Code dictates against miscegenation ensure that these women do not survive such unions long, their murder at the hands of racist whites provides an increasingly conventional source of narrative motivation, the site of a trauma out of which action is generated. This individualized trauma relates to ascendant themes and structures within the genre, "in which the contradictions of American conquest—a kind of generalized trauma—become invested in particular narrative scenarios."[21]

The realignment of the white Western hero with the Indian as a victim of white racist violence functions to resecure his own moral legibility in line with the story of "a nation that had sinned but was on the road to redemption."[22] This story of redemption is one to which melodramatic conventions are particularly well suited. As Linda Williams has argued (and as I outlined in the last chapter), melodrama in American culture has provided the most powerful mechanism for the transformation of national guilt into an assurance of national virtue. Through scenarios of victimization and suffering, American culture enacts an assertion of national innocence and goodness, ascribing to its protagonists the moral virtue of the powerless, even (or especially) in the context of representations of nationalist violence and aggression. These melodramatic scenarios, as Williams illustrates, have often pivoted around scenes of racialized suffering, as melodrama has provided a means through which to negotiate questions of race and moral legibility in the United States. Ever since the publication of Harriet Beecher Stowe's *Uncle Tom's Cabin*, the "spectacle of racialized bodily suffering" has served as a signifier of moral virtue in the context of a national culture in which suffering provides a basis for claims to democratic inclusion and the rights of citizenship.[23]

The pro-Indian Western offers one powerful example of this "peculiarly American form of melodrama in which virtue becomes inextricably linked to forms of racial victimization."[24] As the authority previously granted to the hero is represented as increasingly bankrupt, the very conventions of action and violence that had once assured his moral stature come to render him morally suspect. In response to these pressures, the Western shifts emphasis, expropriating the moral claims of contemporary civil rights discourse by aligning the hero with the position of victimization and with the virtue accruing to that position. As I shall argue, it is the white Western hero for whom and with whom the spectator is encouraged most emphatically to feel in these films, as he is shown to suffer both through the force of his internalized guilt and shame and through his alignment with the Indian as the morally endowed victim of racialized violence.

The White Man's Indian: Race and Redemption in the Pro-Indian Cycle

Although Delmer Daves's *Broken Arrow* (1950) is most often credited with inaugurating the pro-Indian cycle, consideration of the changing coordinates of racialized violence and moral authority in the Western usefully begins with a discussion of William Wellman's *The Ox-Bow Incident* (1943), a film generally left outside such discussions. An immediate critical success (and nominated for Best Picture in 1943), though for many years a popular failure, *The Ox-Bow Incident* has been recognized since the time of its release as breaking new ground for the genre, moving it toward darker and more morally ambiguous terrain. In its representation of the lynching of three innocent men, the film introduces what will become a central trope in Westerns of the 1950s, as the positive values of community morph into the ruthless anarchy of the mob. While the B Westerns evidenced discomfort with the image of vigilante violence in more subtle and ambiguous ways, after World War II the generic representation of such violence becomes far less ambivalent. Warshow expresses irritation over this development, noting that "it is no longer possible to present a lynching in the movies unless the point is the illegality and injustice of the lynching itself." He credits *Ox-bow*, as an "anti-Western," for making this point explicit.[25]

The Ox-Bow Incident focuses on the efforts of a hastily convened posse to track down and bring to justice three men suspected of cattle rustling and murder. On its most explicit thematic level, the film (like the acclaimed novel upon which it is based) is concerned with violence and its legitimacy, mob mentality, and the breakdown of moral authority that mob mentality is understood to represent. The mob, which seeks and fails to constitute itself as a legitimate posse, is marked from the outset by association with the socially marginal forces of the community—with drunkenness, aggression, and undisguised sadistic glee. The representation of the mob resonates with contemporary anxieties over the status of the individual in an age of fascism and the mass, and with the image of affect itself as a contagious, mimetic force operating in opposition to reasoned, rational discourse. As in representations of the mass spectator as a hysterical figure or the crowd as a site of unruliness and violence, affect registers as a destructive force, an undisciplined and unregulated set of intensities that the Western, like all melodrama, seeks to harness.

More than simply highlighting the mob as an embodiment of the breakdown of moral authority, *The Ox-Bow Incident* links this breakdown to the specter of racialized violence. For even though the lynching around which the narrative revolves is not represented as racially motivated, the film insistently encodes the history of racialized violence that the lynching scenario serves inevitably to signify.[26] At the level of narrative and dialogue, it both highlights and represses the significance of race to the moral dilemma it stages, intensifying moral condemnation of the mob while omitting references to white supremacy original to the novel.[27] Even as it downplays the novel's more overtly racist rhetoric, however, the film renders good and evil in highly racialized terms, embodying villainy in the faux Confederate Major Tetley (Frank Conroy), the leader of the posse, and locating the film's moral center in the ostracized figure of Sparks (Leigh Whipper), the African American preacher whose prominence on both sound and image tracks underscores his significance to the film's indictment of violence.

In addition, and importantly, the film begins to adumbrate the significance of racialized violence to the moral resuscitation of the Western hero himself, suggesting how the hero will achieve a new moral clarity through this violence. Structurally, the film is bookended by the arrival and departure of two cowboys (Henry Fonda and Harry Morgan). The men are not strangers to the scrappy community of Bridger's Wells, Nevada, but their marginal position in relation to it will make them nominally suspect and, initially at least, tenuous in taking a stand against the lynching. Their failure to take a strong stand against the posse implicates them in the miscarriage of justice that ensues, and their marginal position relative to the film's primary action maintains them primarily in a position of spectatorship. However, the careful visual rhyming of the opening and closing sequences of the film—the men depart up the same sloping street down which they had arrived, the dog that had crossed before them now crosses back behind—both obscures and underscores an important transformation: the men had arrived in Bridger's Wells aimless and frustrated of purpose; they depart morally enlightened, on a mission to right in some small way the wrongs committed over the course of the film.

The negative energy of the mob is associated with what the film presents as exaggerated or misplaced forms of traditional white masculine authority, embodied both by the obsessively militant Tetley and the bullish "Ma" Grier (Jane Darwell). Ma operates as a gendered signifier of the grotesque that resonates with and confirms the mob's perverse miscarriage of justice. Although her leadership role is downplayed relative to the novel, her raucous offscreen laughter repeatedly underscores the disjunction between the boisterous affect of the mob and the gravity of their actions, casting this disjunction as non-normative. Despite the mobilization of queerness to signify the perversity of the film's lynching scenario—a conjunction that represses acknowledgment of racialized violence as a normative, institutionalized force—the film does not subscribe to gender conservatism in any consistent way. Indeed, a rejection of masculine hardness, represented by Tetley, provides the primary rhetoric through which the film decries the mob's violence; and conventionally stigmatized representations of masculine softness—the town's shopkeeper and Tetley's nervous and cowardly son—provide the most explicit arguments against injustice, their association with the feminine animating rather than circumscribing their moral authority.[28]

The repudiation of the mob's violence alongside the masculine hardness that Tetley embodies is articulated in relation to a set of racialized representations and the history they encode.[29] Tetley's position as a Confederate veteran here is key; through it, the film encodes a racialized violence that, on a narrative level, it denies. Presenting Tetley as the closest thing to a villain, the film emphasizes his association with the South through repeated cuts to the conspicuous plantation-style home in which he lives (and ultimately dies) and the equally conspicuous presence of a Confederate insignia on the uniform he wears. In line with the novel, and with dominant discourses of race and region in American culture more generally, the film mobilizes Tetley's association with the South to signify the moral bankruptcy of his position.

It is through the figure of Sparks, however, that *The Ox-Bow Incident* most affectingly inscribes the history of lynching as a mode of white racial terrorism. In its impulse both to highlight and to deny the significance of racism to its problematic, the film expands the role of Sparks as an embodiment of moral goodness and purity even as it evacuates the novel's original racist rhetoric.[30] Sparks's moral function is announced in stylistically explicit ways that stand apart from the film's otherwise spare sound and image tracks, in line with the melodramatic impulse to produce as incontrovertible the signs of moral goodness. Isolated in the frame at key moments, awash in a soft-focus "heavenly" light, and accompanied on the soundtrack by a mournful angelic chorus, Sparks functions as a signifier of spiritual enlightenment and integrity, a lone figure standing in gentle yet unyielding opposition to the will of the mob. A site of "true feeling" rather than rational argument, he functions as an irrefutable signifier of goodness.

Fig. 13. Isolated in the frame at key moments and accompanied by an angelic chorus, Sparks stands as a signifier of moral integrity shadowed by the history of racialized victimization. *The Ox-Bow Incident* (Wellman 1943).

From his initial introduction, the film invites identification with Sparks's goodness as he is leeringly called out by the town drunk to join the lynch mob in a shot that briefly collapses his offscreen position with that of the audience. The angelic chorus that breaks in at the moment Sparks's name is called is the first nondiegetic sound since the film's opening sequence, and it continues as Sparks moves with slow dignity to join the group as conscientious objector and spiritual guide. The chorus will return when Sparks— in a departure from the novel—rises as the first man to stand in opposition to the lynching, underscoring his moral function (fig. 13). Again, the camera stakes out a position behind Sparks from which to survey the sadistic Tetley and his posse, aligning itself with his vision. In contrast, the small group that rises to stand with Sparks will be shot straight on from an objective point of view, their stance speaking, in the film's terms, for itself.

Sparks's embodiment of true feeling is shored up through his positioning as a racialized victim, even as his spiritual authority works to activate and confirm race as a meaningful term within the moral logic of the film. His victimized status is suggested first in the leering manner in which he is called out by the mob and later, in the film's only explicit reference to racially motivated lynching, when Sparks confides to Henry Fonda's Gil Carter that he witnessed the lynching of his own brother. More subtly, but significantly, the film's association of Sparks with the image of the lynched bodies highlights both his moral function and his implicit positioning as a victim within a history of racialized violence the film both references and denies. After the lynching, Sparks is left alone in the frame, kneeling and singing as the camera pans to take in the shadows of the hung men swinging above him. In a film whose soundtrack is notably spare, the choral music and Sparks's hymnal singing are particularly significant. While the former functions as a moral register, the mournful recitations of the latter speak of and to a history of violence the film otherwise works to repress. Sparks's song carries over the subsequent cuts, as the sobered posse—whose hanging of three innocent men has now been established—is revealed slowly filing out of the valley, the poignancy of the tune inseparable from the shadow of racialized violence and guilt that hangs, like the bodies of the men, in the air.

The popular failure of *The Ox-Bow Incident* at the time of its release relates both to its unflinching attitude toward so-called Western justice and to its persistent destabilization of the generic expectations of the Bs. While *Stagecoach* (Ford 1939) condensed and refined B stereotypes into a new feature format, *Ox-Bow* offers their sinister recasting: the town drunk as an undisguised sadist; the Southern gentleman as a murderous sociopath; and Rose Mapin, standing in for "the whore with a heart of gold," fleeing the scene. A requisite early barroom brawl, likewise, is followed by the unconventional image of the fallible hero vomiting outside the saloon. In addition, by emphasizing the community's eager anticipation of the spectacle of violence itself—and by positioning the film's protagonists primarily as witnesses to rather than participants in the action—the film implicates its audience in its critique of the generic conventions of Western violence. Highlighting the relationship of violence to its public staging, *Ox-Bow* invites an uncomfortable identification with spectatorship itself and with the circuits of pleasure animating its conventional investments.

Through significant departures from the novel, however, Fonda's Gil maintains his status as hero, even as he represents a significant deviation from generic expectation. The lack of any dramatic action or clear moral conviction on his part and the acquiescence implied by his presence at the lynching deny him the conventional function of the protagonist as an agent of justice. But under ideological and industrial pressures (the censors required a clear condemnation of the film's violence), Gil is granted a stronger moral substance than the novel ever suggests. In Walter Van Tilburg Clark's book, Gil and his buddy Art are not among the few men who take a stand against the lynching when a final vote is called; in the film, Gil is hesitant to acquiesce to the false deputizing process, quick to jump to the defense of the less powerful, and visually framed from the beginning alongside representatives of legitimacy and justice, namely, Sparks, the shopkeeper Davies (Harry Davenport), and Tetley's son Gerald (William Eythe). As in the case of Jimmy Stewart in the Anthony Mann Westerns discussed below, the presence of Fonda in the role also exerts a certain pressure, suggesting an underlying decency despite the lack of strong action on Gil's part.

These revisions, like the heightening of Sparks's role, provide the film with a narrative structure lacking in the original novel. While the film in closing entrusts to an enlightened Gil a clear moral mission, the novel makes precisely the opposite point, underscoring the extent to which Gil and Art remain outsiders to the moral drama. In its need to restore some of what the original story has eroded, the film reinvigorates the position of the Western hero, making Gil into the literal mouthpiece for the call to moral conscience as he reads aloud the letter written by one of the condemned men to his wife. As he departs on a mission to deliver this letter to the new widow, the film grants Gil a nobler purpose in his departure from Bridger's Wells than the one with which he arrived, adumbrating a connection between the lingering shadow of racialized violence and the revitalized moral purpose of the Western protagonist.

Despite the partial resuscitation of Gil Carter, however, *The Ox-Bow Incident* remains a dark and fairly unforgiving film, one that goes out of its way to deprive the spectator of conventional generic pleasures. The film is conspicuous in its stillness, for instance, in the static composition of its shots and the lack of motion across its frames. One of the only exceptions to this stillness underscores the film's revisionism: a sequence of the posse on the ride is accompanied by a ponderous and ominous soundtrack, undercutting the visceral and moral satisfactions of fast action. The sequence constructs this rare moment of vigorous motion not as a triumph of justice but as the foreshadowing of its miscarriage, offering a critical reflection on generic convention itself.[31] The film eschews the pleasures of pathos as well, as the sheriff's arrival on the scene of the lynching "too late" provides none of the moral satisfaction conventionally secured through an identification with loss. Offered as a coda to the violence rather than an integral component of its constitution—with no intercutting to build suspense and no score to orchestrate the emotions—what is lost here is the moral clarity of melodrama itself.

Although *The Ox-Bow Incident* provides a suggestive precursor to the genre's reformulation of race, morality, and violence, in its negativity the film fails to address the contemporary ideological requirements of the Western to mobilize a critique of white supremacist violence while maintaining a strong image of moral authority at its core. The films conventionally taken to herald the inauguration of the pro-Indian cycle—Delmer Daves's *Broken Arrow* and Anthony Mann's *Devil's Doorway*, both released in 1950—move away from this negativity, offering different affective solutions. While both films mobilize a critique of the Western's conventional racial paradigm and of the relationship between violence and morality it proposes, they do so in ways that recuperate the hero as a moral center, infusing this figure with a new kind of authority grounded in pathos and an association with racialized victimization.

In *Devil's Doorway*, the genre's conventional conflict between the rancher and the encroaching sheep farmers who threaten the openness of the range is given a new twist, as the "cow man" in question is the Shoshone Indian Broken Lance, known as Lance Poole (Robert Taylor), a sergeant major returned from the Civil War to build up his family's cattle interests in Wyoming.[32] Though his efforts are initially successful, his lucrative business inflames racialized resentments that lead to a call for homesteading on Sweet Meadows, his edenic ancestral home. As is revealed over the course of the film, Native Americans, as wards of the state, are ineligible to own land under the Homestead Act. Despite his status as a decorated veteran and recipient of the Congressional Medal of Honor, Lance is forced to relinquish his dreams of building an integrated race-blind community and to take up arms in a suicidal last stand to protect Sweet Meadows and his Shoshone brethren, who have fled the reservation to seek refuge there.[33] The film underscores the contemporary resonance of the question of civil rights in a postwar context, emphasizing the hypocrisy of a system of institutionalized discrimination that would deny Lance these rights and making explicit the dream of a racially harmonious society as forged through the intimacy and sacrifice of war.[34]

Here the familiar melodrama of Griffith's Indian pictures—in which a Native American protagonist tries and fails to integrate into white society—meets up with the genre's contemporary critique of the cattle baron as a figure of outsized masculine authority to significant, if dissonant, effect. In many ways, *Devil's Doorway* replays the conventions of Griffith's earlier films: the protagonist's efforts to integrate fail despite his evident credentials—his education, manners, and high moral standing, or, as here, his business success and military service—and despite (or because of) his love of a white woman. Like his predecessors, Lance reverts over the course of the film to a strong identification with the Native heritage from which he is initially represented to have strayed, shedding his cavalry uniform and later his rancher's garb for an open-necked shirt, beads, and a headband. In this respect, *Devil's Doorway*, like Griffith's earlier films, exhibits only a partial critique of dominant racial ideology, challenging constructions of

Native otherness even as this otherness is confirmed through the gradual resurfacing of an "authentic" Native identity.

A strong sense of both generic convention and deviation is underscored at the beginning of the film. After a classic opening credits sequence—a montage of vast western landscapes across which a lone figure rides—the film's action begins much as does *Ox-Bow*'s. A man rides into town, down a dusty street, and hitches up his horse outside a saloon. As in *Ox-Bow*, the street is deserted but for a lone scrappy dog, yelping aggressively at the heels of our protagonist in a show of hostile foreshadowing. When we cut in to a shot of the rider, the camera reveals Robert Taylor in red face and a cavalry uniform. In this cut, the film introduces itself as an exploration of the impact this racialized difference will make on the conventional set pieces of the genre.

This difference is quickly given narrative and formal weight in the sequence that follows, which opens with a subjective shot of Lance's entrance into the saloon from the perspective of a black-clad figure fore-grounded at the far edge of the frame (his black mustache, once revealed, will further confirm his villainy in the conventional melodramatic stylis-tics of the film). The shot registers a sense of foreboding, signified through the blackness of the man's attire, but most affectingly through its removed and slightly distorted angle on Lance. The sequence returns repeatedly to this shot, shadowing Lance's homecoming with a sense of menace. When the gaze is eventually assigned to the town's lawyer, Verne Coolan (Louis Calhern), his racist invective confirms what the mise-en-scène has already suggested: that menace will take a specifically racialized form.

The hostility structuring this initial encounter erupts into physical vio-lence in a subsequent barroom sequence, in which a mobilization of noir stylistics—a heavy use of shadows punctuated by occasional flashes of lightning, low-angled shots of the fighting intercut with looming close-ups of the sweaty, leering faces of the men who watch—links the formal sense of menace to the spectacle of racialized violence.[35] In this second sequence, we return to the earlier composition, with the figure of Coolan now in the left foreground, doubled by his sadistic sidekick, Ike Stapleton (James Millican), who takes up Coolan's original spot on the right. The visual rhyming of the shots presents the second encounter as the sinister unfolding of the first. The sequence recasts the brutality of the genre's con-ventional barroom brawl, implicating the white community in the public spectacle of racialized abuse (a spectatorial role eagerly undertaken, as the close-ups assert). That it opens with a shot of a crude sign above the bar stating a prohibition against the sale of alcohol to Indians emphasizes again the question of civil rights. The film echoes contemporary challenges to dis-criminatory access and mobility within public space and self-consciously parrots the discourse of miscegenation as it animates segregationist rhetoric. "Let you in the saloon and the first thing you know, you'll want to mix with us socially," Ike taunts, as he shoots at Lance and his companion.

In these sequences and elsewhere, the film deploys conventional set pieces of the Western while recalibrating the moral coordinates of their violence. A sequence in which Lance and his men attack a wagon train of largely sympathetic Irish sheep farmers, for instance, is reproduced in visually familiar terms, as is a later sequence in which Lance and his Shoshone brethren silently stalk and kill their aggressors in the night. These familiar images of the Indian as an agent of violence, however, circulate within a narrative emphasis on the status of the Indian as a racialized victim of both individual and institutional discrimination and abuse. Thus the film challenges the presumptions that animate conventional images of Indians on the rampage, offering these images as the desperate—even heroic—actions of a beleaguered community. In contrast to the violence of the Shoshone as they fight for a chance at survival off the reservation, the violence of the white community is mobilized, as in *Ox-Bow*, through the formation of a posse of dubious legitimacy and the specter of mob violence this engenders.

In the end, Sweet Meadows will be surrounded by a white lynch mob and by the U.S. Cavalry in a battle sequence that reproduces both the iconic "Attack on the Settler's Cabin" (and its rearticulation in *The Birth of a Nation*) and the heroic fatalism of the Last Stand scenario. Sweet Meadows has been given a narrative and a formal centrality throughout the film, emphasized repeatedly onscreen and in dialogue as an idyllic place of peace and plenty, "the dream all men have when they ache for home" (fig. 14).[36] The visual constitution of Lance's ranch as a traditional log cabin resonates with the history of racial melodrama stretching from *Uncle Tom's Cabin* forward. As Linda Williams argues, home provides one of the central defining features of melodrama, a locus of innocence and purity from which the protagonists have been estranged and to which they long to return.[37] *Devil's Doorway* resignifies the iconic image of the besieged homestead as the last refuge of the dying Indian and recasts the attack upon it as the act of white men driven to violence by the admonitions of an inveterate racist. By anchoring the attack sequence with conventional images of defenseless women and children huddled within the homestead, the film redeploys familiar melodramatic structures in the context of their critique. When the cavalry's traditional "ride to the rescue" devolves into a fatal showdown between the forces of white society and the few remaining Shoshone survivors of the raid, the film abandons the conventional configuration of violence, race, and moral authority even as it relies upon the affective structures of melodrama to do so.

Fig. 14. The constitution of Sweet Meadows as an idyllic space of peace and plenty resonates with the melodramatic construction of home and its loss while recasting the conventional homestead as a site of Native refuge. *Devil's Doorway* (Mann 1950).

Importantly, however, Sweet Meadows functions not only as the ancestral home of the Shoshone people but also as the vast estate of an individual man's empire, just as Lance occupies both the role of the Indian as a racialized victim and the conventional role of the cattle baron—a doubleness that complicates the question of what, precisely, is being negotiated or reinvigorated in the pathetic image of his downfall.[38] Embodying a collapse of the conventional figures of the noble (yet doomed) Indian with the powerful (yet doomed) rancher, Lance infuses the former figure with a strong masculine identity generally reserved for the white Western hero, while lending to the latter figure a new kind of moral authority. In the film's final shot, Broken Lance emerges from the homestead in his cavalry uniform, offering the epitaph—"We're all gone"—before collapsing, with a salute, at the feet of the cavalry officer. Thus the film infuses the genre's image of the inevitable passing of the resolute, powerful figure of the rancher with the pathos and moral authority of racial melodrama, gesturing toward new thematic and affective registers that would become increasingly prominent in the genre across the 1950s.

Delmer Daves's *Broken Arrow* is likewise suggestive in sketching out the terms by which the Western hero will be reinvigorated as a locus of moral authority in the pro-Indian cycle. Like *Devil's Doorway* and *The Ox-Bow Incident*, the film represents the racial intolerance of a white western community while contextualizing Native American aggression with a backstory of abuse. The film traces ex-army scout Tom Jeffords (Jimmy Stewart) on his journey of racial enlightenment and subsequent efforts to bring peace to the warring white and Chiricahua Apache communities in Arizona in the early 1870s. The narrative focuses on Jeffords's growing friendship with the Apache chief Cochise (Jeff Chandler) and his romance with and eventual marriage to the young Apache maiden Sonseeahray (Debra Paget). The film opens and closes conventionally: a lone man rides toward the camera and into a space of encounter with the Indian and later rides away, back into the landscape from which he emerged. As in *The Ox-Bow Incident*, arrival is marked by questionable aims and a relative lack of direction—released from the Union army, Jeffords has been "prospecting for gold, off and on"—whereas departure will be imbued with a higher moral purpose. Again as in *Ox-Bow*, though far more explicitly, racialized victimization will be central to this process of moral reinvigoration.

Like *Devil's Doorway*, *Broken Arrow* is explicit in revisioning the racialized conventions of Western violence. Scalping is evidence of white rather than Apache brutality, for instance, and a wagon train attack illustrates not Cochise's savagery but his military skill and precision, as well as the fatal hubris of the American colonel who would underestimate such things (not incidentally, the sequence scrupulously avoids conventional point-of-view shots from within the wagons' circle). Later, the conventional function of the cavalry itself is usurped when Cochise's men ride to the rescue of a besieged stagecoach that has come under a renegade Indian assault. Although the treacherous acts of both Indians and whites challenge the peace process throughout the film, it is the white community that will bear ultimate responsibility for its breakdown; and, importantly, it is Jeffords's own suffering and loss that will resecure it.

The film has been noted for these revisionist moments, as well as for its positive representation of Native American rituals and celebrations. This latter point can be easily overstated, given the ethnographic conventions that dominate such sequences. But it is nonetheless true that ceremonies that have traditionally served as the generic emblems of white civilization, undergirding arguments as to its superiority, are sited in *Broken Arrow* within the Apache community instead. A coming-of-age celebration, a dance, a wedding, and a funeral stand in positive contrast to the animosity and violence that mark the streets of Tucson, revising familiar Fordian conventions to challenge rather than shore up the claims of white civilization as measured against the "primitive" landscape of the West. The Apache community is represented as strong and vibrant, in contrast to the selfishness, corruption, and hypocrisy of its white counterpart, whose "civilization" is represented as analogous to crass commercialism. As Peter Biskind has noted, within the mise-en-scène of the Indian stronghold, even the Technicolor brilliance of the "majestic bluffs and mesas . . . take on the force of a moral critique of the town."[39]

Although *Broken Arrow* is most often read as a liberal critique of white racial intolerance, my interest in the representational paradigm it inaugurates is somewhat different. For, rather than the Indian as a noble victim of white racism, *Broken Arrow* is focused primarily upon the moral standing of the white man who would take a stand against such racism. Where *Devil's Doorway* negotiates the contemporary challenge to the morality of the Western hero by merging him with the figure of the Indian, *Broken Arrow* offers an alternative solution in the increasingly intimate alignment of the white hero with this figure. In the case of Tom Jeffords, this alignment is evident early on: he nurtures an injured Apache boy; he quickly learns the lesson that Indians are humans and not "wild animals"; and he desires to approach Cochise on the latter's own terms, to learn Apache "in here" (said with a gesture toward the heart that will be repeated later by both Sonseeahray and Cochise, signaling, as Michael Walker has noted, a shared "authenticity of feeling").[40]

While Jeffords's fraternal and romantic bonds with Cochise and Sonseeahray serve as emblems of moral integrity that will be quickly conventionalized in 1950s Westerns, the film makes its greatest affective investment in the image of Jeffords's own suffering. Though Jeffords's reasoned and principled stance in the ongoing conflict between the Apaches and the whites distinguishes him from the racists within his own community, his moral stature derives as much from his own status as a victim as from his defense of the Apaches' rightful grievances. More than on the plight of the Indians—whose death and destruction history has already foreseen, the "pastness" of their fate underscored by Jeffords's own voice-over narration—the film is focused on the status of Jeffords himself as one who suffers. In this respect, *Broken Arrow* adumbrates the movement of the white Western hero from a posture of sympathy and fraternity with to a gradual appropriation of the position of the Indian as victim, suggesting a potent solution to the generic problem of race and morality in this period.[41]

Jeffords's abuse at the hands of racist whites provides the visual register of and the means of securing his moral authority. Though the first images of Jeffords as victim reference more conventional assault scenarios—with his face framed in anxious close-up by a pair of Indian arrows—the film's primary agents of racialized violence soon emerge as members of Tucson's white community, with Jeffords as their primary victim. Dialogue early on attests to the racist antagonism of this community and its distrust of

Fig. 15. The Indian wars are represented as a story of the white hero's own victimization, as when the impulse to hang every Apache from a tree manifests as the stringing up of Tom Jeffords himself. *Broken Arrow* (Daves 1950).

Jeffords's loyalties in the context of his friendship with Cochise. As this friendship grows, accusations of Jeffords's racial treason become more explicit. Ultimately, he is dragged into the street by a lynch mob in a sequence that moves quickly from the assertion that peace will come only "when every Apache is hung from a tree" to the stringing up of Jeffords himself (fig. 15).

The sequence plays out, as it happens, on the recycled set of *The Ox-Bow Incident*, in another example of the increasingly conventional casting of the white community as violent mob. As in the earlier film, the mob's victim here is a white man, though the violence of the mob is now explicitly racialized. In offering up Jeffords as the victim of such violence, the film grants to him (rather than to Cochise or Sonseeahray, for instance) the moral currency associated with the melodramatic spectacle of racialized abuse. It is Jeffords with whom we are encouraged to feel as he struggles desperately against the noose, his pain and outrage with which we are invited to identify.

The film's conclusion underscores even more powerfully the assignment of Jeffords as the primary victim of racialized violence, a man whose personal suffering and loss are raised to a new level of historical and national significance. In the final battle sequence, Jeffords, Sonseeahray, and Cochise are figured as innocents under attack, rendered vulnerable in high angle shots while the white rancher Slade and his gang take up the conventional position of menacing Indians, merging into the rocks and trees on the cliff above. After Sonseeahray is killed trying to defend Jeffords against the bullets, the camera closes in on Jeffords as he cradles her body in his arms, tightening on the image of his twisted face, his anguished cries accompanied by an anxious swell of strings on the soundtrack.

The camera's attentiveness to Stewart's face in moments of physical and psychological suffering provides the most powerful and insistent register of affect across the film, a function particularly apparent in this sequence. Rhyming shots of Jeffords and Cochise have been employed to establish and emphasize a camaraderie and moral equivalence between them (dialogue has likewise underscored their common bond, in part through Jeffords's adoption of a stiff and awkward syntax that echoes Cochise's own). In this penultimate sequence, however, the death of Sonseeahray interrupts this formal rhythm of equivalence. While Jeffords contorts in agony, shots of Cochise emphasize his stoicism, his immovable features reinforcing his stubborn commitment to principle, here the principle of nonviolence from which Jeffords in his grief threatens to stray.[42] Suffering accrues around the image of Jeffords while Cochise remains firmly within the representational confines of the stoic Indian; and although his stoicism is represented as a source of strength and integrity, his affect is contained within the well-established repertoire of the Indian as the noble victim of systematized racial violence. "As I bear the murder of my people, so you shall bear the murder of your wife," Cochise solemnly intones, lending to the image of Jeffords's own suffering a greater moral and historical weight, even as the sense of pastness signified by the image of the stoic Indian serves to underscore the palpably present intensity of Jeffords's pain in contrast.

When Jeffords rides away in the film's final shot, he is imbued with a new moral legibility as the protagonist of a racial melodrama. Although the good General Howard (Basil Ruysdael) acknowledges that there is no way to compensate Jeffords for "the terrible thing that's happened," Jeffords's loss, we are assured in the closing voice-over, brings the warring parties closer together and "[puts] a seal upon the peace." In sealing the peace, Sonseeahray's death also seals the function of the Indian wife as generic shorthand for the hero's own goodness, a figure whose death provides for the righteousness of his violence.[43]

The implications of Broken Arrow's victimization of the "Indian-loving" white man emerge more clearly in The Last Wagon (Daves 1956). Here the position of the racialized victim and the white Western hero collapse into one another through the buckskinned figure of the emphatically fair Richard Widmark's Comanche Todd. Orphaned as a boy, Todd was adopted by an Indian chief and raised as a Comanche.[44] He is being taken to trial for the murder of four white men when the wagon train he and his captor have joined is attacked by Apaches; the only survivors of the massacre are six young people who must now rely on Todd, the epitome of the genre's conventional "man who knows Indians," to lead them through Apache country to safety.

Although Todd's moral identity is initially ambiguous—the film's opening sequence both underscores his status as a cold-blooded murderer and visualizes him as ruthlessly hounded prey—the public spectacle of his racialized brutalization serves as an early register of his goodness. The opening sequence has already established Todd's suffering and vulnerability, but his torture at the hands of the sadistic Sheriff Harper (brother to the murdered men) secures him as the film's primary victim. In Harper's custody, Todd is beaten, manacled, dragged behind a horse, lashed to a tree, denied food and water, and roped to a wagon wheel, where he will remain throughout the first half of the film (fig. 16).

Fig. 16. In Richard Widmark's Comanche Todd, the figures of the white Western hero and the Indian as racialized victim fully collapse. *The Last Wagon* (Daves 1956).

Importantly, the film is explicit in racializing this abuse; Harper's racist invective positions Todd as an Indian during the sequences of his mistreatment. ("Don't be fooled by the color of his eyes and his skin," Harper warns, "he may be white but inside he's all Comanche!") Todd's brutalization thus operates within the traditions of racial melodrama discussed by Williams, generating moral legibility through the racialized spectacle of bodily suffering. Even after he is freed from the wagon wheel, the manacles stay on Todd's wrists through most of the film, underscoring his status as a racialized victim: they reference the diegetic antipathy toward him as an Indian while visually invoking the history of slavery, as Michael Walker has argued.[45]

The public nature of this suffering is redoubled by the presence of an onscreen audience, as in the films discussed above. Here, however, in contrast to the image of the townsfolk as spectators in *The Ox-Bow Incident*, *Devil's Doorway*, or *Broken Arrow*, the white community provides a source of moral authority rather than a locus of racial animus (this function is not unrelated to the wagon train members' own generically coded vulnerability, a status soon confirmed by their offscreen massacre). Formally arranged in a semicircle behind the figures of Harper and Todd, the "Christers," as Harper mockingly refers to them, stand in silent condemnation before the scene of racialized abuse. When they do speak up, it is as the mouthpiece for a liberal rhetoric of tolerance, insisting that, whatever else he's done, Todd is "still a human being" and hence deserving of humane treatment.[46]

Thus the film's own audience is offered a different point of entry into the scene of violence, invited to identify with the moral condemnation of racism mirrored and confirmed by the diegetic audience. Through the leering, venal figure of Harper, who takes a gleeful pleasure in Todd's abuse, the image of racialized villainy is set apart from that of the white community, again in contrast to the films discussed above. In this respect, *The Last Wagon* highlights the function of racist villainy in constituting the moral credentials of those who would react against it; within the tradition of racial melodrama and the discourse of true feeling it constructs, our own identification as racially just is solidified through our vilification of figures such as Harper.[47] By inviting its audience into a more comfortable identification with a white community that stands in moral judgment against racist violence, *The Last Wagon* suggests the success of the genre in incorporating a contemporary critique of white supremacism while maintaining an image of white righteousness at its core.

Part of this restoration involves a return to the very scenarios of racialized violence from which the pro-Indian cycle had initially turned. *The Last Wagon* makes evident the ideological ground that has been cleared through the generic innovation of the white man as racialized victim, as Todd's appropriation of this position enables the film's return to more conventional representations of Indian violence. While Todd combines the traditional image of the Western hero—strong, resolute, resilient, and self-contained—with the moral appeal of racialized suffering, the film's Apaches revert to a state of generic cliché, a dehumanized force of narrative violence and occasional ethnographic interest. For all its liberal rhetoric, the film evidences no thematic or formal discomfort with this regression to the Indian war scenarios of its generic past.

The casting of the white hero in the role of racialized victim is a convention that returns forcefully in the closing decades of the twentieth century and has generally been attributed to the influence of the civil rights movements of the 1960s and 1970s, the upheavals of the Vietnam War, the economic crises of the 1970s, and the emergence of so-called identity politics in the 1980s.[48] An examination of the narrative and representational strategies of this earlier period, however, suggests that an affective lineage can be traced back to the melodramas of the Cold War Western. As noted in the previous chapter, Linda Williams has identified the post-Vietnam function of action melodrama as addressing "the moral dilemma of bad conscience." In the Cold War Western, where the culpability of white supremacist violence hangs heavy, the hero's alignment with—and ultimate appropriation of—the position of racialized victimization strives to reconsolidate a claim to moral authority on the part of the protagonist, the genre, and the nation itself. "The greater the historical burden of guilt," Williams notes, "the more pathetically and the more actively the melodrama works to recognize and regain a lost innocence"—a function we witness in the hero's racialized suffering, and beyond.[49]

"What am I supposed to do, cry? Feel sorry for him?"

This question is posed sardonically by villain Ben Vandergroat (Robert Ryan) in Anthony Mann's *The Naked Spur* (1953) in relation to the suffering of his captor, Howie Kemp (Jimmy Stewart). While intended as a barb—in contrast to Vandergroat, bounty hunter Kemp is held captive only by his own demons—the film's answer to this question is a resounding affirmative. In this film, as in the rest of the Mann/Stewart cycle (*Winchester '73* [1950], *Bend of the River* [1952], *The Far Country* [1954], and *The Man from Laramie* [1955]), empathy is the attitude we are encouraged to feel toward our battered and beleaguered protagonist. The Mann/Stewart Westerns are particularly emphatic in the degree to which they offer up a traumatized, beaten, and bruised protagonist as an object of our pity, although the appeal of pathos these films represent is an undeniable force in the Cold War Western more generally. As Thomas Pauly has noted, the hero in this period was a man audiences respected, "but he was also someone they felt sorry for."[50]

It is the force and function of this feeling sorry to which we must attend, as pathos more than strong action becomes the basis of an attachment to the Western hero and the imperialist legacy he embodies. Pathos has played a key role in Western melodrama from the beginning, of course, as the thrill of the genre's early assault scenarios pivoted around the pathetic image of suffering innocents under attack. In addition, the image of the cowboy as a cultural hero emerged through a lament over his historical passing, and a sense of loss and longing have provided a constituent aspect of the Western hero's appeal at least since Owen Wister's Virginian. What changes after the war is the centrality of pathos over action. As the moral status of action becomes more qualified, pathos provides the central means through which identification with the hero is solicited and secured. The ostensibly negative affects of guilt, shame, and suffering come to provide an affective alchemy through which contemporary ambivalence surrounding traditional Western action may be managed. Such affects serve to negotiate shifting ideological terrain while maintaining—and in important ways invigorating—a strong attachment to the image of the Western hero.

Pity is entangled with questions of race and morality in this period. Even outside the pro-Indian cycle, films are haunted by questions of moral culpability, troubled by the genre's conventional violence and the implication of the hero in such violence. Sometimes the disruption registers only fleetingly, as in *Winchester '73*, when a scene of carnage following an Indian attack casts a brief shadow across the genre's conventional thrills. After the battle sequence, which has underscored the efficacy of the Stewart hero's violence, the camera pans over the image of Indian bodies littering the ground. While the soundtrack swells on a brief note of pathos, the composition of bodies strewn across the field replicates Mathew Brady's canonical Civil War photograph, *The Harvest of Death* ("a crucial part of the visual grammar for representing modern war," as Geoffrey Klingsporn has suggested), offering an alternative reading of the scene as one of nationalized loss and mourning.[51]

As in *The Naked Spur*, however, sometimes the hero's implication in massacre is made more explicit. Here, Kemp and his party are drawn into a gunfight with the peaceful Blackfeet tribe, against Kemp's own judgment and will, by the treachery of Roy Anderson (Ralph Meeker), a dishonorably discharged cavalry lieutenant whose moral laxity and mental instability the film has already established. Anderson is being hunted by a band of Blackfeet after his sexual assault of a Blackfeet woman, which grants moral legitimacy to their pursuit. Formally, however, the battle sequence is entirely conventional, punctuated by Indian war cries on the soundtrack and cut to emphasize either the vulnerability of the white protagonists or the precision of their gunfire (the Indians tumble off their horses with

every shot, while the white protagonists—classically outnumbered—
survive almost unscathed). The conventional editing of the sequence works
to construct white violence as entirely defensive in nature, in keeping
with the genre's longstanding melodramatic structures. Tellingly though,
it is Anderson—concealed from the view of both parties—who brazenly
disrupts the initial nonviolent exchange. His unprovoked shooting of an
Indian chief provides a subtle acknowledgment of white culpability and
aggression, suggesting the way purportedly defensive violence conventionally dissembles through the denial or erasure of this culpability.

In a film centrally concerned with the compromised integrity and ultimate redemption of its hero, the battle sequence and its echoes, though
minor in their narrative significance, assert the racialized guilt through
which the genre encodes moral transgression. Stewart's Kemp is drawn
fully into the battle, which ultimately leaves all twelve Indians dead. The
silence of the shot that follows—in which the gentle fluttering of leaves
emphasizes the contrasting stillness of a battleground littered with Indian
(and only Indian) bodies—amplifies the sense of loss and remorse. The
film's closing shot will provide a subtle rhyme with this earlier moment,
as Kemp and the waifish Lina (Janet Leigh) ride off through a barren field
littered with fallen trees, an "extraordinarily bleak final image" that hints at
the way racialized guilt haunts both the film and its ambiguous resolution.[52]

Kemp is shot in the leg during the battle after bludgeoning an Indian
to death—a "savage" act we witness in medium close-up—and bears his
wound as a badge of shame. The wound figures prominently in inaugurating a series of injuries, accidents, and illnesses that incapacitate Kemp
over the course of the film. That his pain and anguish are not limited to a
physical cause is emphasized in the battle sequence's closing shot, in which
the demoralized Kemp—slumping dejectedly on his horse—pauses in the
middle of the frame, foregrounded against the body-strewn field (fig. 17).
He is haunted by the specter of guilt later in the night, when he wakes fever-
wracked in a state of hysterical paranoia. His mental instability is linked
to the morally dubious violence that preceded it, as he wildly demands,
"Where are they? Where are they?"

As the ambivalence surrounding the Western hero's conventional violence increases in the years following World War II, his onscreen brutalization likewise intensifies. It is not simply that the hero must be "literally
beaten into line," as Jim Kitses has suggested of the Mann Westerns, for
rather than resisting such a beating, the hero appears to invite it.[53] This masochistic impulse can be read along the lines suggested by Paul Willemen
and Steve Neale, who have analyzed the onscreen assault of the male body
as a symptom of homosexual voyeurism and its requisite disavowal.[54]
While recognizing the relevance of these readings, I am concerned here

Fig. 17. Even when not explicitly narrativized, the specter of guilt hangs over the generic conventions of Western action and violence in the 1950s. *The Naked Spur* (Mann 1953).

with the melodramatic function of such bodily suffering. In melodrama, as I have noted, suffering and vulnerability are emblematic of moral goodness, and the spectacle of bodily assault frequently bestows upon its victims the stamp of moral authority. As the Cold War Western takes up the hero's compromised claim to moral integrity as a central concern, scenes of physical battery and wounding can have a paradoxically resuscitating effect, providing for the public spectacle of suffering upon which moral legibility depends. Though the battery of the hero has been a feature of the Western ever since Wister's *Virginian* and has been argued in various ways to be constitutive of his status,[55] the increasingly explicit and extended assault upon the hero in the Cold War period provides both a register of his guilt and, simultaneously, a move toward his redemption.

No single star embodies this dynamic more than Jimmy Stewart. His credibility as a decent man who suffers was a well-established aspect of his persona, forged in classics like *Mr. Smith Goes to Washington* (Capra 1939) and *It's a Wonderful Life* (Capra 1946) and mobilized in *Broken Arrow*. Stewart functions in these films as a nationalized image of moral goodness, an American Everyman who, like the nation, may have sinned but is on the road to redemption. In contrast to this persona, the moral digressions of the Stewart hero in the Mann Westerns are emphasized through his literal and figurative kinship with the films' antagonists and his unmanly allegiance to fiscal rather than chivalric motives.[56] The hero starts out in pursuit of money or land (or, in *Winchester '73*, revenge) and only reluctantly throws off the mantle of self-interest to take up the generic burden of right action.

The guilt of the Mann/Stewart hero finds an outlet in scenes of brutality, as the Mann Westerns are drawn to the spectacle of the hero as he is burned, beaten, and shot. The camera lingers on Stewart's face in such moments, as it twists in paroxysms of anguish; such images, as in *Broken Arrow*, provide a primary register of affect across these films. Stewart's presence serves to infuse this brutalization with a strong sense of internal conflict, a tension between essential decency and its violation. The guilty conscience of the Stewart hero recodes his onscreen battery as displacement; his own failures and inadequacies return to haunt him through the aggressions of his adversarial doubles and through the precipitous hazards of a landscape rendered as an increasingly hysterical mise-en-scène. In the image of his suffering, the spectator is encouraged to read a register of the hero's underlying moral goodness, a symptom of the internal conflict between the moral weakness of the Mann heroes and the essential decency encoded through Stewart's star persona.

In a discussion of the new and "specifically American" sense of shame that accrues around the Stewart persona in the postwar period, Amy Lawrence has noted an "undercurrent of confusion, guilt, and shame that is historically specific but can never be articulated."[57] Though Lawrence reads the image of Stewart "with blood on his hands" in relation to his role as a fighter pilot in the war, the sense of shame she identifies might be fruitfully considered in relation to the Cold War critique of racism that I discuss here. And while the masochistic impulses of these wounding sequences may hint at conflicts underlying the production of normative masculinity, Stewart's anguish generates out of such contradictions a melodramatic spectacle of suffering.[58] Though the violence is represented as an externalization of the Stewart hero's own guilt and shame, this hero nonetheless occupies a position of victimization within a melodramatic structure in which suffering connotes goodness. Stewart suffers because he is good—that is, because he is morally conflicted—and his goodness is at the same time secured through the spectacle of his suffering, embodying what Linda Williams has referred to as "melodrama's alchemical transformation of suffering into virtue."[59] The function of victim-heroes like Stewart, as Williams maintains, "is to demonstrate a virtue proven through the very acts of struggle and suffering," regardless of whether these struggles should succeed or fail.[60]

Suffer and Be Hard: The Power of Pathos

The Mann Westerns expose and explore the impossibility of what Jane Tompkins has described as the generic imperative to come, suffer, and be hard.[61] This sense of impossibility provides another aspect of the hero's recasting as the genre's primary victim, what Jim Kitses describes as a "plaything of a cruel world . . . at the mercy of paradox and contradiction."[62] To locate the Western hero as such a plaything is to appreciate the pressures on constructions of normative white masculinity in this period and the extent to which the impossibility of their resolution aligns the Western hero with the protagonists of contemporary domestic melodrama, who have often been apprehended in these terms. As with his domestic brethren, the pathos of the Western hero is produced through the impossibility of either fully embracing or fully rejecting a traditional image of white masculine authority, the inadequacy of "manly" responses alongside the ongoing imperative to "be a man."[63]

While the woman's films and maternal melodramas of the 1930s and 1940s explored the contradictions and restrictions of women's identity under patriarchy, the domestic melodramas of the 1950s and early 1960s are often oriented around issues of masculinity and its failures.[64] This cycle of "male weepies" offers, in Laura Mulvey's terms, "an insight on man as victim in patriarchal society," featuring as the terms of narrative resolution a "positive male figure who rejects rampant virility and opposes the unmitigated power of the father."[65] Tom Lutz, in his critical investigation of crying, argues that weepies depend for their affective intensity upon the representation of social role fulfillment—both the filmic resolution of its contradictions and the audience's knowledge that such resolutions are, in life, impossible.[66] In the male weepies of the 1950s, protagonists are caught between a rejection of strong patriarchal authority and a phobic relationship to masculine softness, echoing the broader discourse of masculine crisis. While traditional values of masculine hardness are understood as out of step with the currents of postwar social and economic life, the competing values of softness are associated with impotence and weakness, often figured through the specter of homosexuality and the nationalized paranoia this figure, in the context of McCarthyism, represents.

In a discussion of the domestic melodramas of this era, David Rodowick has argued that the genre's inability to find resolution through a secure identification with patriarchal authority produces a generic terrain in which "madness and authority" become "two expressions of the same term." Rodowick reads the merger of these terms as symptomatic of the contemporary destabilization of patriarchal authority, which he regards as a "representation of social power per se." "Either pathetically castrated, or monstrously castrating," patriarchal authority emerges in this context as a sign of the broader ideological conflicts of the 1950s, confounding the formal conventions of the genre and generating textual instabilities and contradictions.[67] Films center on narratives of the Oedipus complex gone astray— maladjusted sons and their tyrannical (or, alternately, weak and ineffectual) fathers, sexual impotence and phallic hysteria, homosexual impulses and fratricidal rage. The era's fascination with a watered-down version of Freudian psychoanalysis mobilizes the inherent instabilities of psychosexual development to both explain and, to some extent, explain away the inadequacies and insecurities of its protagonists; the Freudian framework exposes while working to contain the failures and contradictions of normative masculine identity, registering while individualizing these failures.

In its dynastic iteration, the domestic melodrama focuses on the father as a caricature of virile, aggressive masculinity in films such as *Written on the Wind* (Sirk 1956), *The Long Hot Summer* (Ritt 1958), and *Home from the Hill* (Minnelli 1960). The western-themed *Giant* (Stevens 1956) also highlights the implication of racism in this critique. Authoritative, resolute, and driven, the patriarch in these films is a nineteenth-century ideal of self-made masculinity run amok, his acquisitive drive represented as an excessive, destructive force aligned at once with aristocratic privilege and an outdated imperative of manly self-making.[68] The rejection of the authoritative masculinity represented by the father is never unequivocal, however, as the act of turning away from this figure flirts with the more anxious implications of masculine softness, embodied by the weak and impotent son, whose masculine inadequacy shades into homosexuality. In this iteration of the formula, the son will ultimately be cast off in favor of a surrogate who eschews both weakness and rigidity by incorporating the patriarch's strength alongside the sensitivity of an updated masculine ideal.

In its middle-class guise, the domestic melodrama of the 1950s highlights the plight of the modern suburban "dad"—the protagonist of the contemporary discourse of white masculine crisis—who has sacrificed every vestige of "inner-direction" and relinquished every claim to authoritative individualism. Such men function in the misguided service of larger social organizations, both corporate and domestic. Through the figures of the overworked husband and feminized father (in films such as *Rebel Without a Cause* [Ray 1955], *The Cobweb* [Minnelli 1955], *Bigger Than Life* [Ray 1956], and *The Man in the Gray Flannel Suit* [Johnson 1956]), the domestic melodrama offers a critique of over-compliance with the contemporary imperatives of male domesticity, conformity, and consumption. Though authoritative masculinity is critiqued and rejected in these films, in general they are more concerned with the lack of masculine authority than with its excess.

In both of these iterations, domestic melodramas have been explicitly contrasted with the Western. With its emphasis on action, its predilection for wide open spaces, and its focus on an authoritative male protagonist, the Western is seen to provide a stark contrast to the social restrictions, claustrophobic mise-en-scène, and feminized protagonists of domestic melodrama. Unlike the latter, who are confined to interior spaces, crowded into cluttered frames, and restricted to limited and ineffectual actions, the Western hero is associated with his freedom to move across an expansive landscape and to resolve his conflicts through violence. These differences are understood to grant an agency to the Western hero, which locates his struggles outside the affective terrain of suffering, as in Geoffrey Nowell-Smith's definition of the Western hero as "an active hero, inured or immune to suffering," in contrast to the hero of melodrama, "whose role is to suffer." According to Nowell-Smith:

> Broadly speaking, in the American movie the active hero becomes protagonist of the Western, the passive or impotent hero or heroine becomes protagonist of what has come to be known as melodrama. The contrast active/passive is, inevitably, traversed by another contrast, that between masculine and feminine. Essentially the world of the Western is one of activity/masculinity. . . . The melodrama is more complex . . . where the central figure is a man there is regularly an impairment of his "masculinity"—at least in contrast to the mythic potency of the hero of the Western.[69]

Stylistically and thematically, however, a close kinship exists between the Western and the domestic melodrama in the Cold War era, an unsurprising point when we consider the Western as one of the most culturally influential articulations of American melodrama in this period as in others.[70] Both forms pivot around restricted action and the spectacle of suffering. The small-town claustrophobia and latent hysteria Thomas Elsaesser identifies with domestic melodrama are notable conventions of the Cold War Western, as in the example of the town as lynch mob.[71] Additionally, the Cold War Westerns replay many of the same familial scenarios: Oedipal scars, sexual betrayals, and incestuous liaisons figure centrally; and the relationships of fathers, sons, and brothers are prominent, providing the terms through which masculine identity and authority are negotiated.[72] The fantasy of a self-generating hero (conventionally supported by the genre's erasure of the figure of the mother) is threatened by the insertion of the hero into broader social and familial networks, signaling a diminished faith in the absolute integrity and moral authority of his image.

Like the domestic melodrama, the Western is shaped by the paradox of traditional patriarchal authority. The driven and obsessive patriarch is conventionally embodied by the cattle baron in films like *Red River* (or, more complexly, *Devil's Doorway*) that question his ability to reproduce an adequate masculine heir—a question that figures the social reproduction of hegemonic masculinity more generally. Other Westerns explore the impairment of a hero who is reluctant or incapable of taking strong action within the conventional codes of the genre, as in *The Gunfighter* and the overtly Freudian *The Fastest Gun Alive* (Rouse 1956). In the latter, the twitchy and nervous George Temple (Glenn Ford) must overcome his life-long fear of a gunfight to take up his rightful place as the titular fastest gun, using the weapon of his dead sheriff father to do it. Even in films less explicit in their Freudianism, heroes are haunted by the ghosts of childhood trauma and shadowed by dark fraternal doubles, caught in a web of familial dysfunction that at once defines and constrains them. In tension with those elements of the pro-Indian Westerns that lean toward a broader social indictment, the emphasis on a Freudian framework functions to contain critique, individualizing the pathology at the genre's core.

Although Western protagonists are privy to a range of actions denied their domestic counterparts, it is important to note the degree to which this action lacks its former efficacy. In contrast to the constitutive opposition Elsaesser draws between the protagonists of Westerns and those of domestic melodramas, what is striking about the Cold War Western is how problematic direct action has become, how often and in how many ways it is qualified and constricted. Rather than the fulfillment of the protagonist's desire, action often represents its failure or frustration, a sign of neurosis or instability in keeping with Elsaesser's assertion that "[i]n melodrama, violence, the strong action, the dynamic movement . . . become the very signs of the characters' alienation."[73] In the Western, this alienation is inseparable from the critique of white supremacism, as I have suggested. Yet, while strong action is increasingly problematic, the failure to act is also represented as a sign of impotence or maladjustment, a formal and ideological contradiction the genre seeks to solve.

Rather than direct and linear in its progression, as Elsaesser argues, action in the Cold War Western displays a kind of repetition compulsion, its linearity undercut by the inevitability of return. Heroes tend to move in circles that are signified both visually (as in Will Kane's endless pacing in *High Noon* or Ethan Edwards's cyclical journey in *The Searchers* [Ford 1956]) and thematically (through the emphasis on childhood trauma and the return of the repressed). Elsaesser notes how, in domestic melodrama, "the cathartic violence of a shoot-out or a chase becomes an inner violence, often one which the characters turn against themselves."[74] But in the Cold War Western, too, violence is more hysterical than cathartic—acting out rather than resolving conflict—and, as in the Mann Westerns, often takes the hero himself as its object. To the extent that such violence is represented as the externalization of the hero's own inner struggles, a process of self-destruction conditioned by his guilt, it exhibits the same masochistic impulse Elsaesser discusses.

High Noon offers a suggestive example of the changing status of action (despite the extended shoot-out at its close) and a testament to the contemporary merger of power with vulnerability. Marshal Will Kane (Gary Cooper) is the epitome of the man who "walked more than he rode and brooded more than he acted."[75] In his guise as a frontier town lawman, Kane still carries the generic weight of the traditional hero, but he is burdened by this weight, as emphasized in his reluctant capitulation to the requirements of strong action. The low-angle shots of Cooper as he paces the dusty, desolate streets alone register Kane's mounting anxiety, while the repetition of these shots across the film underscores the futility of his search for support among the disaffected townsfolk. The gradual tightening of the frame around Cooper's face as the film progresses intensifies the sense of approaching doom, while the deepened lines creasing his skin add poignancy to the recurring close-ups.[76]

The suspense generated through these walking sequences is produced through a set of formal and thematic contradictions; we are offered a conventionally heroic angle on the marshal, whose stature is shored up by Cooper's star persona, alongside the suggestion that his authoritative action is something we can no longer take for granted. Like the walking sequences, the swooping crane shot toward the film's conclusion—in which a twitchy Kane awaits the imminent arrival of the vengeful Frank Miller and his men—constructs anxiety through an emphasis on Kane's vulnerability. The pathetic appeal of these images is bound up in the narrative insistence on Kane's abandonment by the community he has served; the lack of popular endorsement for the traditional authority Kane embodies, alongside the visual and thematic constitution of his vulnerability, secures an attachment to his beleaguered image precisely to the extent that it is represented as beleaguered. The community's moral failure in *High Noon* participates in a broader trend; even outside the pro-Indian cycle, the town figures regularly as a source of violent menace as well as social restriction— "a rotten town, with a lot of rotten people in it," as hero Wes Steele (Ray Milland) maintains in *A Man Alone* (Milland 1955).

The mise-en-scène of action changes in this context, as I have noted. The hero is increasingly restricted to interiors, as in *The Gunfighter*, in which the gunslinger hero holes up in a saloon ("You better wait in here, not move around much," he is warned), or in *A Man Alone*, in which the wrongly accused hero is captive within a middle-class home for most of the film. Meanwhile, the genre's conventional landscapes—rather than the nationalist fantasy of "open space"—are recast as a projection of the hero's own distorted psychic terrain, "the unnatural world of a disturbed mind."[77] Even in his discussion of the distinction between melodrama and the Western, Elsaesser recognizes this resemblance. Although he maintains that "the assumption of 'open' spaces is virtually axiomatic" in the Western, he acknowledges that "openness becomes problematic in films that deal with potential 'melodrama' themes and family situations"—themes and situations central to the Western in this period.[78]

Indeed, nowhere is the collapse of madness and authority that Rodowick discusses in relation to domestic melodrama more evident than in the Western, where generic conventions forcefully collide with contemporary pressures on the construction of normative masculinity. The genre's configuration of this collapse highlights how the critique of strong action and of the traditional hero as its agent operates within the negotiation of racism as both a foundation of the Western and an ideological formation it must now (on some levels) eschew. This critique was evident as early as *The Ox-Bow Incident*, in which the repudiation of Major Tetley aligned the image of authoritarian masculinity with the specter of white racist violence (and masculine softness or effeminacy with the voices of moral reason). It is evident more explicitly in Ethan Edwards, hero of *The Searchers* (and, like Tetley, an ex-Confederate soldier), a figure whom Douglas Pye has aptly described as "both monstrous *and* John Wayne" (italics in the original).[79]

Although much has been written about *The Searchers*, it nonetheless bears noting how the tensions I have been tracing manifest in the film's incoherent attitude toward its protagonist, whom it can neither fully accept nor fully disavow.[80] Wayne's persona, consolidated across a decade of B Westerns and launched into feature stardom by the success of *Stagecoach*, embodies the Western hero's traditional appeal. As he appears in the film's famous opening shot, riding toward his brother's ranch from out of a vast landscape, Ethan recalls the expansionist fantasy of freedom, motion, and open, empty space upon which the genre is founded.[81] The majestic buttes of Monument Valley, lone statues in the distance, suggestively echo the figure of Ethan himself. The longing gaze of his sister-in-law Martha (Dorothy Jordan), standing in the doorway that frames his arrival, and Wayne's own towering frame in the domestic sequence that follows confirm his heroic stature, his place at the center of the film's interests and investments.

This same sequence, however, introduces the moral flaw that will drive and qualify Ethan's actions across the film. His adoptive nephew Martin Pawley (Jeffrey Hunter) arrives for dinner, to Ethan's hostile reception. Like Ethan, he approaches on horseback and is framed by a doorway (although he rides bareback and it is the back door this time). Identified at the outset as one-eighth Cherokee, Martin will signify in complex ways as Indian

("A fellow could mistake you for a half-breed," Ethan accusingly notes).[82] As Brian Henderson has argued, in Ethan's refusal to accept Martin's literal and figurative place at the family table, the film establishes the question of race and belonging as central to its problematic.[83] Indeed, the issue of home and its threshold—what crosses over into domestic space, and who or what regulates that passage—is made visually explicit in the rhyming opening and closing shots, whose composition is echoed across the film.

The film's ambivalent relationship to strong action cannot be understood apart from its negotiation of racism. In the case of Ethan, the moral culpability of his onscreen violence crescendos as the titular search plays out, finding its most shocking manifestation in Ethan's intended murder of his abducted niece Debbie (Natalie Wood), now acculturated to Native society and married to the Comanche chief Scar (Henry Brandon). The racist dread animating Ethan's obsessive quest to find Debbie—and to kill her if she is found "too late" (in Ethan's view, when interracial sex will have obliterated her essential whiteness)—is visualized in his deranged shooting of a buffalo herd partway through the film, an incident Martin "still hasn't gotten straight" in his mind when he narrates it in a letter to his sweetheart, Laurie (Vera Miles). The slaughter is interrupted by the sound of a bugle call, which heralds a more explicit scene of racialized violence. Ethan's crazed attempt to starve the Comanche by killing off the buffalo herd anticipates the subsequent sequence, which reveals the assault by the U.S. Cavalry on a Comanche winter camp, an act the film represents as reprehensible ("What'd them soldiers have to go and kill her for, Ethan, she never done nobody any harm?" Marty cries when he comes upon the body of the sympathetic Look amid the carnage).[84]

Alongside its partial critique of both individual and systemic white racial violence, The Searchers participates in the conventions of the pro-Indian cycle in other ways. Ethan's racist animosity, for instance, is coupled with his intimate knowledge of Native customs and language, aligning him with the Indian even as his racist obsessions drive both the search and the film itself.[85] Meanwhile, Martin and Debbie, the film's hybrid whites, remain sympathetic characters throughout, their goodness secured in part through their different modes of kinship with the Indian. This kinship is coupled in both cases with their status as victims of Indian attacks, a more confused version of the racialized victimization we witnessed in the pro-Indian cycle. Through Ethan's ultimate acceptance of Marty and Debbie's integration into home and family—his recognition of the "half-breed" Marty as kin and his return of Debbie to the Jorgenson's ranch (a domestic space that mirrors and overlays his brother's homestead)—the film represents his evolution away from both madness and moral darkness. Nonetheless, in the final shot, Ethan will turn with hesitancy from the space of home, from which his own proximity to violence—paradoxically encoded through racialized ideologies of savagery—precludes his entry.[86]

The incoherence of *The Searcher*'s attitude toward Ethan is instructive, for his monstrosity and his authority derive from a shared source. Wayne's Ethan represents a figure whose generic legacy mobilizes a pleasurable association with action and whose onscreen persona embodies the conventions of the strong, resolute Western hero, even as his commitment to white supremacist violence shades increasingly into madness. Through him, the film offers both a critique and a complex shoring up of the Western hero, revealing a deep attachment to a figure whose complicity with the genre's foundational racism provides both the source and the limit of his authority. The impossibility of resolving this tension within generic terms produces a potent sense of mourning, a lament (and directive) offered in the theme song's remorseful refrain ("ride away"). That this song blends in both the opening and the closing sequences into the tune of the antebellum "Lorena" (reportedly popular with Confederate soldiers) suggestively amplifies the significance of white supremacism to Ethan's turn from home. As Henderson suggests, Ethan is "excluded for our sins; that is why we find it so moving."[87]

As exemplified in this ending, the critique of the Western hero is accompanied by an intense nostalgia at his passing. Ethan's racist obsessions do nothing to qualify the pathos of the film's closing image, with its poignant confirmation of an impossibility Ethan has embodied from the outset, his status as a disruption to the image of family he both threatens and secures. The function of nostalgia is in fact key to the Western hero's authority; the appeal of canonic figures like Wayne is constituted only through a relentless assertion of their inevitable loss.[88] This pathetic image of loss is crystallized in the closing shots of Cold War Westerns, as in Joey's plaintive cry after the receding figure of Shane, the retreat of Wayne's Ethan Edwards, or the crumpling collapse of the dying Joel McCrea in Sam Peckinpah's *Ride the High Country* (1962). That the soundtrack plays such a crucial role in constituting the appeal of these images underscores their melodramatic function, the affective investment that surrounds and saturates them.

Indeed, rather than qualifying the poignancy of such shots, the critique of the hero heightens it by foreshadowing his ultimate exclusion from and unfitness for the broader social world the films envision. The primary vector of suspense in films like *The Searchers* operates through the impossibility embodied by the hero himself rather than the hero's triumphant race to the rescue of innocence assaulted (or, alternately, his arrival too late upon the scene of its devastation). Linda Williams has described how "the feeling or threat of loss" functions within the affective dynamics of melodrama, suffusing the form with "the sense that something has . . . 'gone with the wind.'"[89]

In *The Searchers*, it is the loss that Ethan has embodied from the beginning, more than the quest for the abducted Debbie, that generates the film's affective intensity. We know there is no place for Ethan in the domestic world into which he arrives at the film's opening;[90] his alignment with strong action and his casting at the outset in explicit opposition to the forces of racial integration guarantee his unfitness. The anticipation of this loss across the film intensifies the pathos of his ultimate passing out of the diegetic world and, implicitly, out of the social world of its audience as well.

The emphasis on pathos in the Cold War Western produces what I call the John Wayne paradox. As the persistent attachment to the figure of Ethan/Wayne indicates, the critique of the Western hero does not diminish the affective investment in his image. Indeed, though the pressures on the genre cannot be fully resolved within it, the Cold War Western hero— hailing from the genre's most popular and productive period, it is useful to recall[91]—comes to signify the very essence of white masculine authority, an image of strength and resolve that the films themselves cannot (and do not) fully endorse. Despite the contradictions attending his representation, this hero has managed to shed most of his troubled, anxious, and unstable associations; he persists in scholarly and popular imagination as an icon of stability against which late-century crises may be measured and evaluated.[92] John Wayne in particular tends to serve as an incontrovertible signifier of authority, a manly relic from a mythic time before masculine representations became troubled and conflicted, though he rises to stardom as the embodiment of a masculine authority "overshadowed by the prospect of extinction."[93]

What is remarkable about this legacy is the extent to which it conflicts with the formal and thematic emphases of the films themselves, their qualifications on action, focus on failure and suffering, and tendency to cast traditional forms of masculine authority as signifiers of mental as well as moral instability. To make sense of this paradox is to come to terms with the force and function of pathos, the extent to which images of failure, suffering, and loss help to secure an attachment to the fantasy of white masculine authority they would seem to destabilize or disavow. By casting the hero as a victim of racialized violence, of physical assault, of psychological distress, or of the intractable contradictions of gender ideology, the Cold War Western works not to limit but to intensify an attachment to his image. As a victim—even or especially a troubled and compromised one— he emerges as a paradoxical icon of masculine, moral, and national authority, a locus of intense and persistent affective and cultural investment.

The Western's ideological power traditionally stemmed from its construction of an onscreen hero from whom authority seemed naturally to emanate; this is the implication of the merger of visceral with moral thrills discussed in the last chapter. During the Cold War period, the stylistic and thematic contours of the genre begin to bend away from an uninflected representation of masculine authority and the formal emphasis on exciting, morally invigorated action in which it had been grounded. Pathos becomes invested with a new function in this context, crystallizing the position of the hero as one who suffers and tethering our identification of his goodness not to onscreen action but to the spectacle of this suffering. Cast as a victim of externalized physical abuse and internalized guilt and shame, the hero is positioned as the genre's primary site of suffering, embodying the pathetic impossibility of reconciling generic with contemporary ideological pressures.

The genre's emphasis on suffering, however, should not lead us to think of power and pathos as oppositional forces. On the contrary, as we have seen, the Western hero suffers precisely because he is powerful; his suffering is a constitutive element of the authority he embodies. At the same time, and crucially, the suffering of the hero confirms his virtue; it produces for us his status as something worthy, something good, something to be mourned. The potency of the Western hero is inextricable from his impairment, and this impairment works to amplify our attachment to his image. It is not simply that an impulse toward both power and pathos creates formal and ideological tensions in this period, but that pathos is produced through and in relation to the image of power itself. Thus the genre is marked by "heroic melancholy," a "sense of being at once supremely powerful and utterly vulnerable," its hero in "flight from the power which gave him distinction."[94] In the words of Richard Slotkin, the hero is "rendered isolated and vulnerable by the very things that have made him victorious in the past."[95]

In the articulation of a figure defined through the power that renders him vulnerable and of the vulnerability that constitutes power itself as moral, innocent, and benign, we begin to see the ultimate significance of the Cold War Western hero. For in this paradox, the hero echoes the contemporary construction of the nation itself, likewise constituted through the melodramatic conjunction of victimization and virtue and cast as the simultaneous locus of supreme power and supreme vulnerability. By constituting this hero as a site of affective investment, a figure through which to negotiate contemporary ideological challenges to white masculine authority while reconstituting the grounds of this authority, the Western provides an efficacious vehicle for the nationalist imagination of power and virtue both—renewed in its innocence and more precious in its perceived instability.

The fantasy that the genre here enacts of a power that, through its very strength and authority, has been rendered vulnerable or subject to extinction resonates in crucial ways with broader national structures of feeling. As Joseph Masco has argued, vulnerability is an immensely productive affect in the Cold War era; the summons to identify with fear, insecurity, and anxiety crucially underwrites the emergence of the national security state, helping to remake both the geopolitical and the domestic spheres in profound and lasting ways.[96] In Elisabeth Anker's view, melodramatic conventions themselves shape political discourse in newly emphatic ways after World War II, casting international politics in strictly Manichean terms and animating the expansionist activities of the state both domestically and abroad.[97] Thus the pathetic mode of the Cold War Western resonates with the contemporary melodramatic constitution of American national identity more broadly, as a nation enjoying unprecedented wealth, military strength, and global dominance made central to its self-conception the fantasy of its own vulnerability. Through the Western, the affective logic of this conjunction is deeply felt, providing a powerful vehicle for nationalist feeling in the decades to come.

4

The Subject of
Imperiled Privilege

Victimization and Violence in
Late-Century Action Cinema

The action cinema of the late twentieth century would demonstrate both the intensification and the diffusion of the melodramatic pleasures of cinematic violence, drawing upon earlier traditions of thrilling, morally authorized action and pathetic spectacles of suffering, while wedding these to a newly explosive repertoire of technologically enhanced attractions. The figure of the white man as racialized victim, consolidated in the Cold War Western, would be conventionalized as a central generic element of the action cinema of the 1980s and 1990s. The spectacular appeals of violence would intensify in this context, reinvigorating the aggressive direct address of the early cinema, alongside an insistence on the hero's status as a victim of social and institutional, as well as personal and bodily, forms of injury and abuse. At the same time, new affective notes would enter the register of sensational melodrama, including humor and, by the early 1990s, a kind of moral queasiness. The conjoined appeals of vulnerability and violent agency would nonetheless continue to shape the production of imperialist affect, even as the moral underpinning of this conjunction would become increasingly unstable by the twentieth century's close.

In this final chapter, I trace the evolution of sensational melodrama through the late-century action cinema: from the unexpected success of the inaugural Rambo film, *First Blood* (Kotcheff 1982), and the global phenomenon of *Rambo: First Blood Part II* (Cosmatos 1985); to the canonic *Lethal Weapon* and *Die Hard* films as they establish the conventional contours of the genre in this period; to the introduction of a new moral instability circulating around the spectacle of violence in films like *Falling Down* (Schumacher 1993) and *Unforgiven* (Eastwood 1992). Across all of these films, I am interested in the production of what Lauren Berlant has called "the subject of imperiled privilege." This subject, constituted as both white and masculine, is defined by nostalgia for a lost national iconicity and for the fantasy of unmarked and unmitigated access that underwrote it. In the context of the action cinema, the subject of imperiled privilege himself becomes iconic, as the action hero emerges as a new kind of national icon, one whose iconicity incorporates the very premise of its loss.

The action cinema's construction of this subject position as a broadly appealing point of identification derives from its circulation of the melodramatic conventions I have been tracing. As ever, the invitation to identify with this position is not limited to white men; instead, it revolves around fantasies of vulnerability and agency that resonate with a much broader field of social and psychic desires. As Berlant notes, even the period's ubiquitous discourse of white masculine crisis, which posits white men as a newly disenfranchised population, highlights a set of appeals and anxieties that apply broadly, as "many people of color and women identify with the world of desire for accumulation and self-extension attributed, here, to 'white men'"—and hence, implicitly, with the specter of their loss.[1]

This discourse of crisis, rising in the 1980s and peaking in the early 1990s, echoes in many ways the crisis discourse of the twentieth century's turn while raising new questions about the status of white men in late capitalism. Articulating aspects of this crisis, a variety of men's movements emerge in this period to decry the domestication and feminization of American men. As before, ideas about masculine physicality animate understandings of manliness in this context, replaying the fantasy of the strenuous life. Blaming both feminist and corporate power for the denigration of men's leadership roles and circulating fantasies of the primitive as an avenue of manly rejuvenation, these movements urge the reinvigoration of modern men through more traditional modes of gendered being.[2] While echoing the rhetoric of Theodore Roosevelt and his contemporaries, this discourse also emphasizes the contemporary character of this crisis, reading it broadly as a response to second-wave feminism, affirmative action, and a masculine and national malaise following from the military and moral quagmire of Vietnam. The economic recession of the 1970s, the outsourcing of industrial labor, and the continued ascendance of the service sector are frequently cited in such discussions, although in general social and cultural factors are emphasized above economic ones, inviting a cross-class identification with the plight of white men as a newly imperiled demographic.

In its more virulent strains, the late-century discourse of crisis holds that, in the context of identity politics and the alleged hegemony of "political correctness" that followed upon the civil rights and liberation movements of the 1960s and 1970s, the rights of white men are being ruthlessly trampled. In the rush to acknowledge and redress the collective struggles of populations historically marginalized within the social, cultural, and economic institutions of the nation, it is argued, the legitimate claims of white men—the alleged beneficiaries of social and institutional privilege—have been unfairly denied. Rather than icons of privilege and access, white men are recast as society's most aggrieved and least understood victims.

At the same time, it is suggested, white men cannot fight back aggressively against these encroachments because the very image of a strong, authoritative masculinity has been impugned by second-wave feminism and the failures of Vietnam and hijacked by a commodity culture in which its fetishization announces its very instability.[3] Even self-identified feminists could take a sympathetic view of this "betrayal" of American men, as in journalist Susan Faludi's *Stiffed*, a melancholy ode to male mistreatment in the context of postindustrial consumer society. According to Faludi, a "society of utility," in which men's roles were stable, productive, and well-defined, has given way, in the face of corporate downsizing and outsourcing, the growth of the service sector, and the imperatives of consumerism more generally, to a vacuous society of spectacle in which "manhood is defined by appearance."[4]

The question of spectacle is central to the action cinema, of course, where it serves as a site of identification and pleasure rather than a simple marker of instability. In this context, the spectacularization of white masculinity can function to visualize the power of self-extension that Berlant identifies as so central to its social construction. This notion of self-extension resonates with Judith Butler's discussion of the imperialist subject, a subject constituted through the fantasy of unimpeded agency, the "apparently seamless realization of intention through an instrumental action without much resistance of [sic] hindrance."[5]

Butler first discusses the mediated production of this subject in the context of the televisual discourse of the Persian Gulf War and returns to it in the aftermath of 9/11, when she considers the relationship between state violence and the sovereign subject it posits. This sovereign subject denies its own constitutive injurability through the doing of injury to others, working "to secure an impossible effect of mastery, inviolability, and impermeability through destructive means." Such a subject "poses as precisely not the one who is impinged upon by others, precisely not the one whose permanent and irreversible injurability forms the condition and horizon of its actions."[6]

In many ways, and especially in its emphasis on an affective sense of unimpeded agency, Butler's imperialist subject mirrors the subject of the late-century action cinema, "whose will immediately translates into a deed, whose utterance or order materializes in an action which destroys the very possibility of a reverse-strike, and whose obliterating power at once confirms the impenetrable contours of its own subjecthood."[7] The violence of the action cinema, in constituting agency through the spectacular display of destruction onscreen, plays to infantile aggressions and to a sadism that underwrites the fantasy of sovereignty itself. The ability of the cinematic apparatus to perform magical feats of destruction—in which the force of a gaze can be obliterating, the act of taking aim perfectly efficacious in its annihilative realization—imbues the action hero with tremendous power and appeal, constituting him as the privileged embodiment of the kind of agency Butler describes.

Rambo (like the Persian Gulf War some years later) is explicitly associated with "righting" the failures of Vietnam, restabilizing the image of imperialist subjectivity and the affect that sustains it. Thus we might usefully consider a figure like Rambo, who makes his first appearance onscreen in 1982 and returns more spectacularly in 1985, as a precursor to the affective and visual logic Butler diagnoses at work in the televisual production of the Gulf War in 1991. Indeed, it is in the action cinema of the 1980s that these logics are first conventionalized, helping to reanimate the imperialist subject of war.

At the same time, however, and crucially, the action cinema speaks to another set of appeals accruing around the very terms of injurability and violability, upon whose denial, Butler argues, the imperialist subject is predicated. Rambo, again, provides a useful example based on the escalating physical and psychological suffering to which he is subjected. He is constituted primarily as one who acts and one who suffers, highlighting the two poles of action and pathos whose alternation defines the melodramatic form more generally.[8]

By situating action cinema within the traditions of sensational melodrama, we can appreciate the central role vulnerability plays in the cinematic fantasy of violence and in the production of the imperialist subject more generally, a subject whose power depends upon a simultaneous repression of and insistence on the conditions of injurability. Indeed, the affective power of the action cinema resides in its ability to give spectacular expression to the doubled appeal through which imperialist subjectivity is constituted, speaking at the level of both form and narrative to the attractions of violent agency and embodied vulnerability and, most emphatically, to their persistent conjunction. Identification with injurability and insecurity are central to identification with sovereignty and agency in this context and to the explosive show of force and destruction in which the spectator is invited to take pleasure.

In its invitation to identify with both victimization and omnipotence, the late-century action cinema harkens back to the military actualities discussed in chapter 1. As in the early charge films and battle reenactments, the pleasures of cinematic motion and violence circulate here through a particular kind of body and a particular kind of spectacle. As in the military actualities and early Westerns, cinematic motion in films like *Rambo* is both masculinized and nationalized. But such motion is not the sole generator of pleasure in late-century action cinema, any more than it was in the early cinema; instead, the spectator is regularly invited into an embodied identification with vulnerability, thrilled and agitated by the formal conventions of cinematic assault. In both animating and qualifying the fantasy of unimpeded agency, the cinematic apparatus continues to serve the affective rhythms of melodrama in complex and multilayered ways, situating the spectator as at once an agent and a victim of the technological powers of force and speed.

Such conventions return us to the conjunction of white masculine representation and the technological thrills of the attraction. Enfolded within a classical fabric, the attraction has always animated genres like the Western, but in late-century action cinema it breaks out of the confines of narrative and character-bound structures to become, again, a dominant mechanism of cinematic address. As in the early cinema, the appeal of the attraction is inseparable from the technological novelties of the cinematic apparatus. As it circulates around "the male body as a machine for generating and undergoing aggressive assault," in Sharon Willis's terms, the action cinema of the 1980s and 1990s heralds a new age of technologically sophisticated film violence.[9] At the same time, though it represents the culmination of many of the trajectories I have been tracing, it also breaks with these conventions, most conspicuously in the degree of moral instability that begins to accrue around the hero and his violence, loosening the conjunction of visceral with moral thrills that the Western had worked to secure.

Spectacular Agonies, Sensational Redemptions: *Rambo* as Melodrama

No one more than Rambo attests quite so clearly to the operations of sensational melodrama as they structure the action cinema. In the Rambo films, we see the construction of innocence through victimization, the relationship of suffering to spectacular outbursts of destructive violence, the technological intensification of the attraction as it undergirds both agency and vulnerability, and, most emphatically, the way this melodramatic alchemy transforms a scene of national guilt into a scene of national virtue and, indeed, pleasure.

Popular and scholarly accounts have often emphasized the cultural emergence of the white male as victim in the 1980s and early 1990s as a specific product of contemporary social, cultural, and economic dislocations. But in articulating these dislocations, the representational strategies of the action cinema draw upon and extend the conventions of the Cold War Western: the emphasis on pathos and loss; the spectacle of bodily trauma and wounding; and the alliance between the white male protagonist and a racialized other as a mechanism of moral authorization. Where the anguish and battery of the Jimmy Stewart hero signaled a departure from dominant generic conventions, however, the beleaguered protagonist would become central to the thematic and stylistic vocabulary of late-century action cinema, in which the hero's physical and psychological sufferings condition spectacular resuscitations of strength and aggression onscreen.

If the melodramatic articulation of white masculine authority, which highlights the protagonist as the primary source of both pathos and action, is well established by the 1980s, the figure of the Vietnam veteran provides for its intensification. As Susan Jeffords has argued, the Vietnam vet circulates in cultural discourse of this period as emblematic of "a more widely based victimization of 'man and the idea of manhood.'"[10] In the Rambo films, this victimization animates a reallocation of guilt and innocence in the wake of Vietnam, resecuring identification with the image of white masculine authority while struggling to solve, as Linda Williams has noted, "the overwhelming moral burden of having been the 'bad guys' in a lost war."[11]

This is a burden that Cold War Westerns had already moved to address, as I discussed in the last chapter. In the shadow of Vietnam and the social and economic upheavals of the 1970s, however, this burden shifts away from the Western, which moves increasingly toward postures of parody and critique. It migrates instead into the Western-influenced action cinema, which takes up as a central project the rearticulation of imperialist affect away from registers of guilt and shame and toward an intensified identification with the screen-based pleasures of action and violence.

First Blood is unusually explicit about the problem of guilt and its allocation. The film traces the arrest, escape, and recapture of Vietnam veteran John Rambo by a small-town sheriff and his deputies. Throughout his extended pursuit through the punishing terrain of the Pacific Northwest, Rambo insists that he "didn't *do* anything." And, indeed, the film's diegesis is dedicated to Rambo as the misunderstood and unfairly persecuted protagonist of melodrama, one whose identity is misconstrued from the outset and whose moral legibility must be established through the public spectacle of his suffering. At the same time, an acknowledgment of Rambo's complicity in morally dubious violence is repeatedly voiced by his old commander, Colonel Trautman (Richard Crenna), who highlights the indiscriminate killing that characterized Rambo's official mission in Vietnam.[12] As the film makes clear, it is precisely what Rambo *did* do in Vietnam that animates both his anguish and his military prowess, the conjunction of which it is one of the film's primary purposes to display.

The film opens like a conventional Western with the arrival of a stranger to town, though here on foot rather than on horseback. The opening sequence introduces, fleetingly, the fantasy of home as a space of innocence and tranquility, an image to which the film (and, indeed, the franchise) will not return. The constitution of home as the locus of lost innocence is a crucial element of melodrama, as Linda Williams has argued, and the fantasized resurrection of such a space animates the longing at melodrama's core. In classic stage melodrama, gardens and rural domiciles provided the most conventional icons of home. *First Blood* opens on the image of a rustic community set against a backdrop of natural beauty, establishing briefly the domestic fantasy whose betrayal the film will mourn.[13]

The opening shot of a dilapidated cabin hints at both the ruined nature of home and the extent to which the idea of home and its loss will animate the action to come. As Rambo moves down a tree-lined dirt road past the cabin, he pauses to gaze smilingly on a group of children at play. The camera follows the laughing children down a sloping hillside, coming to rest upon a few small houses gathered on the shore of a mountain lake (fig. 18). The visual drama of the Northwest landscape, which will transmute into harshness after Rambo's flight to the forest, is figured here as the sparkling backdrop for a modest yet homely ambition—a small house by the water, women hanging clothes on the line—albeit one, the film is quick to assert, that exists only at the level of Rambo's hopeful fantasy.

In other ways, too, *First Blood* attests to the melodramatic conventions that shape and drive the action cinema. The film's hyperbolic score, alternately mournful and jubilant, orchestrates a landscape of physical extremes, in which dark forests, precipitous cliffs, fast-moving rivers, and cavernous mines provide the dramatic register of a film notoriously scant on dialogue. Crashing thunder and flashes of lightning punctuate Rambo's battle with Sheriff Will Teasle (Brian Dennehy) and his men, while the muteness of the hero himself is legendary. In keeping with melodrama's tendency to "externalize the inner states of characters" and their conflicts through elements of the mise-en-scène, the film's landscape materializes through stark contrasts and physical dangers the psychic as well as moral stakes around which its action circulates—questions of guilt and innocence, suffering and virtue.[14]

Fig. 18. Rambo is first introduced to the screen through the fantasy of home as the locus of desire in a fleeting image of domestic tranquility to which the film and its sequels will not return. *First Blood* (Kotcheff 1982).

Rambo's disinclination toward speech, like that of the laconic Western hero, is reminiscent of the historical emergence of melodrama through a prohibition on the spoken word.[15] The role of the mute is well established in the melodramatic tradition, corresponding "first of all to a repeated use of extreme physical conditions to represent extreme moral and emotional conditions."[16] In the more recent context of the American cinema, the intensification of onscreen violence in genres like the Western and the action cinema has correlated with a decreasing emphasis on dialogue, often understood to signal these genres realist affiliations. As Christine Gledhill has suggested, however, "the taciturnity of masculine realism is the seedbed of melodramatic emotion."[17]

Through its collection of musical, gestural, and spectacular signs, Peter Brooks argues, melodrama reaches out toward "meanings which cannot be generated through the language code," and this sense of striving toward fuller meanings is a source of its power and appeal.[18] Indeed, the film asserts that Rambo's muteness speaks louder and more fully than words through its emphasis on the nervous chattering of his adversaries, which demonstrates the capacity of verbal expression to say very little. In contrast, muteness allows for a fuller articulation of meaning through nonverbal modes of expression, including the physical extremes of the mise-en-scène, the hyperbolic score, the spectacle of speechless suffering, and the visceral appeals of onscreen action.

In the absence of verbal expression, Rambo's body takes on a heightened burden of signification, in line with melodrama's emergence through performance traditions that emphasized body rather than voice as the primary site of expressivity.[19] Up until the film's polemical coda, in which the taciturn hero erupts in a torrent of tears, recriminations, and regrets over society's betrayals of the Vietnam veteran, Rambo's melancholy is constructed primarily at the level of his body. The constitution of Rambo as one who suffers is amplified by his dejected, mournful gaze, emphasized by Stallone's darkly hooded, deep-set eyes. In *First Blood* in particular, attention to this gaze speaks to the melodramatic pressure on the body to express the inner truth of its characters (in Christine Gledhill's terms, the pressure on characters and actors to "body forth in their physical presence . . . the cause of innocence, justice, hope").[20] Given the melodramatic imperative to announce through the play of surface appearance what resides beneath, Stallone's hangdog look speaks to the inner truth of his suffering, and thus to his goodness, within a melodramatic logic by which one circulates as the primary signifier of the other. In addition, Stallone's star persona—cemented by *Rocky* (Avidsen 1976) and its sequels—pivots around the image of his woundedness and the virtue accruing to his melodramatic positioning as an underdog.[21]

It is Sheriff Teasle's initial misreading of this body, when Rambo wanders into the ironically ordained town of Hope, that inaugurates the string of misrecognitions that will structure the film. This early misreading raises the question of Rambo's legibility—and his moral legibility in particular—that it is the project of *First Blood* to address. Teasle interprets Rambo as a threat, a hippie drifter set against the normativity of small-town life, when in fact, the film insists, he is a victim (as well as a Special Forces soldier and Medal of Honor recipient). This theme of misrecognition runs throughout the action cinema, highlighting the genre's problematic of moral identity. (The convention itself becomes a self-referential joke by the time of *Rambo III* [MacDonald 1988], in which Rambo's now iconic body is misread as that of a tourist.)

To establish the moral identity of its hero, the action cinema must abuse him, in keeping with melodrama's construction of virtue through suffering. In contrast to Westerns in which the hero fights to protect or avenge aggrieved communities or individuals, there is no one to save or protect in *First Blood* but Rambo himself. Rather than an image of female and domestic imperilment, then, the film revolves around the spectacle of Rambo's own vulnerability and violability, establishing a central feature of late-century action cinema. Rambo is bludgeoned with a billy club, blasted with a high-powered hose, sliced open in a torture flashback, shot at while he dangles from a sheer cliff, and impaled by a tree branch when he falls (an injury that gives rise to the queasy spectacle of his self-suturing). Underscoring melodrama's insistence on the public function of such suffering, shots of Rambo's abuse are intercut to highlight the presence of diegetic spectators, amplifying the spectacularization of the scene of torture.

These representations circulate within the melodramatic history of racialized suffering. As in the pro-Indian Westerns, *First Blood* codes the figure of the white man as Indian to consolidate the moral authority accruing to his victimization. The extent to which Rambo's affinity with the resources of the forest is coded as a kind of "going native" aligns him with heroes like Comanche Todd in *The Last Wagon*, as well as Broken Lance in *Devil's Doorway*, who like Rambo is subjected to both personal and institutionalized forms of abuse.[22] Rambo's signature knife and bow and arrow, as well as his attire (in *First Blood*, a makeshift canvas tunic suggestive of animal hide), underscore his coding as Indian. The unique source of his strength is offered as the conjunction of his primitive instinct with his modern military know-how; *Rambo: First Blood Part II* will make this union explicit by identifying Rambo as "of Indian-German descent."

The animosity directed at Rambo by Teasle is expressed as an irrational and visceral form of loathing, aligning his persecution with a history of racialized violence. (Rambo "smells like an animal," and Teasle wants to kill him "so bad [he] could taste it.") Rambo's status as a victim generates the terms of his moral legibility while casting a morally dubious light on his abusers (most particularly, the sadistic deputy Galt, the only character killed in the course of the film's violence). As Sylvia Shin Huey Chong suggests, Rambo "derives the righteous indignation of his victimization from the civil rights movement."[23] In the 1972 novel upon which the film is based, Teasle is a Southern sheriff, an identity that highlights his interpellation of Rambo "into the subject position of blackness." As Chong notes, the blasting of Rambo with a high-powered hose in the film adaptation fulfills a similar function, recalling "the posture of African American abjection" in news footage of civil rights protestors buckling under the force of fire hoses in Birmingham, Alabama.[24]

In both mobilizing and repressing the racial contours of American melodrama, *First Blood* replaces the social history of racialized violence with an assertion of the white man as the primary victim of institutionalized abuse. The film's opening fantasy of home, for instance, is immediately betrayed through the revelation that the last surviving member of Rambo's unit, the object of his visit to this remote spot, died the previous summer. The comrade, Delmar Berry, is offered as a casualty of malignant government neglect, eaten away by cancer after exposure to Agent Orange. That Berry is African American is not incidental; for if this opening invokes, as Susan Jeffords has argued, "an absent strong body" in the loss of Berry (whose stature is emphasized in dialogue but whose photograph is kept out of view), it is Rambo's body that will move in to occupy the space Berry's evacuates.[25] Catalyzed by Berry's death, Rambo takes up his position as a victim of both institutionalized discrimination and individual bodily suffering, absorbing the moral claims that accrue to this suffering and fore-closing its assignment along other axes of gender or race.[26] This alignment with an African American buddy provides the mechanism for an appropriation of the position of racialized victimization and will become conventional in mainstream action cinema across the 1980s.

In the context of its persistent abuse, however, Rambo's body has a double status—ruthlessly battered yet unbreakable, vulnerable yet endlessly resourceful—and it is through this doubleness that action cinema constructs its appeal. If, as Sally Robinson has argued, "white men can most persuasively claim victimization by appealing to representations of bodily trauma," the Rambo films offer an emphatic case study.[27] But the status of this bodily trauma is complex, as the spectacle of wounding opens out in two different but interrelated directions. We are invited to identify with Rambo as violable, even as the scene of wounding provides for the display of his superhuman resilience, that is, for the very denial of his injurability. This dynamic is particularly apparent in sequences of self-suturing, which linger on the spectacle of the wound in the context of its self-repair. In *First Blood*, for instance, we pull in close to watch Rambo stitch a deep gash sliced across his arm; the gaping lips of the wound, gushing curtains of blood, highlight the gendering of the violable body, producing an uneasy spectacle of vulnerability alongside a testament to Rambo's resilience.

Such moments recur across the Rambo films, although the balance between emphasizing Rambo's violability while attesting to his powers of self-repair can slip into a suggestive kind of excess. Such is the case in *Rambo III*, when Rambo removes a wooden spike that has penetrated his body. The insistent return of the camera to close-ups of the wound as Rambo presses the spike slowly through the hole in his flesh conditions a profound unease on the part of the spectator.[28] When Rambo cauterizes the wound, flames leaping straight through him, he embodies for a moment the kind of fiery spectacle more conventionally visited upon his adversaries. In its fascinated attention to the violability of Rambo's body and its exploration of his agony as a kind of orgiastic release, the sequence gestures toward the gendered instabilities animating action cinema and the relationship between moral guilt and masochistic ecstasy that these films otherwise disavow.

In his ability to withstand pain and deny bodily need, Rambo recalls Judith Butler's imperialist subject, who is able to realize his intention in a world hostile to the same, inured to the conditions of precariousness, the physical and social contingencies that constitute human life. In *First Blood*, Colonel Trautman enumerates the deprivations Rambo has been trained to endure ("to ignore pain, ignore weather . . . to eat things that'd make a billy goat puke"), and we are constant witnesses to the ravages he suffers and survives. Rambo's ability to withstand abuse, deny need, and survive independent of social networks participates in the fantasy of sovereignty around which imperialist subjectivity pivots. *Rambo: First Blood Part II* will conclude like a conventional Western: Rambo walks away alone into a vast landscape "where no supporting social network seems necessary."[29]

But it is not simply the case that Rambo's resilience cancels out the spectacle of his wounding or negates the appeal of his vulnerability; indeed, in the context of American culture, the sovereignty of the imperialist subject has depended upon a paradoxical emphasis on its curtailment. Thus the invitation to identify with vulnerability in social as well as bodily registers represents a key feature of late-century action cinema and of the imperialist subjectivity it works to construct. The efficacy of Rambo as a cultural icon—his ability to magnetize cultural attention and investment—is not solely an attribute of the films' fantasies of omnipotence. The insistence and inventiveness with which these films return us to the spectacle of Rambo's wounding attest to the importance of the vulnerability such wounding encodes. While Rambo may embody a denial of precariousness, his appeal is significantly constituted through an insistence upon it.

Rambo's suffering can be understood both as an extension of longstanding melodramatic conventions and as a response to pressures specific to the post-Vietnam era, in which the moral and psychic exhaustion of a failed war couple with economic recession to produce a widespread sense of national malaise. In this first register, the Rambo films rehearse what Jane Tompkins has called the "moral ecstasy" of the Western, in which "the hero is *so right* (that is, so wronged) that he can kill with impunity" (emphasis in original).[30] As Linda Williams similarly argues, heroes in contemporary action blockbusters are identified "not only by their heroic actions but also, first and foremost, by their suffering of some outrage. . . . The hero's suffering seems to earn him . . . the moral right to kill the enemy with impunity."[31] This conjunction of embodied vulnerability and violent agency has a long history in American cinema, as I have argued. In mobilizing this tradition, late-century action cinema draws upon and extends a melodramatic structure of feeling oriented around the attribution of goodness through suffering and the constitution of righteous violence through identification with victimization—a hallmark of imperialist affect.

In the second register, in which Rambo's suffering responds to specific contemporary pressures, we might remember that melodrama emerged historically to address a sense of dislocation, an epistemological rupture in which established ways of knowing are destabilized in the face of profound structural change. The reinvigoration of melodrama in action cinema of the 1980s makes sense in this light. These films address significant social and economic shifts and a feeling of impeded national agency in the aftermath of Vietnam—a wide-scale disruption in the nationalist fantasy of sovereignty that is the fulcrum of imperialist subjectivity.[32]

Like the contemporary discourse of white masculine crisis within which it circulates, the action cinema invites identification with states and conditions of vulnerability and insecurity at a time of social and economic upheaval. We should understand this invitation, like the fantasy of self-extension that Berlant discusses, as broadly issued and received. As in *First Blood*, in which Rambo laments his inability to find even menial work as a civilian despite his elite military training, the action cinema conventionally pairs bodily abuse with social and economic marginalization, constituting the hero's victimization across multiple dimensions. On the one hand, these representations are addressed to the imagination of white men as newly disenfranchised, their authority undercut by economic crisis, the failures of Vietnam, and the liberation struggles of the 1960s and 1970s. On the other hand, Rambo's insecurity also speaks to broader conditions of precarity in the context of post-Fordism, as well as to a general condition of precariousness upon which identification with vulnerability may be based.[33]

In keeping with the affective logic of melodrama, white masculinity itself may be a particularly compelling point of identification in the context of its disappointments, identification with the fantasy of self-extension most inviting and accessible when accompanied by an assertion of its tenuousness. The films propose a melodramatic solution to a contemporary sense of crisis, offering to redress the insecurities of identification with vulnerability through explosive, consuming displays of power.[34] As the tremendous global success of the films suggests, the appeal of identification with this position is not restricted along national lines, but may extend to audiences attuned in a variety of localized ways to conditions of precarity.[35] At the same time, we might consider how the action hero's resilience obscures the structural entrenchments of precarity, with which he at the same time invites identification.

The efficacy of onscreen violence differs across the first two films, however, as each takes a distinct position on the question of guilt and complicity around which the problem of Rambo's moral legibility circulates. In *First Blood*, the impulse both to acknowledge and to bracket Rambo's complicity leads to a degree of instability. Despite Rambo's insistence on his own innocence—"I didn't *do* anything!" he repeatedly asserts—and despite the film's focus on his unjustified persecution, an ambiguity accrues around the image of his violence. Rather than righteously retributive, this violence becomes increasingly hysterical across the course of the film, displaced from its original targets and manifesting instead as a spectacular though increasingly illegible display of destruction. Chong's discussion of the original novel is suggestive in understanding this incoherence, as the novel more directly links Rambo's violence to the moral instabilities of Vietnam. The "smell of death" that travels in the novel through Rambo back to small-town America operates as a condensed signifier of national fallibility and the abuses of institutionalized authority represented both by Vietnam and by racialized state violence.[36]

In the film, this function manifests in the illegibility of Rambo's violence and any moral critique it might levy. The register of this violence shifts from actions we might cast in the mold of self-defense to a broader-based assault; in his final extended rampage, it seems that Rambo exacts revenge on the town of Hope itself. Without dialogue or character development to lend a clear motive, Rambo's violence is noteworthy mostly for its spectacular destructive force. The film revels in this excess but also, through Colonel Trautman's final rejoinders and Rambo's own eventual breakdown, maintains a degree of distance from it. If Rambo is revenging himself upon a nation that would not love or accept him, in destroying the infrastructure of Hope he destroys the very home for which he had longed.

What is striking here is the extent to which this final spectacular rampage fails to suture the pleasures of onscreen violence either to a tightly honed identification with Rambo as their agent or to the recognition of a moral foundation as their cause. In the initial explosive sequence, for instance, Rambo throws his lighter into a pool of gasoline and retreats back into the darkness as flames ignite in the foreground. We then cut to a choppy montage of explosive force and destruction, as the fire engulfs first the army truck Rambo has stolen and eventually the gas station itself. As the screen erupts in flame and smoke, shattered glass and debris, Teasle and his men look on in aghast wonder from inside the police station. Across the ensuing sequence, which intercuts between the police arriving on the scene and the ongoing, spectacular explosions, we see Rambo only once, a shadowy figure cutting briefly across the dark foreground of the frame.

The effect of this sequence is to displace the spectacular display of violence away from the figure of Rambo himself, undercutting any visual or rhythmic sense of his agency. Violence manifests instead as a series of explosive symptoms, an hystericization of Rambo's grief and anger, traveling independently of his direct actions, consuming the screen as it consumes Hope itself. Rambo is not a visual focus; he moves through the sequence as he moves through the townscape, a restless catalyst of destruction. Rather than redress the prior spectacle of his victimization through a reassertion of his mastery, the spectacle of destruction suggests Rambo's intemperance, his inability to direct or contain the violence within him—a violence, as Chong suggests, that carries within it the complex specter of Vietnam.

The failure of *First Blood* to produce Rambo as a site of self-mastery qualifies the film's production of imperialist affect, to the extent that self-mastery is a precondition of sovereignty. As Chong articulates, "the action film . . . depends on the ability of narratives to make causal links between agents and their actions, thus imputing agency to the transformation of situations and circumstances."[37] *First Blood* fails to secure such a link, and although Rambo's hysterical grief is re-embodied in his final breakdown in Colonel Trautman's arms, his plaintive paean to his sense of powerlessness further underscores the frustration of his agency. The mournful note upon which the film ends, as the closing credits roll over a frozen image of Rambo as he's taken into custody, emphasizes the futility of his actions even as it supports his pathetic status. The fantasy of mastery upon which imperial subjectivity is founded is thus largely evacuated here. To borrow Chong's description from another context, this closing image "does not salvage American subjectivity in the face of defeat; it embraces defeat as the very condition of American subjectivity, after Vietnam."[38]

It is this unfixed quality of guilt and innocence that *Rambo: First Blood Part II* will move to stabilize, tightly choreographing its violence to construct a sense of Rambo's powers of self-extension and redirecting its aggressions along sharper and more explicitly nationalist lines. The pyrotechnic chaos that concludes the first film is recomposed in sequences emphasizing the precision of the hero's violence and its awesome, spectacular effects. Rambo's will is visualized as a controlled force of destruction, its target not small-town America but Soviet soldiers and their Vietnamese allies. Violence is reconstituted as both pleasurable and righteous in this context, addressing "American spectators weary of failures of the body incontinent exhibited in the Vietnam War" and of the cinematic echoes of these failures across the 1970s and early 1980s.[39]

Rambo is insistently visceral in its address, assaulting the spectator through a barrage of visually and aurally aggressive techniques, even as these same techniques prop up a narcissistic identification with Rambo's omnipotent violence. The film style *Rambo* consolidates is constituted through the amplification of both sound and image, the increasing pace of editing (in which "rapid multiple cuts become a cinematic analogue to the represented action"), and an emphasis on special effects, among other features.[40] The success of what William Warner has referred to as the film's "bracing and inventive spectacularizing of action" would directly impact the development of action cinema going forward, heralding the return to prominence of the attraction.[41]

Into sequences already oriented around spectacular representations of motion and violence, *Rambo* incorporates an aggressive direct address, both in shots nominally motivated by the position of Rambo's onscreen targets and in less mediated instances of violent action oriented toward the camera. The insistent appeal of the attraction highlights the complex pleasures of a spectator position that seeks to be, like its early predecessor, simultaneously shocked and reassured. Thus the thrill of mediated violence—and the imperialist affect it here supports—continues to rely upon an identification with both omnipotence and vulnerability, coded through formal as well as narrative registers.

While First Blood's emphasis on Rambo's dejection largely falls away in this second film, the narrative and visual insistence on Rambo as the victim of past and present abuse continues, encouraging pathetic identification with a figure whose rampages become increasingly lethal and destructive. As Linda Williams has aptly noted, this second film "rechannels" the pathos of the first into action, "as Rambo is given his chance to 'win this time.'"⁴² Winning in this context does not imply an eradication of vulnerability, however, but the reintegration of vulnerability with a position of mastery within an ongoing dialectic of pathos and action. While the pleasures of action unravel in First Blood, moving from the pyrotechnic chaos of the final rampage to the pathetic spectacle of Rambo weeping in his colonel's arms, in Rambo the identification with vulnerability lends a moral and affective charge to the identification with lethal violence. Whereas in First Blood Rambo is responsible for the death of only one man (and that by accident), in Rambo he blithely cuts down dozens. That we are not invited to feel any ambivalence or remorse before the spectacle of these killings is owing to this reintegration, which constitutes Rambo's violence as a felt good, in keeping with the conventions of sensational melodrama.

One aspect of this shift is the emergence of the prisoners of war Rambo has returned to Vietnam to rescue; they grant to his mission a stamp of moral authority, while in their abjection they deflect the feminized image of weakness away from Rambo himself.⁴³ At the same time, the brutalization of Rambo's own body becomes more extended and intense. His torture is conventionally staged as a crucifixion—his body stripped, stretched, and suspended in leech-infested slime, with his eyes turned mournfully upward, or lashed to an upright bed spring and electrified—bringing an explicit moral valence to the image of his suffering.⁴⁴ Alongside the constitution of Rambo as one who suffers, the brutality of these sequences continues to establish his superhuman toughness, his ability to withstand intense pain without "breaking."⁴⁵

While such sequences constitute Rambo's moral legibility as well as his resilience, their address is nonetheless complex. They are structured to solicit identification with sadistic as well as masochistic positions, as Warner has discussed, placing the spectator in a fluctuating relationship to the spectacle of Rambo's pain—at once aligned with his suffering and, through camerawork and editing, implicated alongside the agents of his torture.⁴⁶ In addition, the sequences highlight the uneasy implications of

Rambo's own positioning as an explicit object of the gaze: he is feminized in his quality of to-be-looked-at-ness even as the genre pivots around the conventionally masculine prerogatives of his action.[47]

The "fascinated unease" these sequences produce lends to Rambo's subsequent show of violence a quality of catharsis, intensifying the felt good of this violence as it releases the spectator from the instabilities of this sadomasochistic circuit into a more unified identification with Rambo as a site of agency. At the same time, the spectacle of destruction (like the scene of torture) pivots around a sadism that a melodramatic logic of virtuous suffering and retributive violence works to contain. The satisfactions of "winning this time" are never separable from the sadomasochistic economies of such films but are constituted through the ordering of these economies in accordance with the broader conventions of melodrama, an ordering that animates and authorizes the exuberant, cathartic pleasures of screen violence. *Rambo*'s ability to redress the uneasy spectacle of its hero's torture through spectacle of another kind arguably accounts for its tremendous success, a success that helped inaugurate the era of big-budget action as the most profitable and popular of Hollywood genres.

Comparing the explosive violence of this second film to its hysterical articulation in the first is instructive in this regard. Unlike the final rampage of *First Blood*, the violence of *Rambo* is intricately linked to the figure of Rambo himself. Here we move from a close-up of an explosive arrow tip as Rambo twists it into place, to a close-up of Rambo's face as he looks up with a glower, to a medium shot of his well-muscled body as he pulls back the bow, to a rack focus shifting quickly from a close-up of Rambo's eye as he takes aim to another close-up of the arrow head, now pointed directly at the camera (fig. 19). The lethality of Rambo's gaze, which this sequence works to construct, is confirmed in the ensuing cut from a behind-the-shoulder shot of Rambo letting loose the arrow, to the fiery engulfment of the mise-en-scène below (figs. 20–21). Such sequences produce the anticipation of violence through an alignment with Rambo's gaze and a fetishization of his body, highlighting the paradoxical implication of the camera as it both empowers and objectifies the hard body of action cinema.

Onscreen violence operates as a signifier of Rambo's powers of self-extension across the sequence; every new explosion is preceded by the image of Rambo twisting on an arrowhead, taking aim, or letting loose the bow. The spectacle of destruction is constructed as a direct expression of Rambo's intent and skill, his willingness and ability to destroy. The steady rhythm of the sequence as it alternates between the image of Rambo—calm and focused in his preparations, as the soundtrack quiets and the camera slows—and the fiery destruction below produces a sense of both

Figs. 19, 20, 21. *Rambo* invites pleasure in the scene of violence through identification with the lethality of the hero's gaze and the efficacy of his intent in a powerful example of imperialist subjectivity onscreen. *Rambo: First Blood*, Part II (Cosmatos 1985).

anticipation and inevitability, constituting his violence as an inexorable force, its arrival inescapable, its precision unerring.

In contrast to the pyrotechnic chaos of the first film, it is precisely the image of control that the second film works to construct, emphasizing the satisfactions of an identification with Rambo's aggression. As Warner suggests, sadistic infantile energies animate the violence here, as "these scenes of destruction realize a child's fantasy of total control, of effortless mastery of every conceivable impediment to the self."[48] The complete destruction of the enemy—in Butler's terms, the destruction of "the very possibility of a reverse-strike"—is given striking visualization when Rambo fires his arrow at a pursuing Vietnamese soldier and (through a cut that resembles nothing so much as an early trick film) obliterates him into nothingness.[49] Occasional ruptures in conventional continuity—at one moment Rambo appears at the edge of a field, lighting it on fire; in the next moment, he is shooting from the rocks above—also harness the apparatus of the cinema to lend an almost magical quality to Rambo's powers of self-extension.

The specter of Vietnam surfaces here through images recalling news coverage of the war, including canonic still photographs that came to signify the moral reprehensibility of violence. Far from destabilizing or interrupting the representation of violence in *Rambo*, the recirculation of these images within a new sequence of action recasts them as a source of pleasure. Quite strikingly, for instance, the film makes a point of underscoring the inhabitants of a hamlet through which Rambo flees—women, children, a group of monks at prayer, an old man, a baby crying on the soundtrack. The visual emphasis on the villagers as anxious and vulnerable spectators to a set of actions in which they are in no way implicated both refigures wartime military discourse in which the categories of enemy combatant and civilian often merged and replays the image of the Vietnamese village as a site highly vulnerable to U.S. militarized violence.

The spectacular destruction of the hamlet two minutes after Rambo runs through it does not occasion any slowdown in the action. Instead, the panicked soundtrack of the village disappears, along with any images of the villagers themselves, replaced by the cries of the swarming soldiers whom Rambo seeks to repel with his explosive arrows. The film does not hesitate over the image of the immolated soldiers as they run, bodies blazing, from the flaming fields. Rather, this image—which recalls that of the self-immolation of the Buddhist monk Thich Quang Duc and the iconic Nick Ut photograph of Phan Thi Kim Phuc running from the site of a napalm attack[50]—is stitched seamlessly into the sequence, offered as one more detail in the catalog of Rambo's efficacious violence. In both this case and that of the hamlet, civilian casualties are absorbed back into the more normalized image of military casualty, further qualified by the prior spectacle of Rambo's abuse at the hands of both the Vietnamese and the Soviet soldiers.

That these images do not undermine or disrupt the flow of action attests to the success with which the film absorbs the moral crisis of Vietnam into a spectacular display of force and destruction constituted as both right and pleasurable. Despite these images, or indeed through them, *Rambo* moves away from the moral instability of *First Blood*, reconstituting onscreen violence as a site of both moral and visceral satisfaction. While the mass slaughter of the depersonalized swarm of Vietnamese soldiers may discomfit some viewers—and while it is not insignificant to the film's racism that we witness the graphic deaths of only the Vietnamese, though Soviet soldiers are visible across the sequence—the film itself evidences no discomfort here. Instead, the sound and image tracks collude to produce a rhythmically satisfying sequence pivoting around an identification with Rambo and the lethal power of his gaze.

The primary means of weaponizing Rambo's gaze is the Ram-bow itself, a specially designed bow outfitted with explosive arrow tips.[51] Rambo's gaze, which in *First Blood* signified the wounded inner truth of his suffering, is transmogrified through the Ram-bow into a testament to his violent efficacy, his ability to materialize his intentions through the conjoined technologies of cinema and war. Here we appreciate, in Paul Virilio's famous phrasing, "the eye's function being the function of weapon," as the film explicitly aligns Rambo's gaze with its lethal trajectory, recalling familiar conventions of the Western.[52] In *Rambo*, however, the satisfactions of self-extension operate on a different scale; rather than the quick seizure or tumble of a hapless outlaw or Indian, Rambo's intent manifests in spectacular explosions engulfing the film's sound and imagescapes.

Rambo's relationship to technology is deeply paradoxical, however, as has often been noted. On the one hand, in *Rambo*, the technological attractions of screen violence are celebrated as a source of pleasure, morally anchored by Rambo's status as both victim and hero. But while action sequences emphasize how Rambo's body merges with the technology of war—as well as, importantly, with the technology of the cinema—his power is simultaneously proposed as a measure of his distance from and disdain for modern technology.[53] Like the fantasy of manliness animating the discourse of the strenuous life, Rambo's power is understood to derive from his rejection of the modern, signified here by bureaucratic hierarchy, computer technology, and the technicians responsible for managing the mechanisms of both. In contrast, Rambo represents the virtues of the primitive, even as he himself is cast as "a pure fighting machine." His Ram-bow speaks to this paradoxical relationship: it collapses a signifier of Rambo's "nativeness"—in line with his Indian-German descent and his appropriation of guerilla fighting tactics—into a piece of sophisticated military hardware, of which Rambo is in general both an expert handler and, arguably, himself the prime example.

Rambo's uncanny ability to merge with the natural world—another racialized marker of his "native" guerilla expertise—also reflects this paradoxical relationship. His blending into his surroundings constitutes one of the trademark pleasures of the films, as we are invited to guess from what unexpected corner of the mise-en-scène Rambo may next spring to violent action. Indistinguishable from his natural surroundings in one instant, he is lethally distinct in the next.[54] Rambo's celebrated ability to disappear into the landscape of war interestingly reverses the terms of visibility and manliness established in Spanish-American War discourse. While the ability of the Cuban rebels to blend into the terrain was cast as a mark of their racialized inferiority and associated explicitly with cowardice, Rambo's appropriation of guerilla tactics signifies his ability to control the very terms of visibility itself. He appropriates the racialized category of the primitive through his fighting techniques; but, at the same time, his ability to merge with and violently emerge from the mise-en-scène suggests his intimate alignment with the cinematic apparatus, which works to constitute his powers of self-extension.

Rambo's appeal is constituted through his ability to mobilize the technologies of cinema and war toward the production of pleasure, through an invitation to identify with technologically amplified powers of self-extension. As in the early military actualities, the visceral and visual appeals of mobility are central to these pleasures, providing a key feature of the cinematic articulation of imperialist affect. As Warner has argued, in the film's swooping final helicopter ride, in which Rambo triumphantly appropriates the machine that has menaced him, "everything depends upon the mobility of the hero, his control of his own visibility, and his ability to destroy anything that stands in his way."[55] The technological pleasures the film offers—as novel in the 1980s as were the pleasures of onscreen motion in the 1890s—are hereby aligned with Rambo as their agent.

Identification with Rambo thus opens out in a number of different directions: onto the image of the primitive white man as he circulates through the discourse of the strenuous life and into later articulations of white masculine crisis; onto a restabilized image of national mastery and morally authorized aggression; and onto the power of technology itself—weapons of spectacular destruction as well as the cinema's ability to figure them—which both animates and exceeds the image of Rambo's self-mastery. In relation to this last point, action films like *Rambo* may signal a shift away from more tightly embodied modes of identification, or more precisely, may signal a shift toward the coupling of character-based modes of identification dominant in classical Hollywood cinema with other, more loosely embodied registers.

Thus, while *Rambo* pivots on a fantasy of self-mastery along the lines Butler discusses, the cinematic apparatus works to shape this fantasy in ways that move beyond identification with Rambo as the locus of agency, to open out onto identification with the disembodied force and mobility of technological violence itself.[56] To be swept along through time and space, to experience the vertiginous thrill of the helicopter ride alongside the assurance of its control, to identify with the limitless abilities of self-extension fantasized through such action sequences—these are the central pleasures *Rambo* offers. Through such appeals, the film proposes as a solution to "anxiety about American loss (of strength, of the pleasures of mastery, of pre-eminence) . . . the audience's acceptance of our 'natural' place in the machine."[57]

In this compensatory formulation—in which the spectator is invited into an identification with the technological force of destruction as a source of pleasure, one anchored if not fully contained by a moral claim to righteousness—the film anticipates the mediated appeals of war as Butler diagnoses them in the Persian Gulf War six years later. The kind of bomb's-eye view that circulated as shockingly novel in this context would become entirely conventional, of course, as identification with the speed and obliterating force of missiles and bombs comes by the twenty-first century to function as a mainstay in both the imaging and the waging of war.

In its intensification of the sensational address of cinema, *Rambo* returns us to what Matthew S. Buckley has argued is the foundational impulse of melodrama: not, primarily, the recognition of good and evil, but the capacity "to produce affective and emotional sensations of great intensity." In seeking to explain this impulse, Buckley emphasizes the profound and traumatic dislocations that structured the lived experience of contemporary audiences in late eighteenth- and early nineteenth-century France and England and hypothesizes that, for these audiences, melodrama spoke to a heightened need for sensational stimuli. As he describes, the traumas of that age arrived not as a single, cataclysmic upheaval but as "an almost unbearable series of unexpected and uncontrollable political and social conflicts, each seeming to mark a logical endpoint, each leading . . . to a previously unthinkable collapse."[58] For audiences habituated to this extended, agonizing devolution of traditional ways of ordering the world, an intensified mode of dramatic representation was necessary to render a lived experience shaped through radical and ongoing rupture and through newly spectacular (and newly mediated) experiences of violence and war.[59] Thus melodrama turned early not to moral redemption but to "affective redemption and the legitimation of violence as right . . . a world in which moral virtue is safeguarded only by the unhesitating use of murderous force," resulting in "a militant, primarily sensationalist genre of imperial power."[60]

Buckley's discussion is suggestive in contemplating the resurgence of sensational melodrama in action cinema of the 1980s, in which the conventionalization of explosions circulates as perhaps the single most defining feature. As Buckley notes, the "unprecedented force, speed, and intensity" of early theatrical melodrama dovetailed with the development of spectacular war, a relationship also relevant to special effects–laden action cinema of the late twentieth century. Geoff King, in questioning the ubiquity of explosions in this cinema, emphasizes visual and technological factors—the ability of the fireball to materialize "force and intensity" while still allowing for the representation of human action in its path.[61] Though an interesting argument, it leaves unaddressed the question of why the attraction itself enjoys a resurgence in this period. I will return to some of these issues in the Epilogue, but for now it is worth noting that the intensified visceral address of action cinema may speak both to longstanding melodramatic traditions and to a historically specific set of requirements conditioned in part by the intensification of mediated, spectacular war. Under the pressure of this intensification, new pleasures and new modes of identification emerge.

While the Rambo films continue to do the affective work of the Western—welding moral and visceral appeals to construct the felt good of cinematic violence—they also gesture in the direction of things to come. In *Rambo*, identification is solicited both with the morality of violence and with its spectacular technological force. The moral force of melodrama has always been propped up by the affective intensity of other modes of responsiveness. As the action cinema develops, however, the interweaving of moral with visceral satisfactions becomes looser, as the sensational pleasures of the genre circulate with an increasing independence from conventional structures of moral authorization. Thus, as Buckley observes of early melodrama, the moral and affective structures of melodrama may not always align, because "if its moral structure appears to offer a consoling vision, its affective structure fosters instead quite the opposite perspective, encouraging and reinforcing infantile processes of defensive withdrawal and violent projection."[62] The action cinema is fueled by such energies—by fantasies of omnipotence as well as powerlessness—in ways that continue to animate, even as they increasingly exceed, the effort of melodrama to frame them in explicitly moral terms.

Lethal Weapon, Die Hard, and the New Pleasures of Action

The loosening of the conjunction between visceral and moral appeals that the Western did so much to naturalize marks the action cinema as it develops forward from *Rambo*'s tremendous global success. Invigorated by this success, Hollywood would turn out a slew of big-budget, effects-laden features oriented around the violent antics of white male victim-heroes, including the popular and influential *Lethal Weapon* and *Die Hard* films of the late 1980s and early 1990s.[63] Like *Rambo*, these films insist on the generally beleaguered status of their loner protagonists, asserting the social marginalization and ongoing physical abuse of their heroes while binding the cinema's sensational pleasures to their violence. The films' investments in velocity, force, and impact—speeding vehicles and massive pyrotechnic displays, imploding structures and shattering fountains of glass and steel, relentless blasts of gunfire and crashing falls from dizzying heights, all shot and edited to maximize their visceral, kinesthetic impact—highlight the primary importance of sensation to the genre's appeal. Although the moral constitution of violence is not absent from these films, the visceral appeals of action are more central, circulating in excess of and sometimes even in opposition to the genre's moral claims.

Even as they attest to the increasingly spectacular investments of action cinema, however, the *Lethal Weapon* and *Die Hard* films, and those for which they become a template, continue to mobilize conventional structures to authorize their heroes' violence. These are melodramas first and foremost, and operate within longstanding traditions of the form. Producer Joel Silver (responsible for the *Lethal Weapon* franchise and the first two *Die Hard* entries) identifies the foundational melodramatic structure of these films: "There are good guys and bad guys, and the bad guy does bad things, so the good guy chases him . . . at the end of the movie—in this genre of mov-ies—the bad guy loses and the good guy wins. And that has proved to be a commercially viable formula."[64] The formula is a familiar one, of course, and its sensational iteration in late twentieth-century action cinema rehearses scenarios from the earliest blood-and-thunder melodramas onscreen, in which "abundant rapid action, stimulating violence, spectacular sights, and the thrills of physical peril, abductions, and suspenseful rescues" defined the genre.[65] Action cinema incorporates new appeals alongside these familiar pleasures, including humor, the intensification of technologized violence, and an increasingly self-referential relationship to spectatorship itself.

Like the *Rambo* films, the first *Lethal Weapon* (Donner 1987) plays upon the image of the violently unstable Vietnam vet, making the social rein-tegration of this figure a primary narrative project. As in *First Blood*, the mental instability of the vet—here a renegade cop rather than a rootless loner—generates much of the film's action and excitement, as the represen-tation of Martin Riggs (Mel Gibson) allows "the negative ideas about the Vietnam vet (as haunted, 'crazy,' a social cripple) to be assumed and trans-valued, until they become sources of his uncanny strength."[66]

Although Riggs, like Rambo, is an ex–Special Forces soldier, in *Lethal Weapon* the very problematic of Vietnam is disavowed by casting the hero's psychosis not as the result of his military past but as the result of the sudden, violent death of his wife. Trauma and loss are reinscribed at the site of the domestic, and the hero is repositioned less ambiguously as their victim. At the same time that Riggs's military service is figured as incidental to his mental instability, the film casts his adversaries as ex–Special Forces soldiers as well, men whose sadistic perversions are eagerly underscored. This doubling allows for the positive valuation of Riggs's resilience, strength, and lethal resourcefulness, while displacing any implication of his guilt or complicity—a testament to the success of *Rambo*'s recasting of the vet as a hero whose wartime experience endows him with special powers and no particular moral burdens.[67]

A sequence early in the film suggests how the reinscription of trauma at the site of the domestic moves away from the shadow of morally dubious violence to emphasize the hero as victim. Craning down through a dark, rainy night to the window of Riggs's mobile home, we cut in upon the grieving Riggs sitting on his couch, cradling his wedding picture in his lap. As Christmas cartoons babble mindlessly on the television, Riggs takes a loaded pistol first to his forehead, then to his mouth, before breaking down in tears before the photograph. Across the sequence, the lingering, extreme close-ups of the weapon being readied for deployment—the insertion of the bullet into the chamber, the release of the safety, a view directly down the dark barrel of the gun, the finger on the trigger—recall similar shots in the *Rambo* sequence discussed above. Here, however, the protagonist is positioned as the pathetic victim rather than the triumphant agent of this—his own—violence. The sequence ends with Riggs, unable to pull the trigger, crumpled and weeping before his dead wife's image. *First Blood* leaves us with a similarly broken-down Rambo, but *Lethal Weapon* moves from this early scene of hopelessness and despair toward Riggs's social and domestic reintegration and the redirection of his violence toward his adversarial double, the evil Mr. Joshua (Gary Busey) of the aptly named Shadow Company.[68]

A particular racialized dynamic structures the action cinema, which conventionally involves a relay between the white protagonist and his African American buddy or sidekick. This pattern repeats across the *Lethal Weapon* and *Die Hard* films, as many scholars have discussed.[69] The alliance recalls the racial melodramatics of the Cold War Western, in which the hero's increasing alignment with the position of the Indian as a racialized victim secures his own moral authority. In the context of the late-century action cinema, however, the marginalization of the white male hero operates through the denial of any claims to victimization on the part of his African American buddy.[70] That the normative middle-class home into which the undomesticated Riggs is gradually integrated is that of his

African American partner Robert Murtaugh (Danny Glover), for instance, highlights how the marginalization of the white hero pivots on the evacuation of this position by an African American ally, instituted here as a site of social and economic security.

Such appropriations must be shored up by a reassurance of the film's non-racist project, however; hence a cast of Aryan antagonists explicitly or implicitly aligned with the specter of racist violence helps to secure the moral credentials of both the film and its hero. The elisions and refusals animating this logic are expressed in condensed form in an early sequence of *Die Hard: With a Vengeance* (McTiernan 1995), in which Bruce Willis's John McClane is impelled by his sadistic nemesis to don a sandwich board with the inscription "I hate niggers" while parading the sidewalks of Harlem. When he is attacked by a group of neighborhood thugs, McClane occupies a position of victimization even as he embodies, quite literally, an expression of white supremacist hate speech. In staging this scene of ventriloquized bigotry, the film both raises and anxiously disavows the specter of white racism, as McClane is impelled to don the sign by an adversary who is himself mobilizing racism as cover for his purely mercenary intentions.

At the same time, the film is eager to emphasize McClane's vulnerability on the streets of Harlem as constituted through his whiteness, and it will continue to assign him a position of racialized victimization through the introduction of the separatist, race-proud storekeeper Zeus Carver (Samuel L. Jackson), who is reluctantly recruited into the film's buddy role. Zeus's fixation on race will be cast as the source of racialized animosity throughout the film, allowing for the reconfirmation of McClane as a victim of racial intolerance. The film's articulation of the contemporary rhetoric of reverse racism exposes the extent to which an appropriation of racialized victimization continues to underlie the white male hero's marginalization, rendering his claims to moral authority legible while evacuating the institutionalized history of racism itself.

Although pathos and victimization continue to play a role in these films, new affects also surface to constitute the felt good of cinematic violence. In contrast to Rambo's stony solemnity, the manic capers of *Lethal Weapon*'s Riggs and the incessant wise-cracking of *Die Hard*'s McClane provide trademark attractions of the genre, essential to their tone and rhythm.[71] If the satisfactions of Rambo's violence relied upon the steady alternation of shots of Rambo taking aim with shots of the explosive impact of his actions, violence in these later films often takes the structure of a joke, with the lethal dispatches delivered as the ultimate punch line. While the Cold War Western introduced shame into the affective register of sensational melodrama, mobilizing it to reference and redress the moral culpability of its hero, late-century action cinema integrates humor as a central aspect of its appeal, signaling the ascendance of pleasures less tightly secured by earlier structures of moral authorization.

While this development references and amplifies conventions of the Western, in which the hero's dry wit is mobilized to underscore the potency of his violence, the action cinema's more explicit integration of humor with extreme violence marks a significant shift. Marsha Kinder suggests, for instance, that the association of violence with humor in the anti-Westerns of the late 1960s and 1970s generates guilt and a degree of self-conscious discomfort.[72] In late-century action cinema, in contrast, the comic representation of violence is significantly stabilized. As Leo Charney and others have suggested, humor both manages and intensifies the eruption of violent action here, minimizing it through the pretense of levity while accentuating its startling intensity and brutality through contrast.[73] As the integration of humor and violence is itself conventionalized, however, rather than simply a sense of contrast, the genre constructs an affective resonance between them.

The action cinema's ironic, self-mocking tone, its pastiche of earlier genres, its spectacular intensification of violence, and its investment in style over narrative substance have been read as symptoms of its postmodernism, signaling an evacuation of the category of the moral itself.[74] While this reading might be seen as resonant with my own, to argue that the moral foundation of violence is less central to the constitution of the action cinema's pleasures is not to suggest that it falls away entirely. Indeed, despite the integration of humor and a self-conscious irony into the genre, melodramatic structures continue to shore up the goodness of protagonists and to animate identification with their violence.

To represent this violence apart from such structures of moral authorization would be to offer sadism as a much more explicit point of identification. Instead, though its pleasures run along sadistic (as well as masochistic) currents, the action cinema works to manage and direct these currents in particular ways. Meanwhile, the narrative emphasis on the unrepentant sadism of the films' antagonists both acknowledges and seeks to manage the hero's (and the genre's) own sadistic appeal by assigning it elsewhere. That the sadism of these antagonists is frequently underscored by their failed attempts at humor—that their jokes are not funny highlights the status of their violence as pathological—attests to how humor has come to function as an arbiter of righteous violence in this context. Thus, the genre does not evacuate its moral claims or move entirely away from conventional melodramatic structures to make them. Rather, an alternate set of appeals ascends alongside these structures, namely, humor and, as suggested by *Rambo*, an intensified identification with the force of technological violence itself.

The final action sequence of *Die Hard 2* (Harlin 1990) highlights how humor can operate within conventional scenarios of victimization while amplifying the pleasures of technologized violence as a point of identification. A battered and bloodied John McClane has been thrown off the wing of a taxiing airplane and lies writhing on the runway. The plane carries a renegade band of paramilitary fanatics and the South American dictator they have freed from U.S. custody; having shut down all runway lights and taken over air traffic control, the men have willfully endangered the lives of hundreds of airline passengers. From his prone position, and with his characteristic underdog tenacity and calm under pressure, McClane flips open and ignites his lighter (fig. 22). The soundtrack's insistent crescendo—mounting in the face of the bad guys' impending escape—comes to a sudden, momentary halt. The pause is punctuated by a close-up of McClane's bloodied face as he utters his trademark retort, "yipee ki-yay, mother fucker," and hurls the lighter into the plane's trail of leaking jet fuel. As the soundtrack returns to its pulsing crescendo, the flames race down the snow-covered runway and jump to the tail of the plane just as it lifts off the ground, incinerating it in a massive, orange fireball (fig. 23).

An emphasis on McClane's wit and his vulnerability at this decisive moment of his most deadly action works to intensify pleasure in the image of destruction itself. The high-angle shots of McClane lying bloodied on the runway visually reaffirm this vulnerability, even as the sequence constructs his omnipotence, rehearsing melodrama's conventional doubling of the positions of victim and agent. In *First Blood*, the similar tossing of a lighter into a trail of gasoline served to displace the explosive spectacle of violence away from the figure of Rambo himself, suggesting the hysterical instability of his violence; in *Die Hard 2*, in contrast, the suturing of McClane as a spectator to his own destructive agency sets up a very different kind of affective relay. As the sequence cuts from shots of the plane exploding spectacularly against the night sky to a close-up of McClane's giddy delight in its image, his position as a spectator is offered as an explicit point of identification—a reflection and confirmation of our own (fig. 24). Rather than undercutting a sense of agency, the sequence underscores McClane's power, asserting his almost magical ability to overcome barriers of space and time to impel the destruction of an accelerating, airborne adversary while lying wounded in the snow—a position of passive omnipotence that mirrors the spectator's own narcissistic identification with the cinematic spectacle of destruction.

Although such structures work to direct pleasure and aggression along particular lines, the spectacular appeals of action cinema always function in excess of these directives. At the same time that it celebrates the pleasures of violence as spectacle, for instance, the sequence above gestures toward

Figs. 22, 23, 24. The action cinema increasingly offers the position of the spectator as a point of explicit identification—the hero as gleeful witness to his own spectacular powers of destruction. *Die Hard 2* (Harlin 1990).

more unstable implications circulating through and around the image of destruction. These are implications that *Die Hard 2* invites by intercutting interior shots of the getaway plane into the final sequence, highlighting how the melodramatic conventions of suspense can pivot on a fleeting

identification with the imperiled position of antagonists as well as protagonists. Shots of the fire as it races down the runway and roars through
the plane are intercut with shots of the plane's occupants, at first unaware
and then increasingly panicked, as flames consume the cabin. The reaction
the film invites in the seconds before the plane's spectacular explosion is
thus an unstable one, pivoting on a sadistic identification with the force of
violence—stabilized if not fully secured by the status of the doomed men as
"bad guys"—as well as an identification with the vulnerable position of the
men themselves.

Identification with vulnerability is frequently incorporated into action
sequences through subjective point-of-view shots from the position of
enemy targets as lethal projectiles race toward them, raising questions
about the fluid circuits of identification that structure the "thrills" of action
cinema more generally. In such shots, the position of the enemy and that
of the audience briefly coalesce through the aggressive direct address of
the attraction. The visceral appeal of such sequences is intensified through
identification with the position of the enemy as a site of embodied vulnerability, even as the pleasure of such sequences conventionally culminates
in the spectacular destruction of that very position. This point suggests
the complex and myriad ways in which action cinema solicits identification with vulnerability, not simply through narrative and thematic means,
but also—as I have argued—through the persistence of the attraction as a
mode of address. Both when shots of objects moving forcefully and directly
toward the audience are assigned as subjective point-of-view shots, and
when such shots are stitched into action sequences without assignment to
any onscreen character, an identification with vulnerability is solicited at
the level of film form itself, both in accordance with and in excess of narratively conditioned modes of identification.

Similar kinds of instability are found in images of spectacular violence.
In *Rambo*, this violence is explicitly aligned with the hero's powers of self-
extension, but bad guys, too, have the means of spectacular destruction at
their disposal. Indeed, in *Die Hard 2*, of four sequences featuring the action
cinema's requisite explosions, three are attributed to bad guys. In the first
of these, McClane's failure to avert a passenger jet's disastrous crash landing ends in a fiery inferno. As the plane bursts into flame, the film cuts
from the explosion to zoom in on horrified reaction shots from each of the
ineffectual good guys, making explicit the significance of the disaster as,
precisely, spectacle, something to be witnessed, to be watched.

Thrown back into the snow by the force of the explosion, McClane lies
sobbing on the runway in a close-up that matches the later image of his
giddy pleasure. The trauma here is presented in spectatorial terms: the
onscreen characters are made to watch without the power to change the

course of events. The final sequence will work to supplant this trauma, reproducing the earlier spectacular explosion but shifting the roles by filling the plane with bad guys and casting its destruction as the heroic work of McClane himself. The earlier spectacle provides an affective foundation for the final one, animating identification with McClane's virtue as well as his powerlessness, which the latter sequence will redress by restoring him to agency as well as, importantly, to pleasure.

We might read the destruction of the passenger jet as fixing the identification of the bad guys, attesting to the sociopathology of their ringleader, Colonel Stuart (William Sadler), and intensifying an emotional investment in his destruction. It is important to note, however, that pleasure in the image of spectacular violence may exceed these structures. As Fred Pfeil has argued, Stuart's orchestration of the plane crash evidences an efficacy lacking in the film's official authority figures; his "ability to lay down the Law, be obeyed, and be effective" aligns him with no one so much as the imperialist subject himself.[75] Thus we might consider how the spectacle of destruction may animate identification with the aggressive force of violence and the fantasy of self-extension it visualizes, even when this identification runs in opposition to the trajectory of narratively based affiliations.

As has often been asserted, the appeals of spectacle are distinct from those of narrative, opening out in different directions, although such appeals still represent "sedimented ways of seeing," as Dana Polan has usefully asserted.[76] In this respect, the film's impulse to restage the earlier explosion as a site of pleasure through which moral and visceral satisfactions realign may be read as the impulse to stabilize attractions that always exceed the moral dictates of narrative. *Lethal Weapon*, too, evidences this impulse toward realignment, as when Murtaugh revels before the fiery wreckage of the would-be getaway car of Shadow Company's General (Mitchell Ryan) as it explodes in a spectacular, heroin-filled cloud. Murtaugh's righteous pleasure in this explosion can be seen to replace an earlier, less stable instance of spectatorial glee, in which four six-year-old boys stand in appreciative awe before the flaming inferno of a house in which, incidentally, their neighbor has just been incinerated. ("Do it again, do it again!" they cry, echoing the genre's own reiterative compulsions.)[77]

Against the instabilities of pleasure and identification, action cinema works to anchor its affective relays through the conventional narrative structures of melodrama. A pathos-infused coda follows the final spectacular explosion in *Die Hard 2*, for instance, in which the battered McClane stumbles through the disaster scene desperately calling for his wife, Holly (Bonnie Bedelia), whose position among the imperiled passengers has provided emotional ballast throughout the film. In place of the more unruly attractions of the preceding violence, the scene offers McClane as the locus of a stabilized and more "mature" pleasure, signified through the reunion of the heterosexual couple and the resurrection of home this union encodes. Holly's presence works to frame McClane's violence in the conventional terms of rescue; he calls her name from the runway as he rocks like a baby with delight at the sight of the exploding plane, whose flaming path will now serve as the landing lights for Holly's imperiled aircraft.[78] In the context of a franchise that mocks the very pretense of domestic security, both familial and national, the impulse to play this final reunion fairly straight is conditioned at least in part by McClane's prior glee—a sadistic delight whose aggressions the sentimental coda works to recontain.[79]

There's No Place Like Home: *Falling Down* and the Subject of Imperiled Privilege

As I have argued, an identification with both omnipotence and vulnerability structures action cinema's appeal. The heroes of this cinema are at once the most masterful and the most vulnerable of men, and the films invite identification with these positions in ways that both affirm and unsettle narratively conditioned and morally authorized modes of identification. This duality speaks, again, to a central function of sensational melodrama, which renders violence as righteous in relation to a vulnerability that both animates and qualifies this violence. These films work to create and sustain an "affective structure in which we are, on the one hand, victimized and, on the other, engaged in a righteous cause of rooting out terror."[80]

The *Lethal Weapon* and *Die Hard* films conventionalize the conjunction between white masculinity and imperilment. As in *First Blood* and *Rambo*, they figure precariousness in multiple terms, through bodily vulnerability and through their heroes' shaky hold on normative forms of social and economic security. In addition to their social marginalization as loners, the films' protagonists hold a tenuous position in relation to work (as signified by Riggs's jeopardized status in the police department and McClane's disrespected role as a New York City cop in the context of larger bureaucracies of finance, security, and defense) and in relation to family (as signified by Riggs's murdered wife and girlfriend and McClane's insecure relationship to Holly, whose career aspirations constantly draw her away from her husband, creating the conditions for the endangerment of both).

Riggs and McClane represent generalizable conditions of human vulnerability alongside more particular forms of disenfranchisement in the context of late-capitalist America. *Die Hard* is particularly explicit in defining McClane against a host of forces represented in contemporary discourse as a threat to American global and white masculine dominance and authority, most particularly a multinational corporate power associated with both the

foreign and the feminine. As Fred Pfeil has suggested, the particular association of both McClane and Riggs with the inner workings and cordoned-
off, noncommercial spaces of the buildings they inhabit—the air ducts,
elevator shafts, and drippy, pipe-ridden backrooms and basements—aligns
them with an earlier era of industry (even as it speaks to these heroes'
uncanny ability to navigate a new postindustrial world, "their weirdly intimate knowledge of their way around the very spaces they do so much, to
our delight, to destroy.")[81]

These films argue both for the victimized position of white men as a
newly visible—because newly suffering—demographic and for the ongoing status of straight, middle-class white men as the privileged icon of the
American national body, the unmarked center against which a variety
of margins, borders, and peripheries may be defined. That middle-class
white men embody both the condition of precariousness and the means
of its violent redress is relevant to the films' widespread appeal, which is
based in the assertion of vulnerability and victimization and in identification with a historically and formally constituted position of entitlement.
This doubling is emblematic of the discourse of white masculine crisis
more broadly, in which identification with victimization and entitlement
collude.

The film *Falling Down* (Schumacher 1993) is particularly useful in delin-
eating how the white male protagonist is constituted as occupying both
a particular and a highly generalizable position in the landscape of late-
capitalist America. From its hyperbolic opening sequence onward, the film
shuttles between the pathologized perspective of its victimized antihero
(Michael Douglas, the era's poster-boy for beleaguered white masculinity)[82]
and a perspective whose unmarked status, assigned both to D-Fens and to
the film itself, is naturalized in contrast as the site (and sight) of the normal.
Douglas's character is known throughout most of the film only by his
license plate moniker, D-Fens, a reference to the defense industry and to
the notion of imperiled national sovereignty, which the film both endorses
and critiques.

Like *Rambo, Falling Down* was greeted as emblematic of its cultural
moment, its popular success read as a testament to contemporary anxieties
surrounding the displacement of white middle-class men and the attendant threat to American national identity. The film's prominent media coverage highlights the paradoxical function of crisis discourse in recentering
a subject whose marginalization it at the same announces—a function the
film itself repeats.[83] Though many reviewers emphasized the film's reaction-
ary impulses, reading its attitudes as coterminous with those of its paranoid protagonist, others focused on the film as a critique of these attitudes,
albeit a partial and largely incoherent one. Ultimately, however, the film

reinscribes its protagonist's perspective even as it represents this perspective as distorted, emphasizing his marginalization through formal and thematic structures founded upon the assumption of his centrality.

The film traces the violent last day in the life of D-Fens (or Bill Foster, as we come to learn), a divorced and recently laid-off defense industry worker. Its action is set in motion when Bill abandons his car in the midst of rush-hour gridlock and sets off across the urban "jungle" of Los Angeles with the simple declaration that he is "going home."[84] The mounting desperation with which he repeats this mantra as he cuts an increasingly violent swath across the city reflects his growing realization of the impossibility of this return. For, as it is the film's project to assert, Bill's home is a place that no longer exists, if indeed it ever did.

In cataloging the ways in which the space of Los Angeles destabilizes its white middle-class male protagonist, the film plays upon the city's contemporary image as the epicenter of an increasingly globalized, privatized, multicultural America.[85] From its kaleidoscopic, polyglot streets to its lavish, exclusive enclaves, Los Angeles is a space in which the film's Everyman hero—a Cold War caricature of the straitlaced, buzz-cut middle-man whose patriotic stripes are earned working to "protect us from the communists"—is constituted as an intruder. Carved into myriad private fiefdoms lorded over by a host of hostile inhabitants (Latino gangbangers, aggressive panhandlers, wealthy country club snobs), the city offers no refuge to the physically and spiritually exhausted D-Fens, but only endless assertions of his redundancy to its daily machinations.

Likewise, the white picket–fenced house in which his young daughter prepares to celebrate her birthday (its mythic status qualified by its peeling paint and "bohemian" Venice Beach siting) is officially sealed off from him, his ex-wife Beth (Barbara Hershey) having taken out a restraining order against him. As Bill makes his way toward the birthday party uninvited, Beth warns him, "This is not your home anymore." Denied a familial or national space in which he can be "at home," Bill will act out with increasing violence until, pushed to the edge of the continent, he teeters dead off the Venice Pier.

Falling Down is influenced by the Western, and the Western hero, of course, is never at home. Defined through his distance from spaces of domesticity, he is positioned at the margin between home and what is constituted as foreign (and threatening) to it, aligned with the forces of wilderness and savagery even as he sets up to battle these forces. *Falling Down* rehearses this dynamic in D-Fens's violent association with and escalating appropriation of the weapons of his adversaries (a baseball bat, a switchblade, a gym bag full of guns, a bazooka, and ultimately—in a pathetic turn—his daughter's water pistol). Like the traditional Western hero, D-Fens fights in the name of civilization against the savagery of contemporary society as he perceives it; he (like the film) is unable to recognize home in the already inhabited spaces of the city he traverses.

The fantasy and the impossibility of home are ongoing melodramatic investments of the action cinema. Home, as the primary site of loss and longing, is a landscape at once psychic, temporal, and geographic, a space of innocence, order, and security, whose betrayal and violation animate the films' action and violence. The *Rambo* series is explicit in framing the loss of home as a loss of national innocence; a longing for return to home excites Rambo's violent agonies. In the *Lethal Weapon* films, home is signified most explicitly through Murtaugh's suburban colonial (and the nuclear family housed therein), a structure whose idyllic façade masks its essential insecurity. The films underscore the susceptibility of this home to invasion and destruction in what becomes a running joke across the series; it is ruthlessly battered and literally blown apart (or, in a more mundane variation on the theme, overrun with termites). The battery of the house is played for laughs, but the vulnerability of Murtaugh's family serves a more conventional melodramatic purpose, as when the abduction of Murtaugh's daughter and the threat of her sexual assault provide the catalyst for action in *Lethal Weapon*. In *Die Hard* (McTiernan 1988) and *Die Hard 2*, the captivity of McClane's wife serves a similar function, providing the narrative motivation and justification for violence.

More than anywhere, however, the loss of home is registered in the instability of the hero himself. In the *Lethal Weapon* and *Die Hard* films, the abandonment of the protagonist by his wife (whether through death or career ambition) is thematized as the source of the hero's particular anguish and, as an extension of this anguish, of his particular propensity for violence. The disorder produced through this loss is at once social and psychic, signifying both a changing socioeconomic landscape and the unmooring of the hero from traditional structures of patriarchal authority and identity. This unmooring produces both grief (as in the suicidal distress of Riggs) and resentment (as in McClane's complaints over his wife's reversion to her maiden name in deference to her multinational corporate employer). Whereas *Lethal Weapon* emphasizes the loss of home as the source of an agonizing inner disequilibrium—one that covers over and stands in for the emotional trauma of Vietnam—*Die Hard* represents the loss of home as a gendered betrayal associated explicitly with the shifts of global capitalism.[86]

Falling Down makes unusually explicit the extent to which such dislocations relate not simply to a domestic discourse of white masculine crisis, in which the incursions of feminism and multiculturalism impinge upon the institutionalized privileges of white masculinity, but also circulate within a broader discourse of American geopolitical decline. In this context, the loss of home represents a loss, precisely, of the naturalized space of privilege, mobility, and self-extension through which the imperialist sub-ject has been constituted. As Liam Kennedy has argued, in D-Fens's jour-ney across Los Angeles, we can recognize the shadow of familiar narratives of imperial history—which are also narratives of the Western—including "colonization, expansion, regeneration through violence, and dependency upon the racial other."[87] But rather than a fantasy of the sovereign subject of Manifest Destiny, the film traces "an inversion of the national allegory of American expansion," in which Bill's access and mobility are inhibited.[88] Construction crews meet him at every turn, holding up stop signs in his face, and all the spaces he encounters have been territorialized already.

Reading the film alongside other contemporary "requiems for the American Empire," Kennedy suggests the relationship between *Falling Down*'s representation of besieged white manhood and its representation of the disintegration of imperial subjectivity more broadly.[89] Domestic cul-tures and mythologies, he reminds us, are "shaped by the global workings of empire building," and expansionist ideologies undergird the social con-struction of normative masculinity. The invisibility of empire is strongly correlated with the invisibility of whiteness and "has long worked to secure the white male's privileged role of universal subject—at once central and invisible."[90] To the extent that the marking of white male subjectivity as a particular rather than a universalized position challenges this invisibility, the imperialist subject is implicated as well.

Falling Down suggests the role of imperialism in securing the status of the white male as ordinary, although, as Kennedy argues, "even as D-FENS' imperial subjectivity disintegrates the film sustains an imperialist vision of 'the things going wrong' in the society around him."[91] The film inaugu-rates this process in the opening sequence, establishing the terms of Bill's paranoia while distancing itself from them through an emphasis on their distortion. We first hear Bill's heavy, strained breathing over a blackened screen; as the opening credits appear, the camera zooms out from between his lips to track over his sweating face in an extreme, distorted close-up. As we drift out to the grid-locked traffic beyond the claustrophobic con-fines of Bill's car, the distorted image of Bill is echoed all around him. The soundtrack opens up to a montage of Spanish and English talk radio, an angry car phone conversation, and the screams of a busload of rowdy chil-dren, underscored by a high, piercing whistle, percussive beats, and a dron-ing buzz. Through an accelerating tempo, marked by the mounting strains of the percussive score and increasingly rapid cuts between fragmented and distorted images of the occupants of other cars, we are invited—in for-mal and visceral terms—to share in Bill's growing panic.

Bill views his fellow travelers as just so many signs of social and cultural collapse, and by assigning this perspective to him at the moment of his psychological breakdown, the film both defines and distances itself from the imperial subjectivity at its center, whose position it at the same time secures.[92] The coordinates of this collapse are visualized through the terms of gender, race, and ethnicity: the image of the Third World in the First, embodied by a young Latina girl in the car ahead, whose mournful gaze out the back window and blond, blue-eyed doll suggest her own displaced "otherness"; the feminine as a site of dread, suggested in the distorted image of a middle-aged woman applying lipstick in her side-view mirror; two men in a convertible (one feminized in his open-collared shirt and gold chain), shouting across a car phone, their "loudness" an infringement on the space and comfort of others; and the multiracial face of the nation, signified by the students on a school bus draped conspicuously with a massive American flag. The image of the flag recurs across the film, but in this opening sequence defined by Bill's perspective, it serves as an emblem of loss, a loss represented by the distorted faces of a diverse national body—diversity functioning as the very sign of distortion here.

Intermixed with these images are other signs of breakdown and delay: crude bumper stickers, the car's broken air conditioner, lines of grid-locked traffic, sputtering tailpipes, blinking construction lights. The helicopter that rises to dominate the sound mix at its breaking point, the clouds of exhaust that drift through the sequence, and the constitution of racialized otherness as the site of a vague but undeniable dread, all suggest the scene as one of a war zone. Under threat is the presumed mobility of white masculinity itself across the mise-en-scène of a city that is, as Kennedy suggests, "very much an imperial city, economically and culturally formed by the dynamics of American empire building."[93]

If the hyperbolic stylistics of this opening sequence qualify this vision of diversity as a sign of national distortion by positioning it as a symptom of Bill's own imbalance, other sequences work more subtly to reinforce the film's racialized imagination of space and belonging. The film visualizes Bill's alienation, for instance, through a spectacularization of the urban poor—a homeless vet, a street person, an immigrant selling oranges—bodies criminalized and pathologized as the site of difference itself. Rather than locate these bodies within broader social or familial contexts or mobilize their vision as an alternative or competing point of view, the camera isolates these figures within the frame, offering them as spectacles that need no further backstory or explication; they speak, in this context, for themselves as signifiers of the degeneration of the city.[94] Such images are constructed as subjective point-of-view shots, intercut with Bill gazing out at the city. Their stylistic neutrality functions to naturalize the status of Bill's gaze in this context, associating it not with Bill the nascent sociopath but with another Bill who shadows the first throughout the film: Bill the middle-class voyeur.

The ideological particularity of Bill's gaze passes unmarked in this second context; its point of view, one that defines the multicultural space of the city as precisely not the space of home, is normalized through the weight of its ethnographic conventionality. In contrast to the way his own gaze circumscribes and defines its others, the sequence imagines Bill himself as outside the point of view of any onscreen figure. His vision, measured here against the particularity and embodied contingency of others, is aligned with that of the film itself.

The film thus works to recenter the imperialist subject, whose presumed displacement provides its thematic content but whose ongoing assumption organizes its perspective. We might think of this perspective along the lines of the First Worldism that Judith Butler discusses in *Precarious Life*, a position here posited as under threat even as the film works actively to reproduce and naturalize its ordering of the world, its mechanisms of framing, the experiences it constitutes at its center. To the extent that a decentering of this First Worldism is marked precisely at the site of its pathologization, we might consider—along with Butler—how this decentering is itself visualized as a kind of wounding, a site of pathos, a loss to be mourned (and, as I shall argue, ultimately redressed).

The public park sequence midway through the film provides another example of how these strategies pathologize the city and its inhabitants. The sequence is particularly significant in relation to the presentation of Bill as a kind of populist Everyman hero, "an ordinary man at war with the everyday world," because the park represents the only instance of a noncommercial public space within a film that seems to decry the privatization and territorialization of space itself.[95] Rather than a site of community or democratic possibility, however, the park (like the traffic jam) is represented as a site of urbanized degeneration and decay, underscoring diversity itself as a condition of unsavory proximity. This vision is presented in a sequence preceding Bill's introduction to the scene through alternating shots that cut between close-ups of children frolicking on the playground and images of poverty, homelessness, and disease: a man crumpled against a pole holds a sign that reads "We are dying of AIDS, please help us"; another in a wheelchair holds a sign that reads "Homeless vet need food need money"; a man and woman fight over a shopping cart of cans as police intervene. Rather than Bill's subjective view, this montage naturalizes the very terms of imperial paranoia that the film elsewhere assigns to Bill's distorted vision.

The oscillation between the representation of Bill, on the one hand, as an Everyman whose unmarked vision echoes the film's own and, on the other, as a particularized subject whose distorted outlook casts the decentering of imperialist subjectivity as a site of pathology informs the film on

other levels as well. It finds a formal rhyme in the long, high-angle establishing shots and the off-center, drifting close-ups that constitute the film's
visual approach to Bill, "pushing him in our face one minute, dissolving
him in the Brownian movement of the street in the next."[96] Bill's Everyman
credentials are nominally based upon his status as a citizen and, most
significantly, a consumer, as in the famous Whammyburger sequence, in
which Bill rails against the substandard fast food experience. However, the
implicit racialized and gendered coordinates of this position are suggested
from the opening sequence onward. While the Whammyburger sequence
offers D-Fens's populist appeal free from any racialized taint, for instance,
his earlier violent encounter with a Korean shopkeeper has already underscored the racist, anti-immigrant animosity that informs the discourse of
consumer rights he mobilizes.[97]

Nonetheless, the film offers Bill's status as a citizen-consumer as a point
of identification; we are invited to take pleasure in Bill's violent defense
of his rights and to identify with a sense of their wrongful curtailment.
This process is supported by the construction of Bill as a site of "ordinariness," which is to say, a site of naturalized access and mobility; as Richard
Dyer argues, the film represents "both extreme whiteness, ambivalently
perceived, and ordinary whiteness, that is, whiteness as ordinariness."[98]
Identification is thus invited *both* with the white male protagonist as a
representative national subject—a subject constituted through the endow-
ment of particular rights and privileges—*and* with the notion of this subject's decentering. The film's "confusions of agency and powerlessness"
resonate with the appeals of action cinema more generally.[99] They draw
upon the contemporary audience's very real identification with precarity,
while mobilizing a fantasy of self-extension, a dynamic supported by the
long melodramatic tradition of articulating American national identity as
founded in both victimization and violence.

Blocked in this attachment to the fantasy of privilege and its curtailment
is a recognition of the unequal allocation of rights within a politics and
history of exclusion and the racism and xenophobia underwriting this allocation. Instead, the assertion of Bill's rights and their denial solicits identification with Bill himself as a site of institutionalized neglect. To secure
this marginalized position requires, as in *Lethal Weapon* and *Die Hard*,
its evacuation by an African American ally. Thus the space of "whiteness
as ordinariness" paradoxically relies upon an alignment with blackness,
where blackness operates as the culturally legible site of marginalization
(a site both mobilized and denied through Bill's appropriation of it). While
the representation of "extreme whiteness" is particularized through its
association with racially motivated hostility and violence—emphatically
embodied in the homophobic, misogynistic, racist, and anti-Semitic

neo-Nazi surplus store owner Nick—"ordinary whiteness" relies upon an identification with the position of racialized victimization itself.

This alignment with African American boys and men operates across the film, offering Bill rare moments of connection. In the opening sequence, for example, the steady, contemplative gaze of a young African American boy on the school bus provides the only point of quiet and stillness. This fleeting sense of allegiance is repeated during the Whammyburger episode, when an African American boy is the only patron brave enough to raise his hand in answer to the rampaging Bill's query about the substandard burger he's been served, and at a construction site, when a boy on his bike pauses to give Bill instructions on the use of his bazooka (uttering an awestruck, "Cool, man!" when Bill fires it).

This connection manifests most significantly in Bill's brief communion with an African American protester—a man dressed, as has frequently been observed, as Bill's double. As he pickets a bank that has denied him a loan, he carries a sign that reads "Not Economically Viable," a phrase that Bill will later repeat in respect to his own downsizing. In the midst of encounters based around hostility and aggression, the shared moment between Bill and the protester is marked out for our attention. As the squad car carrying away the protestor lurches into the center of the frame and pauses, the man's face framed by the open car window, he beseeches Bill, "Don't forget me." Bill solemnly nods. The irony of the moment is considerable, as Kennedy has suggested, as it is precisely upon such an amnesia that the film's construction of white victimization is founded.[100] This connection and its paradoxical legitimation of Bill's grievances operate in explicit contrast to his encounters with the Latino gangbangers and the Korean shopkeeper, who, in keeping with anti-immigrant discourse of the 1990s, embody the breaching of national integrity and the decentering of the imperialist subject himself.[101]

Even as *Falling Down* works to naturalize its vision of whiteness as ordinariness, the film makes gestures toward a critique of the action cinema's conventional pleasures and the extent to which identification with white male victimization serves as their impetus. Stylistically, it eschews the visceral, kinetic satisfactions of accelerated action in favor of a languid pace calibrated to the slow burn of Bill's resentment. In contrast to the explosive spectacles and rapidly edited, fast-paced violence of the *Rambo*, *Lethal Weapon*, and *Die Hard* films, *Falling Down* favors long takes and a drifting camera that circles slowly, taking in the quiet menace of its hero. The film's style has been described as "queasy" or "nauseous," suggesting both the visceral and the moral instability of its perspective.

The representation of Beth as a vulnerable damsel in distress replays certain conventions of melodrama, but the film departs from the dominant rhythms of the form even when melodramatic structures of parallel action are mobilized. In a sequence leading up to the drive-by shooting of Bill by the Latino gangbangers he has beaten, for instance, Bill menaces Beth over a pay phone while the avenging gang approaches. The sequence shuttles between three shots: Beth, nervous and alarmed; Bill, focused on Beth and unaware of the approaching danger; and the gang members, armed and eager as they move in for the attack. The doubled position of Bill as simultaneously victim and victimizer intensifies and confounds more conventional circuits of identification and suspense; the increasingly claustrophobic framing of Bill's face on the phone with Beth—her anxiety mounting—underscores his own status as threat, while cuts to the gang-bangers' approach emphasize Bill's vulnerability. The sequence renders our identification with Bill as fundamentally unstable; we can neither comfortably inhabit nor fully withdraw from it.

In undermining any stable identification with Bill, the film undercuts the conventional rhythmic satisfactions of violence, refusing or extending only partially the conjunction of visceral with moral thrills. Long takes invite identification with Bill's victims as they lie wounded and cowering under his gaze, while Bill himself takes a smug satisfaction in their condition. His sarcasm is offered as literally and figuratively off-beat. For example, after firing point-blank into the leg of one of the gang members as he lies face down in a pool of blood amid the wreckage of a fatal car crash, Bill offers as a parting shot, "Take some shooting lessons, asshole." Rather than underscoring the status of violence as a punch line, the quip serves as a symptom of Bill's psychosis, a reaction confirmed by the horror of the onscreen spectators. Though the crash is the result of the gang's vicious drive-by attack, the sequence works against any easy pleasure in Bill's shooting of the injured man. Alternating between high-angle close-ups of the gangbanger's upturned face as he begs for mercy and low-angle shots of Bill aiming his gun down at the incapacitated man, it highlights both the power and the sadism of Bill's position, casting an ironic shadow across the notion of his decentering (fig. 25).[102]

Despite such sequences, reports of wildly enthusiastic responses to Bill's violent outbursts circulated widely as part of the film's contemporary mythos, and criticism often pivoted around the question of audience pleasure. Conventional satisfactions do persist in *Falling Down*, as the film's attitude toward violence, like its attitude toward Bill himself, vacillates between "ordinary" generic pleasures and a queasier impulse toward critique.[103] The calm confidence with which Bill dispenses his brutal correctives operates within the conventions of the action hero, for instance, even as it hints at the sociopathic constitution of this figure. In contrast to the destruction of the Korean shopkeeper's store or the shooting of the

Fig. 25. In the queasiness of its representation of D-Fens, *Falling Down* hints at the aggression animating the conventional spectacle of righteous retributive violence. *Falling Down* (Schumacher 1993).

Latino gangbanger, other encounters (Bill's assault on a public phone booth and his punching out of a profane road-rager) are presented in snappy, abbreviated form, their staccato violence and dry wit restoring the genre's conventional imbrication of humor and violence. Similarly, the audience is invited to enjoy the spectacle of Bill using a bazooka to blow up what he deems to be unnecessary roadwork (an enjoyment both confirmed and parodied in the appreciative reaction of Bill's young interlocutor). Here the film plays upon the "visceral satisfaction at seeing life's little irritations resolved swiftly and violently," in ways that cover over—again—the white supremacist foundations of Bill's resentments, ironically inviting identification with his position of privilege and the powers of self-extension it entails through an assertion of their frustration.[104]

Although the film refuses to authorize Bill's actions in full, it nonetheless concludes conventionally, with a resuscitated image of redemptive violence and the poignant fantasy of home. Against the queasy implications of the powerful if partial identification with Bill, the film offers a kinder, gentler incarnation of white masculine crisis and redemption in the figure of Martin Prendergast (Robert Duvall), a police detective on his last day on the job, who tracks Bill's movements across the film and will kill him at its close.[105] Prendergast's plight, including his loss of job and family, in many ways parallels Bill's own, and the film sets him up explicitly as Bill's double.

In contrast to the film's vacillating attitude toward Bill, Prendergast travels a more conventional path from browbeaten nice guy to take-charge avenger. While Bill rails against the incivilities of daily life and the inconstancy of institutional rewards, Prendergast takes these obstacles in stride, countering a variety of affronts with patience, humor, and forbearance. It is Prendergast, as Dyer has argued, who "resecures the centrality—the invisibility, the ordinariness—of the white male."[106] In the end, he will assert himself against his wife's relentless nagging, cuss out his derisive boss on live television, and take up the role of paternal counselor to Bill's ex-wife and daughter. Through his transformation, the film reaffirms the generic myth of regeneration through violence and restores at least in part the conventional pleasures of watching a beleaguered protagonist violently redeemed.

Like so many Westerns, *Falling Down* ends on a note of pathos as well as redemption.[107] Among the film's many misrecognitions, the most poignant is articulated in the final stand-off on the pier, when Bill asks in blinking disbelief, "I'm the bad guy? How'd that happen? I did everything they told me to. Did you know I build missiles? I help to protect America."[108] Though Prendergast responds with a regretful affirmative, both the intermittent pleasures of Bill's violence and the pathos of his death cast doubt on his status as "the bad guy," suggesting this as a final, fatal misrecognition. In the tradition of the Western, Bill is most compelling at the moment of his departure: after Prendergast takes his reluctant shot, we are offered the slow-motion image of Bill—with a pathetic squirt of his water pistol—tumbling backward over the edge of the pier. The camera lingers on the ocean as it consumes him, the soundtrack swelling up in melancholy lament. His death is offered as a confused protest over the displacement of the imperialist subject himself; we are encouraged to recognize in Bill (rather than in the many folks he menaces) the film's true victim.

If, ultimately, the project of the film is "to turn a sociopath into a martyr," the fantasy of home is key to this alchemy.[109] Unlike *The Searchers*, however, where the hero recedes in the final shot from an idealized domestic space that his violence has worked to secure, home is positioned in *Falling Down* as a site of both violence and delusion. Nonetheless, the film in its last moments returns to an old home movie, with its reinscription of both the fantasy of home and the poignancy of its loss. Its searching final shot echoes and intensifies Bill's insistent longing ("I'm going home!"), replaying to an emptied-out room the emptied-out image of a happy nuclear family that, though it never existed as such—and indeed, the more so for our knowledge of this fact—retains all the pathetic force of melodrama. The camera floats like a ghost into the little house, drawing nearer and nearer to the television screen as it replays the wavering, unsteady picture of Bill and his family, until the edges of the screen disappear and the washed-out image of Bill's face—a close-up of a close-up—is offered as the film's own look, its distortion not grotesque, as at the film's opening, but poignant in its simultaneous and impossible distance and proximity (fig. 26).

Fig. 26. *Falling Down* comes to rest in closing on a home video image of home, its distortions offered through the lens of pathos rather than paranoia. *Falling Down* (Schumacher 1993).

Beyond Forgiveness: *Unforgiven* and the Limitations of Critique

Another film released around the time of *Falling Down*, Clint Eastwood's Oscar-winning *Unforgiven* (1992), provides a fitting coda to the question of moral queasiness and turns us back explicitly to the terrain of the Western, upon which—in some sense—we began. The film, credited alongside Kevin Costner's *Dances with Wolves* (1990) with a late-century revitalization of the Western, suggests both the moral instability surrounding generic representations of violence and the extent to which this instability and the critique it maps may nonetheless fail to interrupt the pleasures of the form.[110]

Drawing on the elegiac Westerns of the early 1960s, *Unforgiven* is both revisionist and deeply nostalgic, refusing to authorize fully the violence of its protagonist while evidencing an unabated longing for the conventional modes of authority he represents. Like *Falling Down*, *Unforgiven* exhibits both the impulse of critique and the limitations of this impulse, concluding like the former on a note of both pathos and violent regeneration. Debate on the film's generic and ideological significance has focused on the question of this ending and the extent to which it is felt to solicit or to frustrate an identification with the Eastwood hero. For, despite a critical reception that celebrated the film's success in complicating longstanding generic conventions, *Unforgiven*, in its final moments, circles back around to the very pleasures it has sought to trouble, underscoring their persistence and the extent to which moral authority may have become a gratuitous aspect of their appeal.

The film traces the journey of widower William Munny (Clint Eastwood), a repentant retired gunfighter laboring as an unprosperous hog farmer, who is seduced into one last bounty hunt by the promise of quick money and the possibility of a better life for himself and his two young children. Much has been made of our visual introduction to the middle-aged Munny as he scrambles about in the hog slime in a futile effort to separate out sick hogs from the healthy ones. The disappointment of generic expectation that this introduction represents is made immediately explicit: the offscreen voice of the young Schofield Kid (Jaimz Woolvett) exclaims, "You don't look like no rootin', tootin', son-of-a-bitchin' cold-blooded assassin." The Kid himself, who arrives seeking a partnership with the legendary gunfighter, likewise represents a disappointment. Although he is introduced through visual conventions that suggest his violent prowess, his bragging gives the lie to his tough-talking charade long before we learn that his near-sightedness renders him incapable of striking all but the most proximate of targets.

The introduction to Munny in the mud—like his ongoing difficulty mounting a horse, which will provide for recurrent images of him collapsed and scrambling—announces the film's revisionist leanings. Such failures mark the distance between Munny and the physical prowess and moral infallibility conjoined in the hero's conventional ability to ride and shoot. To fail at target practice or stumble about in the mud is not to embody a classic Western hero, in whose actions moral and visceral satisfaction coalesce. Nor is Munny, on the surface at least, the action hero as imperialist subject, a site of mastery and self-extension.

Following on the Cold War Western's reinscription of the hero as a site of physical and psychological suffering, however, Munny's failures in fact signal his heroic credentials. The film builds upon the Cold War Western's image of a fallible, vulnerable hero—a man whose past is positioned as a source of failure and shame, if also of prowess, who seeks and fails to escape its violent legacy. Like Jimmy Stewart in *The Naked Spur*, Eastwood spends a good deal of time on the ground, falling off his horse, scrambling in the dust, crawling in agonizing close-up across a barroom floor, crying out in anguish through a fevered night of guilt-ridden dreams. Dennis Bingham has identified the film's style as "masochistic" for its tendency to anticipate and reinforce such postures ("When a body falls from a horse, the camera is there to meet it").[111] As in the Cold War Western, the hero's physical degradation signals both an acknowledgement of the moral implications of the genre's conventional violence—a kind of generic mea culpa—and the production of the hero as a site of pathetic identification.

The theme of inadequacy introduced in these early sequences circulates around the contingent, unreliable status of Eastwood/Munny's body and, by extension, of the male body more generally. The failure of this body to live up to its phallic pretensions—or, put differently, to its iconic status as the site of self-mastery—provides the film's narrative catalyst, as in the

moment of sexual insecurity that sets the action in motion (a young prostitute is brutally attacked for giggling at the small penis of her client, a man
nicknamed "Quick Mike," suggesting again a lack of sexual prowess).[112] This
phallic dressing-down will continue across the film, as the prosaic status of
the male body is asserted through the highlighting of defecation, disease,
death, and decay (the murder of Quick Mike as he sits in the "shithouse"
suggests some of the anxiety attending this emphasis). In its assertion of
fluid boundaries and compromised postures, this emphasis on bodily
functions breaks emphatically with a generic tradition oriented around
the male body as a site of imagined sovereignty—a well-bounded locus of
agency and self-mastery through which the fantasy of national sovereignty
itself takes shape.

In the end, however, *Unforgiven* cannot escape its own investment in the
spectacle of violence and the status of the hero as an omnipotent agent at its
core. Munny's reawakening to violence—his phoenix-like rebirth from the
hog slime back into the thrillingly cold-blooded, terse-talking Eastwood
persona—is the path along which the film inexorably moves. The initial
withholding of the conventional pleasures of narcissistic and sadistic identification with the hero as violent agent only intensifies the anticipation of
their eventual restoration.

The film cues these expectations in a number of ways. To a significant
extent, this dormant persona is never far from the surface of Eastwood's
performance, legible in Munny's sparse dialogue, dry humor, stoicism, and
resolve. The status of Munny as a reformed man, softened through that
most conventional agent of domestication, the pious wife, is one toward
which both Munny and the film evidence ambivalence from the start.
Munny's lingering gaze at the tiny, receding figure of the Kid, whose initial offer of a partnership he has rejected, underscores both his own and
the film's sense of longing. The soundtrack breaks in with a wistful refrain
as the camera floats forward to frame Munny's weathered, muddied face
gazing out at the distant horizon. From within this ambivalence, the film
encodes its promise of resurrection; Munny's oft-repeated refrain, "I ain't
like that no more," operates (like Bill Foster's insistence that he is "going
home") to assure us to the contrary.[113]

Most significantly and insidiously, however, the film's reverent nostalgia
for the traditional ethos of the Western and its hero manifests in recurrent sequences of Munny, the Kid, and Munny's old partner, Ned Logan
(Morgan Freeman) as they traverse the landscape on horseback. In contrast to the degradations and violent contrivances of its human inhabitants, the physical landscape of the West emerges here as an idyllic, majestic
counterpoint, both beautiful and—crucial to my argument—free from
impediment or restraint (fig. 27). While other sequences emphasize the

compromise and disappointment of conventional action, these montages of unfettered plains, clear-running rivers, and forests of autumnal splendor, accompanied by a wistful, elegiac score, reach toward the genre's expansionist fantasy of "open" space and the pleasurable identification with motion across it.[114] These images, central to the ideological project of the Western from its inception, are presented as beyond reproach, set apart from the space of critique that other episodes animate. Naturalized here is the generic fantasy of mobility and self-extension as foundational to imperialist subjectivity—the ideology of Manifest Destiny as signified through the cinematic appeals of white men on horseback.

In contrast to these uncritical appeals, up until its final shoot-out, *Unforgiven* (like *Falling Down*) undermines the conventional generic pleasures of onscreen violence. The agonizingly extended killing of the cowboy Davey (Rob Campbell), for instance, is structured in stark opposition to the genre's traditional rhythms. In place of quick cuts between the hero's violent action (the raised gun, the taking aim) and the efficacy of his violence (the adversary's dying clutch at the heart, the Indian's tumble to the ground), this drawn-out sequence—designed, in Carl Plantinga's terms, "as a painful spectatorial experience"—emphasizes the ambivalence and imprecision of the protagonists and the pain and fear of their victim.[115] "Davey Boy" (whose nickname underscores his essential innocence) is a largely sympathetic character, implicated in the attack on the prostitute Delilah (Anna Levine) but not responsible for it and eager to make amends. There is no clear moral victory in watching him suffer. Yet the camera lingers over him lying injured under his horse, framing him in tight close-up as he crawls

Fig. 27. Against the critique of conventional Western violence it mobilizes elsewhere, *Unforgiven* maintains an uncritical investment in the genre's expansionist fantasy of wide "open" space. *Unforgiven* (Eastwood 1992).

desperately for cover, and then, after Munny has shot him through the gut, sticks around to witness his slow and painful death.

More than a sympathetic alignment with Davey as victim, the sequence produces an uncomfortable identification with the guilt and ambivalence of Munny, Logan, and the Kid as they awkwardly deliberate the shooting and then sit, frozen in a tableau of anxiety and shame, listening to the protestations of the dying man below. The later killing of Quick Mike (David Mucci) in the outhouse will also frustrate the conventional rhythms of generic violence. The act is offered both formally and thematically as a disappointment of its extended anticipation, leaving the Kid—in the aftermath of this, his first killing—shaken and weepy with remorse.

Despite the film's refusal to align the violence of its protagonists with either moral authority or rhythmic, visceral satisfactions, however, the conventions of racial melodrama continue to operate within it, providing narrative and affective impetus for violence. For even as it disavows the status of its hero as a morally endowed avenger, *Unforgiven* mobilizes the spectacle of racialized suffering to stabilize identification with Munny as a violent agent. The unflinching brutality of the film's final shoot-out both stems from and requires the scenario of racialized suffering that precedes it, in which the hapless Ned, picked up by a cowboy posse as he makes his way home and innocent of the killing with which he is charged, is beaten to death by the sadistic sheriff Little Bill (Gene Hackman). Although Ned's death is kept offscreen, the brutal whipping he receives at Little Bill's hands replays a central set piece of racial melodrama, suggesting a familiar allocation of innocence and guilt even as the film presumes to complicate their conventional assignment. Race itself comes into focus only through such violence, as the image of Logan/Freeman's bloodied back asserts a racialized history of violence that the film (and its director) have elsewhere sought to evacuate (fig. 28).[116]

The episode allocates a crucial measure of righteousness to Munny's subsequent violence, while branding the sadism of Little Bill with the mark of racial injustice. The sequence cuts between the grunting Ned, naked from the waist up and framed behind the bars of the cell to which he is chained, and reaction shots of the deputies in the jailhouse and the townsfolk gathered beyond, as they cringe and flinch with every crack of the whip. As Linda Williams has argued, racial melodrama revolves around such public spectacles of bodily suffering, for which Uncle Tom's whipping at the hands of Simon Legree serves as the prototype.[117] The racialized significance of Little Bill's sadism will be further implicated by the public display of Ned's body, illuminated by torchlight before the saloon; the scene, revealed in a subjective tracking shot attributed to Munny, while Little Bill's voice barks out offscreen, recalls once more the spectacular history of racialized

Fig. 28. The spectacle of racialized victimization animates and stabilizes the retributive violence that follows, enfolding its brutality within the moral fabric of melodrama. *Unforgiven* (Eastwood 1992).

violence. Depriving Little Bill of any credible moral purpose, the killing of Ned allows Munny's murder of Little Bill to be cast within the generic mold of the paradoxically violent restoration of order.[118] Through this specter of racialized violence, the Eastwood persona will be reborn: the affective logic of racial melodrama combines with the generic attractions of the Western hero to locate the final shoot-out within rather than outside of the realm of conventional pleasure.

Much critical debate has circulated around how to read this final shoot-out, in which a now whiskeyed-up Munny wreaks lethal havoc in retribution for the murder of Ned, killing in cold blood the saloon's unarmed proprietor, Little Bill, and a handful of his deputies (one in the back as he tries to escape). Critics dispute the extent to which the sequence reinscribes or further undermines the generic attractions of violence, eviscerating them of any code of honor or reanimating them through a thrilling, cathartic display. Although within narrative terms Munny's violence is cast as a moral failure, within generic terms—terms intensified by the presence of Eastwood himself—the exuberant return of the omnipotent hero restores a set of satisfactions that the film up to this point has steadfastly withheld.

In place of a clear moral authority, it is the authority of a particular style—its mediated history, its visceral satisfactions—to which the sequence, like the film, attests. Spectatorial anticipation of the shoot-out is cued, as Bingham notes, by the return of old Eastwood motifs, including "the slow ride into town, the subjective track to the saloon, and, most startlingly, the surprise emergence of the stranger figure . . . from out of an 'objective' camera position."[119] The film's reverent attitude toward Munny is echoed in the glances of the awestruck men as they turn their heads in a quick, rhythmic series of shots to stare toward the doorway in which Munny has magically materialized, hyperbolically underscored by a thunderclap from the raging storm outside. The camera moves as if magnetized, zooming in slowly on the figure of Munny—now ramrod straight and unflinching, his rifle raised, his allure confirmed by the saloon's riveted spectators, who dare not and cannot turn away. And while the misfire of his rifle as he aims it at Little Bill might be read as a qualification of Munny's omnipotence, the explosion of violence that follows stands in stark contrast to the earlier shootings of Davey and Quick Mike. As Munny grabs for his pistol in time to shoot Little Bill and his deputies in a sequence of sharp cuts and fast, frenetic action, the film returns in closing to the familiar rhythms of Western violence.

Although Bingham interprets Munny's retort to the dying Little Bill, "deserve's got nothing to do with it," as evidence of generic departure, the shoot-out affirms the extent to which the generic attractions of violence do not rely on their overt moral affirmation. The space between the imperialist subject as action hero and the moral critique of generic violence is, in this period, a muddy and uncertain terrain. Nonetheless, the film mobilizes a variety of conventional methods to authorize Munny's violence and render it cathartic, including the beatings of Ned and Munny himself and the representation of Little Bill as an unrepentant sadist (which serves to qualify Munny's own sadism). And while Munny's murder of Little Bill registers some of the unease we witnessed in *Falling Down*—we pause to take in Bill's fear; Munny towers in menacing low angle over the wounded man he is about to kill—*Unforgiven* also moves to stabilize this sense of queasiness (we see the flinching regret on Munny's face after he pulls the trigger, for instance).

In this sense, Munny's assertion that "deserve's got nothing to do with it" is disingenuous, a point recognized by the film's contemporary audience, whose evident satisfaction in Munny's violent rebirth was noted with dismay by many of the film's contemporary critics.[120] As Carl Plantinga observes, "the deep satisfaction some audience members took when Munny blows away his enemies . . . [suggests] that for many of us, the myth of redemptive violence has become so entrenched, and the pleasures expected of Eastwood's violent persona so firmly ingrained, that they conflict with and perhaps override our desire for Munny's redemption."[121] It is Munny's violent outburst itself, however, that signifies as redemption within the thematic and affective rhythms of the film. The final framing of this violence as within rather than beyond the moral fold is registered in the image of Ned's body as Munny pauses on his way out of the saloon and in the small smile on the scarred face of Delilah, to whom the film repeatedly cuts in its final montage. As the townsfolk gather to watch Munny ride away into the night, both instances underscore the wrongs that Munny's violence may be felt to right.

Like the dime novelist Beauchamp (Saul Rubinek), whose gleeful response to seeing a legend come to life the film both ridicules and invites us to share, we are positioned to recognize that, in Munny's violence, we are witness to the "real thing," an authentic Western icon whose potency derives not from the righteousness of his cause but from the force of its articulation. Beauchamp's function throughout the film is to highlight the wide-eyed, theatrical, and self-aggrandizing constitution of Western heroism, in particular its false idols of authenticity and historical veracity (values to which Eastwood the director has been noted for his "meticulous adherence"). It is revisionism itself that the film ultimately debunks, however, the fiction of the West, as Paul Smith has argued, "returning in overpowering form to literally blow away" the film's demythologizing impulse.[122]

In its partial evacuation of the moral authority of its hero, *Unforgiven* suggests the extent to which such authority may be increasingly subsidiary to the generic appeals of violence. In this respect, the film participates in those "fantasies that bind pleasure to aggression," affirming the centrality of sadistic and narcissistic appeals to the attractions of screen violence.[123] Earlier in its generic history, the project of the Western was to bind the visceral appeals of cinematic action to an assertion of their moral virtue and to anchor both pleasure and virtue to the image of the white male body in motion. By the end of the twentieth century, however, an identification with the figure of the Western hero—as with the action hero more generally—no longer relies in the same way on this conjunction.

In its movement away from a moralizing discourse, *Unforgiven* reflects tendencies evident in the genre since Sam Peckinpah's *The Wild Bunch* (1969) and Sergio Leone's Spaghetti Westerns, in which the orchestration of violence becomes increasingly stylized and visceral in its appeal. As Bingham argues, more recent Westerns "compensate for the loss of values, even those about which the classical Western was ambivalent, by hyperbolizing the model, intensifying the spectator's egoistic investment in the hero's violent response."[124] Generic convention (compounded here by the pressures of Eastwood's star persona) holds forth the promise of violent action, and identification with this action constitutes the particular satisfactions of the form; although the position of moral authority is never fully evacuated, the appeals of sensational violence do not depend on it.

In late-century action cinema, an increasing investment in the technologized spectacle of violence begins to overwhelm the narrative trajectory through which the hero's moral authority has conventionally been founded. Much of Eastwood's earlier work already centered violence in the image of its hero, "knowing that no moral code could truly contain such brutality."[125] Yet, ultimately, one of *Unforgiven's* most significant impulses is not to eschew but to stabilize the attractions of brutal violence. Even as it guts the conventions of sensational melodrama of their more explicit moral claims, the film rehearses the familiar rhythms of victimization and violent resurgence. This is the appeal around which the action cinema of the 1980s and 1990s revolves, mobilizing discourses of crisis and critique while affirming the pleasure of their refutation through persistent fantasies of violent self-extension, celebrating even as it qualifies the appeals of imperialist subjectivity onscreen.

The early years of the twenty-first century would bring a resurgence of the cultural fantasy of unimpeachable moral authority, however, as embodied in the image of the Western cowboy hero and the action hero more generally. Drawing upon the history of sensational melodrama, popular and political discourse in the wake of 9/11 would reassert the melodramatic constitution of this authority as it animates the visceral pleasures of violence, along with the image of the strenuous white male body in which the appeals of nationalist virtue and aggression coalesce. The tremendous success of action films in the burgeoning home video market of the 1980s and 1990s presage and help to condition affective rhythms that would come to structure the televisual discourse of war—briefly during the Persian Gulf War in 1991, and more persistently in the twenty-first-century wars in Afghanistan and Iraq—a discourse predicated upon the fantasy of embodied vulnerability and technologically enhanced omnipotence. While the sensational appeals of action have always operated both in relation to and in excess of morally authorized identifications, the spectacular attractions of the war on terror would reconfirm the extent to which American nationalism still prefers its sadistic pleasures contained within the affective and narrative frameworks of melodrama, joining the thrills of violence to a morally reinvigorated narrative of national innocence and righteous retribution.

Epilogue

To Be Real

Virtual Violence in the Twenty-First Century

> In times of real or manufactured political crisis, it is espe-
> cially likely that the dead speech of the cliché will return
> in its ghostly garb not only as senseless farce, but also
> as a genuine and interested attempt to create continu-
> ity with the precrisis world. In this way some potentially
> destabilizing aspects of the crisis being managed can be
> neutralized or even reclothed as stabilities.
>
> —**Lauren Berlant,** *"The Epistemology of State Emotion"*

In the days and weeks after 9/11—stretching into months and years—the
dead speech of cliché seemed to surface with considerable efficacy: the
cowboy rhetoric, rehearsing violent scenarios from a cultural imagination
of the West; the Manichean structures of good and evil; the promise and
anticipation of righteous, retributive violence as it grew out of the public
spectacle of suffering and victimization—and of thrilling, spectacular violence at that, the visceral and moral conjunction of shock and awe. The
formal and narrative conventions of sensational melodrama provided an
affective structure to shape and direct public feeling in this context. In
producing a "national present tense from the materials of the past,"[1] these
conventions worked to stabilize the "potentially destabilizing aspects of the
crisis," to make a familiar kind of sense—a moral sense—out of events that

seemed to rupture the precepts of American national identity, threatening to recast national feeling in a new affective mold. The mix of sense and sensation that followed in the mediated unfolding of war was both novel and familiar, replaying established rhythms to orchestrate a new set of mechanisms, new modes of organizing, imaging, and engaging in nationalist violence.

The efficacy of the melodramatic framing of 9/11 and the ensuing war on terror speaks to affective structures made habitual across a century of cinema, as I suggested in the Introduction. It speaks as well to the appeals of virtual violence in televisual war discourse and videogames from the early 1990s forward: the invitation to identify at once with technologically enhanced omnipotence and an embodied sense of vulnerability. These appeals were presaged by the cinematic history of sensational melodrama, as I outlined in the last chapter. In closing, then, I wish to make a slight pivot to suggest, in an admittedly preliminary way, how the solicitation to identify with violent agency and embodied vulnerability shapes imperialist representation into the twenty-first century and how ideas of both realness and righteousness undergird this production. Although the moral appeals of mediated violence had become increasingly unstable by the end of the twentieth century, as I have argued, the ascendance of realness as its own kind of virtue—evidenced in the emphatic turn toward a "you are there" aesthetic dominating war representation across genres and media— is nonetheless still implicated in the conventions of sensational melodrama whose genealogy I have traced.

Realness is produced as an affective category, a category of feeling. The notion of realness speaks to the operations of affect in relation both to dominant systems of meaning and value and to the imagination of a feeling or experience located somehow beyond or outside these systems. Within cultural discourses of war in particular (and despite the interpenetration of war and daily life in the context of the military-industrial-entertainment complex), experiences that challenge mundane forms of responsiveness are the ones classified most insistently as signifiers of the real—signifiers, that is, of a kind of overwhelming sensory response that absorbs us in an immediacy of feeling believed to stand apart from regular processes of ordering or cognition. The real is thus constructed at least in part through a fantasy of its outsideness, its lack of capture by the structuring constraints of the social or the cultural. As we saw in the discourse of the strenuous life, the realness of combat in this respect has been understood as its virtue, to the extent it is felt to interrupt the enervating aspects of experience in the context of modernity.

Our experiences of the real, however—the things with which we identify and to which we give credence; the intensity, texture, and direction of our responsiveness; how we recognize and classify the way things *feel*—are shaped of course through the forces of history and culture that situate us, even as these experiences may exceed or interrupt the forms these forces lend. Realness circulates as an ideological as well as a visceral or affective arrangement, then, such that the realness of strenuous experience embodied ideas of white masculine as well as national superiority, for instance, and the further migration of these ideas into the Western cast fast-paced action as a signifier of the conjoined values of the authentic, the manly, and the American.

Indeed, realness in American culture is produced as an explicitly mediated category, intertwined with the conventions of sensational action and violence, as I have argued. Like the fantasy of immediate experience off-screen, screen-based violence is classified as authentic or realistic to the extent that it is able to solicit embodied responses intense enough to take us out of a mundane sense of ourselves in the world. Such responses are understood as determined by the exigencies of the moment, unsullied by the workings of culture, power, and the social, which processes of mediation might otherwise be understood to represent (such that authentic modes of representation are understood as authentic to the extent they are felt to operate despite rather than through these processes). As we have seen, however, viscerally intense modes of address take shape through specific ideological and moralistic frameworks, and the feeling of realness—like the feeling of goodness—represents a powerful combination of affects, the fusing of sensation with morality.

The cultural preoccupation with realness results in a striking circularity. While combat experience is valued as standing outside of the experiential categories of the everyday, for instance, the textures, rhythms, and intensities of that experience are most readily recognized as real insofar as they replicate mediated expectations. Relative to the expectations of awe-inspiring spectacle and intense, enveloping sensation that mediated violence has worked, in part, to produce, war may "[underperform] as entertainment or shock or even as a forum that can reveal something essential about the human condition."[2] The dissonance between these expectations and the embodied experience of war is conventionally registered not as a challenge to sensationalized notions of realness, however, but as their more temporary disappointment.[3] Thus, even immediate, overwhelming, and category-defying experiences get looped back into processes of mediation, represented and narrativized not in opposition to but very much in accordance with the mediated expectations and experiences of a screen-driven culture.

At the same time, in this uneasy, inextricable shuttling between "real" and virtual experience, mediated representations are themselves measured against the imagination of real experience and often found wanting. As Jan

Mieszkowski argues, "war stories—whether verbal narratives, photographs, or films—are perpetually attacked for not seeming real enough. The standards of 'reality' that reality fails to meet are themselves the very real products of such war stories."[4] Similarly, with regard to Vietnam War representation, "popular films have come to represent the 'authentic' story of the war," according to Marita Sturken. And yet they are considered inevitably inadequate to this task, as, in the words of one veteran, "no matter how graphic and realistic, a movie is after all a movie, and war is only like itself."[5]

In relation to war and violence, then, ideas of realness merge with the experience of virtual forms, such that the category of experience itself must be understood as a powerfully hybridized one, composed of a dynamic interchange between these different modes of being in the world. When the experience of violent rupture is later described as being "like a movie," for instance (in combat, as in the attacks of September 11), this description is offered as a marker both of its unreality (the extent to which it is understood to exceed or evade the categories of everyday experience) and of its authenticity (the extent to which it meets the sensational requirements of rupture itself). Thus we might best think of realness as the mediated fantasy of an unmediated experience, a fantasy that may be disappointed by, but can never stand apart from, the representational conventions that construct it.

This imbrication of war and virtual experience is not new, of course. As Mieszkowski argues in his investigation of mass spectatorship's emergence in the Napoleonic era, the reality of battle has been complexly intertwined with its representation for the last two centuries. When an expanding field of battle coincided with the ascendance of print media to produce war as a spectacle, something to be viewed by an audience, an imagination of combat as centrally informed by its representation became a defining feature of war, for combatants as well as for a remote mass audience.[6] A "vexed interdependence" has persisted ever since, in which firsthand experience and secondhand interpretation of war—both understood as incomplete—rely upon each other even as each undercuts the other's authorizing functions. Indeed, according to Mieszkowski, the modern concept of the mass first takes shape in this context, identified foremost with the "mass of spectators consuming war."[7] That origin hints at the role mediated constructions of war play in the visceral politics whose emergence Lauren Berlant traces to this same period, a period coincident with the cultural ascendance of melodrama.[8] If the mass learns to feel together as "embodied members of a sensuous social order,"[9] then the representation of war—and perhaps more specifically its melodramatic representation—plays a starring role in this process.

Realism, as Christine Gledhill articulates, is "that modality which makes a claim on the real, in a bid to redefine what counts as reality."[10] Thus it is necessary to consider the mediated processes of attunement that orient us to particular contours of the real at a given time. Codes of the real crisscross between generic and cultural contexts, as what is taken to constitute cultural reality bends and sways under the pressure of generic verisimilitude. Genre conventions produce signs of the real that circulate back through the extrafilmic world, granted a credence in that broader context through the reiterative force of their generic status. Questions of realness and authenticity are challenged in their particulars but very rarely in their general impulse, however; individual instances of representation may be debated as more or less realistic, while the constitution of realness as such is rarely scrutinized. Thus, realness remains a powerful legitimizing force, helping to institute a set of affective responses by which sensation is culturally categorized and experienced. Part of what gets naturalized through this discourse of realness is the affective structure of melodrama itself, not simply the construction of good and evil, but the merger of visceral with moral appeals and the vacillation between positions of vulnerability and omnipotence that has defined imperialist subjectivity at least since the late nineteenth century.

In the context of the late twentieth and early twenty-first centuries, the virtues of authenticity and the real continue to accrue to representations of speed and impact, visceral, aggressive forms of address, and the modes of responsiveness these are imagined to condition. Such appeals continue to be associated with male-identified genres and entertainments; the more aggressively visceral the form, the more strongly gendered it appears. Videogames figure prominently in evaluations of the realness of screen-based violence, as do the sensationalist conventions of filmic war representation, in their emphasis on intense sensory address as a marker of authenticity. We might think here of the famous Omaha Beach landing sequence of *Saving Private Ryan* (Spielberg 1998), which heralded a new era in the "you are there" aesthetics of mainstream war representation ("absolute realism," in the words of one review),[11] or the celebrated stylizations of *Black Hawk Down* (Scott 2001), received as both the "most extravagantly aestheticized" and "most realistic" representation of war on film.[12] In these and other examples, the real is associated with a high degree of graphic realism combined with heavily stylized conventions oriented toward a representation—or, better, a reproduction—of the visceral and affective intensity of violence. While these may appear to be distinct or even contradictory aesthetic impulses, the conjunction is consistent with the broader traditions of sensational realism and with precedents like the sensation scenes of the melodramatic stage, which combined sophisticated feats of scenic realism with a dramatic form oriented around exaggerated modes of expressive address. And indeed, in these films as in their nineteenth-century precedents, melodramatic conventions of pathos as well as action provide the affective context for the realism of mediated violence.

While the imbrication of sensationalism and realism is not new, video-games drive an intensifying "you are there" aesthetic that combines increasingly sophisticated graphic fidelity with an aggressively visceral mode of address, one that continues to stake its claim upon the real through a combination of affective appeals. In the genre of the first-person shooter in particular, a fantasy of mastery is inextricable from identification with a state of embodied vulnerability; the imbrication of these two positions—which form the grounds of imperialist subjectivity as I have traced it—is constitutive of gameplay itself in this context. Identification of the player with the avatar onscreen hinges on the fantasy of both vulnerability and control (control of mobility and violence, in particular). The actions of the player are felt to control the movements of the avatar, even as onscreen environments and the available field of action within them are understood as circumscribed and pre-programmed.[13] This point may seem obvious, but it bears remarking nonetheless, because the fantasy of control may function to naturalize precisely the kinds of framings that Judith Butler has highlighted as so essential, reinforcing the normative "schemes of intelligibility" through which we can recognize, for instance, a subject or a life.[14]

The "you are there" impulse of first-person shooter games, war movies, and other action-based forms extends in the twenty-first century to war reporting as well. The rise of embedded reporting (in its own way also resonant with the melodramatic conventions of "reality television") works to reinforce the primacy of a first-person point of view organizing the representation of war, a point of view that pivots around the notion of feeling as the privileged signifier of the real.[15] Intensely visceral and kinesthetic, these conventions propose knowing or understanding along the axis of feeling. You cannot know or understand war unless you have been there, as is commonly asserted, and yet, through the conventions of contemporary war representation, it is the virtual experience of "being there" that we are invited to share. As Marita Sturken has argued in relation to the codes of realism that emerge with Vietnam War films, spectatorship itself is cast here "as a kind of veteranness," located explicitly within the mise-en-scène of violence. Such spectatorial appeals harken back to the end of the nineteenth century, when the thrill of "how it feels to be under fire" circulated as an experience to be consumed. A similar transaction occurs today, when, "[f]ar from an irreducibly personal ordeal, absolutely singular in its particularity and specificity, 'being under fire' has become a generic electronic good that is shuttled between various broadcasting and consumption formats."[16]

The first-person vision that defines realistic war representation today mobilizes the credence of what Sturken has called the "grunt's eye view"—the notion, closely related to the epistemological status of the real I have been tracing, that the truth of experience is best found "on the ground." This view from the ground alternates with another, a god's-eye view that has conventionally defined war representation as spectacle. We might be tempted to think of this vacillation as a shuttling between the positions of actor and spectator, with the former corresponding to the embodied vulnerability of the combatant, for instance, and the latter to a protected position of voyeuristic omnipotence. But, of course, the doubling inheres in both these positions, as was the case with Henry Fleming on the field of battle, embodying an object of a gaze he himself projects out across the landscape, or Stephen Crane on the hilltop, surveying the scene of battle while he stands amid a hail of bullets. The precise dynamics of oscillation may vary in television newscasts, films, and videogames, as they shuttle from first- to third-person points of view, but the oscillation continues to construct imperialist affect out of the conjoined appeals of agency and vulnerability. As with Crane on the hilltop, a different kind of credence may attach to each of these positions, but the significance continues to be found in their interrelation.

Within the contemporary military-entertainment complex, the doubled positions of the spectator-soldier and soldier-spectator are ubiquitous, as virtual, screen-based experience is integrated into war making at every level. Examples of this complex extend beyond its institutional structures and include the broader militarization of American culture, the ascendance of militainment, and the increasing merger of militarized entertainment with the experience of warfare "on the ground."[17] In the context of the twenty-first-century wars in Afghanistan and Iraq, for instance, soldiers play first-person shooter games on their Xboxes after a day of patrol, the army deploys online gaming machines to boost troop morale, and combatants persist in the tendency to represent their own experiences as "like a video game." Screens have long mediated the experience of war, of course, with aerial reconnaissance and aerial combat serving as primary examples.[18] With technologies like vision-enhancing prosthetics and networked communications feeding into helmet-mounted displays, the virtual aspects of combat are becoming more integrated even on the ground. Finally, the rapid ascendance of drone warfare in recent years makes the merger between combat and screen-based experience, between fighting and spectating, between the real and the virtual evermore complete.

The increasingly intimate alignment between the military and the entertainment and technology industries is marked by the ready flow of technology and personnel from the military to the private sector and back again, by the adaptation of military simulations for commercial release, and by the military's frequent modification of popular videogame platforms for training (as well as rehabilitation) purposes.[19] Simulation technologies merge military with industrial and academic endeavors until the distinction between these institutional spaces collapses. This conflation is particularly explicit in the case of the University of Southern California's Institute for Creative Technologies (ICT), a joint venture of the defense and entertainment industries launched in 1999 through a $45 million grant from the Department of Defense (and it has received hundreds of millions more since). Drawing upon expertise in the entertainment and software industries to advance simulation technologies in the interests of both military and commercial sectors, the ICT highlights the centrality of screen-based experiences to the imagination and enactment of state-sponsored violence.

This merger of the entertainment industry and the military around the question of the real and its reproduction highlights how centrally film and videogames provide the terms through which realness itself is apprehended. The ICT's mission is "to build a partnership among the entertainment industry, Army, and academia with the goal of creating synthetic experiences so compelling that participants react as if they are real" (or, more specifically, "to create veterans who've never seen combat"). The aesthetic and affective conventions of realism are central to this process, as is the notion of immersive technologies in their impact on the body. The effectiveness of visual fidelity and the degree of realness granted to a simulation are understood to rely significantly on a user's emotional engagement with the onscreen environment. In conceptualizing the ICT and its benefits, then, story and character (and the expertise that Hollywood brings to their development) have been understood as key, alongside other affective elements, such as "wind, temperature, humidity, and odor,"[20] a suggestive angle on the complex of factors that constitute mediated realness and its affects and a reminder, again, of the centrality of generic convention to this process.

Another prominent example of the military-entertainment complex is the Army Game Project, which encompasses the online tactical first-person shooter game America's Army alongside a multitude of related ventures. America's Army was the first instance of a videogame specifically developed and marketed by the U.S. military for a civilian audience, with the aim of providing its players with a "virtual Soldiering experience." The game was conceived as a recruitment effort at a time of unprecedentedly low numbers in the late 1990s (and considered the most effective recruitment strategy since the Uncle Sam "I Want You" ads of World War II). It was developed at an initial cost of approximately $8 million and launched online on July 4, 2002 (and has been available for free download since). The game has spawned dozens of versions (including console, cell phone, and arcade editions) and serves as a platform for a variety of government and military training applications, including individual weapons training and large-scale battlefield simulations.

Promotional trailers for America's Army stitch together different codes of realism, shuttling between aesthetic traditions of documentary realism and sophisticated high-fidelity gameplay graphics and incorporating the first-person shooter perspective into this diversely rendered landscape of the real. The trailers are scored to emphasize both a sense of noble mission (the documentary-style footage) and a sense of excitement (the gameplay graphics), shifting like the image track between these different modalities of the real. Taglines highlight this doubleness through wordplay that bridges the real and the virtual. The trailers make an argument for gameplay as both coextensive with and equivalent to the experience of combat, a conjunction of pleasure and violence, entertainment and military service, that pivots on the status of screen-based technology as the means of both playing at and waging war. Like the broader Army Game Project, America's Army highlights the extent to which the skill sets for these activities converge, the extent to which war itself has come to look and feel like a videogame, through the fusion of simulated and material enactments of violence.

Among the other projects encompassed by the Army Game Project is the Virtual Army Experience (VAE), a large-scale mobile combat simulator, which since 2007 has traveled to state fairs, NASCAR races, amusement parks, and air shows, transforming the original game into a multisensory thrill-ride cum recruitment center (fig. 29).[21] Another is the Army Experience Center (AEC), a $12 million "virtual experience center" that opened in the Franklin Mills Mall in Pennsylvania in 2008 (and closed in 2010 in the face of ongoing protests). In these two examples, the relationship between recruitment and gameplay is made explicit and hinges upon the status of military simulations as thrilling or fun. One mall poster advertising the AEC made light of the conjunction: "Shop for Socks. Grab a Bite. Pilot an AH-64 Attack Helicopter." Though protesters rejected the blithe equivalence between entertainment and state violence, simulated fun and its lethal implications, we might read the advertisement as a dead-serious joke on the mundane nature of war making in an age of the drone pilot who is home for dinner. The center was thus haunted by the equivalence upon which it was founded: the extent to which playing at and waging war converge.

In one credible revolution through this circuit, then, civilians acclimated through the simulated thrills of screen-based violence encounter army recruiters as they exit the Virtual Army Experience at their local state fair. Once enlisted, soldiers train using simulation technologies adapted from the entertainment sector; some may serve as drone pilots, waging war with a joystick designed off the Xbox, in a screen-based environment that resembles one of the Army Experience Center's simulation stations. After deployment, veterans may spend their off-duty hours playing

Fig. 29. The Virtual Army Experience, an interactive army recruiting exhibit that simulates real-life combat missions. Courtesy of the U.S. Department of Defense. Photo by J. D. Leipold.

war-themed videogames. Those who return home suffering from post-traumatic stress disorder may encounter these games again, in the context of their increasingly common therapeutic application, preparing these soldiers for redeployment. In the blurry merger of gameplay, training, war, and rehabilitation, the tendency of soldiers to narrate their combat experiences as "like a videogame" takes on a different valence.

The tracing of this circuit and the integral role of screen-based violence through every stage of its process does not touch upon broader or more abstract questions of how videogame conventions may shape or structure soldiers' experience of warfare. Some of the most interesting ways in which America's Army works to shape or direct affective experience reside in its deviations from more common conventions of gameplay: its enforcement of a singular identification with the U.S. soldier, refusing the genre's standard option of playing the game from a variety of subject positions, including that of the "enemy;"[22] its incorporation of the official army values of LDRSHIP (Loyalty, Duty, Respect, Selfless Service, Honor, Integrity, Personal Courage) into the experience of gameplay by rewarding actions deemed to represent these values with the opportunity to take on a wider range of roles, take up a wider range of weapons, and engage in a wider range of missions; and its eschewal of graphic images of death or dismemberment (in contrast to the game's otherwise obsessive attention to the vivid and specific rendering of visual detail, death is represented as a sterile, noiseless, and sanitized affair).[23]

We might consider the function of these conventions as they work to construct a specific imagination of imperialist violence—a cleaner and less ambiguous fantasy, in which violence is both moralized and nationalized—and question how this image coexists with or implicates the training and recruitment functions of the game. We might also ask how ideologies of American exceptionalism map onto the imagination of geopolitical space in this context, through a violent mobility marked explicitly with the U.S. Army brand, or ask how gameplay here encodes an exceptionalist image of American state-sponsored violence as legitimate, honorable, and necessary.

In addition, and perhaps even more importantly, in tracking the appeals of America's Army and of first-person shooter games more generally, we might consider how the construction of imperialist violence resonates with conventions forged across a century of cinema: how the conventions of sensational melodrama subtly shape the structure and experience of gameplay; how this relationship is underwritten by a discourse of the real; and how this dynamic relates to a broader structure of feeling governing the cultural imagination of war today. In the context of these questions, we might consider more specifically our identification with a mobility tracked through and as a trajectory of violence, the centrality of the weapon as the site and means of this identification, and the constitution of space and our movement through it as defined by a shifting interplay between positions of embodied vulnerability and violent agency, with one state always harboring within it the promise and possibility of the other. While recognizing how these impulses resonate with the longstanding traditions of sensational melodrama, we might also consider how the constitutive merger of violent agency and perpetual vulnerability serves an age of terror and counterterror in particularly compelling ways, encouraging an affective and embodied identification with a subject position ever vigilant, ever vulnerable, and endowed with a violent agency subtly (and not so subtly) underwritten by the assurance of righteousness.

In the world and on the screen, a vacillation between positions of vulnerability and omnipotence has organized imperialist affect, structuring the imagination and experience of war. The fantasy of embodied vulnerability coexists with the invitation to identify with the powers of technologized violence—with the appeals of self-extension and control represented through digital and cinematic as well as weapons technologies and, most emphatically, in their merger. When we question how the melodramatic contours of imperialist affect are conditioned and circulated as part of a structure of feeling in the late twentieth-century United States, providing an affective repertoire that would be tapped to quick and deadly ends at the opening of the twenty-first century, we must look to videogames as well as Hollywood films and other fictions of war. We must consider how this structure of feeling persists or transforms in the context of the wars of the twenty-first century, questioning the imbricated postures of vulnerability and omnipotence as they inform screen-based experience and experience on the ground.

In relation to the latter—never fully separable from processes of mediation, as I have argued—we might consider how the embodied experience of combat on the ground may be structured through the dynamic interplay of power and vulnerability. The status of the soldier as an object, as well as agent and instrument, of sovereign violence produces a powerful sense of precariousness, as Kenneth MacLeish has compellingly discussed in his ethnographic account of present-day soldiers and the affective experience of war. The "killing technologies" designed both to subject and to protect the body of the soldier produce, more so than a sense of technologized invincibility, a heightened identification with the condition of vulnerability. Weapons and armor "are material, bodily environments through which [soldiers] understand their *vulnerability* to violence just as much as their ability to produce and withstand it" (italics in original).[24] The soldier's body emerges in this context as the locus of "terrible power and terrible vulnerability"—a formulation striking in its resonance with the imperialist subject whose genealogy I have traced through the mediated conventions of melodrama.

Indeed, as I have suggested, a sense of precarious life seems to inform identification with imperialist subjectivity in essential and foundational ways. In respect to its specific appearance in the twenty-first century, Judith Butler has suggested the felt need "to shore up the first-person point of view, and preclude from the telling accounts that might involve a decentering of the narrative 'I' within the international political domain."[25] This process of recentering, according to Butler, "emerges to compensate for the enormous narcissistic wound opened up by the public display of our physical vulnerability," that is, to compensate for the general challenge to a first-person point of view represented by the events of 9/11.[26] While Butler speaks of this first-person view in general terms, leaving aside questions of representational aesthetics and their political significance, we might well wonder if the energetic embrace of this aesthetic in war representation of the twenty-first century relates to the compensatory dynamic of repression and denial that Butler diagnoses.

Thus we might return in closing to Matthew Buckley's question as to the significance of melodrama as a form of affective conditioning—and an "addictive" one at that.[27] In the "gradual melodramatization of psychological and social reality" across the nineteenth century, Buckley identifies an "affective structure becom[ing] a normative form of feeling and thought," highlighting melodrama's "domination, by the turn of the twentieth century, of perceptual modes of apprehension."[28] Although we might interrogate further the mechanisms through which this conditioning is transmitted, both within and across different structures of feeling, the notion of such conditioning is nonetheless suggestive in considering the extent to which sensational melodrama continues to shape both popular and political representations of war. If melodrama has conditioned us, what has it conditioned us toward? If the vacillation between vulnerability and omnipotence is one piece of an answer to this question, it seems certain that psychic as well as ideological economies are addressed in the rhythm of this vacillation; that is, these processes shape not only the social structures that subjects inhabit but also the psychic means of inhabiting these structures themselves.

As training regimes incorporate the simulation technologies of entertainment platforms like America's Army, and as combat itself becomes—for U.S. military personnel at least—an increasingly mediated affair, the relationship of spectatorship to war becomes an ever more pressing concern. Even as the first-person perspective has ascended, however, and even as the solicitation to identify with vulnerability may have served the war on terror in particular ways, it is necessary to emphasize the different status of bodies rendered vulnerable in these contexts. In an age of drone warfare, it is crucial to underscore the lethal persistence of the aerial view as well as the view from the ground—the god's-eye view alongside the "you are there" imperative (an imperative that aligns ironically in this context with the removal of U.S. combatants from the material scene of violence). Indeed, for the drone pilot, the god's-eye view emerges as a new mode of first-person perspective, with lethal implications for the material bodies, and embodied subjects, on the ground.

How the sensations of war are ordered, or how their disorderings may be recontained, relates perhaps to the dead speech of cliché to which Berlant gestures, an ossified structure of feeling that retains something of its original force even as it casts the uncanny shadow of its own inadequacy, conditioning the possibility of critique. Across this book, I have endeavored to trace something of the "affective structure in which we are, on the one hand, victimized and, on the other, engaged in a righteous cause of rooting out terror."[29] I have asked how a melodramatic framing—of victims and heroes, of the vulnerable and the powerful, and, most persistently, of the collapsing of these positions—continues to organize our experiences of nationalist violence in the hope that, by identifying and understanding something of the history of this structure and the visual and affective logics that sustain it, we might endeavor to be differently moved, or moved, at least, toward different ends.

ACKNOWLEDGMENTS

In the undertaking of this project, I have incurred many debts, an adequate accounting of which is impossible to give. But I am deeply appreciative of the wealth of folks who have nurtured this work, and me in it, in meaningful and myriad ways. Accepting the necessarily partial nature of the gesture, I am very happy to have the chance to acknowledge a few of the people and places that have facilitated the project and made its completion a possibility.

First, my sincerest thanks to Leslie Mitchner for her enthusiastic support of the project, to Leslie, Lisa Boyajian, and the staff at Rutgers University Press for making the publication process such a smooth and efficient one, and to the careful eye and considerate efforts of copyeditor Gretchen Oberfranc. My great thanks and appreciation also to Sarah Hagelin and Susan Jeffords for their generous engagement with the work, understanding of its larger stakes and investments, and productive insights, questions, and suggestions. The book is stronger for their input and engagement, although its shortcomings, of course, remain entirely my own.

Sincere thanks also to my mentors and advisors along the long way. For Wendy Brown, whose early support enabled my first forays into the psychic and social formations of gender—and whose own work provides enduring inspiration—I have always been extraordinarily grateful. To Mary Ann Doane, Philip Rosen, and Mari Jo Buhle, I likewise owe a great debt, for providing avenues into the initial questions about the gendered and racialized function of crisis discourse out of which the present project grew, and for the impetus to push those questions further and in more fruitful directions than I would have on my own. My appreciation as well to Susan Smulyan for her support of this journey, and to the staff of the Library of Congress Motion Picture and Television Reading Room, who, in the first years of my research, before early films had become so wondrously available through digitization, facilitated crucial access to the archive there. A special thanks also to the indefatigable Robyn Wiegman for her endless generosity and for welcoming me into the Women's Studies Program at Duke, and to all the faculty, students, and staff for such rich and rewarding experiences during my years teaching there.

I am truly lucky to have made my institutional home over the last five years in the Department of American Studies at the University of Hawai'i at Mānoa, and my profound gratitude and appreciation go out to all my colleagues. Their drive and dedication set an inspiring example, and their collective, unwavering support and encouragement have been essential to the completion of this project. I am also grateful to the department and to the College of Arts and Humanities for a little time away from teaching toward the completion of this book, and to all my students for the energy and interest they have brought to our shared endeavors. Particular thanks to Vernadette Gonzalez for her early cheerleading; to David Stannard, whose belief in my efforts has meant so much to me; and to Lori Mina, for facilitating so smoothly the business of daily life. The fates smiled very brightly indeed in granting me colleagues who are also dear friends. A very special thanks then to Kathleen Sands, for her generous spirit, her warm and ready ear, and the timely loan of her magical headphones; to Mari Yoshihara, for her excellent advice and her unflagging faith, which—since she is always right, or almost—has helped so much to fortify my own; and to Elizabeth Colwill, whose dauntless encouragement, patience, and insight have allowed me to feel and to remember, in the face of challenges large and small, that the effort is both meaningful and possible.

To other far-flung friends and those closer to home, I am ever grateful, for the levity and sustenance they have provided over the many years it has taken me to bring this project to fruition. A special shout-out to the illustrious Vicki Walden for her humor, strength, and wisdom, and for the legions of cheering mice who have sometimes made all the difference, and to Mira Hinman, for her life-long friendship and unwavering interest and concern. Finally, to my family, the deepest gratitude and appreciation for shoring me up, unconditionally and in so many ways, and for the many forms of refuge they have offered: to Megan and Devin Eagle, for their unflagging love and support; to my mother, Barbara Eagle, who sets such an inspiring example in all the things that matter most; and to my father, Herbert Eagle, who, with keen eye and ready interest, has been my sole reader and sounding board through much of this long process. To Will, Kaia, and Theo, for enduring all and brightening so much, no thanks is great enough. It is to them this work is dedicated.

Portions of chapter 1 appeared in an earlier version as "A Rough Ride: Strenuous Spectatorship and the Early Cinema of Assaults," *Screen* 53 (Spring 2012): 18–35. Portions of my broader argument first appeared in an earlier form as "Virtuous Victims, Visceral Violence: War and Melodrama in American Culture," in *The Martial Imagination: Cultural Aspects of American Warfare*, edited by Jimmy L. Bryan Jr. (College Station: Texas A&M University Press, 2013). My appreciation to the publishers for permission to reprint this material here.

NOTES

Introduction

1 George W. Bush, Proclamation, "Patriot Day 2002," September 4, 2002, and Proclamation, "Patriot Day 2003," September 4, 2003.

2 One might think here of how the American flag functioned in the weeks and months after 9/11, both as an expression of affective alignment with loss and as a bellicose assertion of nationalism in the lead-up to war.

3 See Benedict Anderson, *Imagined Communities: Reflections on the Origin and Spread of Nationalism* (London: Verso, 1983).

4 Lauren Berlant, *The Queen of America Goes to Washington City: Essays on Sex and Citizenship* (Durham, NC: Duke University Press, 1997), 31.

5 For a seminal account of melodrama in political as well as cultural life in the United States, see Linda Williams, *Playing the Race Card: Melodramas of Black and White from Uncle Tom to O.J. Simpson* (Princeton, NJ: Princeton University Press, 2001), as well as her "Melodrama Revised," in *Refiguring American Film Genres: History and Theory*, ed. Nick Browne (Berkeley: University of California Press, 1998), and most recently, *On The Wire* (Durham, NC: Duke University Press, 2014). For my own initial articulation of the prominence of melodrama in American cultural life, see "Making a Spectacle of Himself: White Masculinity, Melodrama, and Sensation in the American Cinema, 1898–1999" (PhD diss., Brown University, 2006). For a recent investigation of melodrama and American political discourse, see Elisabeth R. Anker, *Orgies of Feeling: Melodrama and the Politics of Freedom* (Durham, NC: Duke University Press, 2014). For other influential examinations of melodrama as a cultural mode, see Christine Gledhill, "The Melodramatic Field: An Investigation," in *Home Is Where the Heart Is: Studies in Melodrama and the Woman's Film*, ed. Christine Gledhill (London: British Film Institute, 1987); Gledhill, "Rethinking Genre," in *Reinventing Film Studies*, ed. Christine Gledhill and Linda Williams (London: Arnold, 2000); and Ben Singer, *Melodrama and Modernity: Early Sensational Cinema and Its Contexts* (New York: Columbia University Press, 2001).

6 See *Playing the Race Card*, and Williams's discussion of the trans-media travels of *Uncle Tom's Cabin* in particular.

7 As Elisabeth Anker usefully reminds us, in the context of melodramatic political discourse, only certain forms of injury and suffering emerge as legible; see *Orgies of Feeling*.

8 Matthew S. Buckley cites Carolyn Williams's discussion of Victorian melodrama here; see, "Refugee Theatre: Melodrama and Modernity's Loss," *Theatre Journal* 61 (2009): 182.

9 See, for instance, Thomas Elsaesser's seminal "Tales of Sound and Fury: Observations on the Family Melodrama," first published in *Monogram* 4 (1972): 2–15; Mary Ann Doane, *The Desire to Desire: The Woman's Film of the 1940s* (Bloomington: Indiana University Press, 1987); and Christine Gledhill's influential collection, *Home Is Where the Heart Is*.

10 Williams, "Melodrama Revised," 42.

11 In addition to Williams, Gledhill, Singer, and Buckley, see also Steve Neale, "Melo Talk: On the Meaning and Use of the Term 'Melodrama' in the American Trade Press," *Velvet Light Trap* 32 (1993): 66–89, and Tom Gunning, "The Horror of Opacity: The Melodrama of Sensation in the Plays of Andre de Lorde," in *Melodrama: Stage, Picture, Screen*, ed. Jacky Bratton, Jim Cook, and Christine Gledhill (London: British Film Institute, 1994).

12 Neale, "Melo Talk," 72.

13 Ibid.

14 Williams, "Melodrama Revised," 57.

15 Gledhill, "Rethinking Genre," 227.

16 See Peter Brooks, *The Melodramatic Imagination: Balzac, Henry James, Melodrama, and the Mode of Excess* (New Haven, CT: Yale University Press, 1976).

17 Ibid., 67.

18 Ibid., 42.

19 Buckley, "Refugee Theatre," 181.

20 Gunning, "Horror of Opacity," 51.

21 Williams discusses "the achievement of a felt good, the merger—perhaps even the compromise—of morality and feeling" ("Melodrama Revised," 55).

22 Though the interaction between cultural forms and the social and political contexts they shape and represent is not so direct, Gerould makes an important argument with regard to the resonance between melodrama and the political, ideological, and economic currents of the new nation; see Daniel Gerould, ed., *American Melodrama* (New York: PAJ Publications, 1983), 7.

23 Gledhill, "Melodramatic Field," 25.

24 Williams, "Melodrama Revised," 50, 83n15.

25 William Mazzarella, "Affect: What Is It Good For?" in *Enchantments of Modernity: Empire, Nation, Globalization*, ed. Saurabh Dube (London: Routledge, 2009), 296.

26 Hugo Munsterberg, *The Film: A Psychological Study* (1916; New York: Dover, 1970), 95.

27 Ibid.

28 Singer, *Melodrama and Modernity*, 40.

29 See Linda Williams, "Film Bodies: Genre, Gender and Excess," *Film Quarterly* 44 (Summer 1991): 2–13.

30 As early as 1800, William Wordsworth noted the "craving for extraordinary incident" that urbanization and the increasing "uniformity" of occupation

produces; cited in Jan Mieszkowski, *Watching War* (Stanford, CA: Stanford University Press, 2012), 15.

31 This view is not necessarily opposed to the previous, as the sensationalism of modern culture was thought to enervate its citizen-spectators, producing a compensatory need for greater stimuli. For a significant example of this argument in relation to cinema, see Singer, *Melodrama and Modernity*. As Singer suggests, the works of Siegfried Kracauer, Walter Benjamin, and Georg Simmel are key to the conceptualization of modernity here (Freud's discussion of the stimulus shield in *Beyond the Pleasure Principle* is also relevant).

32 Buckley, "Refugee Theatre," 180.

33 Suspicion might attach to visceral modes of responsiveness even in this context, as evidenced by the comments of Ludwig Lewisohn, writing in *The Nation* in 1920 on the violent pleasures of action-based melodrama that masquerade as righteousness; see Singer, *Melodrama and Modernity*, 40.

34 Judith Butler, "Survivability, Vulnerability, Affect," in *Frames of War: When Is Life Grievable?* (London: Verso, 2010).

35 Lauren Berlant, "The Epistemology of State Emotion," in *Dissent in Dangerous Times*, ed. Austin Sarat (Ann Arbor: University of Michigan Press, 2004), 47.

36 Williams, *Playing the Race Card*, 35.

37 Joseph Masco, *The Theater of Operations: National Security Affect from the Cold War to the War on Terror* (Durham, NC: Duke University Press, 2014), 20.

38 Brian Massumi frequently emphasizes this as a "base definition," citing Spinoza; see, for example, *Politics of Affect* (Cambridge: Polity Press, 2015), ix.

39 Mazzarella, "Affect: What Is It Good For?," 298–299.

40 On the significance of *Uncle Tom's Cabin*, see Williams, *Playing the Race Card*. For thoughts on the political possibilities of melodrama more broadly, see Williams, *On The Wire*, and Anker, *Orgies of Feeling*.

41 He prefers this term over that of imitation or contagion as it allows for a sense of "difference within unison"; Massumi, *Politics of Affect*, 56.

42 Ibid., 115.

43 Ibid., 114–15.

44 Butler, *Frames of War*, 50.

45 Though the work that has been animated through and around the concept of public feelings is too extensive to cite here in full, the scholarship of Lauren Berlant, Ann Cvetkovich, Katie Stewart, and others active in the Public Feelings and Feel Tank collectives has contributed in particularly fruitful ways to its germination.

46 Raymond Williams, *Marxism and Literature* (Oxford: Oxford University Press, 1977), 132.

47 Ibid., 133.

48 Butler, *Frames of War*, 67.

49 Mazzarrella references Massumi here; see "Affect: What Is It Good For?" 301.

50 The spectator-subject is "solicited to feel the impact that provides evidence that she belongs to the public constituted as a mass of spectators who see what she sees and feel what she feels, within a range of appropriate variation"; see Berlant, "Epistemology of State Emotion," 49.

51 Ibid., 52–53.

52 Munsterberg, *The Film*, 96.

53 For different approaches to the periodization of affect as an organizing mode of public life, see, for example, Massumi, Berlant, Mazzarrella, Masco, and Anker.

54 Massumi, *Politics of Affect*, 31.

55 Buckley, "Refugee Theatre," 186.

1 A Rough Ride

1 No moving pictures of live conflict were made in Cuba, and, like other cavalry units, the Rough Riders were dismounted at the outset of the war, ascending Kettle Hill (smaller and less well defended than the adjacent San Juan) on foot. Nonetheless, the "charge of San Juan Hill" persisted in popular imagination, essential to the construction of the Rough Riders as paragons of manhood, associated with both medieval knights and Western cowboys.

2 Richard Harding Davis, "Our War Correspondents in Cuba and Puerto Rico," *Harper's Monthly*, May 1899, 938–48.

3 George Parsons Lathrop, "Edison's Kinetography," *Harper's Weekly*, June 13, 1891. As Bill Brown notes, "when movies do not yet know what movies should be about, it seemed that soldiers and athletes would fit the bill, that war and sport would satisfy the medium's desire for content and for mass spectatorship"; see *The Material Unconscious: American Amusement, Stephen Crane, and the Economics of Play* (Cambridge, MA: Harvard University Press, 1996), 136.

4 See, for instance, Charles Musser, *Before the Nickelodeon: Edwin S. Porter and the Edison Manufacturing Company* (Berkeley: University of California Press, 1991), 126–37; Musser, *The Emergence of Cinema: The American Screen to 1907* (New York: Scribner's, 1990), 225–61; Robert C. Allen, *Vaudeville and Film, 1895 to 1915: A Study in Media Interaction* (New York: Arno Press, 1980); Douglas Gomery, *Shared Pleasures: A History of Movie Presentation in the United States* (Madison: University of Wisconsin Press, 1992); James Castonguay, "The Spanish-American War in U.S. Media Culture," *American Quarterly Experimental Online Issue* (June 1999), http://chnm.gmu.edu/aq; and Kristen Whissel, *Picturing American Modernity: Traffic, Technology, and the Silent Cinema* (Durham, NC: Duke University Press, 2008). For a discussion of imperialism and masculine spectacle in relation to early cinema and more generally, see Amy Kaplan, *The Anarchy of Empire in the Making of U.S. Culture* (Cambridge, MA: Harvard University Press, 2002).

5 For other discussions of the cinematic production of white masculinity as a figure for imperial mobility, see Kaplan, *Anarchy of Empire*, and Whissel, *Picturing American Modernity*.

6 The full passage (which quotes poet James Russell Lowell) reads: "The timid man, the lazy man, the man who distrusts his country, the over-civilized man, who has lost the great fighting, masterful virtues, the ignorant man, and the man of dull mind, whose soul is incapable of feeling the mighty lift that thrills 'stern men with empires in their brains'—all these, of course, shrink from seeing the

nation undertake its new duties; shrink from seeing us build a navy and an army adequate to our needs; shrink from seeing us do our share of the world's work, by bringing order out of chaos in the great, fair tropic islands from which the valor of our soldiers and sailors has driven the Spanish flag. These are the men who fear the strenuous life, who fear the only national life which is really worth leading." From "The Strenuous Life," a speech delivered before the Hamilton Club of Chicago on April 10, 1899.

7 Gender deviance pertains to Anglo-American women as well. As Roosevelt explains in "The Strenuous Life," "When men fear work or fear righteous war, when women fear motherhood, they tremble on the brink of doom, and well it is that they should vanish from the earth, where they are fit subjects for the scorn of all men and women." In concert with concerns over Anglo-American women's decreasing birth rates, immigrant women were cast as excessively fertile, echoing anxieties about the problem of "overproduction." For consideration of issues of sexuality in relation to Roosevelt's strenuous rhetoric and fears of social breakdown, see Sarah Watts, *Rough Rider in the White House: Theodore Roosevelt and the Politics of Desire* (Chicago: University of Chicago Press, 2003).

8 The notion of a widespread crisis of masculinity in this period is a familiar chapter in U.S. historiography, influenced by discussions of a broader "psychic crisis" and a "crisis of cultural authority." For particularly influential accounts, see Richard Hofstadter, "Cuba, the Philippines, and Manifest Destiny," in *The Paranoid Style in American Politics* (New York: Knopf, 1965); John Higham, "The Reorientation of American Culture in the 1890s," in *Writing American History: Essays on Modern Scholarship* (Bloomington: Indiana University Press, 1970); and T. J. Jackson Lears, *No Place of Grace: Antimodernsim and the Transformation of American Culture, 1880–1920* (New York: Pantheon Books, 1981). For discussions of masculine crisis in particular, see Joe L. Dubbert, "Progressivism and the Masculinity Crisis," in *The American Man*, ed. Elizabeth H. Pleck and Joseph H. Pleck (Englewood Cliffs, NJ: Prentice Hall, 1980); E. Anthony Rotundo, *American Manhood: Transformations in Masculinity from the Revolution to the Modern Era* (New York: Basic Books, 1993); and Michael Kimmel, *Manhood in America: A Cultural History* (New York: Free Press, 1996). The years 1898–1904 also mark an intensive period in the corporate consolidation of America; see, for instance, Allen Trachtenberg, *The Incorporation of America: Culture and Society in the Gilded Age* (New York: Hill and Wang, 1982); and Martin J. Sklar, *The Corporate Reconstruction of American Capitalism, 1890–1916* (Cambridge: Cambridge University Press, 1988).

9 Scholarship on women's increasing public role is extensive, but for examples pertaining specifically to the cinema, see Lauren Rabinovitz, *For the Love of Pleasure: Women, Movies, and Culture in Turn-of-the-Century Chicago* (New Brunswick, NJ: Rutgers University Press, 1998), and Miriam Hansen, *Babel and Babylon: Spectatorship in American Silent Film* (Cambridge, MA: Harvard University Press, 1991). For other accounts focused on popular culture, see Kathy Peiss, *Cheap Amusements: Working Women and Leisure in Turn-of-the-Century New York* (Philadelphia: Temple University Press, 1986); Nan Enstad, *Ladies of*

Labor, Girls of Adventure: Working Women, Popular Culture, and Labor Politics at the Turn of the Twentieth Century (New York: Columbia University Press, 1999); and Susan A. Glenn, *Female Spectacle: The Theatrical Roots of Modern Feminism* (Cambridge, MA: Harvard University Press, 2002).

10 See, for instance, Mary Liu, *The Chinatown Trunk Mystery: Murder, Miscegenation, and Other Dangerous Encounters in Turn-of-the-Century New York City* (Princeton, NJ: Princeton University Press, 2007).

11 For a useful summary of the modernity thesis, see Ben Singer, *Melodrama and Modernity: Early Sensational Cinema and Its Contexts* (New York: Columbia University Press, 2001).

12 In addition to Singer, for accounts of the relationship of cinema to modernity, see, for instance, Tom Gunning, "An Aesthetic of Astonishment: Early Film and the (In)Credulous Spectator," in *Viewing Positions: Ways of Seeing Film*, ed. Linda Williams (New Brunswick, NJ: Rutgers University Press, 1994), 114–33; Mary Ann Doane, *The Emergence of Cinematic Time: Modernity, Contingency, the Archive* (Cambridge, MA: Harvard University Press, 2002); Leo Charney and Vanessa R. Scwartz, eds., *Cinema and the Invention of Modern Life* (Berkeley: University of California Press, 1995); and Miriam Hansen's introduction to Siegfried Kracauer's *Theory of Film: The Redemption of Physical Reality* (Princeton, NJ: Princeton University Press, 1997), vii–xlvi. For material upon which this scholarship draws, see Kracauer, "The Mass Ornament," in *The Mass Ornament: Weimar Essays* (Cambridge, MA: Harvard University Press, 1995), 75–86; Walter Benajmin, "On Some Motifs in Baudelaire" and "The Work of Art in the Age of Mechanical Reproduction," in *Illuminations*, ed. Hannah Arendt (New York: Harcourt, Brace and World, 1968), 155–200 and 217–52; and Georg Simmel, "The Metropolis and Mental Life," in *The Sociology of Georg Simmel*, trans. Kurt H. Wolf (Glencoe, IL: Free Press, 1950), 409–24. For a discussion of Coney Island as a site of accommodation and disruption, see John Kasson, *Amusing the Million: Coney Island at the Turn of the Century* (New York: Hill and Wang, 1978). As Gunning notes, the term "attractions" refers to the popular tradition of the fairground and carnival, and most particularly its development in modern amusement parks like Coney Island; see, for instance, "Aesthetic of Astonishment," 131n13.

13 For accounts of neurasthenia and its relationship to contemporary social, economic, and cultural change, see Thomas Lutz, *American Nervousness, 1903: An Anecdotal History* (Ithaca, NY: Cornell University Press, 1991); Lears, *No Place of Grace*; and Rotundo, *American Manhood* (as well as George Beard's seminal 1881 account, *American Nervousness: Its Causes and Consequences*).

14 For discussions of the abundant advice literature counseling against wasteful expenditure and linking sexual regulation to success in the marketplace, see Rotundo, *American Manhood*; John D'Emilio and Estelle Freedman, *Intimate Matters: A History of Sexuality in America* (New York: Harper and Row, 1988), 66–69; and Judy Arlene Hilkey, *Character Is Capital: Success Manuals and Manhood in Gilded Age America* (Chapel Hill: University of North Carolina Press, 1997).

15 For contemporary articulations of these fears, see, for example, Theodore Roosevelt, *The Strenuous Life: Essays and Addresses* (New York: Century

Company, 1902), and Brooks Adams, *The Law of Civilization and Decay* (New York: Macmillan, 1896). Gail Bederman offers an excellent account of the paradox of turn-of-the-century conceptions of civilization and decline in *Manliness and Civilization: A Cultural History of Gender and Race in the United States, 1880–1917* (Chicago: University of Chicago Press, 1995). Richard Dyer explores similar issues in *White* (London: Routledge, 1997).

16 Roosevelt and contemporaries like Fredric Remington and Owen Wister were crucial to the establishment of this equivalency; see G. Edward White, *The Eastern Establishment and the Western Experience: The West of Frederic Remington, Theodore Roosevelt, and Owen Wister* (New Haven, CT: Yale University Press, 1968).

17 For a contemporary account of the racial lineage of the cowboy, see Owen Wister, "The Evolution of the Cow-Puncher" (1895), in *Owen Wister's West*, ed. Robert Murray Davis (Albuquerque: University of New Mexico Press, 1987).

18 Amy Kaplan, "The Spectacle of War in Crane's Revision of History," in *New Essays on the Red Badge of Courage*, ed. Lee Clark Mitchell (Cambridge: Cambridge University Press, 1986), 81.

19 Strenuous activities such as football and war encouraged habits deeply aligned with new bureaucratic forms of middle-class labor. As T. J. Jackson Lears has noted, "football instilled self-reliance and regularity—habits which would later prove useful in a business career," and "a weekend of camping returned fitter men to the office on Monday" (*No Place of Grace*, 108).

20 John Kasson makes a similar observation about strongman Eugen Sandow, who "claimed to embody an ancient heroic ideal of manhood that had been lost in the modern world, yet he turned his body into a commercial spectacle and a commodity whose image was widely reproduced and sold"; see *Houdini, Tarzan, and the Perfect Man: The White Male Body and the Challenge of Modernity in America* (New York: Hill and Wang, 2001), 29–30.

21 See Brown, *Material Unconscious*, 136–38.

22 For further discussion of Roosevelt's indefatigable courtship of the press, see Jonna K. Eagle, "Making a Spectacle of Himself: White Masculinity, Melodrama, and Sensation in the American Cinema, 1898–1999" (PhD diss., Brown University, 2006), 29–37. Amy Kaplan also notes this dynamic in "Romancing the Empire: The Embodiment of Masculinity in the Popular Historical Novel of the 1890s," *American Literary History* 2 (1990): 658–90.

23 On the imbrication of entertainment, sports, and war, see Brown, *Material Unconscious*, 125–66.

24 Smith's account is offered in *Two Reels and a Crank* (New York: Doubleday, 1952). For examples of how it has worked its way into cinema history, see Erik Barnouw, *Documentary: A History of the Non-Fiction Film*, rev. ed. (New York: Oxford University Press, 1983), and Anthony Slide, *The Big V: A History of the Vitagraph Company* (Metuchen, NJ: Scarecrow Press, 1976). (Slide notes that neither of the Vitagraph founders appears to have set foot in Cuba.) On the lack of footage of the charge, see Raymond Fielding, *The American Newsreel, 1911–1967* (Norman: University of Oklahoma Press, 1972), and Susan Moeller, *Shooting War: Photography and the American Experience of Combat* (New York:

Basic Books, 1989). The early film industry enlisted Roosevelt's courtship of the camera as an advertisement for the medium's legitimacy, celebrating the "Apostle of Strenuousness" as a true "picture man." See *The Theodore Roosevelt Association Film Collection: A Catalog* (Washington, DC: Library of Congress, 1986), and *Moving Picture World* 7 (October 22, 1910): 920.

25 Moeller, *Shooting War*, 61.

26 Paul Virilio, *War and Cinema: The Logistics of Perception* (London, Verso: 1989), 10.

27 Stephen Crane, *The War Dispatches of Stephen Crane*, ed. R. W. Stallman (New York: New York University Press, 1964), 165. Due to a shortage of appropriate weaponry, volunteer units were issued Springfield rifles that burned black powder, in contrast to the smokeless powder of the Spanish Mausers. These proved such a liability that the volunteer units were ordered to cease firing entirely early in the conflict. See Moeller, *Shooting War*, 39–40. Kaplan also notes the political significance of American visibility in this context; see *Anarchy of Empire*, 129.

28 John C. Hemment, *Cannon and Camera: Sea and Land Battles of the Spanish-American War in Cuba* (New York: D. Appleton and Company, 1898), 268. Hemment's disappointment anticipates D. W. Griffith's during World War I, when, upon arrival at the Western Front, he found himself "very disappointed with the reality of the battlefield." Griffith's deployment of melodramatic conventions in *Hearts of the World* (1918) to compensate for the battle's failure to supply a sense of drama highlights questions of realism and melodramatic affect.

29 Hemment, *Cannon and Camera*, 269.

30 Ibid., 158.

31 The visual obscurity of enemy combatants in contrast to the exposure of American troops served other ideological functions as well, supplanting the history of Cuban resistance with the conspicuous image of Anglo-American heroism; see Kaplan, *Anarchy of Empire*, 121–45.

32 On Manifest Destiny and the construction of Anglo-Saxonism, see Reginald Horsman, *Race and Manifest Destiny: The Origins of American Racial Anglo-Saxonism* (Cambridge, MA: Harvard University Press, 1981).

33 Edward Marshall "A Wounded Correspondent's Recollections of Guasimas," *Scribner's Magazine*, September 1898, 274–75.

34 Kaplan, "Spectacle of War," 104.

35 Richard Harding Davis, "The Battle of San Juan," *Scribner's Magazine*, October 1898, 402. The account still circulates widely in both critical and popular accounts; see, for instance, Kaplan, *Anarchy of Empire*, 125, and Moeller, *Shooting War*, 37.

36 Davis, "Battle of San Juan," 402.

37 Ibid.

38 Crane, *Reports of War*, ed. Fredson Bowers (Charlottesville: University of Virginia Press, 1971), 157.

39 On the gender politics underlying representations of turn-of-the-century imperialism, see Kristin Hoganson, *Fighting for American Manhood: How Gender Politics Provoked the Spanish-American and Philippine-American Wars* (New Haven, CT: Yale University Press, 1998).

40 Kristen Whissel offers a reading of this film very resonant with my own and considers it in contrast to the racialization of the comic body in the visually similar *Colored Troops Disembarking* (Edison 1898); see Whissel, "The Gender of Empire," in *A Feminist Reader in Early Cinema*, ed. Jennifer M. Bean and Diane Negra (Durham, NC: Duke University Press, 2002), 153–58. Amy Kaplan discusses the mediating function of African American soldiers made to play the minstrel's part in Roosevelt's own account of the Battle of San Juan; see *Anarchy of Empire*, 121–45.

41 See Hemment's description of the Cubans' natural affinity for concealment in "Among the Cuban Pickets," in *Cannon and Camera*.

42 See A.C.M. Azoy, *Charge! The Story of the Battle of San Juan Hill* (New York: David McKay, 1961), 137.

43 Brown, *Material Unconscious*, 236.

44 On the gendered dynamics of this gaze, see Kaplan, "Romancing the Empire," 111–17.

45 Kaplan, "Spectacle of War," 79, and Brown, *Material Unconscious*, 145.

46 Kaplan, "Spectacle of War," 100.

47 According to Bill Brown, Henry represents a performer "who has, as it were, internalized the spectacle, performing in response to his own projection. The public scene has been compressed into a private fantasy" (*Material Unconscious*, 132).

48 Stephen Crane, *The Red Badge of Courage: An Episode of the American Civil War* (New York: Signet Classics, 1960). For Brown's discussion of this "compulsion to picture," see *Material Unconscious*, 145.

49 David Axeen, "'Heroes of the Engine Room': American 'Civilization' and the War with Spain," *American Quarterly* 36 (1984): 497.

50 Ibid., 482.

51 Elihu Root, "The American Soldier," in *The Military and Colonial Policy of the United States* (Cambridge, MA: Harvard University Press, 1916), 3–4; cited in Axeen, "Heroes," 481.

52 On the war as a "warrior critique of business civilization," see John Mallan, "Roosevelt, Brooks Adams, and Lea," *American Quarterly* 8 (1956): 216–30.

53 Kaplan, "Spectacle of War," 98.

54 Alan Trachtenberg, *Reading American Photographs: Images as History, Matthew Brady to Walker Evans* (New York: Hill and Wang, 1989), 78.

55 The gendering of this position as masculine does not limit its availability to women, of course, who can and do take up the invitation to identify with the imperialist agency and mobility (as well as the vulnerability) that strenuous spectatorship works to construct.

56 In asserting the importance of the strenuous spectator to the evolution of early cinema, it is not my intention to displace or discredit accounts that emphasize the more unruly or resistant aspects of the institution or those that trace the significance of early cinema as a site of cultural feminization. Rather, my goal is to complicate our picture of early cinema spectatorship by exploring the conventions of direct address within the context of contemporary discourses of gender and

war, and to consider their significance as gendered signifiers of the authentic across the twentieth century.

57 Mary Ann Doane, "Technology's Body: Cinematic Vision in Modernity," *differences* 5 (1993): 2–3.

58 As Doane notes, "The body at issue in these discourses is a sexually and racially unspecified body. Such a configuration always suggests that what one is dealing with is, in fact, the white male body. And indeed, the language of failure or flaw and prosthetic power are those of a masculine scenario in which it is the male body which is put at risk by modernity" ("Technology's Body," 14).

59 Rabinovitz, *For the Love of Pleasure*, 32.

60 Laura Mulvey, "Visual Pleasure and Narrative Cinema," *Screen* 16 (1975): 6–18.

61 Lynn Kirby, *Parallel Tracks: The Railroad and Silent Cinema* (Durham, NC: Duke University Press, 1997), 69–70.

62 "The Nobler Side of War," *Century* 56 (September 1898): 794; cited in Lears, *No Place of Grace*, 112.

63 "How it feels to be under fire" and "the awful sensations of a Naval encounter" appear as entries in *Hero Tales of the American Soldier and Sailor* (Philadelphia: Century Manufacturing Company, 1899); the former account is also cited in John Pettegrew, "'The Soldier's Faith': Turn-of-the-Century Memory of the Civil War and the Emergence of American Nationalism," *Journal of Contemporary History* 31 (1996): 61. The wounded correspondent Edward Marshall wrote the account of "How it feels to be shot," which first appeared in *The Cosmopolitan*, September 1898, 557–58; also cited in Moeller, *Shooting War*, 61.

64 Union veteran B. F. Scribner discussed the "regenerative possibilities" of war in *How Soldiers Were Made* (1887), cited in Pettegrew, "'The Soldier's Faith,'" 58.

65 The quote is from Spanish-American War veteran Charles Johnson Post; see *The Little War of Private Post* (Boston: Little, Brown and Company, 1960), 123.

66 Doane, "Technology's Body," 6.

67 On the imbrication of realism and sensationalism, see, for example, Vanessa Schwartz, *Spectacular Realities: Early Mass Culture in Fin-de-Siècle Paris* (Berkeley: University of California Press, 1998).

68 M. G. Van Rensselaer, "At the Fair," *Century Magazine* 46 (May 1893): 11; cited in Rabinovitz, *For the Love of Pleasure*, 7.

69 Moeller, *Shooting War*, 49. For additional discussion of these activities, see also Brown, *Material Unconscious*.

70 Brown, *Material Unconscious*, 161.

71 Kaplan, "Spectacle of War," 103. On the heroization of the war correspondent, see also Brown, *Material Unconscious*, 125–66.

72 Davis, "Our War Correspondents," 941–42.

73 Crane, *Active Service* (1899), cited in Kaplan, "Romancing the Empire," 678, and Brown, *Material Unconscious*, 160.

74 "Character Sketch. Mr. James Creelman, War Correspondent," *Review of Reviews* 18 (October 1898): 339; cited in Brown, *Material Unconscious*, 160.

75 Davis, "Our War Correspondents," 941.

76 Burr McIntosh, for instance, self-consciously parallels a gunner's preparations to fire the first artillery shot at San Juan Hill with his own preparations to "shoot" the gunner. The simultaneity of these actions is signified by the shaky image that results from the simultaneity of the shots, confirming the location of both gunner and photographer in the midst of violent action. See McIntosh, *The Little I Saw of Cuba* (1899); cited in Moeller, *Shooting War*, 58.

77 According to Hemment, "the successful illustrator nowadays must have something of the athlete, the sportsman, the soldier, and the sailor in his composition"—an evaluation echoed by W. I. Lincoln Adams in his introduction to *Cannon and Camera*, in which he identifies Hemment as an athlete "peculiarly well fitted to undertake the hazardous enterprise" of "shooting" war, noting that it is "to his courage as a man as well as to his skill as a photographer" that the book is owed (*Cannon and Camera*, xi).

78 On the gendered construction of a consumer gaze in relation to the early cinema in particular, see Rabinovitz, *For the Love of Pleasure*. Amy Kaplan's account of the female gaze as it structures the contemporary romance novel is also relevant; see "Romancing the Empire."

79 Brown, *Material Unconscious*, 320n90.

80 Annual report of Harvard president Charles Eliot, quoted in "The Week," *The Nation*, March 1894, 147.

81 J. A. Hobson, *Imperialism* (1902; Ann Arbor: University of Michigan Press, 1965), 215, and Kaplan, "Spectacle of War," 102.

82 *New York Journal and Advertiser*, April 26, 1898, 13; cited in Musser, *Before the Nickelodeon*, 129. For discussion of the war program's significance to the development of narrative, see also Musser, *Emergence of Cinema*.

83 Whissel, *Picturing American Modernity*, 63–116.

84 For the most influential iterations of this thesis, see Tom Gunning, "The Cinema of Attractions: Early Film, Its Spectator, and the Avant-Garde," *Wide Angle* 8 (1986): 63–70, and Gunning, "Aesthetic of Astonishment."

85 Quoted in Jay Leyda, *Kino* (London: Allen & Unwin, 1960), 407–9; also cited in Gunning, "Aesthetic of Astonishment," 118.

86 Rabinovitz, *For the Love of Pleasure*, 147.

87 Cited in Charles Musser, *Edison Motion Pictures, 1890–1900: An Annotated Filmography* (Washington, DC: Smithsonian Institution Press, 1997), 589. The sense of collision is represented with particular force in this film by a cut that covers over a moment of actual impact.

88 Musser, *Emergence of Cinema*, 4.

89 Rick Altman, *Silent Film Sound* (New York: Columbia University Press, 2007), 86; and Musser, *Emergence of Cinema*, 138.

90 Wolfgang Schivelbusch, *The Railway Journey: The Industrialization of Time and Space in the 19th Century* (Berkeley: University of California Press, 1986), 150–58.

91 On the masculine image of American imperial mobility, see Kaplan, "Romancing the Empire," 685–90, and especially Whissel, "Gender of Empire," 141–65.

92 Kemp Niver offers this description of *Skirmish Fight* (AMB 1903) in *Early Motion Pictures: The Paper Print Collection in the Library of Congress* (Washington, DC: Library of Congress, 1985), 300.

93 Quoted in Musser, *Edison Motion Pictures*, 500.

94 For Whissel's incisive discussion of the genre of battle reenactments in this period, see *Picturing Modernity*. Though I came upon Whissel's work sadly late in the development of these arguments, her discussion is highly resonant with my own.

95 For an extended discussion of this function as it animates American cinema across the twentieth century, see Eagle, "Making a Spectacle of Himself."

96 See Hoganson, *Fighting for American Manhood*. Though she does not discuss melodrama specifically, Hoganson provides excellent evidence of the melodramatic conventions shaping contemporary war discourse.

97 For a longer discussion of the relationship between the Wild West and the military actualities, see Eagle, "Making a Spectacle of Himself." Whissel, too, argues for the importance of the Wild West to early cinema; see *Picturing American Modernity*.

98 Kirby, *Parallel Tracks*, 79.

99 For a discussion of how *The Red Badge of Courage* reinterprets war "through the cultural lens of the lens itself" in ways that anticipate Spanish-American War representation, see Brown, *Material Unconscious*, 125–66.

100 See Richard Abel, *The Red Rooster Scare: Making Cinema American, 1900–1910* (Berkeley: University of California Press, 1999).

101 My intention here is to signal the cultural construction of such a pleasure rather than to delimit the gender of subjects who may take up the invitation to identify with it.

2 Manifest Destiny in Action

1 The *BFI Companion to the Western*, ed. Edward Buscombe (New York: Atheneum, 1988), attributes the erroneous date of 1895 to this 1903 painting, leading to some confusion. Buscombe references this earlier date when he notes the painting as anticipating *The Great Train Robbery*; see "Painting the Legend: Frederic Remington and the Western," *Cinema Journal* 23 (1984): 18.

2 In *White* (London: Routledge, 1997), Richard Dyer suggests that "[i]t is in the visceral qualities of the Western . . . that enterprise and imperialism have had their most undeliberated, powerful appeal" (33).

3 See Vachel Lindsay, *The Art of the Moving Picture* (1915; New York: Liveright, 1970), 289–90. Richard Slotkin also cites this passage in *Gunfighter Nation: The Myth of the Frontier in Twentieth-Century America* (New York: HarperCollins, 1992), 237.

4 André Bazin, "The Western, or the American Film par excellence," in *What Is Cinema?* trans. Hugh Gray (Berkeley: University of California Press, 1971), 140–41. Jean-Luc Godard similarly claims the Western as "the most cinematographic genre in the cinema"; see *Godard on Godard*, trans. Tom Milne (New York: Viking Press, 1972), 117 (cited in Buscombe, "Painting the Legend," 19).

5 For exceptions, see, for instance, Linda Williams, "Melodrama Revised," in *Refiguring American Film Genres: History and Theory*, ed. Nick Browne

(Berkeley: University of California Press, 1998), and Charles Musser, "Rethinking Early Cinema," *Yale Journal of Criticism* 2 (1994): 203–32.

6 Richard Abel, *The Red Rooster Scare: Making Cinema American, 1900–1910* (Berkeley: University of California Press, 1999), 171.

7 On the Western's role in negotiating American as opposed to foreign film production, see Abel, *Red Rooster Scare*, especially chapter 6.

8 Christine Gledhill has discussed how aesthetic processes, themselves derived from ideological material, "[hand back] to the social affective experience and moral perceptions"; see "Rethinking Genre," in *Reinventing Film Studies*, ed. Christine Gledhill and Linda Williams (London: Arnold, 2000), 240.

9 For influential examples, see Thomas Elsaesser, "Tales of Sound and Fury: Observations on the Family Melodrama," *Monogram* 4 (1972): 2–15; Christine Gledhill, ed., *Home Is Where the Heart Is: Studies in Melodrama and the Woman's Film* (London: British Film Institute, 1987); and Mary Ann Doane, *The Desire to Desire: The Woman's Film of the 1940s* (Bloomington: Indiana University Press, 1987).

10 Important exceptions to this tendency include calls by Christine Gledhill and Linda Williams to consider the status of male action genres as melodrama; see Gledhill, "Rethinking Genre," and Williams, "Melodrama Revised." Others have noted more casually the status of the Western as melodramatic without considering further this appellation; see, for instance, Philip French, *Westerns: Aspects of a Movie Genre* (New York: Viking Press, 1973); Robert Lang, *American Film Melodrama: Griffith, Vidor, Minnelli* (Princeton, NJ: Princeton University Press, 1989); and Michael Coyne, *The Crowded Prairie: The Hollywood Western and American National Identity* (London: I. B. Tauris, 1997). David N. Rodowick, who contrasts melodrama with action-oriented genres like the Western, nonetheless notes that the Western is "heavily determined by melodramatic content"; see "Madness, Authority and Ideology: The Domestic Melodrama of the 1950s," in Gledhill, ed., *Home Is Where the Heart Is*. Douglas Pye considers melodrama's relevance to the Western, though limits this discussion to the post-*Stagecoach* era, highlighting the association of melodrama with pathos; see his "Introduction" and "The Collapse of Fantasy" in *The Book of Westerns*, ed. Ian Cameron and Douglas Pye (New York: Continuum, 1996). In contrast, studies of other media are quite explicit in recognizing the melodramatic structures undergirding Western action; see, for example, Roger A. Hall, *Performing the American Frontier, 1870–1906* (Cambridge: Cambridge University Press, 2001).

11 See, for instance, Tom Gunning, "The Horror of Opacity: The Melodrama of Sensation in the Plays of Andre de Lorde," in *Melodrama: Stage, Picture, Screen*, ed. Jacky Bratton, Jim Cook, and Christine Gledhill (London: British Film Institute, 1994); Vanessa Schwartz, *Spectacular Realities: Early Mass Culture in Fin-de-Siècle Paris* (Berkeley: University of California Press, 1998); and Shelley Streeby, *American Sensations: Class, Empire, and the Production of Popular Culture* (Berkeley: University of California Press, 2002).

12 Williams, "Melodrama Revised," 42.

13 Steve Neale, "Melo Talk: On the Meaning and Use of the Term 'Melodrama' in the American Trade Press," *Velvet Light Trap* 32 (1993): 66–89.

14 See, for instance, Abel, *Red Rooster Scare*, 152–56, and Scott Simmon, *The Invention of the Western Film: A Cultural History of the Genre's First Half-Century* (Cambridge: Cambridge University Press, 2003). The authenticity associated with the geographical West masculinizes male cultural producers as well, as film actors and directors have joined the ranks of men like Roosevelt, Remington, and Wister in exclaiming over the revitalization that cultural production in the West affords.

15 Simmon, *Invention of the Western Film*, 66.

16 The image of eastern contamination included labor unrest and "class savagery," concerns absent from popular representations of the West; see Alex Nemerov, "Doing the 'Old America': The Image of the American West, 1880–1920," in *The West as America: Reinterpreting Images of the Frontier, 1820–1920*, ed. William H. Truettner (Washington, DC: Smithsonian Institution Press, 1991). The Western's insistence on the cowboy as a paragon of manly self-reliance free from commercial contamination is founded upon denial of his historical status as a wage laborer and of the intensely commercialized process through which he is refigured as a popular hero.

17 "When the horses pound toward the camera and pull up in a cloud of dust, my breath gets short"; see Jane Tompkins, *West of Everything: The Inner Life of Westerns* (New York: Oxford University Press, 1992), 3.

18 Tompkins considers the Western in relation to its "impact on the body and the emotions," an angle largely neglected within film studies (although implicit in the emphasis on the genre's "thrilling" nature). Her account in *West of Everything* takes the genre's assertion of its privileged relationship to the real largely on its own terms, however; and by considering the Western in explicit contrast to the domestic novel, she neglects questions of pathos and sentimentality in the genre.

19 Insistence on the Western as a realist text often entails resistance to consideration of the genre's address at the level of the body, suggesting the extent to which denigration of sensational genres is a selective process. While "body genres," such as pornography, horror, and "women's weepies," are stigmatized on the basis of their call to mimetic bodily response, the visceral impact of the Western is normalized through the discourse of the "thrill." On body genres, see Linda Williams, "Film Bodies: Genre, Gender, and Excess," *Film Quarterly* 44 (Summer 1991): 2–13, and Carol Clover, *Men, Women, and Chain Saws: Gender in the Modern Horror Film* (Princeton, NJ: Princeton University Press, 1992).

20 Paul Willemen raises a similar question in *Looks and Frictions: Essays in Cultural Studies and Film Theory* (Bloomington: Indiana University Press, 1994): "which socio-historical forces are the main determinants generating [melodramatic] discourses; and . . . in which direction do these media discourses actually seek to move their consumers?" (97).

21 Peter Brooks, *The Melodramatic Imagination: Balzac, Henry James, Melodrama, and the Mode of Excess* (New Haven, CT: Yale University Press, 1976).

22 David Mayer, "Theater, Melodrama," in *Encyclopedia of Early Cinema*, ed. Richard Abel (London: Routledge, 2005), 912.

23 Daniel Gerould, ed., *American Melodrama* (New York: PAJ Publications, 1983), 7–9.

24 See Gunning, "Horror of Opacity."

25 See Ben Singer, *Melodrama and Modernity: Early Sensational Cinema and Its Contexts* (New York: Columbia University Press, 2001), and Gunning, "Horror of Opacity," 53.

26 Gunning, "Horror of Opacity," 51–52.

27 The phrase, from publicity material for the 101 Ranch Show, is cited in Paul Reddin, *Wild West Shows* (Urbana: University of Illinois Press, 1999), 175. In addition to Neale, Gledhill, and Williams, on melodrama's investment in producing sensational attractions under the auspices of "lifelike" representation, see Gunning, "Horror of Opacity." For related discussions of the historical imbrication of the sensational and the real, see Schwartz, *Spectacular Realities*, and Streeby, *American Sensation*.

28 On Cody's "characteristic confusion of the theatrical and the historical or political," and the authenticating function of this confusion, see in particular Slotkin, *Gunfighter Nation*, 63–87.

29 Reddin, *Wild West Shows*, 67.

30 Richard B. Wilson, "Music for a Changing Nation: Buffalo Bill's Wild West Goes International," an essay accompanying *Wild West Music of Buffalo Bill's Cowboy Band*, Buffalo Bill Center of the West, Cody, Wyoming, http://www.bbhc.org/explore/buffalo-bill/research/buffalo-bill-band/.

31 Cited in Reddin, *Wild West Shows*, 77, 63.

32 Christine Bold makes a similar point regarding Remington's work, noting that "cavalrymen and cowboys are shown to be engaged in the same activities, working with horses, galloping in groups, firing at enemies: the costumes are different but the purposes are not." See "The Rough Riders at Home and Abroad: Cody, Roosevelt, Remington, and the Imperialist Hero," *Canadian Review of American Studies* 18 (1987): 339. As Bold suggests, casting the contemporary soldier as cowboy hero helps to mediate problematic implications of the nation's imperialist ambitions.

33 Linda Williams, *Playing the Race Card: Melodramas of Black and White From Uncle Tom to O.J. Simpson* (Princeton, NJ: Princeton University Press, 2001), 44.

34 Williams, "Melodrama Revised," 83n15. Ken Burns's PBS documentary *The West* notes the centrality of white victimization to Wild West attractions: "This is a show about conquest . . . yet everything the audience sees is Indians attacking whites . . . it's a celebration of conquest in which the conquerors are the victims . . . what is going on when you celebrate a conquest and you only see yourself being victimized?" Williams cites part of this voiceover in *Playing the Race Card*, 43–44.

35 Buscombe, "Painting the Legend," 13, 25.

36 On earlier traditions of Western painting, see ibid. and Nemerov, "Doing the 'Old America.'"

37 In Carl Wimar's *Attack on an Emigrant Train* (1856), for example, the poses are static and statuesque, the action securely contained within the frame. In George Catlin's *Fire in a Missouri Meadow, and a Party of Sioux Indians Escaping From It: Upper Missouri 1871* (whose title signals its denotative rather than sensationalist representational mode), the battle is represented at a distance, the fleeing Indians are small mounted figures amid an ocean of grass, and the delicate tongues of

flame lick at a distant horizon; there is no effort to encompass the viewer in the space of the action or to render this action in visceral or kinesthetic terms.

38 Cited in Peggy Samuels et al., *Techniques of the Artists of the American West* (Secaucus, NJ: Wellfleet Press, 1990), 180.

39 As Nemerov suggests, Remington signals the legitimacy of violence through the use of clean lines and right angles in representing figures of Anglo-American authority on the western frontier and in eastern industrial cities, and disorderly lines marking the "savage" violence of Indians and working-class immigrants in contrast; see "Doing the 'Old America.'"

40 Buscombe also draws attention to these tendencies, noting that while "Remington's figures characteristically proceed across the frame in long diagonals, Schreyvogel's frequently rush full tilt at the spectator, threatening to jump right out of the frame" ("Painting the Legend," 18).

41 As Buscombe notes as well, "[t]he focus in [Remington's] work is on the moment of action frozen at the point of its maximum impact." He also identifies the tendency toward narrativization in western paintings of this period, suggesting its relationship to their journalistic function; see "Painting the Legend," 17.

42 A similar doubling is witnessed in the right middleground, where an Indian on bended knee raises his rifle toward one cavalryman, while a second cavalryman points his revolver at the Indian's head.

43 See Samuels et al., *Artists of the American West*, 179.

44 For discussion of Remington's Last Stand images in relation to issues of class conflict, racial and ethnic identity, and immigration, see Nemerov, "Doing the 'Old America.'" On these images as capitalist allegory, see also Richard Slotkin, *The Fatal Environment: The Myth of the Frontier in the Age of Industrialization, 1800–1890* (New York: Atheneum, 1985). For more general discussion of Remington's Last Stand images, see Ben Merchant Vorpahl, *Frederic Remington and the West: With the Eye of the Mind* (Austin: University of Texas Press, 1978).

45 In *Caught in a Circle*, even the injured man props himself up on one arm to fire his rifle.

46 Nemerov, "Doing the 'Old America,'" 299.

47 For Remington's disparagement of Schreyvogel's work on the basis of the latter's inauthentic detail, see James D. Horan, *The Life and Art of Charles Schreyvogel* (New York: Crown Publishers, 1969). Horan cites Remington's objection to the "color of Colonel Crosby's pantaloons" in *Custer's Demand*, among many others.

48 Nemerov, "Doing the 'Old America,'" 290.

49 For discussion of western painting and its influence on film Westerns, including the shifting emphasis toward thrilling action in the work of Remington and his contemporaries, see Buscombe, "Painting the Legend."

50 Vorpahl considers this new angle on action as it implies the presence of Remington himself as observer, in line with the "prescriptive point of view" he traces to Remington's work after Wounded Knee (in contrast to the more presentational mode of the earlier Last Stand images); see *Frederic Remington and the West*, 104–26.

51 Filmed live attractions were composed along these lines, as in *Sham Battle at the Pan-American Exposition* (Edison 1901), discussed in the last chapter.

52 Nemerov, "Doing the 'Old America,'" 291.

53 The sentimental "Indian pictures" produced between 1908 and 1910 and shot in the lush woodlands of the Northeast, for instance, rely more on the literary legacy of James Fenimore Cooper than on the sensationalist conventions of the Wild West show. These feature the Indian as a tragic figure in the tradition of the Noble Savage or the Pocahontas myth, portrayed as both a victim of white society and as its self-sacrificing defender. As early as 1909, however, it seems to have been the "Wild West" Westerns for which audiences were "clamoring." As Simmon notes, the consolidation of the Western away from the sentimental occurred at a time when the genre was considered by many to be in decline; the intensification of action and violence contributed to its revival, as "[how to narrate killing] . . . seems to have been the discovery that saved the genre itself from the death so widely predicted for it in 1911." See *Invention of the Western Film*, 45–46.

54 See Simmon, *Invention of the Western Film*, and Eileen Bowser, *The Transformation of Cinema, 1907–1915* (New York: Charles Scribner's Sons, 1990).

55 Since the explosion of cheap storefront theaters around 1905, reformist discourse had focused on the cinema as a site of working-class and immigrant unruliness; by 1907, the industry began incorporating these concerns to an increasing degree. See, for example, Tom Gunning, "From the Opium Den to the Theatre of Morality: Moral Discourse and the Film Process in Early American Cinema," *Art and Text* 30 (1988): 30–40; Anne Friedberg, "'A Properly Adjusted Window': Vision and Sanity in D. W. Griffith's 1908–1909 Biograph Films," in *Early Cinema: Space/Frame/Narrative*, ed. Thomas Elsaesser (London: British Film Institute, 1990); and Lee Grieveson, *Policing Cinema: Movies and Censorship in Early-Twentieth-Century America* (Berkeley: University of California Press, 2004). For examples of early film theory's investment in the discourse of reform, see Hugo Munsterberg's *The Film: A Psychological Study* (1916; New York: Dover, 1970), and Vachel Lindsay's *The Art of the Moving Picture* (1915; New York: Liveright, 1970). The Western suggests a different angle than the working-class masculine reform discussed by Grieveson and Friedberg, however, emphasizing the cinema's investment in a process of masculinization alongside the more familiar impulse of feminization in this period. Richard Abel makes a similar point in relation to the appeal of early Westerns to young male audiences: "The attempt to 'masculinize' moving pictures through 'realist' narratives, and particularly westerns, could be seen, then, as part of a push to transform the 'feminized' space of the nickelodeon into a juvenile or even adult complement to the fraternal organization" (*Red Rooster Scare*, 279n101). Reform discourse itself acknowledged the need to appeal to the male spectator in its desire to supplant the function of the saloon with that of the cinema; see Friedberg, "'A Properly Adjusted Window,'" and Gunning, "From the Opium Den."

56 In contrast to the Western, these urban-themed films featured mostly immigrant and often female protagonists, and focused on issues of sexual alongside other forms of violence.

57 Singer, *Melodrama and Modernity*, 129.

58 Ben Singer cites Ludwig Lewisohn, writing in *The Nation* in 1920, on the pleasure that collective identification with the representation of violence affords. "Nations

addicted to physical violence of a simpler and more direct kind have cultivated the arena and the bull ring," Lewisohn argues. "Those who desire their impulses of cruelty to seem the fruit of moral energy substitute melodrama" (*Melodrama and Modernity*, 41).

59 See Tompkins, *West of Everything*, 228–29.

60 Richard Slotkin suggests how this function extends beyond the cinema, arguing that, with Owen Wister's *Virginian*, a new moral logic emerges, in which "the primary sign of social and moral superiority is not nobility but *virility*," constituted through the white Western hero's status as an agent of action and violence; see *Gunfighter Nation*, 176.

61 Williams, "Melodrama Revised," 52.

62 Roberta Pearson notes at least nine such films produced between 1909 and 1926; see "The Revenge of Rain-in-the-Face?" in *The Birth of Whiteness: Race and the Emergence of U.S. Cinema*, ed. Daniel Bernardi (New Brunswick, NJ: Rutgers University Press, 1996).

63 As Simmon argues, it was the resonance of early Westerns with the Wild West show in particular that impressed contemporary audiences with their realism. See *Invention of the Western Film*, 61–63.

64 On the Custer myth and the silent Western, including *Custer's Last Fight*, see Pearson, "Revenge."

65 Williams, "Melodrama Revised," 61, 80–81.

66 "Surprise attack" is the intertitle reference to the initial attack. In its ambiguity, the film resonates with Griffith's earlier Indian pictures and anticipates the mid-century cycle of "pro-Indian" Westerns discussed in the next chapter. *Custer's Last Fight* also features an initial attack by the U.S. Cavalry upon an "unsuspecting Indian village"; but in contrast to the image of domestic harmony that Griffith offers, the interior space of the teepee in Ince's film is represented as a site of strife and neglect, and the white attack on the Indian village is not shown onscreen. Rather, we see the retreating cavalrymen being fired upon by the Indians, and white bodies litter the ground after the fighting is over, suggesting how—even when Indians are thematically positioned as victims of assault—the Western invests in the suffering of white protagonists.

67 Williams discusses how black bodies signifying "chaos and disorder" are repeatedly flushed from the screen in a flood of whiteness; see *Playing the Race Card*, 120–22.

68 This passage has been widely cited; see, for instance, Richard Schickel, *D. W. Griffith: An American Life* (New York: Simon and Schuster, 1984), 212.

69 Amy Kaplan, "The Birth of an Empire" *PMLA* 114 (1999): 1074.

70 The iconic significance of the cabin is multifaceted and complex. Michael Rogin reads it as a Lincolnesque site of humble origins in "'The Sword Became a Flashing Vision': D. W. Griffith's *The Birth of a Nation*," in *Ronald Reagan, The Movie, and Other Episodes in Political Demonology* (Berkeley: University of California Press, 1987). Linda Williams reads it in the context of *Uncle Tom's Cabin* in *Playing the Race Card*. Richard Slotkin argues, as I do, for its resonance with Western entertainments; see *Gunfighter Nation*, 240–41.

71 Williams, *Playing the Race Card*, 128.

72 This failure is represented most starkly by his inability to save his virginal sister from the sexual rapacity of the freed slave Gus—a failure of chivalric manhood itself.

73 Cited in Slotkin, *Gunfighter Nation*, 250.

74 Hart's visualization of self-control would pass into the sound era in the guise of the laconic Western hero who exemplifies Christine Gledhill's claim that "the taciturnity of masculine realism" serves as "the seedbed of melodramatic emotion" ("Rethinking Genre," 236).

75 These and other contemporary reviews are cited by Coyne, *Crowded Prairie*, 53–54. For a contemporary objection to *Shane*'s aestheticizing tendencies, see Robert Warshow, "Movie Chronicle: The Westerner," in *The Immediate Experience: Movies, Comics, Theatre and Other Aspects of Popular Culture* (Garden City, NY: Doubleday, 1962).

76 Alongside "plenty of action" and "an impossibly incorrigible villain," Mix's wife identified "a very white hero" among the key elements of the highly successful Mix formula; cited in Reddin, *Wild West Shows*, 199.

77 In an indication of how persistently the Western is associated with masculine virtues, even the genre's economic status is noted in terms that highlight its hardness and substance, as the "bedrock" upon which all the "glitter of Hollywood" is founded; see "The Western: A Short History," in *The BFI Companion to the Western*.

78 Simmon, *Invention of the Western Film*, 141.

79 The tendency of the Bs to forgo strong emotional response in favor of a heightened investment in fast, decisive action leads a critic like Thomas Elsaesser to contrast the Western with the domestic melodrama, though such an opposition neglects the centrality of action to the melodramatic tradition; see "Tales of Sound and Fury."

80 Lee Clark Mitchell makes this argument in relation to the onscreen gaze of Joey at Shane; it can be usefully extended to the spectator's own relationship to Shane's image and to that of the Western hero more generally. See *Westerns: Making the Man in Fiction and Film* (Chicago: University of Chicago Press, 1996), 195.

81 Peter Stanfield, "Dixie Cowboys and Blue Yodels: The Strange History of the Singing Cowboy," in *Back in the Saddle Again: New Essays on the Western*, ed. Edward Buscombe and Roberta E. Pearson (London: British Film Institute, 1998), 100. At least since Wister's *Virginian*, the Western has engaged in a complicated dance around its hero's association with the South, nationalizing the image of the cowboy hero while alluding to his Southern origins. The genre employs an association with the South to establish the hero's chivalric claims, heighten his pathos, and explore issues of moral instability (as in the white supremacism of recalcitrant Confederate Ethan Edwards in *The Searchers*). The South, as Richard Dyer argues, "seems to be the myth that both most consciously asserts whiteness and most devastatingly undermines it, whereas the West takes the project of whiteness for granted and achieved" (*White*, 36). However, as Scott Simmon notes, "[t]he fragility of the Western genre's high ethical and democratic claims

would become awfully clear were they to be made about the 'Old South' instead of the 'Old West'" (*Invention of the Western Film*, 160). For additional discussion of the relationship of the South to the imagination of the West, see Slotkin, *Gunfighter Nation*.

82 In *Neath the Arizona Skies* (Fraser 1934), John Wayne is given a similar role as an adoptive father to an Osage daughter. In general, the paternal role is conventionally used to manage the suggestion of interracial romance with which the B Western also plays.

83 This project, evident in the earlier figure of the "good badman," stretches back at least as far as Wister's *Virginian*.

84 Simmons, *Invention of the Western Film*, 168.

85 These films echo earlier images of the charge, but convoluted plots and limited production values can create confusion between vigilante good guys and their bad guy imposters. In *The Purple Vigilantes* (Sherman 1938), for instance, early sequences of vigilantes crashing into town on their nightly crusade represent a legitimate source of violence, while later formally identical sequences represent the misappropriation of the vigilante guise in the service of criminality and crass economic gain. Even within the diegesis, the two groups are composed of many of the same men, further undermining the distinction. Other films negotiate the moral ambivalence of vigilante violence by assigning it to men marked as foreign. In *The Fighting Renegade* (Newfield 1939), Tim McCoy dons the disguise of the heavily accented and mustachioed "El Puma" in his extralegal pursuit of justice, a conceit that distances the McCoy persona from the moral instability of vigilante violence. In *The Night Riders*, the name of the band (Los Capaqueros) functions similarly.

86 The B hero's association with Robin Hood is frequently made explicit through newspaper clippings, soundtrack lyrics, and dialogue.

87 The B Western participates in the long history of popular cultural forms that have consolidated national identity through a cross-class invitation to identify with whiteness. Like its predecessors, the Bs make this invitation with particular force to an economically disenfranchised male audience, associating the image of whiteness with traditional values of masculine independence and authority. Much work has been done on the consolidation of white and national identity across class and ethnic lines and on the role of popular culture in this process. See, for instance, David Roediger, *The Wages of Whiteness: Race and the Making of the American Working Class* (London: Verso, 1991); Robert Toll, *Blacking Up: The Minstrel Show in Nineteenth-Century America* (New York: Oxford University Press, 1974); Eric Lott, *Love and Theft: Blackface Minstrelsy and the American Working Class* (Oxford: Oxford University Press, 1995); Michael Rogin, *Blackface, White Noise: Jewish Immigrants in the Hollywood Melting Pot* (Berkeley: University of California Press, 1996); Alexander Saxton, *The Rise and Fall of the White Republic: Class Politics and Mass Culture in Nineteenth-Century America* (London: Verso, 1990); Nancy MacLean, *Behind the Mask of Chivalry: The Making of the Second Ku Klux Klan* (Oxford: Oxford University Press, 1994); Grace Elizabeth Hale, *Making Whiteness: The Culture of Segregation in the South, 1890–1940*

(New York: Random House, 1998); and Matthew Frye Jacobson, *Whiteness of a Different Color: European Immigrants and the Alchemy of Race* (Cambridge, MA: Harvard University Press, 1998).

88 Consistent with the turn-of-the-century image of the knightly hero, whose claims to whiteness and manliness were constituted through rejection of economic self-interest, the raw drive for economic influence, wealth, and power is decried as antithetical to the substance of the Western hero, who is motivated by fidelity to an inner code of honor rather than commercial gain. In its dissociation of masculine action from materialist aims, the genre is consistent with the discourse of the strenuous life—a discourse that decried the commercial degradation of white masculinity and rallied the nation around an image of manliness revitalized through imperialist action, even as this action functioned in the service of commercial and bureaucratic forces. This point runs somewhat counter to Richard Dyer's representation of the appeals of enterprise and imperialism as more fully merged. It is in the implicit embrace of the latter in the context of a disavowal of the former, I would argue, that the conventions of the Western find their most ideologically powerful form.

89 On the "binding" of the impact of violence within narrative cinema and the production of narrative sense out of kinesthetic sensation, see Marsha Kinder, "Violence American Style," and Leo Charney, "The Violence of a Perfect Moment," both in *Violence and American Cinema*, ed. J. David Slocum (New York: Routledge, 2001).

3 Western Weepies

1 Thomas Pauly describes the Cold War Western in similar terms, noting the genre's "substitution of anxiety for action" and the status of the hero as a man who "walked more than he rode and brooded more than he acted"; see "The Cold War Western," *Western Humanities Review* (1979): 259. Pauly's comments resonate with the earlier complaint of George N. Fenin and William K. Everson: "In older westerns, men acted; for better or for worse, wisely or stupidly, they acted. They didn't ponder, debate, subject their tortured souls to self-examination." See *The Western: From Silents to Cinerama* (New York: Orion Press, 1962).

2 The noir influence emerges most emphatically in 1947 with Raoul Walsh's *Pursued* and is invigorated by Anthony Mann's move from noir to the Western in the 1950s. For specific discussion of the anxiety of noir in relationship to postwar masculinity, see, for instance, Frank Krutnik, *In a Lonely Street: Film Noir, Genre, Masculinity* (London: Routledge, 1991), and Robert Corber, *Homosexuality in Cold War America: Resistance and the Crisis of Masculinity* (Durham, NC: Duke University Press, 1997). Scott Simmon reads the postwar Western as significantly structured through its relationship to noir in *The Invention of the Western Film: A Cultural History of the Genre's First Half-Century* (Cambridge: Cambridge University Press, 2003).

3 David Savran, too, examines the emergence of the white male as victim in cultural discourse of the 1950s, although he focuses on the marginalized image

of the hipster and the gradual transformation of this figure within mainstream discourse; see *Taking It Like a Man: White Masculinity, Masochism, and Contemporary American Culture* (Princeton, NJ: Princeton University Press, 1998).

4 The mid-century surge in crisis discourse is a familiar chapter in the history of masculinity in America. See, for example, Michael Kimmel, *Manhood in America: A Cultural History* (New York: Free Press, 1996); Barbara Ehrenreich, *The Hearts of Men: American Dreams and the Flight from Commitment* (New York: Anchor, 1984); Savran, *Taking It Like a Man*; Robert J. Corber, *In the Name of National Security: Hitchcock, Homophobia, and the Political Construction of Gender in Postwar America* (Durham, NC: Duke University Press, 1996); and Steve Cohan, *Masked Men: Masculinity and the Movies in the Fifties* (Bloomington: Indiana University Press, 1997). Timothy Melley's discussion of "agency panic" and "the paradox in which a supposedly individualistic culture conserves its individualism by continually imagining it to be in imminent peril" resonates with my own consideration of crisis discourse. See *Empire of Conspiracy: The Culture of Paranoia in Postwar America* (Ithaca, NY: Cornell University Press, 2000), 6, and Jonna K. Eagle, "Making a Spectacle of Himself: White Masculinity, Melodrama, and Sensation in the American Cinema, 1898–1999" (PhD diss., Brown University, 2006).

5 Arthur Scheslinger Jr., "The Crisis of American Masculinity" (1958), in *The Politics of Hope* (Boston: Houghton Mifflin, 1963).

6 Robert Warshow, *The Immediate Experience: Movies, Comics, Theatre and Other Aspects of Popular Culture* (Garden City, NY: Doubleday, 1962), 139; Schlesinger, "Crisis of American Masculinity," 237.

7 This is the title of a book by the editors of *Look* magazine, published in 1958 by Random House.

8 Alarm over the national "peril" of American matriarchy increased in the years following World War II. In 1946, for instance, psychiatrist Edward Strecker attributed to maternal influence the mass failure of "psychoneurotic" recruits during the war; see *Their Mothers' Sons* (New York: J. B. Lippincott, 1946). First published in 1942, Philip Wylie's vitriolic *Generation of Vipers* (New York: Farrar & Rinehart, 1942), which ranted against the "megaloid Mom worship" crippling American culture, became a best-seller in the 1950s.

9 The release of the Kinsey Report in 1948 also played a role in denaturalizing the process of heterosexual masculine development.

10 Schlesinger, "Crisis of American Masculinity," 244.

11 Almost every account of the Western in this period notes the transformation of the genre along these lines. For general discussions, see Fenin and Everson, *The Western*; Richard Slotkin, *Gunfighter Nation: The Myth of the Frontier in Twentieth-Century America* (New York: HarperCollins, 1992); Douglas Pye, "Introduction: Criticism and the Western," in *The Book of Westerns*, ed. Ian Cameron and Douglas Pye (New York: Continuum, 1996); and Pauly, "Cold War Western." For more specific consideration of the industrial and social pressures conditioning such shifts, see Philip French, *Westerns: Aspects of a Movie Genre*

(New York: Viking Press, 1973). On the industrial turn toward "adult" themes, see Barbara Klinger, "'Local' Genres: The Hollywood Adult Film in the 1950s," in *Melodrama: Stage, Picture, Screen*, ed. Jacky Bratton, Jim Cook, and Christine Gledhill (London: British Film Institute, 1994).

12 Warshow, "Movie Chronicle: The Westerner," in *Immediate Experience*, 144.

13 See French, *Westerns*, and Warshow, *Immediate Experience*, 143.

14 In contrast to Judith Halberstam's discussion of the queer resonance of failure, my argument here emphasizes the role that failure and its affects may play in shoring up normative subject positions and our attachments to these positions, even while they point up fissures in the uniform or stable constitution of the normative. See *The Queer Art of Failure* (Durham, NC: Duke University Press, 2011).

15 Wister asserts that "the knight and the cowboy are nothing but the same Saxon of different environments"; see "The Evolution of the Cow-Puncher" (1895), in *Owen Wister's West: Selected Articles*, ed. Robert Murray Davis (Albuquerque: University of New Mexico Press, 1987). For a suggestive discussion of the relationship between the Western hero and the fantasy of the Anglo-Saxon knight in the early twentieth century, see Amy Kaplan, *The Anarchy of Empire in the Making of U.S. Culture* (Cambridge, MA: Harvard University Press, 2002), 92–120.

16 The scene at the beginning of the film when Earp literally kicks Indian Charlie out of town has been highlighted in a number of discussions, including Douglas Pye, "Genre and History," in Cameron and Pye, eds., *Book of Westerns*, and Simmon, *Invention of the Western Film*. Earp's relationship to Doc Holiday's Chicana mistress, Chihuahua, is taken up by Corey Creekmur, "Acting Like a Man," in *Out in Culture: Gay, Lesbian, and Queer Essays on Popular Culture*, ed. Corey Creekmur and Alexander Doty (Durham, NC: Duke University Press, 1995).

17 Mary Dudziak, *Cold War Civil Rights: Race and the Image of American Democracy* (Princeton, NJ: Princeton University Press, 2000), 49. According to Dudziak, from the mid-1940s through the mid-1960s "the federal government engaged in a sustained effort to tell a particular story about race and American democracy: a story of progress, a story of the triumph of good over evil, a story of U.S. moral superiority" (13). See also Thomas Borstelmann, *The Cold War and the Color Line: American Race Relations in the Global Arena* (Cambridge, MA: Harvard University Press, 2001).

18 Sara Ahmed, *The Cultural Politics of Emotion* (New York: Routledge, 2004), 109.

19 Pye, "Introduction," 11.

20 Among the starkest examples of this trend is John Sturges's *Bad Day at Black Rock* (1955), in which cowboy iconography is deployed to signify a sinister backwardness harboring the threat of racial violence.

21 Janet Walker, "Captive Images in the Traumatic Western," in *Westerns: Films Through History*, ed. Janet Walker (New York: Routledge, 2001), 221.

22 Dudziak, *Cold War Civil Rights*, 54.

23 Linda Williams, *Playing the Race Card: Melodramas of Black and White from Uncle Tom to O.J. Simpson* (Princeton, NJ: Princeton University Press, 2001), xiv.

Drawing upon the work of Wendy Brown and Lauren Berlant, Williams highlights melodrama's function in producing the suffering subject as deserving subject and the centrality of this function to the negotiation of racialized subjectivity in particular. See *Playing the Race Card*, 43; Brown, *States of Injury: Power and Freedom in Late Modernity* (Princeton, NJ: Princeton University Press, 1995); and Berlant, "The Subject of True Feeling," in *Cultural Pluralism, Identity Politics, and the Law*, ed. Austin Sarat and Thomas R. Kearns (Ann Arbor: University of Michigan Press, 1999).

24 Williams, *Playing the Race Card*, 44.

25 Warshow, *Immediate Experience*, 142.

26 For a discussion of censorship activities pushing racialized violence to the margins of screen treatments of lynching in this period, see Ellen C. Scott, *Cinema Civil Rights: Regulation, Repression, and Race in the Classical Hollywood Era* (New Brunswick, NJ: Rutgers University Press, 2015). Although I came upon Scott's book in the final stages of the preparation of my own, her comments on NAACP head Walter White's commendation of *The Ox-Bow Incident* are especially relevant here; see p. 2.

27 The most overtly racist character of the novel, the southern half-wit Gabe, has been deleted from the film entirely, and the term "nigger," which circulates freely among the novel's protagonists, is likewise omitted. As for Major Tetley, the film suggests he may be an imposter, a faux Confederate veteran rather than a genuine man of the South (a change apparently incorporated so as not to alienate a white Southern audience). At the same time, the film eschews the novel's more ambivalent attitude toward the lynching itself, issuing instead a clear moral judgment. See Walter Van Tilburg Clark, *The Ox-Bow Incident* (New York: Random House, 1940).

28 This characterization is in stark contrast to the novel, in which effeminate or sensitive men retain their stigma of weakness.

29 When Tetley insists on taking his son along to witness the lynching, he hopes "this will do what I've failed to do, make a man of you." In the book, Gil Carter, the character played by Henry Fonda, is sick with the memory of a lynching he witnessed. These scenarios echo Fonda's own youthful experience, when he was made by his father to watch the lynching of an African American man. That the making of *Ox-Bow* purportedly provided cathartic for Fonda adds extratextual shadings to the shadow of racial guilt that hangs across the film. For a discussion of Fonda's experience, see Kevin Sweeney's comments in A&E's *Henry Fonda: Hollywood's Quiet Hero*, included on the DVD release of the film (Twentieth Century Fox, 2003).

30 The film's refusal to credit actor Leigh Whipper—the first African American member of Actors' Equity and a founder of the Negro Actors Guild—ironically highlights the very problematic of racism the film seeks to repress.

31 The original trailer for the film features this same sequence with exactly the kind of thrilling soundtrack the film itself refuses, suggesting an attempt to promote this genre-busting film as more conventional fare.

32 As in all the era's pro-Indian Westerns, the casting of a white actor in red face ironically highlights the institutionalization of racism in Hollywood.

33 The film suggests the relevance of contemporary Indian policy to the pro-Indian Westerns. New questions surrounding the status of indigenous peoples within the American national body were prominent after the war, raised in part by their military service. Notable among these policies was House Concurrent Resolution 108, passed in 1953, which "terminated" the tribal status of Native Americans. Presented as an effort to liberate Indians from the limitations of their dependent status, the resolution revoked many of the rights and sovereignty that tribal status had at least nominally entailed. Massive urban relocations and the so-called reversion of Native lands to the U.S. government resulted, an impact *Devil's Doorway* would seem to anticipate. As Steve Neale has argued, the tendency to ignore this history in discussions of the pro-Indian Western indicates the ongoing ease with which the "vanishing Indian" act—the impulse at the core of the resolution itself—may yet be performed. See Jacquelyn Kilpatrick, *Celluloid Indians: Native Americans and Film* (Lincoln: University of Nebraska Press, 1999), 50–58, and Steve Neale, "Vanishing Americans," in *Back in the Saddle Again: New Essays on the Western*, ed. Edward Buscombe and Roberta E. Pearson (London: British Film Institute, 1998).

34 Here as elsewhere, the film is unusually didactic in underscoring at the level of dialogue the contemporary social issues it addresses.

35 The stylistics of the sequence resonate with Mann's work in noir during the 1940s.

36 The line is offered by the covetous Coolan and resonates with Williams's discussion of melodrama as "suffused with nostalgia for a virtuous place that we like to think we once possessed, whether in childhood or the distant past of the nation" (*Playing the Race Card*, 28).

37 See *Playing the Race Card* and "Melodrama Revised," in *Refiguring American Film Genres: History and Theory*, ed. Nick Browne (Berkeley: University of California Press, 1998).

38 In his guise as cattle baron, Lance is ironically associated with the rhetoric of empire building and undertakes the conventional generic actions of this figure, such as resisting the coming change the railroad will bring and driving the sheep farmers off the road to protect the purity of the land as "cattle country."

39 Peter Biskind, *Seeing Is Believing: How Hollywood Taught Us to Stop Worrying and Love the Fifties* (New York: Pantheon Books, 1983), 233.

40 Michael Walker, "The Westerns of Delmer Daves," in Cameron and Pye, eds., *Book of Westerns*, 125.

41 In this dynamic, the pro-Indian cycle resonates with Sarah Hagelin's discussion of the cultural construction of vulnerability as it pivots on a logic of racial substitution; see *Reel Vulnerability: Power, Pain, and Gender in Contemporary American Film and Television* (New Brunswick NJ: Rutgers University Press, 2013).

42 Hagelin's discussion of Method acting in this period—in which emotionalism comes to circulate as a privileged signifier of male vulnerability and authenticity— is interesting to consider here; see *Reel Vulnerability*.

43 Of the many films in which this convention figures, *The Last Train from Gun Hill* (Sturges 1959) offers a particularly graphic example, opening with a brutal, extended sequence in which an idyllic buggy ride through the woods devolves

into the rape and murder of Marshal Matt Morgan's Indian wife. The marshal's revenge quest will structure the narrative of the film.

44 The film's racial representation of Todd is far from coherent; it asserts his status as Indian while confirming at key points his identity as a white man, as on the brink of his sexual liaison with a white woman, for instance.

45 Walker, "Westerns of Delmer Daves," 140. The collapse suggested between the positions of Indians and African Americans as victims of white racial violence resonates with critical readings of the pro-Indian cycle in the context of black civil rights. See, for instance, Brian Henderson, "*The Searchers*: An American Dilemma," *Film Quarterly* 34 (Winter 1980–1981): 9–23, and Steve Neale's troubling of this approach in "Vanishing Americans." The courtroom coda at the end of *The Last Wagon*, in its articulation of institutionalized racism ("Show me a white jury that would hang four white men for killing a Comanche squaw!"), further suggests the significance of contemporary civil rights discourse to the film.

46 The film denies us any knowledge of Todd's motivation for the murders until the courtroom coda, in which we learn that the four men in question raped and murdered Todd's Comanche wife and beat to death his two young sons. That the narrative justification for Todd's violence is left until the film's closing underscores the extent to which it is superfluous to the constitution of his moral legibility, which the spectacle of his suffering functions to establish.

47 Williams has discussed the way "the white racist stereotype exists . . . only to be hated with a vengeance that makes the majority white audience feel good"; see *On The Wire* (Durham, NC: Duke University Press, 2014), 185.

48 See, for instance, Susan Jeffords, *The Remasculinization of America: Gender and the Vietnam War* (Bloomington: Indiana University Press, 1989); Kimmel, *Manhood in America*; Barbara Ehrenreich, *Fear of Falling: The Inner Life of the Middle Class* (New York: Pantheon, 1989); Savran, *Taking It Like a Man*; and Susan Faludi, *Stiffed: The Betrayal of the American Man* (New York: William Morrow, 1999).

49 Williams, "Melodrama Revised," 61.

50 Pauly, "Cold War Western," 268.

51 Geoffrey Klingsporn, "War, Film, History," in *Hollywood and War: The Film Reader*, ed. J. David Slocum (New York: Routledge, 2006), 36. For more on the Brady image, see Allen Trachtenberg, "Albums of War," in *Reading American Photographs: Images as History, Mathew Brady to Walker Evans* (New York: Hill and Wang, 1990). In case we miss the reference, dialogue shortly afterward references Bull Run, joking over the Stewart hero's Confederate past.

52 Douglas Pye, "The Collapse of Fantasy," in Cameron and Pye, eds., *Book of Westerns*, 172.

53 Jim Kitses, *Horizons West: Anthony Mann, Budd Boetticher, Sam Peckinpah; Studies of Authorship within the Western* (Bloomington: Indiana University Press, 1970), 43.

54 Paul Willemen first suggested the "anxious aspect of the look at the male" that the Mann Westerns in particular represent; see "Anthony Mann: Looking at the Male," *Framework* 16 (1981): 16, and *Looks and Frictions: Essays in Cultural Studies and Film Theory* (Bloomington: Indiana University Press, 1994). Developing this insight

further, Steve Neale argues that scenes of physical battery in Westerns and war films work to repress and disqualify the male body as an erotic object, while at the same time allowing for its fetishistic display; see "Masculinity as Spectacle: Reflections on Men and Mainstream Cinema," *Screen* 24 (1983): 2–16. Such scenes become central to the action cinema of the late twentieth century, considered in the next chapter.

55 Lee Clark Mitchell reads the physical debilitation of the hero as the necessary precondition for his rebuilding, while Jane Tompkins analyzes how scenes of torture generate suspense in anticipation of the hero's breaking point and provide for display of the hero's dominance over the violability of his "fleshly self." See Mitchell, *Westerns: Making the Man in Fiction and Film* (Chicago: University of Chicago Press, 1996), and Tompkins, *West of Everything: The Inner Life of Westerns* (New York: Oxford University Press, 1992).

56 As discussed in previous chapters, an allegiance to commercial interests has long been constructed in complex opposition to the dictates of manliness, both within the Western and beyond.

57 Amy Lawrence, "American Shame: *Rope*, James Stewart, and the Postwar Crisis in American Masculinity," in *Hitchcock's America*, ed. Jonathan Freedman and Richard Millington (New York: Oxford University Press, 1999), 70.

58 There has been a tendency to read spectacles of masculine suffering in relation to issues of castration and lack and to emphasize the disruptive potential of such spectacles; see, for instance, Kaja Silverman, *Male Subjectivity at the Margins* (New York: Routledge, 1992). In the Western as elsewhere, however, it is also important to consider how such spectacles may strengthen rather than challenge identification with dominant masculinity.

59 Williams, *On The Wire*, 130.

60 Ibid., 88.

61 See Tompkins, *West of Everything*, and especially her discussion of landscape; in general, suffering provides a central thematic for Tompkins's analysis of the Western and its appeal.

62 Kitses, *Horizons West*, 35. Douglas Pye makes a similar point in relation to these heroes as "victims of intractable situations"; see "Collapse of Fantasy," 172.

63 The Western hero was never an ideologically singular figure and has from the beginning incorporated a celebration of traditional masculine virtues alongside an emphasis on their inevitable passing. Nonetheless, the Cold War period exerts new and intensified pressures on the image of masculine authority at the genre's core.

64 See, for instance, Mary Ann Doane, *The Desire to Desire: The Woman's Film of the 1940s* (Bloomington: Indiana University Press, 1987), and Christine Gledhill, ed., *Home Is Where the Heart Is: Studies in Melodrama and the Woman's Film* (London: British Film Institute, 1987).

65 Laura Mulvey, "Notes on Sirk and Melodrama," in Gledhill, ed., *Home Is Where the Heart Is*, 76–77.

66 See Tom Lutz's chapter on "Fictional Tears," in *Crying: The Natural and Cultural History of Tears* (New York: W. W. Norton, 1999), and particularly his comments on male weepies such as *Home from the Hill*.

67 David Rodowick, "Madness, Authority, and Ideology," in Gledhill, ed., *Home Is Where the Heart Is*, 278.

68 The association of the aristocracy with both abusive power and gender deviance has a long history within middle-class melodramatic traditions, and the correlation of wealth with sexual power and sexual inadequacy resonates with earlier formulations of the aristocratic villain as at once rapacious and effete. Tensions between economic striving and the ambivalent implications of success have shaped middle-class manhood since its emergence as a category of social identity in the mid-nineteenth century.

69 Geoffrey Nowell-Smith, "Minnelli and Melodrama," in Gledhill, ed., *Home Is Where the Heart Is*, 72.

70 Douglas Pye makes a similar point, asserting that Mann's Westerns, "in their focus on the unstable and tortured masculinity of their heroes, demand to be seen alongside—indeed as part of—the 'fifties cycle of male melodramas." See "Collapse of Fantasy," 173.

71 Thomas Elsaesser, "Tales of Sound and Fury: Observations on the Family Melodrama" (1972), reprinted in Gledhill, ed., *Home Is Where the Heart Is*.

72 Films like *The Fastest Gun Alive* (Rouse 1956) make their debt to popular Freudianism explicit, recasting the conventional figure of the reticent gunfighter as a man wracked by Oedipal guilt. Glenn Ford emerges as an icon of Oedipal angst in this film, as in Delmer Daves's *Jubal* (1956). These trends were not restricted to big-budget features, as attested by films like *Vengeance Valley* (Thorpe 1951), *Horizons West* (Boetticher 1952), and *The Lonely Man* (Levin 1957)—all centrally concerned with the melodramatic articulation of relationships among fathers, sons, and brothers.

73 Elsaesser, "Tales of Sound and Fury," 62.

74 Ibid, 56.

75 Pauly, "Cold War Western," 259. Other films by Stanley Kramer (as producer) and Fred Zinnemann, like *Home of the Brave* (Robson 1949) and *The Men* (Zinnemann 1950), suggest more starkly the fascination with masculine immobility.

76 Pauly argues that "*High Noon* is a collection of close-ups"; see "Cold War Western," 270. Joan Mellen discusses the significance of Cooper's aging face in *Big Bad Wolves: Masculinity in the American Film* (New York: Pantheon Books, 1977).

77 Kitses describes a hysterical landscape in which "action flows below the surface to break out in strangely malignant scenes" that signify and reconfirm the hero's instability, and Slotkin notes a landscape that "mirrors" the hero's own psychology. See Kitses, *Horizons West*, 72, and Slotkin, *Gunfighter Nation*, 382.

78 Elsaesser, "Tales of Sound and Fury," 55.

79 Douglas Pye, "Double Vision: Miscegenation and Point of View in *The Searchers*," in *Book of Westerns*, ed. Cameron and Pye, 229.

80 As Pye argues, the film is unable to provide a comfortable point of identification with Ethan or the means of fully disengaging from such an identification. While we are increasingly encouraged to read Ethan's obsession with miscegenation as irrational and neurotic, the film at the same time confirms and reinforces such views; see "Double Vision."

81 Tom Grayson Colonnese emphasizes in the question "Where does that ranch *come from?*" the repressed history of violence animating this opening image. "Native American Reactions to *The Searchers*," in *The Searchers: Essays and Reflections on John Ford's Classic Western*, ed. Arthur M. Eckstein and Peter Lehman (Detroit: Wayne State University Press, 2004), 337.

82 Martin's identity is unstable, shuttling between Indian and cowboy. Though he is racialized as other in his interactions with Ethan, his heroic status will be secured through his killing of the Comanche chief Scar.

83 Henderson reads the film as a negotiation of the contemporary politics of racial integration; see "*The Searchers*."

84 While the editing here is suggestive in linking individual racist pathology to systemic racial violence, the film's attitude toward racism is highly unstable, as the next sequence—which shifts quickly from a representation of Comanche women herded like cattle by the U.S. Cavalry to an image of recovered white women captives seemingly gone mad through contact with the Comanche—collapses Ethan's racial dread with the film's own. See Pye, "Double Vision."

85 The contemporaneous *The Last Hunt* (Brooks 1956) tries to resolve this conflict by assigning these attributes to two different men, the remorseful buffalo hunter Sandy MacKenzie (Stewart Granger) and his avowedly racist partner, Charlie Gibson (Robert Taylor). The film grants moral authority to the Indian and the "half-breed" as victims of racialized abuse and to Sandy as sympathetic to their cause. Charlie's racist violence—constituted as in *The Searchers* through a doubling of the figures of buffalo and Indian—is cast as a sign of mental instability and moral bankruptcy. Nonetheless, the film depends for its affective intensity and visual interest on the violence it decries.

86 This relinquishment is consonant with the Western hero's conventional status as a man too close to the forces against which he fights, although in the context of the 1950s, his exclusion is linked not just to generic convention but to the contemporary critique of racism.

87 Henderson, "*The Searchers*," 447.

88 We might question whether the loss being mourned encompasses that of unrepentant racism itself, a register of ambivalence surrounding the pressure to qualify, at the level of official policy and discourse at least, the white supremacist assertions that had once provided the genre's uncritical ground.

89 Williams, *Playing the Race Card*, 31.

90 Ethan's love for his sister-in-law Martha operates as another confirmation of this necessary exclusion.

91 While the B Western provided an economic backbone, it was not until the 1950s that the feature Western emerges as a dominant Hollywood product. Westerns constitute as much as 25 percent of all films made in this period and are regularly included among top-grossing titles and award nominees. See Pauly, "Cold War Western," 257, and Slotkin, *Gunfighter Nation*, 347–48.

92 Yvonne Tasker notes the extent to which, "in the context of debates around masculinity John Wayne provides . . . a figure whose meaning seems absolutely fixed"; see "Dumb Movies for Dumb People: Masculinity, the Body, and the Voice

in Contemporary Action Cinema," in *Screening the Male: Exploring Masculinities in Hollywood Cinema*, ed. Steve Cohan and Ina Rae Hark (London: Routledge, 1993), 234. The tendency to cast the Cold War Western hero as a secure site of masculine authority extends beyond Wayne; the leading men of the era's feature Westerns remain the "foremost symbol[s] of moral guardianship and true Americanism" despite their increasingly ambiguous claims to moral integrity. See Michael Coyne, *The Crowded Prairie: The Hollywood Western and American National Identity* (London: I. B. Tauris, 1997), 68. Philip French has noted how little the angst of the postwar hero seems to impact attitudes toward the genre, as "moviegoers and filmmakers alike have continued to carry in their minds a firm notion of the archetypal Western where everything goes according to a series of happily anticipated moral and dramatic conventions" (*Westerns*, 17).

93 According to Thomas Pauly, it was the "melancholy loneliness" of Wayne's Nathan Brittles in *She Wore a Yellow Ribbon* (Ford 1949) that "heralded the emergence of a new type of Western hero, and . . . rocketed John Wayne to stardom" ("Cold War Western," 267–68).

94 See Simmon, *Invention of the Western Film*, 232; Slotkin, *Gunfighter Nation*, 383; and Pauly, "Cold War Western," 266. Christian Appy's discussion of "sentimental militarism" points to a similar impulse in the representation of the authoritative military "Old Man"; see "'We'll Follow the Old Man,'" in *Rethinking Cold War Culture*, ed. Peter J. Kuznick and James Gilbert (Washington, DC: Smithsonian Institution Press, 2001), 91.

95 Slotkin, *Gunfighter Nation*, 390.

96 As Masco argues, nuclear weapons are key to this affective structure in the Cold War era; they constitute "the ultimate weapon and the ultimate vulnerability." See *The Theater of Operations: National Security Affect from the Cold War to the War on Terror* (Durham, NC: Duke University Press, 2014), 126.

97 See Elisabeth R. Anker, *Orgies of Feeling: Melodrama and the Politics of Freedom* (Durham, NC: Duke University Press, 2014), 89.

4 The Subject of Imperiled Privilege

1 Lauren Berlant, *The Queen of America: Essays on Sex and Citizenship* (Durham, NC: Duke University Press, 1997), 261n2. Richard Dyer, in a similar vein, notes the "underlying pattern of feeling, to do with freedom of movement, confidence in the body, engagement with the material world, that is coded as male (and straight and white, too) but to which all humans need access"; see "Action!" *Sight and Sound* 4 (1994): 9. Jane Tompkins's comments on her attraction toward "the power of Western heroes, the power that men in our society wield" is also relevant here, as it suggests the broad appeal of masculine figures of agency onscreen: "I've been jealous of power, and longed for it, wanted the experiences that accompany it, and seen the figures who embody it as admirable. . . ." See *West of Everything: The Inner Life of Westerns* (New York: Oxford University Press, 1992), 18.

2 See Michael A Messner, *Politics of Masculinities: Men in Movements* (Thousand Oaks, CA: Sage, 1997); Michael Kimmel, ed., *The Politics of Manhood: Profeminist*

Men Respond to the Mythopoetic Men's Movement (Philadelphia: Temple University Press, 1995); Michael Schwalbe, *Unlocking the Iron Cage: The Men's Movement, Gender Politics, and American Culture* (New York: Oxford University Press, 1996); Fred Pfeil, *White Guys: Studies in Postmodern Domination and Difference* (London: Verso, 1995); David Savran, *Taking It Like a Man: White Masculinity, Masochism, and Contemporary American Culture* (Princeton, NJ: Princeton University Press, 1998), 169–176; and Kenneth Clatterbaugh, "Literature of the U.S. Men's Movements," *Signs* 25 (2000): 883–94.

3   For further discussion of this dynamic, see Jonna K. Eagle, "Making a Spectacle of Himself: White Masculinity, Melodrama, and Sensation in the American Cinema, 1898–1999" (PhD diss., Brown University, 2006).

4   Susan Faludi, *Stiffed: The Betrayal of the American Man* (New York: William Morrow, 1999).

5   Judith Butler, "The Imperialist Subject," *Journal of Urban and Cultural Studies* 2 (1991): 74.

6   Judith Butler, *Frames of War: When Is Life Grievable?* (London: Verso, 2010), 178.

7   Butler, "Imperialist Subject," 75.

8   On the significance of these rhythms to action cinema, see Linda Williams, "Melodrama Revised," in *Refiguring American Film Genres: History and Theory*, ed. Nick Browne (Berkeley: University of California Press, 1998), and *On The Wire* (Durham, NC: Duke University Press, 2014), 113.

9   Sharon Willis, *High Contrast: Race and Gender in Contemporary Hollywood Film* (Durham, NC: Duke University Press, 1997), 33.

10 Susan Jeffords, *The Remasculinization of America: Gender and the Vietnam War* (Bloomington: Indiana University Press, 1989), 119.

11 Williams, "Melodrama Revised," 61.

12 In *First Blood*, the colonel confides, "It can get confusing sometimes . . . you can bet Rambo and I got confused. We had orders. When in doubt, kill." In *Rambo*, he underscores a similar point: "In Vietnam [Rambo's] job was to dispose of enemy personnel. To kill. Period. Win by attrition. Well, Rambo was the best."

13 See Linda Williams, *Playing the Race Card: Melodramas of Black and White from Uncle Tom to O.J. Simpson* (Princeton, NJ: Princeton University Press, 2001), 28, and "Melodrama Revised," 65.

14 On melodrama's expression of character through mise-en-scène, see, for instance, Christine Gledhill, "The Melodramatic Field: An Investigation," in *Home Is Where the Heart Is: Studies in Melodrama and the Woman's Film*, ed. Christine Gledhill (London: British Film Institute, 1987), 23.

15 See Peter Brooks, *The Melodramatic Imagination: Balzac, Henry James, Melodrama, and the Mode of Excess* (New Haven, CT: Yale University Press, 1976). Gledhill also glosses this history in *Home Is Where the Heart Is*, 15.

16 Brooks, *Melodramatic Imagination*, 56.

17 Gledhill, "Rethinking Genre," in *Reinventing Film Studies*, ed. Christine Gledhill and Linda Williams (London: Arnold, 2000), 236.

18 Brooks, *Melodramatic Imagination*, 72.

19 Such traditions include pantomime, acrobatics, and others; see, for example, ibid. and Gledhill, "Melodramatic Field."

20 Gledhill, "Rethinking Genre," 238.

21 See Sylvia Shin Huey Chong's comments on the character of Rocky in *The Oriental Obscene: Violence and Racial Fantasies in the Vietnam Era* (Durham, NC: Duke University Press, 2011), 255. She also quotes Matthew Frye Jacobson's characterization of Rocky as "a poster boy for white victimization"; see his *Roots, Too: White Ethnic Revival in Post–Civil Rights America* (Cambridge, MA: Harvard University Press, 2008), 100–108.

22 The death of Rambo's native guide Co in *Rambo* replays with striking visual resonance the death of Sonseeahray in *Broken Arrow*, rehearsing the moment at which Jeffords's suffering reaches its apex and secures his moral worth.

23 Chong, *Oriental Obscene*, 63.

24 Ibid., 262.

25 See Susan Jeffords, *Hard Bodies: Hollywood Masculinity in the Reagan Era* (New Brunswick, NJ: Rutgers University Press, 1994), 30. For my own initial consideration of this dynamic, see Eagle, "Making a Spectacle of Himself," 356. Chong also suggests Berry's significance in emphasizing "race as the grounds for Rambo's melancholia" (*Oriental Obscene*, 262).

26 John Wheeler's designation of the Vietnam veteran as the "nigger of the 1970s"—a status constituted in part through the "inflicting [of] traumatic wounds"—is significant in this respect; see Jeffords, *Remasculinization*, 120–21. Robyn Wiegman also references this quote and the broader impulse it expresses in *American Anatomies: Theorizing Race and Gender* (Durham, NC: Duke University Press, 1995), 122–25. On the elision of race in Vietnam narratives of male bonding, see Jeffords, "'That Men Without Women Trip,'" in *Remasculinization*.

27 Sally Robinson, *Marked Men: White Masculinity in Crisis* (New York: Columbia University Press, 2000), 6.

28 Susan Jeffords has noted the extent to which such sequences discomfort male audience members in particular; see *Hard Bodies*, 49–50.

29 See William Warner, "Spectacular Action: Rambo and the Popular Pleasures of Pain," in *Cultural Studies*, ed. Lawrence Grossberg, Cary Nelson, and Paula Treichler (New York: Routledge, 1992), 676.

30 See Jane Tompkins, *West of Everything*, 229.

31 Williams, *On The Wire*, 113.

32 Chong suggestively refers to the "affective disorder" of the Vietnam syndrome in this respect; see *Oriental Obscene*, 2.

33 For discussion of the shared conditions of precarious life—the mutually constitutive dependencies, contingencies, and embodied vulnerabilities that define the experience of being human—and the way the concept of precarity directs critical attention to the grossly inequitable distribution of these vulnerabilities, see Judith Butler's *Precarious Life: The Powers of Mourning and Violence* (London: Verso, 2006), and her *Frames of War*.

34 Elisabeth Anker's discussion of the "orgiastic victimization" offered by melodrama as "a way for political subjects to manage the daily impotence and precarity of

contemporary life" through the promise of eventual agency is resonant here; see *Orgies of Feeling: Melodrama and the Politics of Freedom* (Durham, NC: Duke University Press, 2014), 151.

35 On the global success of *Rambo*, see, for instance, Warner, "Spectacular Action."

36 Chong discusses the complex condensation of black urban and antiwar protest that Rambo embodies alongside the specter of orientalized violence; see *Oriental Obscene*.

37 Ibid., 259.

38 Ibid., 132.

39 Ibid., 213.

40 On the features of *Rambo*'s innovative style, see Warner, "Spectacular Action," 683.

41 Ibid., 681.

42 Williams, "Melodrama Revised," 60. We might also consider the invitation to replace mundane suffering and pain with intensified affect that constitutes melodramatic political discourse, as Elisabeth Anker describes in *Orgies of Feeling*.

43 As Susan Jeffords notes, by the late 1970s, American POWs, in particular, "rate very high in their reception of public sympathy." See *Remasculinization*, 126, and Warner, "Spectacular Action," 674.

44 Warner, too, notes the stringing up of Rambo "crucifix-style" ("Spectacular Action," 678).

45 Jeffords and Yvonne Tasker both emphasize this aspect of Rambo's wounding; see Jeffords, *Hard Bodies*, and Tasker, *Spectacular Bodies: Gender, Genre, and the Action Cinema* (London: Routledge, 1993). David Savran's discussion of masochism and the cultural production of white masculinity in the post-Vietnam era is also relevant; see *Taking It Like a Man*.

46 On the gendered circuitry of sadistic and masochistic identifications structuring these sequences, see Warner, "Spectacular Action," 678–79, and Jeffords, *Hard Bodies*, 49–50.

47 Sequences of wounding and torture provide opportunities for the camera to linger over Rambo's naked body, emphasizing this body as an object of visual pleasure even as the scenario of physical violence seeks to disqualify it from erotic investment. On the homosexual repression enacted through the conventional brutalization of the male body onscreen, see Paul Willemen, "Anthony Mann: Looking at the Male," *Framework* 16 (1981): 16, and Steve Neale, "Masculinity as Spectacle: Reflections on Men and Mainstream Cinema," *Screen* 24 (1983): 2–16. Savran considers this function in relationship to the *Rambo* films in *Taking It Like a Man*. For other readings of masochism, masculinity, and the cinema, see David Rodowick, *The Difficulty of Difference: Psychoanalysis, Sexual Difference, and Film Theory* (New York: Routledge, 1991), and Kaja Silverman, *Male Subjectivity at the Margins* (New York: Routledge, 1992).

48 Warner, "Spectacular Action," 680.

49 That Rambo's lethal shot is taken only after his adversary fires is in keeping with the melodramatic constitution of his violence as essentially defensive.

50 Chong also suggests the way Ut's photograph recalls that of Thich Quang Duc's self-immolation, "another image of immobilized suffering burned into the American public imagination"; see *Oriental Obscene*, 114–15.

51 According to Susan Jeffords, the weapon was marketed as the "Ram-bow," a suggestive condensation of Rambo's body and/as weapon; see *Remasculinization*, 12.

52 See Paul Virilio, *War and Cinema: The Logistics of Perception* (London: Verso, 1989), 4.

53 The most frequently cited instance is Rambo's attack upon the computer bank entrusted with monitoring his mission; the vision of Rambo blasting away millions of dollars' worth of computer equipment offers a cathartic spectacle of technocide to an audience primed to regard this technology as antithetical to Rambo's own brand of embodied authority.

54 Warner offers a compelling articulation of Rambo's ability to control his own visibility in such moments; see "Spectacular Action," 684.

55 Ibid., 682.

56 Warner suggests the "abstract, disembodied, general, empty, and therefore open" subject position through which "*Rambo* becomes the site of moving spectacle itself" ("Spectacular Action," 682). Susan Jeffords's discussion of the technological reintegration of the male body is also relevant, as "in Vietnam representation, technology does not 'stand in for' the (male) body but *is* that body, because the body has ceased to have meaning as a whole and has instead become a fragmented collection of disconnected parts that achieve the illusion of coherence only through their display as spectacle" (*Remasculinization*, 14).

57 Warner, "Spectacular Action," 685.

58 Matthew S. Buckley, "Refugee Theatre: Melodrama and Modernity's Loss," *Theatre Journal* 61 (2009): 179.

59 On this last, see Jan Mieszkowski, *Watching War* (Stanford, CA: Stanford University Press, 2012).

60 Buckley, "Refugee Theatre," 186.

61 Geoff King, *Spectacular Narratives: Hollywood in the Age of the Blockbuster* (London: I. B. Tauris, 2000), 102.

62 Buckley, "Refugee Theatre," 188.

63 The fourth *Lethal Weapon* film was released in 1998, and the fifth *Die Hard* in 2013, but I focus here on the earlier installments.

64 Cited in Leo Charney, "The Violence of a Perfect Moment," in *Violence and the American Cinema*, ed. J. David Slocum (New York: Routledge, 2001), 59.

65 Ben Singer, *Melodrama and Modernity: Early Sensational Cinema and Its Contexts* (New York: Columbia University Press, 2001), 192.

66 Warner, "Spectacular Action," 674.

67 In contrast, the complicity of the Special Forces adversaries is made explicit: "We killed everybody."

68 For a mapping of the structural relationship between protagonists and antagonists in *Lethal Weapon* and *Die Hard*, see Pfeil, *White Guys*.

69 On the interracial buddy pair of late-century action cinema, see, for example, Willis, *High Contrast*; Wiegman, *American Anatomies*; Tasker, *Spectacular Bodies*; and Pfeil, *White Guys*.

70 One implication of this reordering is the assignment of institutionalized racial violence to the African American buddy, who is positioned in the *Lethal Weapon* and *Die Hard* films as the agent of police violence against young black men.

71 For a specific discussion of Willis in this respect, see Yvonne Tasker, "Dumb Movies for Dumb People," in *Screening the Male: Exploring Masculinities in Hollywood Cinema*, ed. Steven Cohan and Ina Rae Hark (London: Routledge, 1993).

72 See Marsha Kinder, "Violence American Style: The Narrative Orchestration of Violent Attractions," in Slocum, ed., *Violence and the American Cinema*.

73 In addition to Charney, "Violence of a Perfect Moment," on violence and humor in the action cinema, see Tasker, *Spectacular Bodies*, and Kinder, "Violence American Style."

74 In scholarly debates across the 1980s and 1990s, postmodernism would be associated with a variety of departures, including the evacuation of truth, sense, politics, and reality. For discussions of postmodernity in relation to the action cinema in particular, see Pfeil, *White Guys*; Charney, "Violence of a Perfect Moment"; and Tasker, *Spectacular Bodies*.

75 Pfeil, *White Guys*, 25.

76 See Dana Polan, "'Above All Else to Make You See': Cinema and the Ideology of the Spectacle," in *Postmodernism and Politics*, ed. Jonathan Arac (Minneapolis: University of Minnesota Press, 1986), 59.

77 That the victim is a prostitute who has been implicated in a murder may bracket our disturbance at the boys' enthusiasm, though the film has not portrayed her as a villain.

78 Holly serves as both a problem and a catalyst across the franchise; in *Die Hard*, her career-driven relocation to California and reversion to her maiden name in deference to her Japanese employer signify a condensation of offenses and provide the context for the film's unfolding violence.

79 Like the conventional siting of diegetic action around the Christmas holiday, the ironic scoring of the chaotic rescue scene with the holiday hallmark, "Let It Snow," qualifies somewhat this sentimentality.

80 Judith Butler articulates this structure of feeling in a discussion of public discourse after 9/11; see *Precarious Life*, 6.

81 See Pfeil, *White Guys*, 29.

82 See, for instance, the image of Douglas's D-Fens gracing the cover of *Newsweek*'s "White Male Paranoia" issue of March 29, 1993, as well as the *Village Voice*'s "Whiny White Guys" issue of March 7, 1995. As Sally Robinson argues, "the announcements of crisis are inseparable from the crisis itself, as the rhetoric of crisis performs the cultural work of centering attention on dominant masculinity." See *Marked Men*, 11, and my own "Making a Spectacle of Himself."

83 Films like *Fatal Attraction* (Lyne 1987), *Basic Instinct* (Verhoeven 1992), and *Disclosure* (Levinson 1994), worked alongside *Falling Down* to establish Douglas as the contemporary paragon of beleaguered white masculinity.

84 As Richard Dyer has argued, the status of Los Angeles as a jungle is "suggested not only because this is a well-known cliché about urban America but by the geographical confusion of the terrain and the often lethal hostility of the natives." See *White* (London: Routledge, 1997), 217.

85 For one of the most trenchant discussions of Los Angeles in this light, see Mike Davis, *City of Quartz: Excavating the Future in Los Angeles* (London: Verso, 1990), which Liam Kennedy takes up in relation to *Falling Down* in "Alien Nation: White Male Paranoia and Imperial Culture in the United States," *Journal of American Studies* 30 (1996): 87–100.

86 The loss of home serves a dual function, marking the hero's suffering while liberating him from any domestic inhibitions of aggressive action (the impact of which is suggested by the tentativeness of Murtaugh, in contrast).

87 See Kennedy, "Alien Nation," 96.

88 Ibid., 97.

89 Ibid., 87.

90 Ibid., 88.

91 Ibid., 92.

92 For resonant discussions of this opening sequence, see Willis, *High Contrast*, 14–16, and Pfeil, *White Guys*, 239.

93 Kennedy, "Alien Nation," 94.

94 Kennedy makes this point as well, arguing that "this is poverty as spectacle, an aesthetic transfiguration of lived experiences into reified images," rendered by a camera that "colonises and exoticises scenes of intractable otherness" (ibid., 95).

95 According to John Gabriel's audience response analysis, Bill's populist appeal is never so great as when he berates a couple of country club retirees for their monopolization of the open green space of a golf course: "You should have children playing here! You should have families having picnics! You should have a goddamn petting zoo!" See "What Do You Do When Minority Means You? *Falling Down* and the Construction of 'Whiteness,'" *Screen* 37 (1996): 129–51.

96 Pfeil, *White Guys*, 240. Willis has noted a similar impulse at work in *Die Hard*, in which, "as the film's editing works consistently to structure an alternation between extremes—claustrophobic proximity and monumentalizing distance—the camera's parallel work alternates high and low angles that, respectively, miniaturize and monumentalize [the male] body" (*High Contrast*, 40).

97 The film goes out of its way to emphasize Bill's lack of racial animosity by highlighting neo-Nazi Nick's mistaken assumption that the Whammyburger incident was targeted at "a bunch of fucking niggers." The encounter with Nick, although seeking to siphon off the racist implications of Bill's own actions, also affirms the distortions upon which Bill's discourse of rights is founded, as he announces to Nick, "Feels good to exercise your rights, doesn't it!" as he blasts him away in the back.

98 See Dyer, *White*, 222.

99 The phrase is Kennedy's articulation of Bill's paranoid state; "Alien Nation," 98.

100 Ibid., 96.

101 In the context of the 1992 Los Angeles riots during which the film was shot, the destruction of the Korean immigrant's store might be viewed as an appropriation of a position ascribed within a dominant cultural imaginary to the African American male.

102 Bill here embodies the insights of Onage Benjamin, quoted in *Newsweek*, March 29, 1994, 50: "European males have always had the propensity to say 'I feel threatened' while holding a gun to somebody else's head."

103 Kennedy makes a similar point in "Alien Nation," 97–98.

104 The phrase is from Terrence Rafferty's review of the film, "Slow Burn," *New Yorker*, March 8, 1993, 98–99.

105 Pfeil (*White Guys*) uses the term "queasy" to describe identification with Bill's violence. Gabriel ("What Do You Do") discusses the powerful though partial identification conditioned by the film in his audience response analysis. Nearly every commentator notes the function of Prendergast as double; for one particularly lucid account, see Willis, *High Contrast*.

106 Dyer, *White*, 221.

107 Making a nod to both the Western and the action cinema's ironic attitude toward it, Bill goads Prendergast into the final shoot-out. "Wanna draw?" he asks. "Aw, come on, it's perfect, the showdown between the sheriff and the bad guy."

108 Across the film, Bill is mistaken for a thief, a vigilante, a filmmaker, and a security guard, as well as, of course, an "average white guy."

109 The phrase is from Rafferty's review, "Slow Burn."

110 Among their many honors, both films garnered Academy Awards for Best Picture and Best Director.

111 See Dennis Bingham, *Acting Male: Masculinities in the Films of James Stewart, Jack Nicholson, and Clint Eastwood* (New Brunswick, NJ: Rutgers University Press, 1994), 238.

112 Bingham makes a similar point, noting that "the cycle of violence is triggered . . . by a woman's failure to respect a man's phallic pride" (ibid., 236).

113 Leighton Grist offers a similar reading of the "inadmissible desire to return to his past life" that Munny's wistfulness encodes. See "Unforgiven," in *The Book of Westerns*, ed. Ian Cameron and Douglas Pye (New York: Continuum, 1996), 298.

114 Lee Clark Mitchell also notes the "sentimentality" of such sequences; see *Westerns: Making the Man in Fiction and Film* (Chicago: University of Chicago Press, 1996), 262.

115 See Carl Plantinga, "Spectacles of Death: Clint Eastwood and Violence in *Unforgiven*," *Cinema Journal* 37 (1998): 76.

116 The evacuation is suggested in Eastwood's insistence on the color-blindness dictating Morgan Freeman's casting and the insignificance of race to Ned's characterization ("it's just hipper not to mention it"). On the ideology of color-blindness and its implications for the film, see Bingham, *Acting Male*, 241, and Paul Smith, *Clint Eastwood: A Cultural Production* (Minneapolis: University of Minneapolis Press, 1993), 282n3.

117 See Williams, *Playing the Race Card*, for a discussion of *Uncle Tom's Cabin* and its resonance across the history of American racial melodrama.

118 This reading is reinforced in Munny's parting warning to the town, "You better bury Ned right. You better not cut up nor otherwise harm no whores."

119 Bingham, *Acting Male*, 240.

120 Noting the audience laughter that greeted Munny's retort to the charge of having shot an unarmed man, Bingham remarks, "perhaps coming from Eastwood, rambling insanity still sounds to some ears like gallows-humor justice" (*Acting Male*, 242).
121 See Plantinga, "Spectacles of Death," 80.
122 Smith, *Clint Eastwood*, 268.
123 The phrase is from Willis, *High Contrast*, 2.
124 Bingham, *Acting Male*, 232.
125 Ibid., 241.

Epilogue

1 Lauren Berlant, *The Queen of America Goes to Washington City: Essays on Sex and Citizenship* (Durham, NC: Duke University Press, 1997), 32.
2 Jan Mieszkowski, *Watching War* (Stanford, CA: Stanford University Press, 2012), 1.
3 When the experience of war disappoints these expectations, it is the experience itself that is faulted on some level as inauthentic, even as these expectations may be critiqued as naïve or impure, derived as they are from mass-mediated representations of war. We see this in the case of Henry Fleming, for instance, whose mediated expectations of war are mocked, even as Crane's novel circulates around the conventional image of combat as an intense and overwhelming sensory experience with the power to absorb temporarily other modes of apprehension and cognition (and is lauded for its realism on this basis).
4 Mieszkowski, *Watching War*, 35.
5 Marita Sturken, *Tangled Memories: The Vietnam War, the AIDS Epidemic, and the Politics of Remembering* (Berkeley: University of California Press, 1997), 86. Sturken considers evaluations of the realism of a film like *Platoon* in terms that emphasize the affective force of onscreen representation—its ability to make the spectator feel "the discomfort, ants, heat, and mud." But precisely this level of feeling is understood to elude representational media, as in Kenneth MacLeish's account of the impossibility of translating from a bodily register embodied experiences like heat and the weight of body armor; see *Making War at Fort Hood: Life and Uncertainty in a Military Community* (Princeton, NJ: Princeton University Press, 2013).
6 See Mieszkowski, *Watching War*, introduction and chapter 2.
7 Ibid., 2.
8 Lauren Berlant, "The Epistemology of State Emotion," in *Dissent in Dangerous Times*, ed. Austin Sarat (Ann Arbor: University of Michigan Press, 2004), and *The Female Complaint: The Unfinished Business of Sentimentality in American Culture* (Durham, NC: Duke University Press, 2008).
9 William Mazzarella, "Affect: What Is It Good For?" in *Enchantments of Modernity: Empire, Nation, Globalization*, ed. Saurabh Dube (London: Routledge, 2009), 300.
10 Christine Gledhill, "Rethinking Genre," in *Reinventing Film Studies*, ed. Christine Gledhill and Linda Williams (London: Arnold, 2000), 235.

11 Quoted in Sarah Hagelin, *Reel Vulnerability: Power, Pain, and Gender in Contemporary American Film and Television* (New Brunswick NJ: Rutgers University Press, 2013), 75. Hagelin's point about the alignment of realism with moral seriousness in the popular reception of the film is also relevant here.

12 Robin Andersen, *A Century of Media, A Century of War* (New York: Peter Lang, 2006), 212.

13 While it is important to consider how agency is circumscribed within these games—and how a fantasy of control may function to naturalize the environments and conventions of gameplay—user-based modifications address this sense of limited agency to some extent (although America's Army, discussed below, is noteworthy for disallowing such "mods").

14 See Judith Butler, *Frames of War: When Is Life Grievable?* (London: Verso, 2010), especially 5–12.

15 This alignment of feeling and authenticity is not unrelated to the concept of true feeling discussed in the Introduction.

16 Sturken, *Tangled Memories*, 96, and Mieszkowski, *Watching War*, 175.

17 Scholarship on the military-entertainment complex is extensive and growing all the time; for some important and useful examples, see Timothy Lenoir, "Programming Theaters of War," in *Bombs and Bandwidth: The Emerging Relationship Between Information Technology and Security*, ed. Robert Latham (New York: New Press, 2003); Roger Stahl, *Militainment, Inc.: War, Media, and Popular Culture* (New York: Routledge, 2009); James Der Derian, *Virtuous War: Mapping the Military-Industrial-Media-Entertainment Network* (New York: Routledge, 2009); Sharon Ghamari-Tabrizi, "The Convergence of the Pentagon and Hollywood: The Next Generation of Military Training Simulations," in *Memory Bytes: History, Technology, and Digital Culture*, ed. Lauren Rabinovitz and Abraham Geil (Durham, NC: Duke University Press, 2003); Nick Dyer-Witheford and Greig de Peuter, *Games of Empire: Global Capitalism and Video Games* (Minneapolis: University of Minnesota Press, 2009); Patrick Crogan, *Gameplay Mode: War, Simulation, and Technoculture* (Minneapolis: University of Minnesota Press, 2011); and Corey Mead, *War Play: Video Games and the Future of Armed Conflict* (New York: Houghton Mifflin Harcourt, 2013).

18 For the most influential account of this imbrication, see Paul Virilio, *War and Cinema: The Logistics of Perception* (London: Verso, 1989).

19 In the much-cited example of Full Spectrum Warrior, a commercial game originally based on a military simulation returns to the military when the console version of the game is redesigned for treatment of post-traumatic stress disorder.

20 Ghamari-Tabrizi, "Convergence," 150.

21 For an ethnographic account of the VAE, see Robertson Allen, "The Army Rolls Through Indianapolis: Fieldwork at the Virtual Army Experience," *Transformative Works and Cultures*, 2 (2009), http://journal.transformativeworks.org/index.php/twc/article/view/80/97.

22 In America's Army, opposing teams in any multiplayer conflict appear to themselves onscreen as U.S. Army personnel.

23 This decision is represented by the game's developers as a principled rejection of the sensationalism of other games, though it is useful to note its alignment with

the broader resistance (official and unofficial) to visual representations of U.S. casualties and the common construction of such representations as antiwar and thus, inherently, antipatriotic.

24 See MacLeish, *Making War*, 54.

25 Judith Butler, *Precarious Life: The Powers of Mourning and Violence* (London: Verso, 2006), 6–7.

26 Ibid., 7.

27 Matthew S. Buckley, "Refugee Theatre: Melodrama and Modernity's Loss," *Theatre Journal* 61 (2009): 175–90. Leo Charney uses similar language in suggesting that "the hunger for kinetic sensations in cinema becomes like a century-long drug addiction in which you need more and more to accomplish less and less"; "The Violence of a Perfect Moment," in *Violence and the American Cinema*, ed. J. David Slocum (New York: Routledge, 2001), 48.

28 Buckley, "Refugee Theatre," 189.

29 Butler, *Precarious Life*, 6.

SELECTED BIBLIOGRAPHY

Abel, Richard. *The Red Rooster Scare: Making Cinema American, 1900–1910*. Berkeley: University of California Press, 1999.

Abel, Richard, ed. *Silent Film*. New Brunswick, NJ: Rutgers University Press, 1996.

Ahmed, Sara. *The Cultural Politics of Emotion*. New York: Routledge, 2004.

Andersen, Robin. *A Century of Media, A Century of War*. New York: Peter Lang, 2006.

Anderson, Benedict. *Imagined Communities: Reflections on the Origin and Spread of Nationalism*. London: Verso, 1983.

Anker, Elisabeth R. *Orgies of Feeling: Melodrama and the Politics of Freedom*. Durham, NC: Duke University Press, 2014.

Axeen, David. "'Heroes of the Engine Room': American 'Civilization' and the War with Spain." *American Quarterly* 36 (1984): 481–502.

Bazin, André. *What Is Cinema?* Translated by Hugh Gray. Berkeley: University of California Press, 1971.

Bederman, Gail. *Manliness and Civilization: A Cultural History of Gender and Race in the United States, 1880–1917*. Chicago: University of Chicago Press, 1995.

Benjamin, Walter. *Illuminations*. Edited by Hannah Arendt. 1955. New York: Harcourt, Brace and World, 1968.

Berlant, Lauren. *Cruel Optimism*. Durham, NC: Duke University Press, 2011.

————. "The Epistemology of State Emotion." In *Dissent in Dangerous Times*, edited by Austin Sarat. Ann Arbor: University of Michigan Press, 2004.

————. *The Queen of America Goes to Washington City: Essays on Sex and Citizenship*. Durham, NC: Duke University Press, 1997.

————. "The Subject of True Feeling." In *Cultural Pluralism, Identity Politics, and the Law*, edited by Austin Sarat and Thomas R. Kearns. Ann Arbor: University of Michigan Press, 1999.

Bernardi, Daniel, ed. *The Birth of Whiteness: Race and the Emergence of U.S. Cinema*. New Brunswick, NJ: Rutgers University Press, 1996.

Bingham, Dennis. *Acting Male: Masculinities in the Films of James Stewart, Jack Nicholson, and Clint Eastwood*. New Brunswick, NJ: Rutgers University Press, 1994.

Biskind, Peter. *Seeing Is Believing: How Hollywood Taught Us to Stop Worrying and Love the Fifties*. New York: Pantheon, 1983.

Bold, Christine. "The Rough Riders at Home and Abroad: Cody, Roosevelt, Remington, and the Imperialist Hero." *Canadian Review of American Studies* 18 (1987): 321–50.

Borstelmann, Thomas. *The Cold War and the Color Line: American Race Relations in the Global Arena*. Cambridge, MA: Harvard University Press, 2001.

Bowser, Eileen. *The Transformation of Cinema, 1907–1915*. New York: Charles Scribner's Sons, 1990.

Bratton, Jacky, Jim Cook, and Christine Gledhill, eds. *Melodrama: Stage, Picture, Screen*. London: British Film Institute, 1994.

Brooks, Peter. *The Melodramatic Imagination: Balzac, Henry James, Melodrama, and the Mode of Excess*. New Haven, CT: Yale University Press, 1976.

Brown, Bill. *The Material Unconscious: American Amusement, Stephen Crane, and the Economies of Play*. Cambridge, MA: Harvard University Press, 1996.

Brown, Charles H. *The Correspondents' War: Journalists in the Spanish American War*. New York: Charles Scribner's Sons, 1967.

Brown, Wendy. *States of Injury: Power and Freedom in Late Modernity*. Princeton, NJ: Princeton University Press, 1995.

Buckley, Matthew S. "Refugee Theatre: Melodrama and Modernity's Loss." *Theatre Journal* 61 (2009): 175–90.

Buscombe, Edward. "Painting the Legend: Frederic Remington and the Western." *Cinema Journal* 23 (1984): 12–27.

Buscombe, Edward, ed. *The BFI Companion to the Western*. New York: Atheneum, 1988.

Buscombe, Edward, and Roberta E. Pearson, eds. *Back in the Saddle Again: New Essays on the Western*. London: British Film Institute, 1998.

Butler, Judith. *Frames of War: When Is Life Grievable?* London: Verso, 2010.

————. "The Imperialist Subject." *Journal of Urban and Cultural Studies* 2 (1991): 73–78.

————. *Precarious Life: The Powers of Mourning and Violence*. London: Verso, 2006.

Cameron, Ian, and Douglas Pye, eds. *The Book of Westerns*. New York: Continuum, 1996.

Castonguay, James. "The Spanish-American War in U.S. Media Culture." *American Quarterly Experimental Online Issue*. June 1999. http://chnm.gmu.edu/aq.

Charney, Leo, and Vanessa R. Schwartz, eds. *Cinema and the Invention of Modern Life*. Berkeley: University of California Press, 1995.

Chong, Sylvia Shin Huey. *The Oriental Obscene: Violence and Racial Fantasies in the Vietnam Era*. Durham, NC: Duke University Press, 2011.

Cohan, Steven. *Masked Men: Masculinity and the Movies in the Fifties*. Bloomington: Indiana University Press, 1997.

Cohan, Steven, and Ina Rae Hark, eds. *Screening the Male: Exploring Masculinities in Hollywood Cinema*. London, Routledge: 1993.

Colonnese, Tom Grayson. "Native American Reactions to *The Searchers*." In *The Searchers: Essays and Reflections on John Ford's Classic Western*, edited by Arthur M. Eckstein and Peter Lehman. Detroit: Wayne State University Press, 2004.

Coyne, Michael. *The Crowded Prairie: American National Identity in the Hollywood Western*. London: I. B. Tauris, 1997.

Crane, Stephen. *The Red Badge of Courage: An Episode of the American Civil War* (1895). New York: Signet Classics, 1960.

_____. *Reports of War*, edited by Fredson Bowers. Charlottesville: University of Virginia Press, 1971.

_____. *The War Dispatches of Stephen Crane*, edited by R. W. Stallman. New York: New York University Press, 1964.

Crogan, Patrick. *Gameplay Mode: War, Simulation, and Technoculture*. Minneapolis: University of Minnesota Press, 2011.

Davis, Mike. *City of Quartz: Excavating the Future in Los Angeles*. London: Verso, 1990.

Der Derian, James. *Virtuous War: Mapping the Military-Industrial-Media-Entertainment Network*. New York: Routledge, 2009.

Dippie, Brian. "The Moving Finger Writes: Western Art and the Dynamics of Change." In *Discovered Lands, Invented Pasts: Transforming Visions of the American West*, edited by Jules David Prown et al. New Haven, CT: Yale University Press, 1992.

_____. *The Vanishing American: White Attitudes and U.S. Indian Policy*. Middletown, CT: Wesleyan University Press, 1982.

Doane, Mary Ann. *The Desire to Desire: The Woman's Film of the 1940s*. Bloomington: Indiana University Press, 1987.

_____. "Technology's Body: Cinematic Vision in Modernity." *differences* 5 (1993): 1–23.

Dubbert, Joe L. "Progressivism and the Masculinity Crisis." In *The American Man*, edited by Elizabeth H. Pleck and Joseph H. Pleck. Englewood Cliffs, NJ: Prentice-Hall, 1980.

Dudziak, Mary L. *Cold War Civil Rights: Race and the Image of American Democracy*. Princeton, NJ: Princeton University Press, 2000.

Dyer, Richard. *White*. London: Routledge, 1997.

Dyer, Thomas G. *Theodore Roosevelt and the Idea of Race*. Baton Rouge: Louisiana State University Press, 1980.

Dyer-Witheford, Nick, and Greig de Peuter. *Games of Empire: Global Capitalism and Video Games*. Minneapolis: University of Minnesota Press, 2009.

Eagle, Jonna K. "Making a Spectacle of Himself: White Masculinity, Melodrama, and Sensation in the American Cinema, 1898–1999." PhD diss., Brown University, 2006.

_____. "A Rough Ride: Strenuous Spectatorship and the Early Cinema of Assaults." *Screen* 53 (Spring 2012): 18–35.

_____. "Virtuous Victims, Visceral Violence: War and Melodrama in American Culture." In *The Martial Imagination: Cultural Aspects of American Warfare*, edited by Jimmy L. Bryan Jr. College Station: Texas A&M University Press, 2013.

Ehrenreich, Barbara. *Fear of Falling: The Inner Life of the Middle Class*. New York: Pantheon, 1989.

_____. *The Hearts of Men: American Dreams and the Flight from Commitment*. New York: Anchor, 1984.

Elsaesser, Thomas. "Tales of Sound and Fury: Observations on the Family Melodrama." *Monogram* 4 (1972): 2–15.

Elsaesser, Thomas, ed. *Early Cinema: Space/Frame/Narrative*. London: BFI Publishing, 1990.

Engelhardt, Tom. *The End of Victory Culture: Cold War America and the Disillusioning of a Generation.* Amherst: University of Massachusetts Press, 1995.

Faludi, Susan. *Stiffed: The Betrayal of the American Man.* New York: William Morrow, 1999.

Fell, John, ed. *Film Before Griffith.* Berkeley: University of California Press, 1983.

Fenin, George N., and William K. Everson. *The Western: From Silents to Cinerama.* New York: Orion Press, 1962.

Fiedler, Leslie A. *Love and Death in the American Novel.* New York: Stein and Day, 1966.

French, Philip. *Westerns: Aspects of a Movie Genre.* New York: Viking Press, 1973.

Gerould, Daniel, ed. *American Melodrama.* New York: PAJ Publications, 1983.

Ghamari-Tabrizi, Sharon. "The Convergence of the Pentagon and Hollywood: The Next Generation of Military Training Simulations." In *Memory Bytes: History, Technology, and Digital Culture,* edited by Lauren Rabinovitz and Abraham Geil. Durham, NC: Duke University Press, 2003.

Gledhill, Christine. "Rethinking Genre." In *Reinventing Film Studies,* edited by Christine Gledhill and Linda Williams. London: Arnold, 2000.

_____. "Signs of Melodrama." In *Stardom: Industry of Desire,* edited by Christine Gledhill. London: Routledge, 1991.

Gledhill, Christine, ed. *Home Is Where the Heart Is: Studies in Melodrama and the Woman's Film.* London: British Film Institute, 1987.

Gregg, Melissa, and Gregory J. Seigworth, eds. *The Affect Theory Reader.* Durham, NC: Duke University Press, 2010.

Gunning, Tom. "An Aesthetic of Astonishment: Early Film and the (In)Credulous Spectator." In *Viewing Positions: Ways of Seeing Film,* edited by Linda Williams. New Brunswick, NJ: Rutgers University Press, 1994.

_____. "The Cinema of Attractions: Early Film, Its Spectator, and the Avant-Garde," *Wide Angle* 8 (1986): 63–70.

_____. "From the Opium Den to the Theatre of Morality: Moral Discourse and the Film Process in Early American Cinema." *Art and Text* 30 (1988): 30–40.

_____. "The Horror of Opacity: The Melodrama of Sensation in the Plays of Andre de Lorde." In *Melodrama: Stage, Picture, Screen,* edited by Jacky Bratton, Jim Cook, and Christine Gledhill. London: British Film Institute, 1994.

Hagelin, Sarah. *Reel Vulnerability: Power, Pain, and Gender in Contemporary American Film and Television.* New Brunswick NJ: Rutgers University Press, 2013.

Halberstam, David. *The Fifties.* New York: Villard Books, 1993.

Halberstam, Judith. *The Queer Art of Failure.* Durham, NC: Duke University Press, 2011.

Hale, Grace Elizabeth. *Making Whiteness: The Culture of Segregation in the South, 1890–1940.* New York: Random House, 1998.

Hall, Roger A. *Performing the American Frontier, 1870–1906.* Cambridge: Cambridge University Press, 2001.

Hansen, Miriam. *Babel and Babylon: Spectatorship in American Silent Film.* Cambridge, MA: Harvard University Press, 1991.

Hemment, John C. *Cannon and Camera: Sea and Land Battles of the Spanish-American War in Cuba.* New York: D. Appleton and Company, 1898.

Henderson, Brian. "*The Searchers*: An American Dilemma." *Film Quarterly* 34 (Winter 1980–1981): 9–23.

Higham, John. "The Reorientation of American Culture in the 1890s." In *Writing American History: Essays on Modern Scholarship*. Bloomington: Indiana University Press, 1970.

_____. *Strangers in the Land: Patterns of American Nativism, 1860–1925*. New Brunswick, NJ: Rutgers University Press, 1988.

Hilkey, Judy Arlene. *Character Is Capital: Success Manuals and Manhood in Gilded Age America*. Chapel Hill: University of North Carolina Press, 1997.

Hofstadter, Richard. "Cuba, the Philippines, and Manifest Destiny." In *The Paranoid Style in American Politics*. New York: Knopf, 1965.

Hoganson, Kristin L. *Fighting for American Manhood: How Gender Politics Provoked the Spanish-American and Philippine-American Wars*. New Haven, CT: Yale University Press, 1998.

Horan, James D. *The Life and Art of Charles Schreyvogel*. New York: Crown, 1969.

Horsman, Reginald. *Race and Manifest Destiny: The Origins of American Racial Anglo-Saxonism*. Cambridge, MA: Harvard University Press, 1981.

Jeffords, Susan. *Hard Bodies: Hollywood Masculinity in the Reagan Era*. New Brunswick, NJ: Rutgers University Press, 1994.

_____. *The Remasculinization of America: Gender and the Vietnam War*. Bloomington: Indiana University Press, 1989.

Jeffords, Susan, and Lauren Rabinovitz, eds. *Seeing Through the Media: The Persian Gulf War*. New Brunswick, NJ: Rutgers University Press, 1994.

Kaplan, Amy. *The Anarchy of Empire in the Making of U.S. Culture*. Cambridge, MA: Harvard University Press, 2002.

_____. "Romancing the Empire: The Embodiment of Masculinity in the Popular Historical Novel of the 1890s," *American Literary History* 2 (1990): 658–90.

_____. "The Spectacle of War in Crane's Revision of History." In *New Essays on The Red Badge of Courage*, edited by Lee Clark Mitchell. Cambridge: Cambridge University Press, 1986.

Kaplan, Amy, and Donald E. Pease, eds. *Cultures of United States Imperialism*. Durham, NC: Duke University Press, 1993.

Kasson, John. *Amusing the Million: Coney Island at the Turn of the Century*. New York: Hill and Wang, 1978.

_____. *Houdini, Tarzan, and the Perfect Man: The White Male Body and the Challenge of Modernity in America*. New York: Hill and Wang, 2001.

Kasson, Joy S. *Buffalo Bill's Wild West: Celebrity, Memory, and Popular History*. New York: Hill and Wang, 2000.

Kennedy, Liam. "Alien Nation: White Male Paranoia and Imperial Culture in the United States." *Journal of American Studies* 30 (1996): 87–100.

Kilpatrick, Jacquelyn. *Celluloid Indians: Native Americans and Film*. Lincoln: University of Nebraska Press, 1999.

Kimmel, Michael. *Manhood in America: A Cultural History*. New York: Free Press, 1996.

King, Geoff. *Spectacular Narratives: Hollywood in the Age of the Blockbuster*. London: I. B. Tauris, 2000.

Kirby, Lynn. *Parallel Tracks: The Railroad and Silent Cinema*. Durham, NC: Duke University Press, 1997.

Kitses, Jim. *Horizons West: Anthony Mann, Budd Boetticher, Sam Peckinpah; Studies of Authorship within the Western*. Bloomington: Indiana University Press, 1970.

Kracauer, Siegfried. "The Mass Ornament." In *The Mass Ornament: Weimar Essays*. Cambridge, MA: Harvard University Press, 1995.

————. *Theory of Film: The Redemption of Physical Reality*. Princeton, NJ: Princeton University Press, 1997.

Krutnik, Frank. *In a Lonely Street: Film Noir, Genre, Masculinity*. London: Routledge, 1991.

Kuznick, Peter J., and James Gilbert, eds. *Rethinking Cold War Culture*. Washington, DC: Smithsonian Institution Press, 2001.

Lang, Robert. *American Film Melodrama: Griffith, Vidor, Minnelli*. Princeton, NJ: Princeton University Press, 1989.

Lawrence, Amy. "American Shame: *Rope*, James Stewart, and the Postwar Crisis in American Masculinity." In *Hitchcock's America*, edited by Jonathan Freedman and Richard Millington. New York: Oxford University Press, 1999.

Lears, T. J. Jackson. *No Place of Grace: Antimodernism and the Transformation of American Culture, 1880–1920*. New York: Pantheon Books, 1981.

Lenoir, Timothy. "Programming Theaters of War." In *Bombs and Bandwidth: The Emerging Relationship Between Information Technology and Security*, edited by Robert Latham. New York: New Press, 2003.

Lipsitz, George. *The Possessive Investment in Whiteness: How White People Profit from Identity Politics*. Philadelphia: Temple University Press, 1998.

Lorant, Stefan. *The Life and Times of Theodore Roosevelt*. Garden City, NY: Doubleday, 1959.

Lutz, Tom. *American Nervousness, 1903: An Anecdotal History*. Ithaca, NY: Cornell University Press, 1991.

————. *Crying: The Natural and Cultural History of Tears*. New York: W. W. Norton, 1999.

MacLean, Nancy. *Behind the Mask of Chivalry: The Making of the Second Ku Klux Klan*. Oxford: Oxford University Press, 1994.

MacLeish, Kenneth T. *Making War at Fort Hood: Life and Uncertainty in a Military Community*. Princeton, NJ: Princeton University Press, 2013.

Mallan, John. "Roosevelt, Brooks Adams, and Lea: The Warrior Critique of the Business Civilization." *American Quarterly* 8 (1956): 216–30.

Masco, Joseph. *The Theater of Operations: National Security Affect from the Cold War to the War on Terror*. Durham, NC: Duke University Press, 2014.

Massumi, Brian. *Parables for the Virtual: Movement, Affect, Sensation*. Durham, NC: Duke University Press, 2002.

————. *Politics of Affect*. Cambridge: Polity Press, 2015.

May, Elaine Tyler. *Homeward Bound: American Families in the Cold War Era*. New York: Basic Books, 1988.

Mayne, Judith. *The Woman at the Keyhole: Feminism and Women's Cinema*. Bloomington: Indiana University Press, 1990.

Mazzarella, William. "Affect: What Is It Good For?" In *Enchantments of Modernity: Empire, Nation, Globalization*, edited by Saurabh Dube. London: Routledge, 2009.

Melley, Timothy. *Empire of Conspiracy: The Culture of Paranoia in Postwar America.* Ithaca, NY: Cornell University Press, 2000.

Mieszkowski, Jan. *Watching War.* Stanford, CA: Stanford University Press, 2012.

Mitchell, Lee Clark. *Westerns: Making the Man in Fiction and Film.* Chicago: University of Chicago Press, 1996.

Moeller, Susan. *Shooting War: Photography and the American Experience of Combat.* New York: Basic Books, 1989.

Mulvey, Laura. "Visual Pleasure and Narrative Cinema." *Screen* 16 (1975): 6–18.

Musser, Charles. *Before the Nickelodeon: Edwin S. Porter and the Edison Manufacturing Company.* Berkeley: University of California Press, 1991.

————. *Edison Motion Pictures, 1890–1900: An Annotated Filmography.* Washington, DC: Smithsonian Institution Press, 1997.

————. *The Emergence of Cinema: The American Screen to 1907.* New York: Charles Scribner's Sons, 1990.

Neale, Stephen. "Masculinity as Spectacle: Reflections on Men and Mainstream Cinema." *Screen* 24 (1983): 2–16.

————. "Melo Talk: On the Meaning and Use of the Term 'Melodrama' in the American Trade Press." *Velvet Light Trap* 32 (1993): 66–89.

————. "Vanishing Americans: Racial and Ethnic Issues in the Interpretation and Context of Post-war 'Pro-Indian' Westerns." In *Back in the Saddle Again: New Essays on the Western*, edited by Edward Buscombe and Roberta E. Pearson. London: British Film Institute, 1998.

Nemerov, Alex. "'Doing the "Old America"': The Image of the American West, 1880–1920." In *The West as America: Reinterpreting Images of the Frontier, 1820–1920*, edited by William H. Truettner. Washington, DC: Smithsonian Institution Press, 1991.

Niver, Kemp. *Early Motion Pictures: The Paper Print Collection in the Library of Congress.* Washington, DC: Library of Congress, 1985.

Niver, Kemp, ed. *Biograph Bulletins, 1896–1908.* Los Angeles: Locare Research Group, 1971.

Pauly, Thomas. "The Cold War Western." *Western Humanities Review* (1979): 256–73.

Pettegrew, John. "'The Soldier's Faith': Turn-of-the-Century Memory of the Civil War and the Emergence of Modern American Nationalism." *Journal of Contemporary History* 31 (1996): 49–73.

Pfeil, Fred. *White Guys: Studies in Postmodern Domination and Difference.* London: Verso, 1995.

Plantinga, Carl. "Spectacles of Death: Clint Eastwood and Violence in *Unforgiven*." *Cinema Journal* 37 (1998): 65–83.

Polan, Dana. "'Above All Else to Make You See': Cinema and the Ideology of the Spectacle." In *Postmodernism and Politics*, edited by Jonathan Arac. Minneapolis: University of Minnesota Press, 1986.

————. "Brief Encounters: Mass Culture and the Evacuation of Sense." In *Studies in Entertainment: Critical Approaches to Mass Culture*, edited by Tania Modleski. Bloomington: Indiana University Press, 1986.

Rabinovitz, Lauren. *For the Love of Pleasure: Women, Movies, and Culture in Turn-of-the-Century Chicago*. New Brunswick, NJ: Rutgers University Press, 1998.

Reddin, Paul. *Wild West Shows*. Urbana: University of Illinois Press, 1999.

Renehan, Edward. *The Lion's Pride: Theodore Roosevelt and His Family in Peace and War*. New York: Oxford University Press, 1998.

Robinson, Sally. *Marked Men: White Masculinity in Crisis*. New York: Columbia University Press, 2000.

Rodowick, David N. "Madness, Authority and Ideology: The Domestic Melodrama of the 1950s." In *Home Is Where the Heart Is: Studies in Melodrama and the Woman's Film*, edited by Christine Gledhill. London: British Film Institute, 1987.

Roediger, David. *The Wages of Whiteness: Race and the Making of the American Working Class*. London: Verso, 1991.

Rogin, Michael. "'The Sword Became a Flashing Vision': D. W. Griffith's *The Birth of a Nation*." In *Ronald Reagan, the Movie: And Other Episodes in Political Demonology*. Berkeley: University of California Press, 1987.

Roosevelt, Theodore. *The Strenuous Life: Essays and Addresses*. New York: Century Company, 1902.

Rotundo, E. Anthony. *American Manhood: Transformations in Masculinity from the Revolution to the Modern Era*. New York: Basic Books, 1993.

Rydell, Robert. *All the World's a Fair: Visions of Empire at American International Expositions, 1876–1916*. Chicago: University of Chicago Press, 1984.

Samuels, Peggy, et al. *Techniques of the Artists of the American West*. Secaucus, NJ: Wellfleet Press, 1990.

Savage, William W. *The Cowboy Hero: His Image in American History and Culture*. Norman: University of Oklahoma Press, 1979.

Savran, David. *Taking It Like a Man: White Masculinity, Masochism, and Contemporary American Culture*. Princeton, NJ: Princeton University Press, 1998.

Saxton, Alexander. *The Rise and Fall of the White Republic: Class, Politics and Mass Culture in Nineteenth-Century America*. London: Verso, 1990.

Schivelbusch, Wolfgang. *The Railway Journey: The Industrialization of Time and Space in the 19th Century*. Berkeley: University of California Press, 1986.

Scheslinger, Arthur, Jr. "The Crisis of American Masculinity" (1958). In *The Politics of Hope*. Boston: Houghton Mifflin, 1963.

Schwartz, Vanessa. *Spectacular Realities: Early Mass Culture in Fin-de-Siècle Paris*. Berkeley: University of California Press, 1998.

Scott, Ellen C. *Cinema Civil Rights: Regulation, Repression, and Race in the Classical Hollywood Era*. New Brunswick, NJ: Rutgers University Press, 2015.

Silverman, Kaja. *Male Subjectivity at the Margins*. New York: Routledge, 1992.

Simmel, Georg. "The Metropolis and Mental Life." In *The Sociology of Georg Simmel*, translated by Kurt H. Wolf. Glencoe, IL: Free Press, 1950.

Simmon, Scott. *The Invention of the Western Film: A Cultural History of the Genre's First Half-Century*. Cambridge: Cambridge University Press, 2003.

Singer, Ben. *Melodrama and Modernity: Early Sensational Cinema and Its Contexts*. New York: Columbia University Press, 2001.

Slocum, J. David, ed. *Violence and the American Cinema*. New York: Routledge, 2001.

Slotkin, Richard. *The Fatal Environment: The Myth of the Frontier in the Age of Industrialization, 1800–1890.* New York: Atheneum, 1985.

———. *Gunfighter Nation: The Myth of the Frontier in Twentieth-Century America.* New York: HarperCollins, 1992.

Smith, Henry Nash. *Virgin Land: The American West as Symbol and Myth.* Cambridge, MA: Harvard University Press, 1950.

Smith, Paul. *Clint Eastwood: A Cultural Production.* Minneapolis: University of Minneapolis Press, 1993.

Stahl, Roger. *Militainment, Inc.: War, Media, and Popular Culture.* New York: Routledge, 2009.

Staiger, Janet, Ann Cvetkovick, and Ann Reynolds, eds. *Political Emotions: New Agendas in Communication.* New York: Routledge, 2010.

Stanfield, Peter. *Hollywood, Westerns, and the 1930s.* Devon: University of Exeter Press, 2001.

Sturken, Marita. *Tangled Memories: The Vietnam War, the AIDS Epidemic, and the Politics of Remembering.* Berkeley: University of California Press, 1997.

Tasker, Yvonne. *Spectacular Bodies: Gender, Genre, and the Action Cinema.* London: Routledge, 1993.

Tompkins, Jane. *West of Everything: The Inner Life of Westerns.* New York: Oxford University Press, 1992.

Trachtenberg, Alan. *The Incorporation of America: Culture and Society in the Gilded Age.* New York: Hill and Wang, 1982.

Virilio, Paul. *War and Cinema: The Logistics of Perception.* London, Verso: 1989.

Vorpahl, Ben Merchant. *Frederic Remington and the West: With the Eye of the Mind.* Austin: University of Texas Press, 1978.

Walker, Janet, ed. *Westerns: Films Through History.* New York: Routledge, 2001.

Warner, William. "Spectacular Action: Rambo and the Popular Pleasures of Pain." In *Cultural Studies,* edited by Lawrence Grossberg, Cary Nelson, and Paula Treichler. New York: Routledge, 1992.

Warshow, Robert. *The Immediate Experience: Movies, Comics, Theatre and Other Aspects of Popular Culture.* Garden City, NY: Doubleday, 1962.

Watts, Sarah. *Rough Rider in the White House: Theodore Roosevelt and the Politics of Desire.* Chicago: University of Chicago Press, 2003.

Whissel, Kristen. "The Gender of Empire." In *A Feminist Reader in Early Cinema,* edited by Jennifer M. Bean and Diane Negra. Durham, NC: Duke University Press, 2002.

———. *Picturing American Modernity: Traffic, Technology, and the Silent Cinema.* Durham, NC: Duke University Press, 2008.

White, G. Edward. *The Eastern Establishment and the Western Experience: The West of Frederic Remington, Theodore Roosevelt, and Owen Wister.* New Haven, CT: Yale University Press, 1968.

Wiegman, Robyn. *American Anatomies: Theorizing Race and Gender.* Durham, NC: Duke University Press, 1995.

Willemen, Paul. "Anthony Mann: Looking at the Male." *Framework* 16 (1981): 16.

———. *Looks and Frictions: Essays in Cultural Studies and Film Theory.* Bloomington: Indiana University Press, 1994.

Williams, Linda. "Film Bodies: Genre, Gender, and Excess." *Film Quarterly* 44 (Summer 1991): 2–13.

————. "Melodrama Revised." In *Refiguring American Film Genres: History and Theory*, edited by Nick Browne. Berkeley: University of California Press, 1998.

————. *On The Wire*. Durham, NC: Duke University Press, 2014.

————. *Playing the Race Card: Melodramas of Black and White from Uncle Tom to O.J. Simpson*. Princeton, NJ: Princeton University Press, 2001.

Williams, Raymond. *Marxism and Literature*. Oxford: Oxford University Press, 1977.

Willis, Sharon. *High Contrast: Race and Gender in Contemporary Hollywood Film*. Durham, NC: Duke University Press, 1997.

Wister, Owen. "The Evolution of the Cow-Puncher" (1895). In *Owen Wister's West*, edited by Robert Murray Davis. Albuquerque: University of New Mexico Press, 1987.

————. *The Virginian*. New York: Macmillan Company, 1902.

INDEX

Page numbers in *italic* refer to figures.

military actualities, 24, 35, 39, 49–50, 52–53, 62, 77. *See also Advance of the Kansas Volunteers at Caloocan; Roosevelt's Rough Riders;* war films

military-entertainment complex, 196, 201–6, 207

military technology, 35–36, 40, 201–3, 206, 207

Mix, Tom, 70, 93, 94–95, 231n76

mob violence, 110–16, 118, 122

modernity: alienation, 10, 47; assaultive properties of, 29, 44–45, 53; economic and social change, 28–29; health effects of, 28–30; mass media, 31–32; melodrama and, 10, 68–69. *See also* consumer culture

morality: of action heroes, 143, 146, 153, 167; of Cold War Western heroes, 102, 105–6, 107, 111, 114–16, 119–20, 121–23, 126, 139–40; feeling and, 3, 6–7, 11–12, 68, 112–14, 164; "good badmen," 91–93; in melodramas, 6–7, 11–12, 68, 69, 85, 164; pathos and, 75, 140; race and, 107, 108; reasoning and, 11; of Western heroes, 84, 91–94, 95–100, 129–30, 140, 153, 233n88; in Westerns, 11, 63, 65, 82, 84, 85, 192

motion: affective experience of, 64; appeal of, 62–63; as assault on spectator, 50–53; imperialist identification and, 50, 57, 62, 88–89; in western action painting, 60, 62, 73, 74, 76; in Westerns, 62–63, 64, 78, 81, 106; white masculine, 63; in Wild West shows, 70, 72. *See also* cavalry charges

Mulvey, Laura, 45, 131

Munsterberg, Hugo, 9, 17

Musser, Charles, 52

My Darling Clementine (Ford), 107

The Naked Spur (Mann), 126, 127–28, *129*

narrative cinema, 44, 57, 58, 63, 64, 79. *See also* Western films

national identity: affect and, 12, 16; American, 2, 8, 25–26, 28, 141, 174, 177, 195–96; B Westerns and, 232n87; feeling and, 12, 16; media and, 3–4, 16; strenuous life discourse and, 25–26, 28; violence and, 2, 8, 18; white masculinity and, 9, 10–11, 25–26, 28, 177

national subject: affect and, 16; identification with, 6; as imperialist subject, 3; white masculinity of, 9, 10–11, 103, 143, 180. *See also* imperialist subjectivity

Native Americans. *See* Indians

Neale, Stephen, 5, 7, 128

Neath the Arizona Skies (Fraser), 232n82

Nemerov, Alex, 73, 75, 78

The Night Riders (Sherman), 97–98, *98*, 232n85

9/11 terrorist attacks, 1–2, 3, 17–18, 195–96, 206

Nowell-Smith, Geoffrey, 133

The Ox-Bow Incident (Wellman), 110–16, *113*, 120, 122, 136, 236nn27–31

pathos: action and, 4; in action films, 184; in Cold War Westerns, 101–2, 106–7, 108, 126–27, 131, 135, 138–41; masculine, 131–32; moral authority and, 75, 140; power and, 140–41; in wartime, 56; in western painting, 74–75, 77; in Westerns, 84, 91, 92, 185; in Wild West shows, 71. *See also* suffering

patriarchy, 131–32, 133–34

Patriot Day, 1–2

Pauly, Thomas, 126

Pearson, Roberta, 85

Persian Gulf War, 3, 144, 145, 163, 193

Pfeil, Fred, 172, 174

Philippine-American War: battleships, 42; films of, 24, 49–50, 53–54, 56, 77

The Photographer's Mishap (Edison), 45, 52

photography: pocket cameras, 40, 49; trick, 45; by war correspondents, 35–36, 40, 48–49, 57, 223n76

Plains War: films, 82, 84; paintings, 59–60, 73

Plantinga, Carl, 188, 191

Polan, Dana, 172

posttraumatic stress disorder, 204, 251n19

postwar period. *See* Cold War period

power: of action heroes, 154, 161, 169, 173; affective forms of, 17–18; corporate, 28, 143, 173–74; of media, 16–17, 18; pathos and, 140–41; of soldiers, 206

precariousness, 5, 152–54, 173–74, 206, 244n33

Progressive reformers, 82

pro-Indian Westerns, 96, 108–10, 116–26, 127–28, 136–39, 236–37nn32–33

The Purple Vigilantes (Sherman), 232n85

Pye, Douglas, 108, 136

Rabinovitz, Lauren, 45

race: changing attitudes in 1950s, 108–9; interracial romances, 120, 123, 137, 232n82;

ABOUT THE AUTHOR

JONNA EAGLE is an assistant professor of film/media in the Department of American Studies at the University of Hawaiʻi at Mānoa, where she teaches in American cinema, war and media, critical and cultural theory, and social and cultural history. Her previous publications have appeared in *Screen* and in the anthology *The Martial Imagination: Cultural Aspects of American Warfare.*